THE
COTTAGE
BOOK

A COLLECTION OF PRACTICAL ADVICE

EDITED BY FRANK B. EDWARDS

HEDGEHOG PRODUCTIONS

Canadian Cataloguing in Publication Data

Main entry under title:

The Cottage Book

Includes index.
ISBN 1-895261-03-1

1. Vacation homes. 2. Vacations. I. Edwards, Frank B., 1952-

GV191.6.C6 1991   643'.2   C91-094837-2

Front Cover Photograph: Ernie Sparks

Trade distribution by
Firefly Books
250 Sparks Avenue
Willowdale, Ontario
Canada M2H 2S4

Printed in Canada for
Hedgehog Productions Inc.
Box 129
Newburgh, Ontario
Canada K0K 2S0

Designed by
Linda J. Menyes

Colour separations by
Hadwen Graphics
Ottawa, Ontario

Printed and bound in Canada by
D.W. Friesen & Sons Ltd.
Altona, Manitoba

Acknowledgements

Completion of this book would not have been possible without the concerted efforts of a small band of talented and hard-working friends. They include: Linda Menyes, Mirielle Keeling, Charlotte DuChene, Dianne Bartlett, Laura Elston, Stacey Anderson, Nancy Cutway, Laura Slade, Seth DuChene and Catherine DeLury.

For their advice and encouragement, I thank Susan Cross, John Bianchi, Tracy Read, Barry Estabrook, James M. Lawrence, Jane Good, Anne Rutherford, Tom Carpenter, Janice McAvoy and Lionel Koffler.

In addition, sincere thanks go to the people at the institutions that I haunted during the research and production of the book: Kingston Public Library, Douglas Library at Queen's University at Kingston, Camden House Publishing and Canada Post's Newburgh, Ontario office.

And finally, special thanks to all those publishers, editors, authors, agents, photographers and illustrators who kindly gave their permission to use the material which has found its way into this book.

Dedicated to Susan and the kids — Kristen, Scott and Hayley — and the summer memories still to come.

Contents

Introduction   8

Cottaging
Slaving Over a Summer Grill by Pamela Cross   12
The Vegetarian Wood-Smoke Barbecue by Tom Ney   17
Memorable Summer Desserts With Blueberries by Janet Ballantyne   18
Getting the Proper Exposure by Daryn Eller   20
Why the Sun Turns Skin Brown by Ira Flatow   25
Deck Lumber Made to Last by Stephen Smulski   26
Beware of Preserved-Wood Guarantees by Merilyn Simonds Mohr   32
The Secret to Exterior Finishes by Leigh Seddon   34
Reaching New Heights Atop the Right Ladder by Leigh Seddon   41
Stripping Wood Before Painting by Janet C. Hickman
         and *Old House Journal* staff   42
Tap Water That's Fit to Drink by Craig Canine   46
Testing the Waters Before Shopping by Craig Canine   52
Avoid That Old Winter Freeze-Up by Charles Long   53
Common Sense and Thick Ice by Yvonne Cox   57
Build Your Own Adirondack Chair by Tony Leighton   60
Laneways That Really Work by Jeremy Schmidt   64
The Secrets of Hauling a Trailer Safely by Tom Wilkinson   70
Crokinole on a Saturday Night by Michael Webster   72
A Few Basic Rules for Cottage Horseshoes by A. Taede Rusty   75
No Escape from Cottage Games by Charles Gordon   76
Our Favourite Family Board Games by The Toy Testing Council of Canada   78

Landscaping
Giving Nature a Helping Hand by Stephen Kress   82
A Private Patch Close at Hand by Lee Reich   89
Planting Trees for the Future by E.E. Vejore   92
Naturally Kept Shorelines by Suzanne Kingsmill   98
Fighting the Weed War With Few Casualties by Gordon Graham   102

Boating
Making Wise Use of Power by Derek Stevenson   106
Achieving the One-Pull Start by Max Burns   111
An Aluminum-Boat Buying Primer by Penny Caldwell   117
A Sleek Craft for Silent Paddling by Sue Lebrecht   118

The Miniature Dreamboat by Craig Canine 121
Riding the Waves in Comfort by Jan Mundy 126
Trailers and Techniques That Work by Sue Lebrecht 128

Fishing

Who Is Really the Smartest by Tiny Bennett 132
A Midsummer's Fishing Scheme by Ken Schultz 138
Catching Fish at Home Is the Key to Success by James Rudnick 140
What It Takes to Win a Walleye by Jake MacDonald 142
A Fish Made for Tossing Back? by Jim Bashline 144
Remember That Fishing With Kids Can Be Fun by James Rudnick 146
Developing Eyes for Big Bass by Cliff Hauptman 148
Mastering the Basics of a Good Tackle Box by John Partridge 150
The Care and Collection of a Favourite Bait by Joseph Bates 152

Pests

Some Are Biters, Others Just Sting by Bev Smallman and Allan West 156
Forcing Pests To "Bug Off!" by Richard A. Casagrande 162
Spring's Clouds of Discomfort by Allan West and Bev Smallman 165
Invasion of the Deadly Ticks by Jean Wallace 168
Bad Reactions to a Pretty Plant by David Seburn 170
Getting Rid of Poison Ivy Plants Safely by Jennifer Bennett 173
Doing Battle With a Mouse by Ronald J. Brooks 174
Are Those Little Ants Chewing up Your Cottage by Adrian Forsyth 177

Nature

Caring For a Bird in Hand by Laura O'Bisco Socha 180
The Magic of the Loons' Songs by Kate Crowley and Mike Link 188
Cold-Weather Dinner Guests by Clive Dobson 191
Singing the Bullfrog Blues by Suzanne Kingsmill 198
A Flicker of Colour by Night by Robert Michael Pyle 202
Protecting the Night Sky by Terence Dickinson 206
Learning to Love Bats by Craig Canine 208
Getting a Sense of Direction by G.I. Kenney 212
Colonizing the Wilderness by Adrian Forsyth 215
Hoarding the Forest's Harvest for the Future by Adrian Forsyth 217

Index 218

Introduction

A Book Plot Hatched in a Boat

The idea for this book was born on a long, hot August afternoon while drifting slowly down a quiet lake in eastern Ontario. I was accompanied by my son, Scott, aged 4 at the time, and we had rowed the heavy, old aluminum boat almost a mile to the far end of the lake, knowing that our reward would be a gentle breeze that would push us home in time for dinner.

He was lying in the bow, and I was draped between the stern and midships, answering his lazy barrage of questions. Where do fish hide? Why do beavers chew down big trees? What kind of bug did I like best? His queries ranged from whys? to what-ifs? and how-do-yous? but they were as much for conversation as for education.

When he bored with academic issues, he grabbed a long wooden oar, mounted it on the bow as a cannon and busied himself playing pirates. I had only to suggest occasional course corrections, made with the remaining oar, and was left to mull over my own what-ifs.

After nine years as a magazine editor and book publisher at Camden House Publishing, I was ready for a change of pace. I had joined *Harrowsmith*, a successful rural-living magazine, during its early years, been part of the launch team of *Equinox*, Canada's answer in 1981 to *National Geographic*, and,

later, headed up the magazines' book-publishing program. But just a few months before that pleasant sojourn down Killenbeck Lake, our perfect little company had been bought by a media corporation, the executives of which regarded our rural location with suspicion. It was clear that a company whose expertise was in television listings and suburban fashion would not tolerate our rather unorthodox approach to publishing for long, and it was a good time to consider alternatives.

As Scott and I drifted closer to our rented cottage, this book, and the company that would publish it, began to take shape in my mind. *The Cottage Book* would *have* to be practical, dealing with topics of interest to anyone with the need for a rural retreat. Fishing, boating, building, landscaping . . . the list seemed endless.

Today, three years later, proofs of the book sit in front of me on my cluttered desk. It is early July, a Saturday, close to midnight, and the book goes off to the printer in less than 24 hours. Having immersed myself in the contents of this book for almost a year, I now have a number of plans to rid our own cottage lot of poison ivy. As well, I have a few ideas where the really big bass are hiding out in our small lake and, with blueberry season upon us, I

am almost ready to swing into some heavy-duty desserts.

But like so many cottagers, the work week threatens to block my good intentions. Next weekend, I promise myself, will be different — when I am not relaxing, I will be clearing brush or picking berries.

The Cottage Book consists of more than 60 magazine articles and book excerpts, drawn from a variety of libraries. It seems that with this project, I created a job for myself that allowed me to find answers to the questions that were always cropping up.

In fact, each chapter in this book represents an answer to a particular concern or interest I have had at one time or another. What do the various loon calls and ululations mean as they drift across a lake? What is the best way to paint clapboard so that it lasts? When is it safe to venture out on the ice in winter? Why do mosquitoes persist in being such pests?

Hopefully, those people who have found their way to this page will take the book to their cottages and leave it out where it can be put to good use for years to come. In cottage country, where a journey to town means time away from the lake or a favourite novel, this book represents dozens of trips to the library and hours of research.

We owe our grandchildren the same natural settings that we have enjoyed. Cottages and the joy around them should not become yet another distant memory.

The Cottage Book is by no means a complete work, and the more I have studied it, the more new questions arise. Certainly, if the demand exists, there will be further volumes. Suggestions and ideas are welcome, as are letters of complaint and compliment. (Address them to The Cottage Book, Box 129, Newburgh, Ontario K0K 2S0.)

Early on in this project, a friend suggested that the book was, perhaps, just a little bit frivolous. After all, were there not larger concerns than how to spend lazy weekends or months at a cottage? I argued that much of the material in the book touched on important matters. After all, with so many North Americans flocking to cottages, camps and various recreational properties, many of which sit on or beside fragile lands, it is important for cottagers, and would-be cottagers, to have solid information on which to base their own plans.

Cottaging has become an important part of our lives, and as the shorelines of our lakes, rivers and oceans grow more crowded, the pressure for improved use has grown. Rising land values are opening up more lakes to development and are encouraging people to try to squeeze more enjoyment from their investment.

To some, that means bigger boats, higher fences and fancier landscaping as they set out to reshape their slice of paradise into a private domain. But to others, increased value simply has put into perspective the true value of what they already have. Who can put a price on the sound of waves lapping at a shore, a bird's far-off cry or the rhythmic din of a chorus of frogs? Those are the sensory pleasures that brought us to the cottage in the first place, and, if we are to preserve them for our children and grandchildren, then we must consider protecting them every time we start another project or a new phase of construction.

For myself, this book has inspired a score or more projects, many of which will never get started. But what better way to spend a summer than to sit on a deck with a cold drink, looking across an expanse of water, thinking of all the things you *could* do and the various ways you *might* do them.

Frank B. Edwards
July 1991

Cottaging

Rediscovering the joys of the barbecue

Slaving Over a Summer Grill

by Pamela Cross

I am an unabashed born-again barbecuer. Until a few years ago, I hated everything connected with barbecuing and refused outright to have anything to do with it. Picnics, for some reason, were different. I have always enjoyed assembling a multicourse feast in a hamper and setting out for some pleasant rural hideaway in which to enjoy it. But barbecues — I couldn't help thinking of the messes, the organization, the fire lighting and, perhaps more than anything else, the memories from my childhood of charred frankfurters (this was long before blackened food became *de rigueur*) and chicken that was burned to a crisp on the outside and still raw and oozing on the inside.

Three years ago, however, I attended a number of barbecue get-togethers and found, to my surprise, that things had changed. I discovered it was possible to sit comfortably outside in a lawn chair and eat any food that could be eaten indoors on plates that didn't suddenly fold in half when held over one's lap. Hamburgers could remain moist and whole. Potato salad could be kept icy cold and served without fear of food poisoning. Chicken could be partially cooked on the stove and then barbecued to give it wonderful flavour, with no

danger of being burned. Best of all, the barbecues I attended seemed to encourage a spontaneous gathering of friends who shared in the meal's preparation and cooking.

Outdoor eating has become very popular over the past few summers, as we seek ways to entertain without overheating the kitchen and cramming the house with guests. And as usual, when a particular cooking style becomes fashionable, a whole industry springs up to provide the equipment and accoutrements deemed necessary to perfect that cuisine. Thus a brief run-through of the barbecuing equipment that is available seems to be in order.

Probably the most basic barbecuing appliance is the hibachi. Literally translated, the name means "fire box." Small, compact and easy to tote (as long as you are sure it has completely cooled before throwing it in the car), a hibachi is an efficient, simple and inexpensive grill for cooking small quantities of food. In fact, I prefer a hibachi to any other kind of barbecue and use three of them when cooking for a crowd. Only slightly upgraded from the hibachi is the kettle barbecue. It is less portable but provides a larger cooking surface. Other options include wheels and a removable lid that aids in heat circulation and offers some protection — to the food, at least — in the event

of inclement weather. Many are supplied with electrically operated spits, indispensable for cooking large cuts of meat or whole chickens or turkeys.

Gas barbecues are convenient, efficient, easy to master and can be used throughout the winter as well as in the summer, and food cooked on them has the delicious smoky taste that we associate with char-broiled food. But there are also significant disadvantages. As well as being expensive, they are heavy and therefore awkward to transport and are so simple to operate that it can be no more fun — or creative — than cooking on a gas stove.

Both hibachi and kettle rely on charcoal for the fire. There are several kinds of wood now available for use as fuel, and their different properties afford lots of elbowroom for debate. Mesquite and hickory are particularly suited for cooking heavy meats (pork and beef), while grapevine cuttings provide a delicate flavour for grilling poultry, fish, lamb and vegetables. Plain charcoal is inexpensive, lights easily and gives a good burn quickly. Charcoal briquettes hold their heat longer but take more time to arrive at the ash stage — 30 minutes, compared with charcoal's 10 to 15. To

Portable and multifaceted, barbecues are the perfect choice for cooking just about anything at the cottage.

Meat is only the beginning for memorable barbecues; a wide variety of vegetables, from tomatoes to green beans, are perfectly suited to the grill as well.

create a pleasant aroma while barbecuing with either form, throw fresh herbs on the coals while cooking.

There are many approaches to lighting a barbecue. Certainly the most reliable is to douse the charcoal or wood with charcoal lighter fluid, let it sit for five minutes and then light. Woodstove aficionados may place paper and kindling at the base of the barbecue, light them and wait for the charcoal or wood to catch. An urban friend of mine places several pieces of charcoal or wood and a few scraps of paper in a waxed milk carton and lights that. But never use gasoline or kerosene — they are dangerous and give the food an unpleasant taste.

The coals are ready to cook over when the ash on them is white. To test the heat more precisely, hold your hand above the coals at the level of the grill. If you can leave it there for three seconds, the fire is what most barbecue recipes call medium-hot; more than three seconds, slow; or less than three seconds, hot. Remember, the true art of

barbecuing lies in getting the food on the grill at exactly the right time. Never begin barbecuing while there are still flames, or the food will taste bitter.

It is not necessary to spend a fortune on barbecuing equipment and gadgets, but there are a few utensils that make outdoor cooking easier and safer. A pair of long, fireproof cooking gloves is mandatory and should be hung close to the barbecue for convenience. Barbecuing tends to result in grease splashes, so a heavy-duty apron is also a good idea. Two sets of tongs are needed — one for moving the coals around, a favourite pastime of the hibachi set, and another for the food. Both should have long, wooden handles, as should the brushes used for basting. If you will be barbecuing fish on a regular basis, it is worthwhile to invest in a hinged wire basket. Using one of these is much simpler than trying to flip a whole fish on the grill without breaking it. Skewers, preferably wooden, and a water sprinkler for dousing sudden flare-ups in the barbecue (or for controlling cooking

temperatures) complete the basic inventory of barbecuing equipment. Extras you may add as you gain enthusiasm and experience include knives, salt and pepper shakers, a carving board and a meat thermometer, but occasional barbecuers can simply borrow these items from the kitchen.

Food that is to be barbecued should be at room temperature before being placed on the grill. If it is too cold, the outside will cook long before the middle. Meat should always be turned with tongs or a spatula. Using a fork will pierce the meat, and valuable juices will run out, causing the meat to dry up and creating flames that will make the meat bitter. When preparing kebabs, soak the wooden skewers in cold water for an hour before using. When barbecuing whole pieces of meat, such as steaks or chops, sear the meat briefly on both sides and then move it slightly farther away from the coals to cook. Large sausages, ribs and chicken wings or legs should be parboiled before being barbecued. A neat trick to keep hamburgers moist while barbecuing is to build each one around a small ice cube. The ice will melt during cooking, keeping the meat juicy and less likely to fall apart on the grill.

To cook corn on the cob on the barbecue, pull back the husks carefully and remove the silk. Replace the husks, tie in place, then boil for 3 to 4 minutes. Cook on the grill over hot coals for 15 minutes or right in the coals for 10 minutes. Potatoes can be baked in the coals as well: scrub them, wrap them in foil, and bury them in the coals to bake for 50 minutes. If sweet potatoes are used, the cooking time will be slightly less.

Following a few simple rules will make outdoor summer eating safe as well as simple and delicious. If you plan to eat in the backyard, keep all salads (especially those with mayonnaise or creamy dressings) refrigerated until the last moment. The same applies to desserts made with cream or eggs. Remove foods to be barbecued from the refrigerator just long enough ahead of time to allow them to reach room temperature. If the salads are left out for more than 30 minutes during the meal, do not keep them. If picnicking, invest in a good cooler that is large enough to hold a couple of blocks of ice, the food and any drinks that need to be kept cold. (Drinks can always be frozen at home and then allowed to thaw in transit, thus leaving more space for food in the cooler.) It does not take long for foods to spoil in hot weather, and this is definitely an area where it is better to be safe than sorry.

Barbecuing can be as simple as digging a pit on the beach, building a fire with dry driftwood and cooking frankfurters on sticks. On the other hand, it can be as elaborate as a pig or lamb roast, involving a huge stone-filled pit, wood and wet leaves for a fire started a whole day ahead of time and a full menu of accompanying dishes, not to mention considerable skills. For most of us, it means something in between — a hibachi or kettle barbecue set up in the backyard, hamburgers, kebabs or steak, a couple of salads and a big bowl of ice cream for dessert, served up with beer and good company. It also means

fine summer fare prepared with a minimum of effort on the part of the cook and maximum enjoyment for all who dine on it.

(NOTE: While some of the quantities in these recipes may seem large, it is our experience that people always eat more outdoors than they do inside.)

CHICKEN WINGS WITH TASTY BARBECUE SAUCE

No discussion on barbecuing would be complete without a recipe for chicken wings. This barbecue sauce can be used with equally tasty results on chicken or pork. Serve the wings with a tangy blue-cheese dip to spice them up even more. Simply combine blue cheese to taste with sour cream and/or yogurt in a blender or food processor, and blend until almost smooth.

20 chicken wings
1½ cups brown sugar
2 Tbsp. apple cider vinegar
4 Tbsp. soya sauce
2 Tbsp. oyster sauce
2 Tbsp. black bean sauce
1 cup tomato sauce
2 cloves garlic, chopped
Juice of 1 lemon
Pepper

Cook chicken wings in boiling water to cover for 15 minutes. Drain, reserving stock for later use.

Meanwhile, combine remaining ingredients in heavy saucepan and cook for 15 minutes, stirring frequently.

Dip wings in barbecue sauce, then place on grill 3 to 4 inches away from white ashes (hot coals) and cook 5 to 10 minutes per side, basting frequently with sauce.

Serves 4 to 6.

ARTICHOKE HEART SALAD

3 cans artichoke hearts
1 red onion
½ cup oil
⅓ cup cider vinegar
2 Tbsp. honey
1 Tbsp. grated onion
Salt and pepper
½ tsp. mustard
1 pkg. spinach, washed and torn

Drain artichoke hearts and cut into quarters. Peel and slice red onion into thin rings. Combine oil, vinegar, honey, grated onion, salt and pepper and mustard in a glass jar and shake to blend well. Mix artichokes and red onion in salad bowl, then pour the dressing over and mix well. Let sit at room temperature for 2 hours. Just before serving, add spinach and toss gently.

Serves 6.

LAMB KEBABS

Assemble the meat and the vegetable kebabs on separate skewers. Although this recipe was created with lamb in mind, other red meats can be used.

Marinade:
1 cup red wine
¼ cup red wine vinegar
½ cup olive oil
2 tsp. thyme
6 peppercorns
2 bay leaves
4 cloves garlic
1 tsp. salt
1 onion, minced
Parsley

Kebabs:
4-5 lbs. lean lamb, cubed
2 large green peppers
1 lb. large mushrooms
3 onions
1 pint cherry tomatoes
Bamboo skewers, soaked in cold
    water for 1 hour

Combine marinade ingredients and mix well. Pour over meat in glass or porcelain bowl. Cover and refrigerate for 24 hours. Drain. When ready to assemble kebabs, cut vegetables into large cubes and place a combination of them on half the skewers and the meat on the remainder. Brush the vegetables with a little marinade if you like. Place the meat kebabs on the grill approximately 4 inches away from the white ashes (hot coals). Cook, turning frequently and basting each time you turn, for 10 minutes, or until the meat is brown on the outside but still pink in the middle. Place the vegetable kebabs on the grill, and cook them in the same manner as the meat kebabs for 5 minutes.

Serves 8 to 10.

PASTA SALAD

2 lbs. fresh spaghetti or fettuccine
2 cloves garlic
2 eggs
6 Tbsp. red wine vinegar
1 tsp. dry mustard
Salt and pepper
2 cups oil
1 cup crumbled blue cheese
2 stalks celery
1 green pepper
1 bunch green onions
1 cup pitted black olives

Cook pasta in rapidly boiling water until just tender — 2 to 3 minutes if fresh pasta is used. Rinse under cold running water, then drain. To make dressing, place garlic, eggs, vinegar, mustard and salt and pepper in blender or food processor. Add 1 cup oil and blend until all ingredients are well mixed. Slowly add remaining oil, with machine running, until a thick mayonnaise results. Add blue cheese and blend until smooth.

Mince celery, green pepper and onions. Toss vegetables, olives and pasta together. Add dressing and toss gently to blend. Chill well.

Serves 8.

GRILLED VEGETABLES WITH PESTO

Take advantage of garden-fresh basil and parsley with this simple recipe for cooking vegetables on the barbecue.

Pesto:
2 cups fresh basil
2 cloves garlic
½ cup fresh parsley
½ tsp. salt
½ cup olive oil
¼ cup Parmesan cheese
4 Tbsp. pine nuts

Vegetables:
4 medium eggplant
Salt
4 medium zucchini
4 large tomatoes
Oil

To make pesto, place basil, garlic, parsley, salt and ⅓ cup oil in blender or food processor. Process, adding oil if necessary, to make a smooth paste. Add cheese and nuts and blend for a few seconds more. Cover and set aside.

Wash eggplant and cut into thick slices. Place in colander and sprinkle liberally with salt. Leave for 30 minutes. Wash and thickly slice zucchini and tomatoes.

Place eggplant on grill 3 inches from medium coals and brush with oil. Grill for 2 to 3 minutes, then turn. Add zucchini, brush with oil and cook for 1 minute, then turn. Add tomato, brush with oil and cook for 30 seconds, then turn. When all vegetables have grilled on both sides, remove to serving dish and top each slice with a heaping tablespoon of pesto.

Serves 8 to 10 as a side dish.

BARBECUED STUFFED SALMON

Oil
1 whole salmon, cleaned, but with head and tail left on
Salt
1 cup pine nuts
1 bunch parsley, chopped
4 carrots, peeled and sliced
2 zucchini, sliced
4 stalks celery, sliced
3 onions, sliced into rings
½ lb. butter, melted
Black pepper
Thyme
4 lemons

Grease a large piece of aluminum foil, and place salmon on it. Salt the cavity. Combine the nuts, parsley and vegetables in a large bowl. Stir in the butter and mix well, adding pepper and thyme to taste. Place the stuffing in the cavity of the salmon. Mound any extra stuffing around the fish. Rub oil over the scales, then squeeze the juice of 2 lemons over all. Wrap the fish gently but securely in foil.

Place the grill approximately 6 inches away from medium-hot coals and cook, turning occasionally, for approximately 30 minutes. Check the fish frequently, as cooking time will vary greatly depending on the heat of the coals. When fish flakes easily but is still moist, it is done. Serve immediately, garnished with lemon wedges, or chill and then serve.

Serves 10 as part of a buffet or 4 as a main course.

BARBECUED SPARERIBS

15 lbs. pork spareribs
2 cups pork stock
4 Tbsp. oil
4 large cloves garlic, minced
2 large onions, finely chopped
1 Tbsp. finely minced gingerroot
2 Tbsp. curry powder
½ cup toasted coconut
½ cup apple cider
5 ½-oz can tomato paste
2 bay leaves
⅔ cup peanut butter
½ tsp. salt
¼ cup soya sauce
Juice of 1 lemon
Tabasco sauce
Worcestershire sauce
½ cup chili sauce
1 cup beer

Cover ribs with water in large pot. Bring to a boil and cook for 15 to 20 minutes, or until ribs are cooked through. Remove ribs from pot, and reserve stock.

Heat oil in heavy skillet, and sauté garlic, onions and gingerroot until onion is translucent. Add curry powder and continue to cook over high heat, stirring, for 5 minutes. Add stock, coconut, cider, tomato paste and bay leaves. Bring to a boil and cook for 10 minutes.

Stir in peanut butter, salt, soya sauce, lemon juice, Tabasco and Worcestershire sauce, chili sauce and beer. Cook for 10 minutes longer, then remove from heat.

Place ribs on grill 4 inches away from hot coals and baste with sauce.

Turn and baste other side. Cook, turning and basting frequently, for 20 to 30 minutes, or until the ribs are crisp and browned.

Serves 10 to 12.

Originally published in Harrowsmith *magazine (Camden East, Ont.).*

The vegetarian, wood-smoke barbecue

by Tom Ney

Cooking out-of-doors arouses my sense of connection to distant ancestors. If I were a hunter, I would grill my prey. But since I'm a gardener, it's vegetables I cook on the open fire.

Last Thanksgiving, for example, I served a rainbow of grilled vegetables on a platter worthy of a 20-pound turkey, to the oohs and aahs of all. Here's how I did it, and how you can too, enhancing that homegrown flavour with a piquant marinade and a robust hint of wood smoke. It's easy and satisfying, whether you're feeding 4 or 40.

Preparation begins several hours before mealtime. Choose vegetables for their colour, such as carrots, zucchini, onions and different-coloured bell peppers. Cut half-inch pieces of carrots and zucchini on the bias for a broad surface. Slice large scallops from red, yellow and green bell peppers. Quarter and separate large sweet onions in creamy petals. For texture and the perfect leafy green, tear clusters of kale leaves into bite-sized pieces. Bag each batch of vegetables separately in plastic food-storage bags, and store them in the refrigerator.

About an hour before dinner, spoon an Italian vinaigrette, preferably one made with balsamic vinegar, over the chilled vegetables in each bag. (You may also want to try the marinade recipe included in this article. At least, brush with vegetable oil.) There's no need to tenderize most vegetables before grilling, but the marinades protect them from drying out and lend a marvellous flavour, especially when they are made with large amounts of chopped fresh herbs. After twist-tying the bags shut, knead the vegetables gently to spread the marinade. Then toss them back into the refrigerator for a rest and a chance to absorb their new flavouring.

The next step is to prepare your grill. I use the Grillery, which is designed especially for wood-fire cooking, but a typical kettle barbecue grill will work too. I have grilled vegetables successfully over a wood fire in mine. You can use regular charcoal or try tossing some hardwood chips or nuggets onto the glowing coals. Flat, portable grills and brick barbecues also work well with wood fires.

Quick-lighting gas grills save a lot of time and effort when cooking outdoors, but you lose the charcoal flavour that a conventional grill gives food, since gas grills normally use flavourless lava stones to radiate heat and absorb juices. Char-Broil has come to the rescue of charcoal lovers with a new kind of briquette developed specifically for gas grills. Char-Broil charcoal briquettes are supposed to provide flavour for up to 10 hours and are designed to retain their shape and not to clog burner ports even after the flavour has been expended. A six-pound bag of briquettes is usually available at home centres, discount stores and garden outlets that sell Char-Broil grills.

Most hardwoods are appropriate for grilling vegetables. However, an interesting kindling ingredient is the prunings from your shrubs and small trees. After talking to Lisa Readie of the Barbecue Industry Association and to other wood specialists, I compiled the following list of recommended woods: alder, apple, American beech, cherry, grapevines, hickory, maple, mesquite, oak, peach, pecan and poplar.

I am sure other types of woody plants would work as well. You may want to try lilac, forsythia, dogwood or others. Avoid softwood conifers or evergreens and obviously any poisonous plants, like poison ivy. If you have any concerns about the suitability of a plant, contact local experts before you try it.

First, stack kindling, sticks and small logs on top of crumpled newspapers in the grill. Light the fire, and when the flames begin to recede, add the grill rack and heat for two or three minutes. Then spoon the marinated vegetables onto the hot grill about four to six inches above the fire. Be sure the grill grates are close enough to support the small vegetables. If not, cover the grill with heavy-duty aluminum foil. Use long-handled tongs or a spatula to keep the vegetables moving. It is impossible to overcook them; they'll char black if you do. Remove them quickly to a bowl or a platter, or serve immediately from the grill.

For your next meal, try grilling the vegetables instead of the meat and watch them disappear first.

CALIFORNIA GARDEN

½ cup freshly squeezed orange juice

2 Tbsp. freshly squeezed lime juice

1 Tbsp. slivered orange zest, blanched 2 minutes

1 tsp. slivered lime zest, blanched 2 minutes

2 Tbsp. chopped fresh French tarragon leaves, or 1 tsp. dried

1 Tbsp. snipped fresh chives or thinly sliced green scallion

2 Tbsp. white wine Worcestershire sauce

¼ cup avocado oil or olive oil

In a small bowl, combine orange juice, lime juice, orange zest, lime zest, tarragon, chives and Worcestershire sauce. Stir with a fork to blend. Drizzle avocado oil into marinade while whisking with the fork.

Let stand at room temperature for 1 hour, or cover and refrigerate overnight.

Makes 1 cup.

Memorable summer desserts with blueberries

by Janet Ballantyne

I love to pick mounds and mounds of blueberries, not only because they are so delicious but also because they are so easy to pick. Compared with thorny raspberries or strawberries that require bending down, blueberries are a snap to harvest. And in a good season, the berries practically fall off the bushes into my pail. Fresh blueberries taste great in the patch and even better at home with a few other ingredients.

During berry season, the sheer volume of fresh fruit means that you can easily eat berries at every meal and still have enough to freeze. However, after the first few bowls of plain blueberries with cream, it's time to find new and creative ways to incorporate blueberries into breakfasts, lunches and dinners.

Since time is always at a premium in the glorious days of summer, I developed a few quick, easy and healthful recipes for you to try. You'll find that the Blueberry Oatmeal Muffins take only 34 minutes from start to tasty finish. They are made with skim milk and less butter or shortening than normal muffins, but the results will never reveal that secret.

The Spiced Blueberry Sauce tastes great on top of pancakes or fresh fruit. It's so quick to prepare that you can whip it up between dinner and dessert. It's sweetened with apple juice concentrate. You'll never miss the sugar or the honey.

The Summer Fresh Blueberry Cheesecake Pie makes an ideal summer treat because it doesn't need baking; once the berry filling heats and thickens — in 10 minutes — the pie just has to be chilled. And again, the small amount of honey helps the natural sweetness of the fruit come through. With only a little time and a little sweetener, the abundant blueberry bounty can provide you with blueberry treats from sunup to sundown.

SUMMER FRESH BLUEBERRY CHEESECAKE PIE

Half the berries are set aside and stirred in after the lush filling heats and thickens — a cooked-pie feel with fresh-berry flavour.

1 single piecrust, prebaked and cooled
3 Tbsp. cornstarch
½ cup water
4½ cups blueberries
½ cup honey
1½ cups low-fat cottage cheese
6 Tbsp. apple juice concentrate

Prepare single piecrust (see recipe below).

Mix the cornstarch into the water until well blended. Place 2 cups of blueberries in a food processor or blender, and pour cornstarch mixture over the berries. Purée.

Pour puréed mixture into a heavy-bottomed, medium-sized saucepan, and add the honey. Cook over medium-low heat for 7 to 8 minutes, or until the blueberry mixture is thick and clear.

Add 2 more cups of blueberries (reserving the last ½ cup for a garnish on the top). Pour the fruit mixture into the prepared, baked piecrust.

For the topping, purée the cottage cheese and apple juice concentrate until smooth and spread evenly over the pie. Decorate the top with the remaining blueberries, sprinkled free-style or arranged in a formal pattern. Chill the pie for 2 hours.

Makes one 10-inch pie (8 servings).

Per serving (estimated): 295 calories, 7.4 g protein, 49 g carbohydrate, 9 g fat, 22 mg cholesterol, 183 mg sodium.

SINGLE PIECRUST

1 cup unbleached all-purpose flour (or see whole wheat variations below)
½ tsp. salt
⅓ cup butter, shortening or margarine
2 - 2 ½ Tbsp. cold water

In a medium-sized bowl, mix the flour and salt.

Cut the butter or shortening into the flour with a pastry cutter until the mixture looks like cornmeal and peas.

Sprinkle the water over this mixture and stir, using a fork, until the dough comes together. Wrap in plastic wrap and chill for 1 hour.

Lightly flour a work surface, and roll out the crust, working from the centre out in all directions. Make a circle 12 inches across and about ⅛ inch thick.

Lift dough gently into pan, folding into quarters, if necessary, to prevent tearing. Fold edges under and crimp. Poke holes in the crust to allow steam to escape.

Bake for 15 to 20 minutes. Cool completely before filling.

Makes one 9-to-10-inch piecrust.

Whole wheat variation: Use 1¼ cups whole wheat flour with 6 tablespoons butter or shortening and 2 to 3 tablespoons water.

Whole wheat and white flour variation: Use ½ cup whole wheat flour and ¾ cup unbleached all-purpose flour, 6 tablespoons butter or shortening and 2 to 3 tablespoons water.

SPICED BLUEBERRY SAUCE

Sweetened only with apple juice concentrate, this sauce can be made between courses.

1 cup blueberries
½ cup frozen apple juice concentrate
⅓ cup water
½ tsp. cinnamon
2 dashes ground cloves
2 Tbsp. unbleached flour

In a small saucepan, combine the blueberries, apple juice concentrate, water and spices. Simmer for 5 minutes.

Place the flour in a small bowl, and spoon in ¼ cup of the hot liquid from the blueberries. Stir until all the lumps are gone. Pour the flour mixture in with the blueberries and stir well.

Cook for 2 more minutes. Serve warm or cold.

Makes 1¼ cups.

Per ¼-cup serving: 74 calories, 1 g protein, 18 g carbohydrate, 0.2 g fat, 0 mg cholesterol, 9 mg sodium.

BLUEBERRY OATMEAL MUFFINS

Add a little cinnamon and nutmeg to these great muffins. They go beautifully with the blueberries. A great recipe that's ready in 34 minutes.

⅔ cup oatmeal (not instant)
1 cup whole wheat flour
¾ cup unbleached flour
1 tsp. baking powder
¼ tsp. nutmeg
1 tsp. cinnamon
1 large egg, beaten
1 cup skim milk
2 Tbsp. margarine or butter, melted
2 Tbsp. honey
1 cup blueberries

Preheat the oven to 400 degrees F. Grease the muffin tin or line with paper muffin cups.

In a large mixing bowl, mix together all the dry ingredients.

In a separate bowl, whisk together the egg, milk, margarine or butter and honey. Stir in the blueberries.

Pour the wet ingredients into the dry ingredients all at once and fold in until the dry ingredients are just moistened.

Spoon batter into the cups and bake for 20 minutes or until lightly browned. Serve warm.

Makes 1 dozen muffins.

Per serving (estimated): 119 calories, 4 g protein, 21 g carbohydrate, 3 g fat, 28 mg cholesterol, 18 mg sodium.

Reprinted by permission of Organic Gardening *magazine (Emmaus, PA). Copyright 1991. Rodale Press, Inc. U.S.A. All rights reserved.*

Suntanning need not be totally shunned, but be careful

Getting the Proper Exposure

by Daryn Eller

Growing up on the beaches of southern California, I was lighthearted and my beach bag was always lightweight, filled with nothing more than a towel, a book and, since I knew I'd be out there for hours, sometimes a piece of fruit. But these days, you'll find me trudging out with a chair — the kind that has an umbrella attached — two bottles of sunscreen (one for my face, one for my body), a lip protector, a hat, a pair of sunglasses and a T-shirt as well as that trusty towel and book (no fruit — I won't be out there that long). Needless to say, my beach bag is a lot heavier now but not as heavy as the weight of indecision on my mind: Do I really need all this stuff? Now that everything from makeups to moisturizers has an SPF and there are T-shirts treated with ultraviolet (UV) blockers and sunglasses containing melanin (the skin's natural sun-protection pigment) on the way, one has to wonder if this might be so much overkill.

Not that the concern isn't real. It's common knowledge that excessive exposure to the sun's ultraviolet rays is primarily responsible for premature ageing and may increase the risk of skin cancer considerably. In fact, the incidence of melanoma, the most serious form of skin cancer, has risen tenfold since 1930. Experts warn that even year-round incidental exposure adds up and can damage skin as much as hours spent lolling on the beach.

Some researchers think that chronic UV exposure may also suppress the immune system. Normally, structures called Langerhans' cells, found in the epidermis, the upper layer of the skin, alert the body to the presence of bacteria, viruses and even cancerous cells that may be developing. When harmed by UV rays, they may lose their ability to trigger immune responses. Scientists haven't pinpointed who is most at risk for having their immune system compromised — skin colour may not make a difference.

What is surprising is that people who are at high risk for sun damage aren't doomed. "It's not clear why some people do and some don't get skin cancer," says Dr. David R. Bickers, professor and chairman, department of dermatology, Case Western Reserve University, Cleveland. "Some skin may possess the ability to repair the injury it has suffered." Nevertheless, everyone needs to be wary of the sun — particularly people with fair skin. "I compare skin damage to a taxi meter," says Dr. Darrell Rigel, clinical assistant professor of dermatology at New York University Medical School. "If you're fair-skinned, your meter runs faster than if you're dark-skinned — although in either case, you can't make the meter go backward."

Doctors warn that children are also vulnerable to UV rays, in part because kids are outdoors three times as often as adults. In fact, by age 18, most people have already received half of the sun exposure they can expect in their lifetimes. A 1983 Harvard study found that one severe sunburn before age 20 may double the risk of developing melanoma later in life. Other factors can also predispose people to sun damage — where a person lives, for one: people in the sunbelt have a much higher incidence of skin cancer than people who live in more northerly areas. An area's pollution level makes an unexpected difference as well. For all its adverse effects, smog just happens to block some UV light.

Finally, although tanning produces melanin, which acts as a defence mechanism against the sun's rays, it does damage skin. "Any tanning reaction is visible evidence of injury. To tan continually is to continually injure the skin," says Bickers.

As the risks of sun exposure have

Melanoma, a form of skin cancer, should be countered with sunscreen and common sense.

become clearer, the specifics of protection have become more and more confusing — sunscreen labels now offer a virtual alphabet soup of acronyms: SPF, APP, APF.

It's the rare sunbather who doesn't know that SPF refers to a suncreen's sun-protection factor — how long it will allow you to stay outside without burning. For example, if you burn in 10 minutes, an SPF 15 will protect you 15 times longer, or 150 minutes. The SPF number is based on how effectively the product blocks UVB rays — strong, short wavelengths that have been linked to sunburn, premature ageing and heightened skin-cancer risk.

Most experts recommend that all fair-skinned people and especially children wear nothing less than an SPF 15 — and that darker-skinned people wear at least an SPF 8 — sunscreen on exposed skin all year long, even when it's overcast (UV rays penetrate clouds). UVB levels that are too low to cause sunburn can still affect your skin over time. But many concede that the need for, say, a woman living in Portland, Maine, to regularly apply sunscreen is not as pressing as for a woman living in southern California. And, perhaps more relevant, the reality is that most people (particularly children) don't wear an SPF 15 daily.

"Not everyone slathers on sunscreen every time they get out of bed, and the fact is, you don't have to," says Dr. John H. Epstein, clinical professor of dermatology, University of California, San Francisco. "Just make sure you use it when it's essential" — when spending an extended amount of time outdoors, especially between the hours of 10 a.m. and 3 p.m., or a day by the pool or at the beach.

You might occasionally want to wear one of the higher-number (18-50) SPFs, although their effectiveness is controversial. Critics say these sunscreens offer only slightly more protection than an SPF 15 (while a 15 screens out 95 percent of the sun's rays, a 30 may screen out only 98 percent) and may lead people to stay out longer than is safe. Still, many dermatologists encourage using higher-numbered products.

As the numbers in SPF sunscreens rise, so does the amount of chemicals used in the formulation. That is the reason super-high-SPF sunscreens are more likely to irritate the skin.

"A 30 won't protect you twice as long as a 15, because it offers only a few percentage points more protection than a 15. But for fair-skinned people who burn easily, it's an important percentage," argues Dr. Nicholas Lowe, clinical professor of dermatology, UCLA Medical School. "It's not necessary to wear an SPF 25 or 30 daily when you're just going to and fro, but it's a good idea if you are fair and are planning to spend a lot of time outdoors."

A sunscreen with a higher-number SPF has another advantage. If you apply it too thinly or inadvertently wipe some off, it will still give you a protection factor of about 15 to 20. "But if you apply an SPF 15 correctly," says Rigel, "that is, use one ounce to cover the entire body, and reapply it hourly, you probably don't need a higher SPF — and higher-priced — sunscreen." One caveat: As the numbers rise, so does the amount of chemicals used in the formulation. That's the reason superhigh-SPF sunscreens are more likely to irritate the skin.

Recently, experts have been emphasizing the potential danger of UVA rays for the fair-skinned. Hence, the rise of new buzzwords on sunscreen labels, such as APF (UVA-protection factor) and APP (UVA-protection percentage).

Decoded, these letters tell you what percentage of UVA rays the sunscreen will block.

Although less powerful than UVB wavelengths, UVA rays penetrate more deeply and are in greater abundance year-round. They can cause wrinkling and photosensitive reactions — rashes, swelling, redness — to medication. They may also exacerbate the cancer-causing effects of UVB rays. "However, they're not as damaging as UVBs nor nearly as efficient at causing cancer," says Epstein.

Even so, "better safe than sorry" seems to be the prevailing attitude these days. Many companies now incorporate UVA- and UVB-blocking ingredients into their sunscreens. The Food and Drug Administration (FDA), which regulates SPF claims, is working on but has not yet established standards for UVA blocking. Not all sunscreens that block UVA rays are labelled as such. Some feature the words "broad spectrum" or "UVA protection" along with their SPF number. Chemicals called benzophenones (oxybenzone, dioxybenzone), listed under ingredients, are another tip-off. Parsol 1789, contained in one sunscreen, has been considered the most effective UVA-blocking ingredient. However, unless a number is provided on the label, there's no way to judge a product's UVA-screening ability. But there's also no reason to agonize over it. "Most good sunscreens with a high SPF offer protection against UVA rays too," says Rigel.

No matter how effectively a product blocks UV rays, it won't protect you if it doesn't stay on. That's why a flurry of research is under way. Some experts, for example, are reportedly trying to develop a sunscreen that will last all day. Estée Lauder, the cosmetic company, recently announced that it is trying to create one that will remain on for several days.

Much of a sunscreen's staying power depends on its delivery system: cream, lotion, gel or oil. Creams and lotions are generally the best performers. "Many have a kind of adhesive ingredient that forms a film on the skin and has the additional benefit of acting as a moisturizer," says Chris Vaughan, a cosmetic chemist and vice president of research and development for Ultimate Contract Packaging, in Pompano Beach, Florida. For that reason, waterproof sunscreens, the longest-lasting products — by FDA regulation, they must stay on for 80 minutes even in water — are usually in cream or lotion form. Waterproof sunscreens often deliver more protection than they advertise. "While they may be billed as an SPF 15, they're usually more like a 20 to 25, so when some decomposes in the water, they'll still offer a protection factor of 15," explains Vaughan. That bonus can spell good news for fast burners but bad news for people who are particularly sensitive to sunscreen chemicals.

Waterproof sunscreens get their staying power in part from innocuous plastic or acrylic polymers. But these also make them feel "gunky" — too gunky, in fact, for day-to-day wear. Oil-based sunscreens are best for hiking and skiing because they protect skin from wind and chill, says Madhukar A. Pathak, senior associate in dermatology at Harvard Medical School. They are usually too heavy and sticky for everyday or beach-day use. If worn while swimming, they could leave behind an oil slick in the pool, meaning your sunscreen is coming off.

Gel formulations differ in how well they stay on the skin; those which are alcohol-based (they feel cool on application) are longer-lasting than those which are oil-based (they feel slick). "Gels have the advantage of spreading easily and covering the skin nicely," says Pathak; and both characteristics make them acceptable for everyday and beach wear.

Almost as important as a sunscreen's delivery system is how long its active sun-blocking ingredients will work and whether they'll irritate your skin. In tests, Vaughan has found ethylhexyl p-methoxycinnamate to be the active ingredient that hangs in there longest. It is usually found in creams and lotions and in PABA-free products.

PABA refers to the chemical para-aminobenzoic acid and its derivatives like padimate O. PABA and its spinoffs are the most effective of all sunray absorbers, but they are surprisingly prone to breakdown. So if you choose a PABA-based product, be sure to re-apply it frequently. Many sunscreens boast that they're PABA-free, because the chemical can cause an allergic reaction in about 7 percent of the population, according to Rigel. Infants under 6 months may suffer adverse reactions to PABA. That's why many sunscreens formulated for children are PABA-free. Otherwise, kids' formulations really don't differ significantly from adult products. "Sometimes, it's just the fragrance that's different," says Rigel.

Other ingredients can also cause irritation. At least one company is working on a sunscreen made with melanin, since it may ultimately be easiest on the skin. Finding a sunscreen that's nonirritating and comfortable can be a matter of trial and error.

Lowe recommends using a separate product for the face, since these formulations are usually lighter and tend not to cause acne. However, because sunscreen chemicals themselves are oils, even "oil-free" formulations are never completely true to the term.

It also makes sense to apply a lip sunscreen; these waxy products don't rub off easily. "When you're choosing any product, though, be aware that you're not necessarily getting more when you pay more," says Lowe.

If there is anything else that's considered a must for outdoor wear, it's a pair of sunglasses: researchers at Johns Hopkins University have found that people who don't shield their eyes from the sun are three times more likely to develop cataracts than those who do. No one is really sure what causes the damage, but it's believed that blue light (part of the visible spectrum) and ultraviolet (invisible) light may alter chemical elements in the eye called chromophores. "Protective sunglasses can't prevent cataracts — they occur naturally with ageing. However, they may slow down their formation," says Dr. Jason S. Slakter, assistant attending surgeon at the Manhattan Eye, Ear and Throat Hospital.

There are other concerns about eye damage from the sun; and if theories about the depletion of the ozone layer — which helps block hazardous rays — are correct, the dangers may be increasing. Some evidence that a diminished ozone layer can contribute to eye problems has already surfaced. Slakter and his colleagues saw 4 out of 12 people who developed solar retinopathy (photochemical burns of the retina) on two days in March 1986. Since cases of solar retinopathy are rare, the doctors investigated and found that the level of ozone in the atmosphere on those two days was the lowest ever recorded by satellite. "It's not that we expect people to start walking in off the streets with solar burns," says Slakter. "This was an unusual incident."

He is concerned, however, that as ozone decreases and UV and blue light increase, macular degeneration, already the leading cause of legal blindness over age 60, may occur more frequently. "People under 30 are most susceptible [because the harmful effects of UV and blue light are cumulative], so they're the ones who need to protect themselves," says Slakter. As in the case of skin and melanoma, there is some correlation between macular degeneration, the region one lives in and the colour of one's eyes: the sunnier the region and lighter the eyes, the more prone to damage a person will be.

Many eye doctors feel that precautionary measures should be taken with children especially, not only because they spend so much time outside but also because "under the age of 10, the human lens allows 75 percent of light to pass through to the retina, while it allows only 25 percent through when we get older," says Dr. Gary Hall, an ophthalmologist in private practice in Phoenix, Arizona. Hall, who had trouble finding sunglasses for his own six kids, has recently developed a line of durable, protective sunglasses for children ages 5 to 15.

Manufacturers of sunglasses rarely specify whether their products block out blue light (if they do, the label will indicate blockage of wavelengths between 450 and 500). Fortunately, the better companies are labelling their products' UV-ray-blocking ability, though the information can be confusing. The American National Standards Institute has designated three categories of sunglasses: cosmetic lenses block 70 percent UVB, 20 percent UVA; general-purpose lenses block 95 percent UVB, 60 percent UVA; special-purpose lenses block 99 percent UVB, 60 percent UVA. "Yes, you should get the most extensive UV- and blue-light-blocking sunglasses you can, but I wouldn't get hung up on the details, especially because it's not clear how damaging each ray is," advises Dr. Richard Koplin, of the eye trauma centre at New York Eye and Ear Infirmary.

Bausch & Lomb has further complicated matters by introducing sunglasses whose lenses contain melanin. Bausch & Lomb doesn't claim the melanin is more effective than other UV-blocking chemicals — it just provides another option for consumers. Yet James Gallas, a researcher at the University of Texas, San Antonio, who developed the synthetic melanin Bausch & Lomb is using, claims it filters out the entire spectrum of visible wavelengths (blue, green, red) more efficiently in proportion to the damage they do.

"While I'm sure the glasses will do some fascinating things, I'm not sure they're something you have to run out and buy," says Slakter. "The sunglasses that block UV and blue light and go for $20 at any supermarket are probably just as good as the expensive kind."

When is it necessary to wear protective sunglasses? Some UV rays do pass through the clouds, so it doesn't hurt to don a pair when it's overcast. However, regular prescription glasses that have been coated with a UV- and blue-light screener (the latter causes a slightly yellow tint) also work fine. "It's essential to wear protective sunglasses when you will be out in bright sunlight for extended periods and when you're exposed to reflective light — from snow or water — which will not only hit your eyes when it comes down but also when it bounces back up," says Slakter. Even then, experts stress darker lenses are not always better: Pupils contract in

Dark lenses are not always better: Pupils contract in light, reducing the number of UV rays that hit the back of the eye; too-dark lenses dilate the pupils, allowing more rays to enter.

reaction to light, reducing the number of UV rays that hit the back of the eye; too-dark lenses can dilate the pupils, allowing more rays to enter.

If you've applied your SPF 15 sunscreen and donned UV- and blue-light-blocking sunglasses, most experts would agree you're in good shape. But you wouldn't know that from the surge in sun-blocking products on the market. The optical industry's zealous response to the news about UV rays and eye damage — the "oat bran syndrome," as Koplin calls it — is echoed in the cosmetic industry. Sunscreens are being added to hundreds of products, even though many dermatologists feel it's not crucial to pile SPF on SPF.

Applying a sunscreen-containing moisturizer when you're already wearing a moisturizing sunscreen, for instance, is redundant. "They serve the same purpose, so why buy both?" asks Rigel. While women have the added option of wearing makeup with an SPF — it certainly doesn't hurt — it's not essential if they're already wearing a sunscreen. "Women may forget to put on a sunscreen but don't usually forget to put on their makeup," notes Pathak. "In that case, makeup with a sunscreen is ideal." Since most people won't put on a lip protectant and a lipstick, wear-

ing lip colour that blocks UV rays makes good sense. One caveat about all sun-protective makeup: Many brands only have an SPF of 4 or 6, "which is pretty useless," says Lowe. Wearing a hat or sitting under a beach umbrella are good additional tactics, though they're not protective enough on their own. "Shade blocks direct light but not scattered light, which can also cause burns." explains Pathak. If you burn under direct sun in 20 minutes, you may burn under an umbrella in 60."

The latest weapon against UV rays is sunscreen clothing. An Arizona-based company called Frogskins offers T-shirts and long-sleeved, high-collared tops made from a synthetic fabric that feels like cotton but is so tightly woven, it has an SPF of 36. A regular cotton T-shirt has an SPF of anywhere from 5 to 12 and allows even more light through when it gets wet. Pathak is also researching ways to make garments more sun-protective. By next year, he hopes to obtain patent approval for a noncarcinogenic chemical treatment for fabrics that blocks UVA and UVB rays at an SPF of 60 to 200, wet or dry.

There's no doubt that some people who don't really need to wear a T-shirt with a super-duper SPF will buy one. Others will be duped into buying a sunscreen, a moisturizer with sunscreen and makeup with an SPF-6 base, all for spending the day working in a windowless office. But at least they'll be erring on the side of caution. "Even if SPFs are being used as a marketing tool, they still represent a good opportunity for people to get added protection," says Bickers. And certainly, the idea that protection sells gives businesses incentive to develop better products.

Meanwhile, researchers are trying to outsmart the sun. Efforts are currently under way at New York University Hospital to develop a vaccine against melanoma. Me, I'm waiting for that ever-rumoured sunscreen pill to surface. Either one will certainly help lighten up my beach bag again.

Originally published in Health *magazine (New York). Copyright 1990 by Family Media Inc. All rights reserved.*

Why the sun turns your skin brown

by Ira Flatow

The reason your skin gets dark and your hair gets light in the sun is because hair is dead and skin is alive.

The business end of the hair is at the follicle, under the top layer of skin. It's in the root where a hair begins to form. Supplied by blood vessels, the root is alive, and as the hair grows, the root gives off a protein material into the shaft. By the time the hair gets to the surface of the skin, it is completely made of protein.

While this protein is being secreted to produce hair, there are pigment cells that are putting in the colour. It's a dark brown pigment, melanin, that makes a brunette dark-haired.

As the hair grows, the melanin reaches the surface of the skin. When the melanin meets the bright sunlight, a chemical reaction takes place that converts the dark pigment to a clear colour. This bleaching is time-dependent. So the longer your hair is exposed to sunlight, the clearer it gets.

While the sun is bleaching the melanin in your hair, it is tanning the melanin in your skin. Unlike the single fibre of dead hair, skin is made of many layers; a dead layer seals the top, while at the bottom, more pigment cells are found.

What happens when you lie on the beach, exposed to the sun? Radiation from the sun begins to warm your body and make you feel good. But your skin panics. Sunlight may be great for your ego, but it's lousy for your skin. Long exposure to the sun's ultraviolet (UV) light can degrade your skin and possibly cause cancer.

Even in a mild dose, ultraviolet light begins to hurt the "prickle" cells in your skin. The blood vessels swell with blood. The skin's sensory receptors are damaged and say, "Ouch!" when touched.

The symptoms are familiar. At this point, you have a mild sunburn. Soak up lots more sun, and your skin starts sending up fluid and white blood cells to protect the area. Your sunburn has advanced to the blister stage — a second-degree burn.

To protect itself from burning and damage, the skin rallies its forces. It begins by thickening its top dead layer. Meanwhile, pigment cells down at the lower skin level rev up to make more pigment, more melanin. The body's game plan is to make enough tough pigment to absorb the ultraviolet light and protect you.

Gradually, the pigment gets spread throughout all the cells. As it spreads toward the top layers and into the prickle cells, the pigment gets darker. A tan is born. A tan is the skin's natural defence against the harmful rays of the sun. Melanin is an excellent sun block. Not only does it absorb UV radiation, but also some of the pigment forms a cap over the living cells in the dermis, protecting the genetic material in the skin. Skin cancer develops when the UV breaks down the strands of the cells' DNA.

It's worth pointing out that the tan takes time to develop. The pigment takes days to work its way up to where you can see it. On the other hand, a sunburn shows up in a matter of hours. That's why it's a common notion to assume that in the course of a couple of days, a sunburn turns into a suntan. But that notion is dead wrong. That process — turning pink to brown — works well when broiling a steak but does not apply to getting a suntan.

In fact, the tanning rays are distinctly different from the burning rays. The sun's burning ultraviolet is called UVA, the tanning ultraviolet UVB. Getting a good burn does not ensure getting a good tan. It does ensure a lot of pain and an increase in the risk of getting skin cancer.

Light-skinned people can get sunburned in only 10 to 20 minutes of exposure during peak sun hours around noon. Black-skinned people can also get sunburned, though it takes 10 to 20 times the exposure.

If you need extra incentive to stay out of the sun, consider this: Not only does extended exposure raise your chances of skin cancer, but sunlight also makes your skin wrinkle and age prematurely. Sun damage is cumulative. Over time, the sun breaks down the elastic material in the skin, replacing it with a substance called elastone. Elastone is a poor substitute for the skin's resilient foundation; it does not hold the skin tightly. The result: sagging, drooping and wrinkled skin.

What should one do? Stay out of the sun; or if being a shut-in is not your life style, try a sun block (see previous story). A sunscreen rated number 15 or higher should allow you to stay outside as long as you want without danger to your skin.

Don't be fooled by cloudy weather. Clouds may absorb the infrared, or heat, rays of the sun, but ultraviolet radiation still reaches the skin. Long exposure, even in the shade of an umbrella, can cause sunburn from scattered and reflected radiation.

Tanning reaches a peak in 4 to 10 days. Fading occurs when pigmented skin gradually sheds. But once skin is sunburned, the damage cannot be undone. The effects are cumulative. Prolonged exposure to UV disrupts the structure of the skin, makes it lose elasticity and, as many people find out too late, causes premature wrinkling and increases the chances of getting skin cancer.

Excerpted with permission from Rainbows, Curve Balls and Other Wonders of the Natural World Explained, © *William Morrow and Co. Inc./Publishers (New York), 1988.*

Understanding preserved wood pays off in the long run

Deck Lumber Made to Last

by Stephen Smulski

Cellulose and lignin, the stuff of which wood is made, are the two most abundant organic compounds on Earth. Without the fungi and insects that biodegrade them, the landscape would be literally covered with downed and dead trees. The problem is that these relentless recyclers don't distinguish between wood lying on the forest floor and wood supporting your first floor.

Humankind has been helping wood-destroying organisms make that distinction ever since the Egyptians first smeared wooden funerary objects with cedar oil. But the wood-preserving industry did not begin in earnest until the late 1800s, when America's railroads, faced with a shortage of naturally durable woods for crossties, started saturating lesser woods with creosote. Today, preservatives protect everything from poles, posts and piles to plywood, millwork and shingles.

Wood rots because it is being eaten by primitive plants called decay fungi, a process aptly termed the "slow fire." Other wood destroyers include carpenter ants, termites and dozens of beetles. Some gnaw tunnels in wood to create places to live, while others use it for food. Crustaceans called marine borers also attack wood, burrowing into ships, piers and other wooden saltwater structures. Even bacteria can degrade wood under the right circumstances.

Four conditions must exist before fungi or insects will attack wood: an oxygen supply; a continuous wood-moisture content of at least 20 percent; a temperature range of 40 to 90 degrees F; and a food source, which is the wood itself. Eliminate any of these conditions, and you eliminate the problem of decay indefinitely.

Of course, it's hard to do much about temperature and oxygen, so the most effective and common method of preventing deterioration has always been to keep wood dry. This explains the long life of wood used indoors. In exterior use or in other circumstances where wood cannot be kept dry, the traditional method of delaying decay has been to use the heartwood of naturally rot-resistant woods, such as western red cedar, redwood, bald cypress and white oak. Nature has kept these and other woods off the menu by depositing in their heartwood unpalatable poisons called extractives. But supplies of naturally durable woods are too small to meet today's demand at an ecologically and economically acceptable price. In imitation of nature's genius, the wood-preserving industry helps fill the demand by impregnating woods lacking decay resistance with preservatives that can extend service life by 30 to 50 years or even longer.

Both nonpressure and pressure processes are used to introduce preservatives into wood. The least effective are nonpressure processes: brushing, spraying and dipping. Brushing and spraying are usually limited to field treatment of wood during construction or remedial treatment of wood in place. Millwork makers routinely dip window sash and other exterior trim in a water-repellent preservative. Poles, posts and piles are sometimes soaked for days or weeks, a process that is really nothing more than extended dipping.

The amount of protection gained with these nonpressure methods is unpredictable. By far the most effective treatments are those in which lumber is placed in a large pressure vessel and preservatives are forced into the wood cells. Although variations abound, the two basic pressure-treating processes are the full-cell, or Bethell, process and the empty-cell, or Rueping/Lowry, process. With both, wood-cell walls are saturated with preservative. After treatment, cell cavities are filled with preservative in the full-cell process but are nearly empty in the empty-cell process.

The attractions of a deck, fresh air and sunshine, also dictate the use of lumber that is weatherproof.

Outdoor lumber, especially any decking that lies flat, should be treated with a repellent that will cause water to bead up rather than soak in.

The full-cell process is needed to protect wood used in severe service environments, including saltwater piles, utility poles and railroad ties. A vacuum of 18-inch mercury is first drawn to remove air from the wood's hollow cells. After the vessel is flooded with preservative, a pressure of 145 psi is applied and the solution is driven deep into the wood. The pressure is later released and the excess liquid pumped to a holding tank. The treated wood is then removed for air drying.

The empty-cell process is used for most over-the-counter pressure-treated woods. No initial vacuum is drawn. As the flooded vessel is pressurized, air inside the wood cells is compressed. When the pressure is released, the expanding air, aided by a small applied vacuum, kicks the preservative out of the cell cavities, leaving them nearly empty. Even though the cell cavities are empty, the cell walls are saturated with preservative.

Regardless of which process is used, green wood is generally dried to around 20 percent moisture content before treatment. Otherwise, the water that saturates its cells would inhibit absorption of preservative. Penetration depends on the type of wood and the size of the lumber being treated. Species that are difficult to treat, such as Douglas fir, are incised with small slits as they pass between spiked rollers to promote penetration. Easily treated species, such as southern yellow pine, are treated without this type of preparation. Generally, lumber up to one inch thick is completely penetrated by preservative. For two-inch-thick stock, easily treated woods will be fully penetrated; more resistant species probably won't. And while the sapwood of some woods is easily penetrated, the heartwood of most resists penetration. Only the sapwood of treated wood has protection against decay greater than what nature already handed the heartwood. Industry standards require 90 percent penetration of the sapwood thickness of timbers four inches thick and up. What is important to remember, though, is that a zone of untreated wood may be exposed during machining, especially in large members; those zones can undermine the treatment.

One indication of the success of treatment is the amount of preservative retained by the wood, which is measured in pounds of preservative per cubic foot (pcf) of sapwood. Retention varies with the preservative and the wood, as well as with the wood's intended use. Retention standards are set by the American Wood Preservers' Association and enforced through chemical analysis of treated wood by an independent third-party agency such as the American Wood Preservers Bureau, the Southern Pine Inspection Bureau or the Timber Products Inspection Agency. When you buy pressure-treated wood, look for an agency tag or quality mark to ensure that the wood has been treated to the retention that's right for its intended use. And don't be fooled by lumber stamped "Treated to Refusal." This misleading label is used for wood that is only superficially penetrated and should be avoided if possible.

Of the countless compounds tested as preservatives, only a handful have the safety, effectiveness, permanence and economy that make them commercially important. Preservatives in use today fall into three classes: creosote, oil-borne and waterborne.

Creosote is a liquid by-product of the carbonizing of coal into coke. It is highly effective against fungi, insects and marine borers. Creosote injected into crossties, marine piles and bridge timbers in a full-cell process may later bleed into the surroundings, causing contamination. Utility and building poles, freshwater piles, fenceposts and industrial wood-block flooring are treated in an empty-cell process that yields a clean, nonbleeding surface. Creosote crossties last about 30 years; utility poles treated with creosote may survive 60 years.

Wood freshly infused with creosote gives off potentially harmful vapours that disappear within a few months. The foliage of plants near freshly treated wood may be killed. Gloves must be worn when handling creosote-treated timbers. Creosote products cannot be painted; coal-tar pitch, urethane, epoxy and shellac are acceptable sealants. Because of its organic origin, creosote eventually biodegrades.

Oilborne products are carried in organic solvents such as liquefied isobutane. The preservatives include pentachlorophenol (penta), iodo propynyl butyl carbamate (IPBC), tributyl tinoxide (TBTO) and copper and zinc naphthenate.

Penta will extend a wood's service life by 20 to 40 years. It has been used since the 1930s to treat utility and building poles, fenceposts and highway timbers. Tinted light to dark brown, penta products glue and finish reasonably well after the noxious oil carrier in it evaporates. Polyurethane, latex enamel, shellac and varnish are all effective sealants.

One problem with penta is that it can migrate to form surface deposits on the wood. It can also leach into the surrounding soil and contaminate the groundwater. Penta slowly breaks down into biodegradable compounds.

Until about 1985, exterior millwork was usually dipped in penta carried in light oil. However, IPBC, with its safer solvents, has replaced penta completely in this application. Because of nagging safety and environmental concerns, pundits predict that penta will ultimately fade from the preservation picture.

The treated lumber and plywood that is now available to do-it-yourselfers and builders is protected with one of a virtual alphabet soup of preservatives that are carried in water. They include chromated copper arsenate (CCA), ammoniacal copper arsenate (ACA), acid copper chromate (ACC), chromated zinc chloride (CZC), ammoniacal copper zinc arsenate (ACZA) and

No one knows how long CCA-treated wood will really last. Treaters guarantee at least 40 years and consider 100 possible.

fluorochrome arsenate phenol (FCAP). These preservatives share similar chemistries and thus have a lot in common. Chromium holds the other components tightly to the wood and prevents leaching. Zinc and copper fight fungi, while arsenic guards against attack by termites and copper-resistant fungi. Ammonia in ACA and ACZA helps carry copper, arsenic and zinc deeper into penetration-resistant heartwood. Douglas fir and other western woods are commonly treated with ACA and ACZA. Southern yellow pine is usually impregnated with CCA.

CCA's effectiveness, permanence, safety and economy make it the workhorse of the waterborne stable. Virtually every pressure-treated stick sold east of the Mississippi has been treated with CCA, as have the majority of those sold in the west. CCA is even making inroads into the creosote and penta pole markets. Agricultural uses of CCA-treated wood include fencing, plant stakes, arbours and greenhouse flats. CCA products are used mainly in

exterior situations where the decay hazard is high, especially where wood is used in ground contact or against concrete and masonry. Aboveground use requires lumber that is treated to 0.25 pcf retention; ground-contact use requires a rating of 0.40 pcf, while treated-wood foundation systems are treated to a retention of 0.60 pcf.

The hallmark of CCA-treated wood is its blue-green tint. It has a residue-free surface and can be used where contact with bare skin is frequent, as in decks and benches. However, watch for the odd piece with a white, gritty surface residue. Though appearing infrequently, this can form when preservative precipitates out of solution during treating in a phenomenon known as "sludging." Leave it with the seller. If on-site, wash the residue off with water, or install the wood so that the residue will not come in contact with skin.

During the treating process, CCA is water-soluble. After the first day or two of post-treatment air drying, CCA is rendered insoluble in water in a process called "fixation." During fixation, chromium reacts chemically with the wood, permanently bonding itself, along with the copper and the arsenic, to the cell walls. For that reason, CCA does not leach from wood in service.

Since use began in the 1930s, three basic formulations of CCA have evolved — types A, B and C, which vary by the amounts of chromiun, copper and arsenic they contain. The newer type C, or oxide form, is now preferred for most applications. Types A and B have had some surface-blooming problems, while type C has not. Because all CCA is applied as a water solution, no vapours are ever emitted.

No one knows how long CCA-treated wood will really last. Treaters guarantee at least 40 years and consider 100 possible. After being in the ground for 50 years, treated test stakes in Mississippi and Florida still show no decay; untreated control stakes lasted fewer than 4 years. Surprisingly, CCA-treated wood is not completely immune to insects like carpenter ants, which do not ingest the wood. And because moulds live in water, CCA products are quite susceptible to surface mould and stain if stacked wet without stickers (solid-piled).

CCA products finish reasonably well. But it is important to remember that when you use pressure-treated wood, you're using basically green wood. Because the wood is saturated with water during treating and rarely kiln-dried afterward, it is often still wet during construction. Water repellents, stains and paints attach themselves to the same sites on the wood cells as does water. Wait at least a week or until the surface is thoroughly dry before finishing. Oil-base semitransparent stains are the best performers on CCA-treated wood, because they are less affected by swelling and shrinking. If the construction cries for colour, follow an oil-base primer with acrylic latex topcoats.

At the very least, always use a water repellent that contains mildewcide (oil-base paint can usually be applied later without trouble). Repellents cause rain to bead on and evaporate harmlessly from a wood surface. Without a repellent, repeated rapid swelling and shrinking will carry surface checks into the untreated core of larger members. Renew repellents every couple of years. Water repellents are critical to extending the life of the wood, so the latest development in pressure treating is to impregnate wood with preservative and water repellent simultaneously.

Treated wood demands that you do more than adjust your finishing technique. If you want to get the most out of this product, you must change the way you think about installation. This is especially true in the case of decking, where some of the rules may seem contradictory. Long before treated wood arrived on the scene, for instance, experience showed that exposed decking should be laid bark side up. This was meant to avoid shelling — loosened grain that appears most commonly on the pith side of flatsawn softwood lumber. Shelling occurs when the rapid swelling and shrinking of exterior wood causes the edges of the darker latewood layer of the growth rings to separate from the wood's surface and curl upward. It is common in uneven-grained softwoods, such as southern yellow pine and Douglas fir.

At least one wood preserver recommends that deckboards be installed bark side up to reduce cupping. But the popular assumption that decking will cup in the direction of its growth rings is true only if its moisture content at installation is lower than the average

---

Without a repellent, repeated rapid swelling and shrinking will carry surface checks into the untreated core of larger members.

---

outdoor equilibrium moisture content.

What confounds the original wisdom of "bark side up" is that nearly all CCA-treated deckboards are sold water-saturated. After being fastened in place, water-saturated, flatsawn deckboards will cup in the direction opposite the curvature of their growth rings as they dry to the locale's year-round average moisture content for exterior wood. One drawback is that water will puddle on their surfaces. But that really isn't a problem as long as a water repellent has been applied. A water repellent will also help reduce shelling and its cousin, raised grain.

Correct fastening can help keep cupping to a minimum. For standard 5/4x6 radius-edge decking, a 10d hot-dipped galvanized ring or spiral-shank nail driven at a slight angle about 1 inch from each edge will do. A smaller nail may pop. Better yet, use the zinc-coated, case-hardened screws developed for this application. From my experience, a good bet is to buy treated lumber a couple of weeks beforehand to permit it to dry partially before building, lay deckboards best face up and generously apply a water repellent as soon as their surfaces have dried.

Plan for shrinkage when laying pressure-treated deckboards. Many builders gap deckboards with a 16d nail, about $\frac{5}{32}$ inch. But because CCA-treated wood is usually wet during construction, you can end up with bigger gaps than you bargained for. A flatsawn southern yellow pine deckboard will be about $5\frac{5}{8}$ inches wide after treating. Used in New England, it will shrink to about $5\frac{7}{16}$ inches as it dries to the region's year-round 16 percent outdoor average moisture content. A $\frac{3}{16}$-inch gap will open even if wet deckboards are butted as they're laid.

CCA, ACA and ACC are corrosive to uncoated metal. In above-grade construction, use stainless-steel, hot-dipped or hot-tumbled galvanized fasteners. Joist hangers, framing anchors and other hardware should also be corrosion-resistant. Types 304 and 316 stainless steel, Type H silicone bronze, ETP copper and Monel fasteners are required for below-grade applications, such as the increasingly popular treated-wood foundation systems.

Southern yellow pine is prone to splitting. When nailing or screwing within 2 inches of the end or close to the edge of lumber, drill a pilot hole. You can reduce splitting by using blunt nails. These punch through wood fibres, rather than cleaving them apart as sharp ones do. Splits caused by careless fastening create water traps that are irresistible to fungi.

Where nails are impossible or objectionable, use lag screws or through-bolts. Put washers under bolt and lag heads, as well as under all nuts. The washers will help to distribute stress. Tighten only until snug. Although a common practice, overtightening fasteners to make sure they are "good and tight" is a mistake, because wet or dry, wood under the washer is easily crushed. Most CCA-treated lumber will shrink after it is in place anyway; even properly tightened lag screws and throughbolts will need to be retightened a few weeks later.

Good design and lumber must be accompanied by conscientious and knowledgeable installation that takes the inevitable shrinking into account.

CCA-treated wood glues well. Phenol-resorcinol, resorcinol and melamine-formaldehyde structural adhesives are used in making laminated timbers from treated dimension lumber. On-site, use only construction adhesives specifically formulated for treated wood.

Treated wood machines the same as untreated wood. Impregnation with CCA increases abrasion to tools slightly, but you can extend blade sharpness by using carbide-tipped blades. As should be done when machining any wood product, whether it is treated or untreated, be sure to wear eye goggles, a dust mask and ear protection.

Remember that large pieces of treated wood may not be fully penetrated. It's important that you treat site-cut surfaces liberally with an over-the-counter preservative. These preservatives usually contain copper or zinc naphthenate, or TBTO. Don't overlook pilot holes, mortises, tenons, bevels and site-sawn stair stringers, either. Whenever possible, use precut stringers, railings, post caps and balusters. Always put the "factory end" of treated posts toward the ground. Cap the site-cut surface with flashing or an overhanging railing. Use a continuous railing to avoid the water trap formed when a joint between segments falls atop a post.

Because of the wide use of CCA-treated wood, questions have been raised about its possible effect on health. As a result, these products have come under increasing scrutiny. Most studies done on CCA products, however, have deemed them essentially safe. For example, a 1987 report by the California Department of Health Services stated that "with the possible exception of creosote," none of the common wood preservatives poses a toxic hazard. But as with any construction material, you should follow certain safety precautions when using CCA-treated wood products.

Use treated wood only where such protection is needed. Wear a dust mask and goggles when machining treated wood, and wash your hands after handling it. Wash work clothes separately before reuse. Do not burn treated wood. Do not use treated wood for cutting boards, countertops, silage or fodder bins or where it could become a component of animal feed. Alhough rarely required, CCA-treated wood can be used indoors without sealing as long as all machining dust is cleaned up.

Only visibly surface-clean CCA-treated wood should be used for playground equipment and picnic tables. For such uses, specify wood treated under AWPA's special standard, C17-88, "Playground Equipment Treated With Inorganic Preservatives." This standard ensures the cleanest surfaces possible. To lessen the potential for skin contact even more, apply a water repellent. Or better yet, use an oil-base stain or paint. Round all edges to prevent splintering, and make sure knots and hardware are flush with surfaces.

To help builders use treated wood wisely, the treating industry publishes an EPA-approved Consumer Information Sheet (CIS) for creosote, pentachlorophenol and inorganic arsenical pressure-treated products (it's supposed to be available from treated wood retailers; it's always obtainable from AWPA and AWPB).

If CCA-treated wood is so safe, then why all the precautions? The answer is that where people's health is concerned, it's best to err on the conservative side. An adage among toxicologists says: "The dose makes the poison."Sensitivity to any substance varies dramatically among individuals.

The two routes by which CCA may enter the body are inhalation and ingestion, especially of airborne machining dust. On the one hand, a forest-service employee showed symptoms of arsenic overexposure after building tables of CCA-treated wood. On the other hand, studies of radial-saw operators and factory employees who build foundation components from treated lumber and plywood found no arsenic concentrations in their systems. The factory workers wore neither masks nor gloves.

There will always be people who are sensitive to the chemicals used in treated wood, as there will always be people who are sensitive to ordinary sawdust. The bottom line appears to be that even without mask or gloves, exposure to arsenic from handling or machining CCA-treated wood is well below the average 80 micrograms Americans get daily from their food and water.

Another waterborne preservative that shows increasing promise is borax, the main ingredient in borates. An old preservative that's been rediscovered, borates protect wood from most fungi and wood-eating insects. Borate-treated wood is the same colour as untreated wood. It is noncorrosive to fasteners and can be readily glued and finished. Nontoxic to people and animals, borates also increase wood's fire resistance.

Borates are applied by dipping-diffusion. Green wood is immersed in a hot, aqueous borate bath, then removed and solid-piled. Over a few weeks' time, the preservative naturally dilutes itself by diffusing into the water in the wood. The sapwood is completely penetrated, as is the heartwood of some woods.

Beware of preserved-wood guarantees

by Merilyn Simonds Mohr

This year, Canadians will hammer 500 million board feet of green-tinged wood into decks, fences and play frames, reassured by the 40-to-60-year or "lifetime" warranty that a chemical-treatment process has rendered the wood virtually immune to rot.

Tests by the Quebec Office of Consumer Protection that were published in its *Protect Yourself* magazine, however, suggest that such confidence may be misplaced. In its random sampling of pressure-treated deck and fence wood sold in Quebec, not a single lot met the industry standard for aboveground use; in fact, much of the wood was from species not deemed "treatable." Although a few treatment companies are complying with quality controls, it is almost impossible for consumers to distinguish wood that has been adequately infused with preservative. The wood often carries an extravagant warranty, which is little more than a marketing gimmick.

"Some of the marketing has painted this stuff as indestructible," says Henry Walthert, executive director of the Canadian Institute of Treated Wood (CITW), an organization comprising about half the 50 companies that produce pressure-treated wood in Canada. "As a result, consumers expect things that the wood can't deliver. It's regrettable, and a lot of people in the industry wish it were otherwise, believe me."

The familiar "green" wood is impregnated with chromated copper arsenate (CCA) — which has emerged as a less toxic alternative to creosote or pentachlorophenol. Tests conclude that chemicals from dry, CCA-treated wood will not leach into the ground or be absorbed by plants.

But will it last 40 years without rotting? That depends on penetration (how far into the wood the chemical seeps) and retention (how much chemical is absorbed and held by the wood). The Canadian Standards Association (CSA) has set standards for pressure-treated wood: CCA must penetrate the wood to a depth of at least ⅜ inch and permeate at least 90 percent of the sapwood. Lumber in contact with the ground must absorb 6.4 kilograms of CCA per cubic metre of wood, while lumber for aboveground use should absorb at least 4 kilograms. Long-term field trials in the United States suggest that wood treated in this way will last 40 years.

"When the CSA standard was introduced, it was intended for industrial applications like highway guardrails

Dry wood is treated in a full-cell pressure process. Spray application shows promise for treating wood in place. Today, the widest use of borates is in the treatment of timbers for log structures and post-and-beam construction.

The big stumbling block with borates is that they remain water-soluble and thus readily leach out of treated wood that gets wet. Until a way is developed to render them insoluble after treatment, borate products shouldn't be used where they are exposed to weather. Unfortunately, this renders them ineffective in the very environments where treatment is most needed.

Other preservatives on the horizon include chlorothalonil and alkylammonium, or AAC, a waterborne preservative already commercially available in New Zealand. Chlorothalonil is an oilborne, EPA-registered agricultural fungicide. With performance on a par with penta, only its high cost needs to be overcome.

With the decline in the use of creosote and penta, the volume of wood treated with waterborne arsenicals and borates will continue to rise. Simultaneous treatment of wood with preservative and water repellent will grow. Tomorrow's products will combine even lower toxicity levels with greater effectiveness at low retentions. With good building practice and preservative treatment, wood can last a lifetime.

(Dr. Stephen Smulski is Assistant Professor of Wood Science at the University of Massachusetts at Amherst.)

Originally published in Fine Homebuilding *magazine (Newtown, CT).*

---

and utility poles," explains Walthert. "In a residential situation, that seemed like overkill. So the CITW developed its own standard. It does not have any scientific basis, really. We took a calculated guess that reflects the best wood treatment we can achieve with the technology available."

The result is PS-1, a standard that reduces the required penetration to $\frac{3}{16}$ inch but increases the retention level to 6.4 kilograms per cubic metre. Wood treated to this standard is appropriate for decks and fences; however, if it cracks and splits, the untreated interior may be exposed to fungus and insect attack over time.

Wood stamped PS-1 is meant for aboveground use only. To comply with building codes, wood for foundations must meet the CSA standard and be stamped PWF — appropriate for preserved-wood foundations. It is up to 60 percent more expensive, it comes only in the dimensions used in foundations — 2-by-4, 2-by-6, 2-by-8, 2-by-10 and plywood — and it is not likely stocked by lumberyards, though it usually can be ordered in large quantities.

Wood stamped PWF has always been inspected at the treatment plant by an independent agency. To give some teeth to PS-1, a handful of treatment companies recently formed The Canadian Wood Preservers' Bureau (CWPB) to operate a voluntary inspection program. At the moment, only 10 companies are regularly inspected, and only 3 produce lumber that qualifies for the PS-1 stamp.

Manufacturers have no legal obligation to meet any standard; the onus is on the builder to buy materials that have passed inspection. As the Quebec study revealed, much of what is sold in lumberyards is highly suspect. Pine, for example, is the preferred species for pressure treatment; spruce and fir absorb CCA poorly. (U.S. manufacturers use mostly yellow pine.) The Quebec study discovered that some batches consisted entirely of spruce. And of more than 700 pieces of wood tested, not one batch met the CSA penetration or retention standard for either aboveground or in-ground use. The average retention rate varied significantly, dipping as low as 1.6 kilograms per cubic metre, and only a quarter of the 4-by-4s showed adequate penetration.

It is 4-by-4s that fall between the cracks when it comes to pressure-treated wood. They are not treated to CSA standards because posts typically have no use in preserved-wood foundations. An industry standard covers 4-by-4s — CSA 080.2 — but a builder is unlikely to find any wood with this stamp at the local lumberyard. According to Walthert, 4-by-4s get the usual deck-and-fence treatment, even though they are often sunk into the ground as fenceposts for porches and decks.

"Some of them probably shouldn't be put in the ground," continues Walthert. "But if you buy a 4-by-4 that is incised — one that has those little staplelike cuts — chances are, it is a better product. Lifetime or 60 years may be an exaggeration, but even poorly treated wood will give 10 or 12 years of service."

Claims against warranties are unlikely, given the loopholes. The buyer has to keep a proof of purchase and leave the stickers stapled to the end of each board. Only galvanized or stainless steel nails can be used. Sawing a board voids the warranty unless the exposed end is treated with a preservative, substantiated by a proof of purchase. And warranties are not transferable to new owners.

Walthert expects that a tighter construction market and consumers keen on quality will eventually drive more pressure-treated-wood manufacturers into CWPB's inspection program. Until then, owner-builders will have to watch for those staple marks, question salespeople closely about species and insist on an inspection stamp — PWF for below-grade applications, PS-1 for above-grade and CSA 080.2 for 4-by-4s used in-ground. If that 40-year wood ends up rotting after a decade, consumers will soon stop buying "green" and switch back to wood such as cedar, which can last 25 years in the ground without any chemical treatment.

Originally published in Harrowsmith *magazine (Camden East, Ont.).*

Relaxing beats having to paint every summer

The Secret to Exterior Finishes

by Leigh Seddon

April Fool's Day brought 70 degrees and sunshine. The garden that last week lay under three feet of snow was now bare and showing signs of life. I knew this was one of nature's little jokes — the next day could easily bring another foot of wet spring snow — but I played along and got out the window and door screens. Imagine, opening a window!

By noon, I was down to T-shirt and shorts, and the house had shed its winter coat of storm windows. The old Victorian was probably as glad as I was to have survived another nasty winter. Surveying winter's damage, I made a mental note of summer's chores: a broken basement window, rotten porch stairs and some painting. Correction — a lot of painting.

A quick inspection of the siding, eaves and trim showed that a good bit of my paint was lying in flakes on the ground or headed there fairly soon. The windowsills were bare, the trim was peeling like mad, and the clapboards looked sandblasted. Overwhelmed by the thought of a summer spent perched on a ladder, scraper in hand, I retreated indoors to the comfort of an armchair and *The New York Times* travel section.

Painting is one of the few maintenance chores I dislike. It's a tedious, time-consuming and recurring headache. Painting is like treading water: if you're conscientious and keep at it, you won't drown.

At $3,000 a crack, hiring out my painting to a professional is not something I can afford, especially when it must be done every five years. Instead, I have instituted a system of rotational painting. I do one side of the house every year, so I have one summer off out of five. But there is obviously more to painting than ingenious planning. The side I did last summer did not look much better than the one done four years ago.

Clearly, I needed to do some fundamental research. There must be a better way to keep up the outside of my house, I thought. And judging from the state of my neighbours' houses, I knew I was not alone.

On a trip to the local library, I learned that my house is a textbook case of paint failure. Nothing unusual had happened; everything that could go wrong simply did. I compared my house to the pictures in the book and discovered that I scored 10 out of 17 on "the signs of paint failure" test.

Paint fails for three principal reasons. The most common of these is moisture, either generated inside the house or leaking in from the outside. As the moisture works its way out of the house through the walls, it becomes trapped behind the paint. After it soaks in for a while, this moisture causes the paint to bubble, then blister and finally peel off the siding. Even $25-a-gallon, guaranteed-10-year paint won't last six months if moisture gets behind it.

Lack of proper surface preparation is another culprit. Paint applied to bare, unprimed wood or over a dirty painted surface simply will not adhere well. Loose flakes of old paint should be scraped and all dirt washed off. Mildew should be killed with a mixture of bleach and detergent, or it may spread to the new paint. (Use a sponge or scrub brush to apply a solution of one-third-cup household detergent, one quart household bleach and three quarts warm water. Make sure the detergent does not contain ammonia, since its combination with bleach creates a lethal gas.) Finally, caulk all cracks and gaps between boards where moisture might enter.

Choosing the right paint for the job is also critical. This is not easy, considering that paints come in oil and latex bases; flat, satin, semigloss or gloss finishes; and in 1,362 different colours.

All paints are a suspension of pig-

Wood siding and trim need not be repainted every year to look their best; careful work is the key.

ments and binder in a thinner, or "vehicle." Traditional oil-base paints use linseed oil as the binder and turpentine as the thinner. Alkyd paints — a more recent invention — have a synthetic polymer binder derived from linseed or other vegetable oils and are thinned with mineral spirits. Latex paints have a latex resin binder thinned with water. The type of paint that will work best depends on the material being painted, moisture conditions and whatever coatings have been put on the surface before. Latex paints are definitely the easiest to apply and clean up, but they are not always the best choice for a durable paint job.

In general, oil and alkyd paints form a hard, nonporous film that makes for excellent durability. Latex paint, on the other hand, forms a more flexible and porous surface film. While not as resistant to abrasion, latex paint is often preferred for problem surfaces. Its flexibility helps lessen cracking on wood surfaces that expand and contract a lot, and its porosity allows it to "breathe" out some moisture.

Fighting Moisture

If you have taken care of moisture problems, prepared the surface well and picked the right paint, you've done the best you can — but paint is still not immortal. Ultraviolet radiation in sunlight eventually breaks down the paint film and causes it to crack. Then moisture can enter to finish it off. In northern climates, homeowners can expect to be back behind the scraper and paintbrush every five years.

Moisture is my biggest problem. Everywhere around doors and windows, paint was blistering and peeling. This is where interior moisture escapes most easily, leaving destruction in its wake. The clapboards along the ground showed the same problem, undoubtedly due to wetness in my basement and the splash of water dripping from the roof.

These were not the only signs of moisture damage. On the north side of the house, the soffits (the underside of the roof overhang) and the topmost clapboards showed watery stains. During the winter, ice had been building up on the roof. When it melted, moisture seeped under the shingles and ultimately into the roof and wall — not enough to do damage on the inside of the house, but enough to strip last year's paint job effectively.

What can be done to control the moisture in old houses is a tricky question, because some moisture is necessary for comfort, but too much can rot your house and peel your paint. I made a list of the things I could do to remedy the moisture problem in my old house.

Activities that generate interior moisture are on the top of my list of suspects. Washing and drying a load of clothes can generate about eight pounds of water vapour. Clothes dryers must be vented to the outside, not just to the basement. Showers and dishwashing are the next biggest sources of moisture. Exhaust fans for the bathrooms and kitchen are the answer.

In the summer, my basement walls are often dripping with water, as warm, moist air condenses on the cool walls. By opening the basement windows and inducing good cross ventilation, this moisture can be reduced. Crawlspaces often have the same problem. The solution is to place a plastic vapour barrier over any exposed earth and to have vents that can be opened in summer.

Since I was already restoring old plaster walls, I decided to install polyethylene vapour barriers on all the exterior walls and ceilings that I had yet to do. This would not only help protect the paint but also keep my insulation drier. For those walls that are still in good shape and will not be opened up, I can use a special vapour-barrier paint as a primer to seal them.

Once interior moisture is under control, my next step is to make sure that any leftover residual moisture can escape without being trapped by the paint. Moisture takes the easiest path out of a house, such as through windows and doors. My old wooden storm windows, which had been caulked in place, were wreaking havoc around my windows as they were actually too tight. Drilling two ¼-inch weep holes on the bottom next to the sill will allow winter condensation to run out. Since moisture rises with warm air, it also likes to escape out the top of buildings. Installing four-inch-diameter screened soffit vents will help moisture escape from the top of the building.

Controlling moisture that comes from the outside is equally important. Aside from the obvious repair of leaking roofs and window caps, caulking cracks and joints in the siding and trim is essential. Use a flexible caulk; acrylic latex caulk is often a good choice because it does not harden like oil caulks and is less likely to crack as the wood joint expands and contracts. Silicone caulks offer a longer life, but most are not paintable.

The Right Paint

During my research, I also learned that my choice of paints had been less than brilliant. Over the years, I've used a number of different latex and oil-based paints — basically, whatever was on sale or left over from another job. The first time I wielded a brush on this house, I applied an inexpensive latex over the existing oil paint. The result was a spectacular reptilian hide of cracked paint. Professionals call this phenomenon "alligatoring," and it is caused by the different rates of expansion and contraction of dissimilar paints and their inability to bond properly. Latex and oil topcoats do not mix well.

I must also confess that my surface preparation was less than diligent. Many old oil paints "chalk" as they weather, forming a fine white dust that covers the surface. Paint manufacturers often encouraged chalking as a way to trap dirt and wash it away with each rain. When you repaint, however, that coat of chalk should be completely washed off, or it will keep the new topcoat from adhering to the old surface. Grease and dirt will have the same effect — the new paint simply flakes off. My surface preparation was limited to a little scraping and rinsing with a garden hose. Not good enough.

After digesting three books on "successful" painting, I knew what I had done wrong. But could I ever possibly do it right?

I continued my quest for answers at a university library. There, I learned that there is certainly no shortage of people working on the problems of paints. If you need to know how to keep paint on a jet fighter flying at Mach 2, the NATO Advanced Study Institute has just the book for you. Down a few shelves, I discovered that 30,000 years ago, my ancestors were painting their caves in southern France with red ochres for pigment and animal fat for binder. Some of their house painting is still visible today, despite the ravages of time. That's the kind of durability I am looking for.

It is hard to read an article about painting without running across the name William Feist. He has studied paints and stains for the past 22 years at the USDA Forest Products Laboratory in Madison, Wisconsin. Excerpts from his 80-odd publications on wood finishes seem to show up everywhere. I settled down to take notes on his 1984 paper "Painting and Finishing Wood For Use Outdoors."

I read that there are two general types of finishes: film-forming paints and penetrating preservatives or stains. Like paints, stains are available in oil and latex bases and are divided into two groups: semitransparent and solid colours.

Both oil and latex paints work best on smooth wood surfaces that don't shrink or swell a lot, such as clapboards. Wood that is quartersawn (the grain running with the edge rather than the face) and low in density (such as spruce or cedar) has a stable surface that will not crack the paint film. Flatsawn wood, such as most vertical siding, is less stable and may cause paint failure. Plywood, which develops checks in its surface and also can have a rough texture, is particularly prone to paint failure. If you must paint rather than stain these difficult types of wood, it is best to use a latex rather than an oil paint, because latexes have a more flexible surface film.

For severely weathered or rough-textured wood and for plywood siding, a filmless penetrating stain is the best choice. Use a semitransparent oil stain, since this will leave no surface film to crack. Solid-colour oil stains are thicker and have better colour that completely

Choosing the right brush for every job

In this era of high-tech spray guns, self-feeding paint rollers and other mechanical applicators, the lowly paintbrush is still holding its own as North America's most popular tool for applying exterior paints.

The main reason for this is that painting with a brush requires no time-consuming setup, such as masking windows and trim. By the time the windows are masked and the sprayer loaded, half the house's walls could have been painted with a brush.

Brush application also makes for a more durable paint job, especially on old wood that has been roughed up by the weather. A brush can work the paint in and around all the irregularities, yielding an even surface film that is less prone to failure.

The one place where spray guns can speed up and improve the quality of a paint job is on irregular or round trimwork, such as porch railings or fences. The use of an airless spray gun can cut application time by up to 75 percent and give a smooth, dripless finish.

Natural or Synthetic
Brushes are available in either natural or synthetic bristles and in a wide variety of shapes and sizes. For oil- or alkyd-based paints, a natural-bristle brush, usually made from hog's hair, will perform best. But the water in latex paints causes natural bristles to go limp, so always use a synthetic-bristle brush, usually made from nylon, with water-based paints.

Both natural- and synthetic-bristle brushes come in various grades. A good brush can last a lifetime if properly used, cleaned and cared for. And the way it spreads paint can make an otherwise frustrating job satisfying.

How do you identify a good-quality brush? It will have fine bristles that spread evenly when pressed against your hand, and they will be supple yet spring back into position when released. The ends of the bristles will be uniformly "flagged," or split, to spread the paint evenly. And, of course, a good brush will cost twice as much as the bargain model.

A Size for Each Job
Brushes also come in different sizes for different jobs. Wall brushes are generally 3 to 6 inches wide and have a square tip. A 4-inch brush is about as big as most "weekend" painters can handle without dribbling paint or getting a sprained wrist. Sash and trim brushes range from 1 to 2½ inches wide and have either a square tip or an angular tip for getting into corners. A 2-inch sash brush is recommended for trim boards and window sashes, a 1-inch trim brush for fine woodwork such as window dividers.

If you're using stain, it makes sense to use a smaller-width brush and one with shorter bristles than you would use for paint. You can also use a foam-pad brush for applying stain to smooth surfaces. The foam pad enables you to cut straight edges and apply a uniform amount of stain. The foam is easily torn up by rough wood, however.

Cleaning both oil and latex brushes only takes a few minutes and, if done properly, will leave the bristles as supple as when new. Latex paint can be cleaned out with warm water. Simply rinse the brush thoroughly, making sure to get all the paint out from under the metal ferrule as well as from the bristles. Then give it one final cleaning with a mild detergent such as kitchen dish soap.

Brushes for oil and alkyd paints must be cleaned up with a solvent and then washed out with detergent and rinsed clean in warm water. Gently shake the wet brush out, then wrap it in newspaper to keep the bristles straight.

conceals the grain of the wood, but they also leave a very thin film. Latex stains are nonpenetrating and will form a paintlike surface film that can fail. Because they are basically watered-down latex paints, they should not be used on jobs where a true penetrating stain is desired.

Water Repellents

To achieve maximum paint life, Feist recommends the following painting procedure. First, treat new wood siding and trim with a paintable (check the label) water-repellent preservative or a simple water repellent. The repellents will keep moisture from entering the wood and will combat shrinking and swelling. Repellents with an added preservative will also help protect wood from mildew and decay. It is especially important to treat windowsills and any trim that gets a heavy dose of weather. In field tests, painted windows treated with a water-repellent preservative were still in good shape 20 years later; the untreated ones had rotted and fallen off the test rack after only 6 years.

Give the repellent several days to dry, then prime the bare wood with a good oil-based primer. Do this whether you are using an oil-based or a latex topcoat. Brushing is the best method of application, as it works the paint into the surface of the wood. The primer forms a good base for the topcoat to adhere to and also seals knots that can bleed through if only a topcoat is used. Feist advises against using a shellac or varnish to seal knots, because it may lead to early paint failure at those spots.

Finally, he recommends using two coats of a good-quality acrylic latex paint. Again, use a brush. Painting should take place within two weeks of applying the primer coat. The temperature must be above 50 degrees F and should not drop below that for 24 hours. Lower temperatures can affect the hardening of the paint and lead to premature paint failure. For northern homeowners, this means that the period from late July through early August is the only dependable season for using a latex paint.

This temperature sensitivity is one

Good preparation of a surface prior to painting will prolong the life of the new paint job. Loose paint should be scraped and the surface washed.

reason so many professional painters in northern states and Canada prefer using oil- or alkyd-based paints. With these, the temperature need only be above 40 degrees F during application. However, avoid painting cool surfaces that will heat up in the sun before the paint dries, since this may cause blistering. Also avoid painting in the late evening when there might be a heavy dew, because surface water can degloss and fade the paint.

Applying two topcoats will double the life of the paint job. And since the time and money spent in preparing the surface may exceed that spent on buying and applying the paint, a double coat often makes economic sense. If you can't put two coats on the whole house, then concentrate on the south side, which gets the most sun, and on heavily weathered areas such as windowsills.

If you are staining the wood, use a water-repellent preservative first and apply two coats of an oil stain over it. Work in the shade, and apply the second coat of stain before the first one dries so that the topcoat doesn't get sealed out. This means working on

small areas (such as several boards) at a time, covering just to the edge of each area to avoid lap marks.

Porches and decks often pose a severe test for any type of finish. They are subjected to constant abrasion from foot traffic. The wood is also in continual movement, as it is wetted by rain and then baked in the sun. Feist advises using a semitransparent stain, preferably of light colour, on decks and roofless porches. This type of finish will wear off in several years, but it is easy to redo without scraping or sanding. A light colour that blends in with the wood will make the worn spots less noticeable. For covered porches that are protected from the sun and rain, a high-quality deck enamel will often hold up well, offering superior protection.

Feist concludes that paint offers the best protection for wood, but its life is dependent on the quality of the wood surface and the control of moisture both outside and inside a building. Paint is an expensive finish to maintain, since surfaces must be painstakingly scraped and cleaned before being recoated. Oil stains, on the other hand, work best on rough, weathered, knotty wood and are relatively immune to peeling because they "breathe." Although they might require more frequent reapplication under heavy weather conditions, the work of preparation is only a fraction of that required for paints.

Paint Snoop

Tom Visser is a house detective of sorts. Not the kind you find hanging around hotels but the kind you would find snooping around old structures destined for the Registry of Historic Places. As head of the Architectural Conservation and Education Service at the University of Vermont, Visser spends a lot of time analyzing peeling paint for the history that lies underneath and recommending appropriate restoration for older buildings. Few people have Visser's combination of academic research qualifications and field experience in restoration.

So I looked up Visser, who, unlike Feist, prefers oil- or alkyd-based paints rather than latex. Oils and alkyds adhere well, are durable and are more compatible with older paints. The choice between a latex and an oil- or alkyd-based paint, however, will often be determined by what is already on your house. Latex doesn't go well over old oil paint, and vice versa. Latex over a chalking oil paint is especially troublesome; an alkyd-based paint is recommended in this situation.

But how do you tell what type of paint is on the house? Look at a chip under a magnifying glass. If the surface is hard and smooth, it's most likely an oil or alkyd paint. If the surface is plasticlike and has craters, it's latex.

Regardless of what type of paint you are planning to use, there are two important things to look for in the paint formulation: the total amount of binder resin and the amount of hiding pigment. Paints that have a high percentage of binder resin are more durable and will last longer, while paints that are made with more hiding pigment will cover more square feet per gallon.

You can determine the total percentages of each of these key ingredients by looking at the label on a can of paint.

The first line on most labels is total vehicle, which includes both binder resin and thinner. The next line should tell you how much of this vehicle is actually binder. Multiplying these two percentages together will give you the total percentage of binder in the paint. For example, a paint that is 60 percent vehicle, of which 30 percent is binder, has a total of .60 x .30 = 18 percent binder. Top-quality flat house paints often have 22 to 25 percent total binder.

In a similar manner, you can figure out the percentage of hiding pigment by taking the total pigment content, which is hiding pigment plus filler, and multiplying it by the percentage of actual pigments. Filler may give a paint body, but actual colouring pigment is what determines the spreading rate (how many square feet you can cover with a gallon) and the appearance of the paint once it has dried.

Is all this label reading necessary? Probably not, if you are buying a manufacturer's top-of-the-line paint. But if you are bargain hunting for a less expensive "good-quality" paint, it might pay to check the label for both quantity and quality of binder and pigments. You should also know that paint manufacturers constantly change their formulas. Buying the same brand and grade of paint you used last year is no guarantee that it is, in fact, the same formulation. (*Consumer Reports* is an excellent source of brand-name ratings. In one recent test, the magazine rated more than 300 paints for their hiding ability and resistance to fading, chalking, mildew and dirt.)

Both latex and oil paints are available in different degrees of gloss, ranging from flat to satin, semigloss and, finally, gloss. Flat paint has a lot of pigment relative to binder, making it softer and less shiny. It is often used for large areas, such as the siding on a house. At the other end of the spectrum, gloss paint has a lot of binder resin relative to pigment, making it hard and shiny. High-gloss or enamel paints are primarily applied to trim and heavily used areas such as porches and entrances. In the high-gloss category, traditional oil paints still give the best finish.

Because paints with a high percentage of binder resin are more durable, satin paints were developed that combine the durability of enamel paints with a fairly nonreflective surface. Thus, it often pays to use a satin paint for siding. But in the case of old siding which is rough and weathered and has an uneven paint surface, a flat paint that doesn't highlight all the imperfections of the surface will look better.

As I stood up to leave Visser's office, he mentioned that we hadn't talked about vinyl siding. Perhaps he feared all this technical talk about painting was about to drive another homeowner to seek the "ultimate solution." Did I know how vinyl siding can trap moisture in an old house? I reassured him that I had no intention of heading in that direction. I've seen too many old houses sadly rot away under the gleaming surface of their new vinyl wrap.

Leonard Spencer describes himself as a "painting contractor with a couple of additional dimensions." Those extra dimensions include a degree in art and a keen interest in the history of painting and architecture. Originally a teacher of art and English in Cabot, Vermont, Spencer has been painting for 23 years — first during summer vacations while teaching but for the past decade as a full-time professional.

Spencer's handiwork is evident on the churches and Victorian buildings of northern New England. Beautiful colour schemes, often of four or more colours, resuscitate the architecture of buildings that were once buried under a coat of white paint. But what is most interesting about these wonderful buildings is that they are not painted at all. They are stained.

According to Spencer, today's solid-colour oil stains are more like old-fashioned paints than modern oil- or alkyd-based paints. The new stains are soft and don't build up a thick film. This is important when it comes time to repaint a building. Instead of spending two days scraping down a side of a building, two hours with a stiff brush will suffice to prepare the surface.

After scouring old painting manuals and photographs, Spencer realized that the paints our forebears used tended to be based on a large percentage of linseed oil and, therefore, were likely to chalk as they weathered. By the time buildings were ready to paint again, the paint film had worn off and a new coat of paint could be put on without the drudgery of scraping made necessary by today's thick paints. Old paint manuals spent page upon page discussing brushes and the proper application of paint, but they had hardly a word to say about scraping and surface preparation. Obviously, it wasn't the problem then that it is today.

The difficulty of finding a paint with these characteristics drove Spencer to start experimenting with oil stains. After 15 years of using stains and perfecting his techniques, he is convinced there is no other treatment for exterior wood that offers the protection and low maintenance costs of an oil stain.

All stains are not created equal, of course. There are latex stains, which form a film that can trap moisture, and then there is a wide variety of oil stains made with fish oil, vegetable oils or linseed oil. These are available in semitransparent or solid-colour formulas. Spencer uses solid stains because he can get paintlike colours, and the extra pigment better protects the wood fibres from ultraviolet degradation. He has two rules of thumb for choosing a stain: go with the one that has the most linseed oil ("not fish oil or cottonseed oil, mind you, but linseed oil"), and choose the one with the most pigment. Unfortunately, stains don't always have a list of their ingredients on the can as paints do, so you may have to find a knowledgeable store manager or call the manufacturer.

Applying an oil stain can take a bit of getting used to. It's much thinner than paint and has a tendency to splatter. If you are doing a four-colour Victorian, this can make application a tricky matter. Spencer has developed a technique of "laying on" the stain with gentle brush strokes and using a brush size appropriate for the area he's working on. It's not uncommon for him to perch on a ladder with a ¼-inch brush in hand to detail some delicate trim work.

Even the best stains don't hold up well on surfaces that are subject to abrasion or continued soaking with water. It is no problem to touch up the skirt of a building every few years, but on high-traffic and high-exposure areas such as porches and railings, Spencer sticks with a good gloss oil paint for durability.

Scraping Secrets

The proper preparation of a house for staining is much the same as for painting. Loose paint must be scraped off with a putty knife or a scraper, and open seams should be caulked. But being a perfectionist and sanding every blistered paint edge does not pay off by increasing the longevity of the finish. Around highly visible areas, however, it may be aesthetically important.

Spencer recommends using a heat gun, which is specially made for removing paint, instead of a propane torch. This is a good idea for several reasons. One is lead poisoning, an occupational hazard affecting many professional painters. Most pre-1970 paints contained lead oxides that made for durable but toxic paints. When heated with a torch, the lead is vaporized and can be inhaled. A heat gun theoretically operates at a low enough temperature that lead is not vaporized. Another reason to use a heat gun rather than a torch is fire. The flame from a torch can be sucked into the wall through gaps in the siding and start a fire that remains invisible and unnoticed until the flames start leaping from the roof, burning out of control.

Since the 1970s, lead has been banned in all commercial paints, but you can be almost certain that the paint on any house built before 1970 contains lead. When you are sanding and scraping old paint, it is always wise to wear a dust mask to avoid inhaling paint dust.

To prepare a building before staining, Spencer advises against washing it. A dry bristle brush will usually clean off any dirt. If you do need to wash with detergent to remove chalk or mildew, do it by hand and not with a high-powered hose, which can drive water up and under the siding and into the walls.

It's already hard enough to find a few dry days in the month of August when the paint or stain will really soak in without drenching the whole building needlessly to begin with.

Like Visser, Spencer wasn't about to end our conversation without a little sermon on the subject of vinyl siding. Rather than competing among themselves by making their formulas a little cheaper every year, he said, paint manufacturers could be taking on the vinyl-siding industry by producing an old-fashioned paintlike stain that would be easy to apply and never flake or peel. That way, the manufacturers could be selling more paint, homeowners would be doing less work, and our buildings would be protected from the sabotage of synthetic siding.

It took me three weeks to sort out my painting problems, but finally, I grew confident about which path to take. I decided to follow Spencer's lead and go with an oil stain instead of paint. Despite my best efforts, I knew moisture would still be a problem in my old house, and a stain is less likely to blister and peel.

A solid-colour oil stain would match the colour and texture of the existing paint much better than a semitransparent stain would. I'd simply have to scrape the loose paint off and apply two coats of stain over the bare areas. If I repeat this every five years, I can let the weather do its work and gradually eliminate the thick buildup that 80 years of painting has left behind.

Sure, it's going to be another 15 to 20 years before all the old paint has finally flaked off the house. But the weather will be doing most of the work, and from the street, you won't be able to tell it is not an impeccably maintained paint job. The best part is that when I am finally down to pure stain, I can almost retire. Then I can implement a new five-year rotational schedule that is positively humane — one summer on duty for a quick scraping and touch-up, and four summers off, each with a good two-week vacation.

Originally published in Harrowsmith Country Life *magazine (Charlotte, VT).*

Reaching new heights atop the right ladder

by Leigh Seddon

All exterior painting entails the use of ladders, whether the job is 10 feet up under the eaves of a single-storey ranch or 50 feet up on a three-storey Victorian. Having the right ladders and using them correctly can make painting go smoothly and safely.

Two types of ladders are generally needed for painting: a small stepladder and a larger extension ladder. The stepladder is used for painting the higher reaches of the first storey, porch ceiling, and the like. An extension ladder is used for the second storey and beyond, reaching up to the eaves.

Both kinds are available in wood or metal. A wooden stepladder with metal reinforcing is a good choice, because it can stand a lot of abuse that might bend and structurally damage a metal one. For larger extension ladders, however, weight is also a consideration, so the best choice is usually an aluminum ladder. Extension ladders are also available in magnesium and fibreglass, but these are more expensive and are usually only justified if you are a professional who works on one every day.

Ladders are divided into three categories of carrying capacity. Type I ladders are heavy-duty and rated at 250 pounds working load. Type II ladders are medium-duty ones, rated at 225 pounds. Type III are light-duty, rated at 200 pounds. In addition, all good ladders are rated by either Underwriters' Laboratories (UL) or the American National Standards Institute (ANSI) and should carry their seal of approval. Consider buying a Type I ladder if your budget can afford it and you are strong enough to manoeuvre it into position (a 40-foot Type I is a real beast). A Type II is usually a good compromise between cost, durability and weight. Type III ladders are so lightweight that they can be easily bent through careless use, damaging their structural integrity and the ability of the sections to slide past one another smoothly and freely.

Be sure to check the label for the working length of the ladder before you buy it. A 40-foot extension ladder can only extend 36 feet, because the sections must overlap to lock together. In the United States, all labels on ladders are now required to list their maximum safe working length.

There are several accessories that can make life on a ladder much easier. The first is a ladder stabilizer, or "stand off." This is a U-shaped aluminum bracket that clamps to the top of the ladder and holds it away from the house. This not only stabilizes the ladder but is handy for working on windows, since the ladder can be set in the middle of the window without touching it. A stabilizer also helps protect the siding from ladder marks. If you're not using one, put a pair of old gloves or heavy socks over the top side rails of the ladder to keep the hard plastic ends from digging into the wood.

Another accessory is a ladder jack. This is a triangulated metal support that clamps onto a ladder and can support scaffolding boards between two ladders. The maximum span between two ladder jacks is about eight feet. Because scaffolding on ladder jacks does not have a guardrail and depends entirely on the stability of the ladders, it is a rather risky place to work. When painting, it is usually quicker to use one ladder and move it along the side of the house. Jacks are useful, however, when you are doing an extended amount of work in one spot, such as taking apart and repairing a window. If you think you would like scaffolding for working on a side of your house, consider renting pump jacks from a building-equip-

What goes up may come down — unexpectedly, if one isn't careful.

ment rental company. Pump jacks will form a safe, steady platform that you can raise or lower with a foot crank.

When setting up an extension ladder, follow these few safety rules. First, set the bottom of the ladder firmly against the house foundation so that it won't kick out when you walk it into the upright position. Before you walk it up, check for power lines or other obstructions overhead. When the ladder is in place against the house, the distance from the house to the base should be one-fourth of the ladder's vertical height. And when you're working on a ladder, use one hand for painting, use a hook to suspend the paint can, and keep one hand on the ladder for yourself.

Originally published in Harrowsmith Country Life *magazine (Charlotte, VT).*

The safest ways to use caustic chemicals

Stripping Wood Before Painting

by Janet C. Hickman and *Old House Journal* Staff

Paint stripping is a messy and potentially dangerous process, and no single method works best for every project. Chemical paint strippers, however, probably see the widest use, because they work on a wide variety of surfaces, offer a reduced health threat from fire or lead-paint dust and are great for a final cleanup after other methods (such as heat tools or mechanical approaches) have done the bulk of the stripping.

Not surprisingly, there's no single, all-purpose chemical paint stripper or one that is completely safe. Each job must be carefully analyzed beforehand and the right stripper chosen.

The chemical strippers on the market today can be broken down into three basic groups: methylene chloride-based (employing this organic solvent as the principal ingredient); caustic-based (relying on the action of alkalies); and alternative systems (those that are neither methylene chloride- nor caustic-based). Each of these distinct types of strippers operates on its own chemical principle and loosens the paint film in a slightly different manner. They also require different handling and health precautions, as well as an understanding of what they can and cannot do to produce the best and safest job.

Methylene Chloride Paint Strippers

Because it is an aggressive solvent with low flammability, methylene chloride forms the basis for most of today's solvent-based chemical paint strippers. These strippers work by partially solubilizing the solids in the old finish. Once the solids are in solution, the methylene chloride molecule, which is very small, can slip between the gaps left by the other, larger molecules and reach the bare wood or other substrate. With the methylene chloride now trapped between the finish and the wood, the finish blisters and peels, leaving behind a softened residue that can be easily scraped away. Many expert refinishers prefer methylene chloride paint strippers, because they are fast and effective and there is the least risk of harming delicate woods or water-based glues.

Solvent-based strippers come in two forms: liquid and semipaste. In general, the liquid form works fastest and is good for removing clear finishes; semipaste works best on paint and vertical surfaces. As a general rule, one gallon of stripper will remove about 75 to 100 square feet of paint, depending upon the number of coats. A chair or small end table, for example, will require about one quart of stripper. Complicated surfaces, such as deep mouldings or wainscotting, may require more. The amount of stripper needed also varies with the number of coats of finish to be lifted. Buy only as much product as you think you will need. Solvent-based strippers do not store well (especially once opened) and, like all hazardous substances, can be dangerous if they should get into the hands of children.

To begin stripping, first prepare a good work area and put on proper protective clothing. The single most important consideration when choosing a work site is the availability of fresh air. The best place to work is outdoors, in an area that affords some overhead protection, such as a canopy or carport. If you are working indoors, open all the windows and doors in the room to permit a strong flow of fresh air through the work area. Use a fan, if necessary, to increase air circulation. Take frequent fresh-air breaks, and leave the work site whenever you are not actually applying or removing the stripper.

Always wear protective clothing when working with solvent-based paint strippers to prevent the chemical from coming in contact with skin or eyes. Clothing should consist of chemical-resistant gloves (neoprene or butyl, not the dishwashing kind) and chemical goggles, long pants, long-sleeved shirt, shoes and socks. The latest information indicates that the use of cartridge respirators is not recommended, because methylene chloride tends to saturate, or "break through," the carbon absorbers fairly quickly, thus rendering the mask an ineffective barrier against solvent vapours. By the same token, ordinary dust masks do not offer a safe alternative to proper ventilation.

Next, carefully pour some remover into a large coffee can or other wide-mouthed metal or glass container with a tight-fitting lid. Dip a wide, natural-bristle brush into the can, and bring out a generous helping of remover. Do not brush the remover on as you would paint. Rather, "lay" it on, working in one direction. When stripping wood, brush with the grain.

If you are working on vertical surfaces, such as doors, walls or trim, start at the top and work down. It is sometimes easier to remove doors and mouldings and strip them outdoors. For indoor work, an old metal dustpan with the rubber edge removed is useful for catching drips from overhead surfaces. When stripping floors, start at one end of the room, approximately four to five feet from the wall (to give yourself enough room to manoeuvre the scraper around), and apply the remover with a scrub brush.

In about five minutes, the surface will begin to peel and blister — a sign that the stripper is working. Leave the work site, and get some fresh air. Solvent strippers work faster on clear finishes, such as varnish, than they do on heavily pigmented coatings, such as oil-based paints. Pigmented coatings are typically made up of tightly cross-linked polymers, which leave fewer molecular gaps for the methylene chloride molecule to slip through. Thus, the same materials that make these coatings so tough make them more difficult to penetrate as well.

Refer to the product label to determine the length of time required for the stripper to work. Usually, it takes anywhere from 5 to 45 minutes, depending on the product being used and other factors, such as weather conditions, type of surface and the age and type of

A careful stripping job should precede any furniture restoration. Too often, an inappropriate chemical stripper will damage the texture of a wood.

finish being removed. After the required time has elasped, return to the work site and gently scrape away the remaining sludge with a dull putty knife or other suitable tool. Scrape away from you, going with the grain.

An old toothbrush or cotton swabs can be used to get into tiny crevices and grooves that the scraper can't reach. Strong twine, burlap or coarse string will remove sludge from leg turnings (use a back-and-forth, shoe-shine motion). As you finish each section, wrap the sludge in a thick fold of newspaper and place it outdoors, where the liquid will

be able to evaporate much more quickly.

To remove the last traces of residue or old finish, wipe the piece with a rag, stiff bristle scrub brush or steel-wool pad, rubbing with the grain. If the stripper leaves a wax film, neutralize it by washing the surface with alcohol, lacquer thinner or a commercial wax remover. Allow the piece to dry for at least six hours before applying new stain or finish. Wait 24 hours to replace doors and drawers, leaving them open for several days after replacing.

The safe use of methylene chloride includes minimizing exposure. High levels of vapours from methylene chloride paint removers can cause irritation to the skin, eyes, mucous membranes and respiratory tract. There should be no problem, however, if there is adequate ventilation and proper safety procedures are followed. The warning signs of overexposure include eye irritation, dizziness, headache, nausea, light-headedness and lack of coordination. If any of these symptoms occur, leave the work area immediately and get some fresh air. Do not return until ventilation has been increased. Individuals who experience severe symptoms, such as shortness of breath or chest pains, should obtain immediate medical attention.

Inhalation of methylene chloride can result in the formation of carboxyhemoglobin, which can impair the blood's ability to transport oxygen. Individuals with cardiovascular or pulmonary health problems should check with their physician if they are planning to use the paint stripper.

If the remover comes in contact with your skin, it may, at first, have a slight cooling sensation. Rinsing the skin with cool water will neutralize the remover. A redness, similar to a minor rash, may appear at the point of contact. Clothing that becomes saturated with remover should be taken off immediately, rinsed in cold water several times, hung to dry and then thoroughly machine-washed by itself. If any of the remover accidentally splashes into your eyes, rinse them immediately with cool flowing water for 15 minutes, keeping the eyelids open to remove the solvent. Consult a physician. If any stripper is swallowed, do not induce vomiting. Instead, call a physician and/or immediately transport the victim to an emergency facility.

In 1985, the National Toxicology Program (NTP) issued a report that linked methylene chloride to cancer in certain animals. Based on the study, the Consumer Product Safety Commission (CPSC) now requires consumer products that contain more than 1 percent methylene chloride to carry a warning label that reads: "Methylene chloride has been shown to cause cancer in certain laboratory animals. Risk to your health depends on level and duration of exposure." There is no evidence of a corresponding risk of cancer in humans, but you should keep your exposure levels as low as possible.

The health profile of methylene chloride is excellent as long as proper safety and handling procedures are followed. For humans, several studies of employees who have worked with methylene chloride (at Eastman Kodak Company, for example) confirm its safety. Adequate ventilation and use of protective clothing are primary safety points, as well as reading the label on the products — the most important guide to their proper use for the casual user.

Caustic Paint Strippers

Caustic-based paint strippers are one of the oldest and simplest formulas for removing paints and varnishes. The active agents in these strippers — caustics — are principally sodium hydroxide (commonly known as caustic soda or lye) and often potassium hydroxide. Rather than softening and swelling the paint film as methylene chloride does, caustic strippers saponify (decompose) the binder in the coating, much as lye or soda ash breaks down fat in old-time soapmaking. Caustic strippers continue to be used, because the ingredients are inexpensive and readily available and because, given enough time, they will eat their way through many types of coatings, from oil-based paints to epoxy-ester finishes. They also do not rely on solvents to do their work.

These strippers probably see their widest use in commercial paint stripping, where they can be found in two forms. Dip-strip paint-removal businesses that specialize in immersion stripping of furniture and doors often use 5 to 10 percent aqueous solutions of caustics in the "hot tank" portion of their process. Some large-scale lead-abatement and paint-removal contractors make use of caustic solutions thickened into a paste with cellulose compounds, which will stick to vertical or inverted surfaces. Paste-type caustic strippers are also sold on the consumer level, and uncomplicated versions have long been made by individual users. A typical recipe is made of one pound lye (available at supermarkets, hardware stores, lumberyards and chemical suppliers) dissolved in one gallon of water and thickened with cornstarch to a suitable consistency.

Choosing a paint stripper

When choosing a paint stripper, look for a product with a formulation along these lines.

Ingredients	Percent (%)	Action
Methylene chloride	82	Dissolves and swells paint
Wax	1.5	Retards evaporation
Toluene	2	Keeps wax in solution
Cellulose derivative	1	Thickener
Methanol	7.5	Keeps cellulose in solution
Mineral spirits	6	Prevents sludge from redrying

Formulations that contain less than 60 percent methylene chloride are likely to be slower and less effective. If the piece you are working on has a lot of vertical surfaces, look for a formula with a slightly higher concentration of thickeners.

Paste-type caustic strippers should be applied in thick coats, with special care taken to cover depressions and moulded details where paint buildup is greatest. Tools that resist the effects of the stripper, such as spatulas or brushes made from polyethylene or rubber, are often used. Caustic strippers work relatively slowly compared with methylene chloride and are left in place anywhere from two to several hours, depending upon the amount of paint being removed and the type of product used. Like other strippers, however, they should not be allowed to dry out, which makes them difficult to remove, and they may need repeated applications to complete the job. Once the stripper has done its work, it is scraped off along with the lifted paint and the surface washed clean with water.

A very important final step with all caustic strippers is neutralization of the surface prior to refinishing. Caustic strippers employ strong alkalies to do their work, and they leave the pH of most surfaces strongly basic, particularly porous ones like wood — a shift that can affect the performance of subsequent finishes. The remedy is to neutralize the surface with an acid wash. Dip-strip shops often use a tank with a 2 percent solution of muriatic acid, but diluted vinegar also works and is handiest for most interior woodwork and small-scale jobs. For exterior stripping projects, some contractors allow acid rain to help with this step by letting the building weather for several weeks before proceeding with a new paint job.

Caustics are effective paint strippers, but they are not ideal for every surface. The biggest problems are with hardwoods — oak, mahogany and walnut, for instance — which tend to darken significantly or change colour when exposed to alkalies. Caustics also attack the glues in veneers and plywoods, which causes them to delaminate. Aluminum, tin and zinc corrode readily in the presence of these compounds as well. Caustic strippers that include water will raise the grain on many kinds of wood — an asset or a drawback, depending upon what the next finishing process is.

Although free of hazardous solvents in most bases, caustic strippers require careful handling for health and safety reasons. Sodium hydroxide, in particular, is very corrosive to human tissue and will cause caustic burns to eyes, respiratory system and skin with a minimum of exposure. Eye and skin protection in the form of goggles, rubber

---

Caustics are effective strippers, but they are not ideal for every surface. The biggest problems are with hardwoods like oak and walnut.

---

gloves and protective clothing are a must, and skin that comes in contact with the stripper should be flushed immediately.

The paint-and-coatings industry in general is moving away from traditional solvent-based products, and a new breed of chemical paint strippers that use neither methylene chloride nor caustics as their active agent has recently appeared. While the chemistry behind these products varies, what they do have in common is their water-based formulations.

Several of these new strippers make use of dibasic acid esters to loosen paint and varnish films. DBEs, as they are called, are a family of organic solvents that have been used for some time in printing inks, automotive finishes and other industrial applications. Although not as active as methylene chloride, DBEs have been reemployed as the major solvents in these new strippers because they are nonflammable, biodegradable and water-rinsing, making them easier and safer to use. Some

manufacturers are turning to surfactants (similar to detergents) to help with the stripping process for the same reasons.

The trade-off for being friendlier to both the user and the environment is that these new strippers are not as aggressive as other chemical strippers. Generally, it is necessary for alternative strippers to be applied as thickly as possible and given plenty of time to do their job — very often hours. Warm temperature is an important factor too, with some products not recommended for use when the temperature is lower than 70 degrees F. They tend to work best on spirit or evaporative finishes such as lacquer and shellac, because these are relatively uncomplicated coatings (basically resin left after the solvent evaporates). They have a harder time with finishes that undergo chemical changes to make them durable — varnishes and enamels, for instance — because they have to break down the cross-linked polymers that give these coatings their strength. It is for this reason that some dibasic ester strippers also include small amounts of solvents made from petroleum distillates. Neutralization, though, is not an issue, because these products do not contain wax or strong alkalies. Cleanup after stripping requires only a thorough washing down with water and then allowing the project to dry completely (at least 24 hours) before refinishing.

Despite their relatively benign nature, alternative strippers should still be used with care. DBEs are organic esters that can irritate eye tissue, and therefore, it is prudent to wear protective goggles. Extended contact can remove the oils from skin and cause drying, so gloves and protective clothing are a wise precaution as well. Skin contact may also cause more severe reactions in those individuals who are allergic to these chemicals.

Last, even though these products are water-based and produce a minimum of odour, ventilation while stripping any surface is always a good idea.

Reprinted with permission from Old House Journal *magazine (New York), January/February 1991.*

Evaluating affordable water-filtration systems

Tap Water That's Fit to Drink

by Craig Canine

Some people call him a "water nerd," and while David Osterberg, a representative in the Iowa legislature, isn't particularly fond of the title, he has been called worse. A tireless champion of Iowa's natural water resources, he knows a lot about groundwater and has been the sponsor of strong laws to protect it.

He has also battled the water-treatment charlatans who rip off consumers. "I went to a farm show once," he says, "where there was a fellow trying to sell a small, pyramid-shaped thing made of tubular metal. You were supposed to set it over your well, and it would clean up the water by 'pyramid power.' There was an optional compartment at the bottom of the pyramid where you could put a Bible or a rabbit's foot, depending on your brand of religion. The guy was charging $340 for it.

"Another time," he remembers, "I heard about an outfit that was selling a black box with a pipe running through it. The thing supposedly removed contaminants by magnetizing the water as it passed through." Hydro-Mag, as its marketers called the device, cost $2,000.

Water-treatment devices have become the patent medicine of the 1980s. A proliferation of newspaper and magazine articles in recent years has documented many alarming cases of groundwater contamination: gasoline seeping into wells from leaking service-station tanks; pesticides and nitrates leaching into groundwater supplies from agricultural operations; industrial and household solvents contaminating aquifers as a result of careless disposal — the list of dangerous pollutants found in drinking water grows longer every day.

In fact, the U.S. Environmental Protection Agency (EPA) has identified some 700 potentially harmful contaminants in our drinking water. These can be divided into five basic categories: bacteria; nitrates; inorganic chemicals like arsenic and the heavy metals, including lead and mercury; synthetic organic chemicals, which include pesticides, PCBs (polychlorinated biphenyls) and industrial solvents; and trihalomethanes, carcinogenic by-products of chlorination. In addition, there are a number of troublesome, though not life-threatening, contaminants that result in bad taste, unpleasant odours and hardness.

As the public's understanding of water contamination has grown, so have its worries — and so has the popularity of equipment to treat water used in the home. Annual sales of in-house filters and other treatment devices now approach $4 billion. The problem with water-treatment equipment, however, is that it is hard to know exactly what you are getting for your money. Many of the filters, pyramids and black boxes on the market come with no guarantee or warranty — and even when they do, measuring the devices' performance against warranty and advertising claims is no straightforward matter. Some potentially harmful contaminants that are found in drinking water, including compounds like pesticides and industrial solvents, have no discernible taste, odour or colour. The maximum allowable limits for many of these chemicals are measured in parts per billion, requiring $70,000 worth of gas chromatography equipment to detect.

Testing for all of the contaminants that you might reasonably suspect in your water supply can cost as much as some of the devices purporting to remove them. Yet such testing is the only reliable way to determine what kind of water-treatment equipment, if any, is needed. Then, after a system of some kind is installed, further testing is the only way to ensure that the equipment is doing its job.

A variety of home-treatment devices are effective in removing contaminants

Families should have their water tested independently and then match water filters to their needs.

from water. The trick is to find the right type of treatment for the specific problems you have with your water supply. In general, home-treatment systems fall into two categories: point-of-entry systems, which treat all of the water that comes into the house; and point-of-use systems, which usually treat only the water used for cooking and drinking (and perhaps bathing). Homeowners with private wells might want a point-of-entry system to deal with problems like excessive iron, bacteria or corrosiveness. The devices used for this type of system are generally more expensive and less precise than those designed for point-of-use systems. So, after you find out what you need to remove from your water, you have to decide how much of your water you want to remove it from.

Some methods of water treatment are fairly specialized. For example, cation exchangers (water softeners) remedy hardness, anion exchangers remove nitrates, and ultraviolet treatment kills bacteria and cysts. But the three methods most frequently employed in point-of-use systems can remove a broad range of impurities. These methods include activated-carbon filtration, reverse-osmosis filtration and distillation. Each method has certain merits and weaknesses. If testing reveals a number of different contaminants in a given water source, a complete remedy may require the combination of two or three devices in a hybrid system.

Carbon filtration is one of the oldest methods of treating drinking water. The ancient Greeks and Romans filtered contaminated water through ashes. Since then, the basic idea has remained the same, although the waste-removal capacity of carbon has been vastly increased by the process of activation. The process begins with carbon-containing raw materials like coconut shells, wood scraps, pulp-mill residue and peat moss. These materials are first dehydrated and carbonized — heated at temperatures up to 1,100 degrees F in the absence of air. The result is "primary carbon," which is then further processed by being exposed to an activating agent, such as carbon dioxide or steam, at 1,400 to 1,650 degrees. This

exposes and enlarges tiny pores in the carbon's surface.

These microscopic pores give activated carbon its filtering capacity. When polluted water passes through the carbon, contaminants in the water are drawn to the pores by molecular attraction in a process known as adsorption. The greater the surface area of the adsorp-

> Carbon filtration is one of the oldest methods of treating water. The ancient Greeks filtered contaminated water through ashes.

tive material, the more contaminants it can remove. One pound of activated carbon has a surface area equivalent to 60 to 150 acres.

The most familiar type of activated-carbon filter uses powdered or granular carbon packed into a cartridge. Filters of this kind are available as whole-house units, as under-the-sink models or as small devices that fit at the end of the kitchen faucet. Because of their size, end-of-the-faucet models have a limited filter life and should not be relied upon in situations where water testing has revealed significant levels of health-threatening contaminants. They serve best as water "polishers," removing undesirable (though not unhealthy) tastes and odours.

Granular-activated-carbon filters can substantially reduce levels of chlorine and many synthetic chemicals, including pesticides.

They cannot remove bacteria, however. In fact, they have been accused of adding bacteria to the water they process, because the bacteria can multiply

in the spaces between the carbon granules. Whether or not the kinds of bacteria that grow in granular-carbon filters are dangerous is a matter of scientific debate. Some manufacturers impregnate their filters with silver nitrate to prevent bacteria from multiplying there. This may or may not be effective, but it raises the concern that silver — a heavy metal — may leach into the water. Another problem with granular-carbon filters is that incoming water can form channels through the carbon, reducing the filter's effectiveness.

A newer, better and more expensive kind of filter uses activated carbon that has been compressed into a solid block. This type of filter has the adsorptive capabilities of activated carbon, combined with the ability to strain out particles down to the submicron level. That means they are effective in removing bacteria, giardia cysts, asbestos fibres, lead and two of the three most commonly found forms of iron — contaminants that granular-charcoal filters can't catch. In addition, solid-carbon-block filters are not subject to channelling, and there is no place for bacteria to grow in them.

Solid-carbon-block filters are available only as under-the-sink or on-the-counter units. They are among the most versatile of the point-of-use options, but they do have some limitations. They have only a small effect on the dissolved minerals that make water hard; they won't remove certain inorganic chemicals and heavy metals; and they won't filter out sodium, nitrates, fluorides or chlorides.

As an activated-carbon filter collects contaminants, the adsorptive sites in the carbon become filled and the filter's effectiveness declines. A fully saturated filter won't remove any organic chemicals at all. And in the case of a solid-carbon-block filter, the pores in the block may become clogged with particulate matter, in which case, water simply won't pass through. The length of an activated-carbon filter's effective life depends on the amount of carbon it contains and on the amount of contamination in the water being treated. Most manufacturers recommend that the filter cartridges on their units be changed once every 6 or 12 months; at least one unit has a built-in monitor that automatically shuts off the water supply after 1,500 gallons or so have passed through the filter — a compelling reminder to replace the carbon cartridge. Of course, the manufacturer's estimate of a filter's lifetime is just that — an estimate. If you suspect that conditions in your water or your home might cause the filter to fail sooner, you might want to seek the advice of an experienced local water-treatment specialist. Or, if you have a chlorinated water supply, you can easily check the filter's effectiveness with an orthotolidine test that you can do at home. This test, commonly used to check the chlorination level in swimming pools, will tell you if the filter is letting chlorine through — a good indicator of its ability to remove chemicals.

Reverse Osmosis

Reverse-osmosis filtration is one of the newer technologies in home water treatment. The process of reverse osmosis (RO) has been used on a large scale for desalination of seawater and in industrial applications for some 40 years. Small home units first appeared on the market in the 1960s. They are popular for their versatility in removing many of the contaminants that activated-carbon filters don't affect: dissolved minerals, salts and nitrates, viruses (which are much smaller than bacteria) and even radioactive particles.

Reverse osmosis is a fancy term that describes a process in which water diffuses through a porous membrane, leaving contaminants behind. This process is propelled by water pressure in the plumbing system. The RO membrane, which is usually wrapped around a central tube and sealed in a compact canister, resembles a piece of cellophane.

Not all of the water that goes into an RO module comes out pure. Most incoming water, in fact, emerges as waste "brine," which goes down the drainpipe. For every gallon of water it purifies, the average RO unit produces six to eight gallons of wastewater. The pace of filtration is somewhat slow, although most home RO filters can

keep up with the average household's demand for drinking water — provided the proper line pressure, temperature and water conditions are maintained. Most manufacturers specify a minimum constant line pressure of 35 to 40 pounds per square inch. Homeowners with private wells may need a booster pump to maintain adequate pressure for an RO filter.

Like activated-carbon filters, RO modules have weaknesses. They are notoriously touchy and expensive to maintain; yearly upkeep may cost $125 to $150 — much more than a solid-carbon-block filter requires. According to some water-treatment specialists in the Dakotas and Canada, RO units do not perform well in extreme cold-weather conditions. And unless a particular unit has a meter on it to indicate the level of total dissolved solids, it's a matter of guesswork to determine when its effectiveness is dwindling. According to David St. Clair of the Water Information Network in Ashland, Oregon, an organization serving independent distributors in the pure-water industry, "We've found that the average consumer is not attracted to RO systems because of the extra expense and the inconvenience of use and maintenance. We tend to view ROs as largely for particular water conditions that solid-carbon blocks can't handle: excessive minerals, nitrates and sodium."

RO systems are susceptible to clogging, so they typically come packaged with prefilters to remove suspended particles and some dissolved solids. And although they will remove some hardness from water, RO units do not hold up well under extreme hard-water conditions. They are frequently coupled with water softeners: the softener removes calcium and magnesium but adds sodium, which the RO unit filters out. RO units are also often paired with activated-carbon filters, since without one, the system would be fairly ineffective in dealing with organic chemicals.

The RO membranes with the highest production capability, called thin-film membranes, are the best choice for treating unchlorinated water, but they are destroyed upon exposure to chlo-

rine. If a thin-film membrane is to be used for chlorinated water, it has to have a carbon filter in front to remove the chlorine. Two other membrane types, cellulose acetate and cellulose triacetate, require chlorinated water to prevent bacteria from growing on them. They cost somewhat less than thin-film membranes, but they are most particular about source-water conditions like temperature and pH.

Distillation

Like charcoal filtration, distillation is another ancient and straightforward form of water treatment. Water is boiled, the steam is condensed on a cool, clean surface, and the purified condensate is captured for future use.

No other technology can beat distillation for removal of minerals, heavy metals, bacteria and particulate matter. But with drinking water, all impurities aren't bad. Some, in fact, are desirable because they impart taste and body. Distilled water is insipid stuff. Small amounts of calcium and iron in drinking water, along with essential trace minerals like zinc and manganese, can help keep the water "balanced." Since pure water is an aggressive solvent, it will tend to leach minerals out of your body. (It will also more aggressively dissolve metals and plastics, which is one reason why distilled water quickly picks up the taste of its container.)

Distillation does not result in absolute purity, since some volatile chemicals boil at a lower temperature than does water and are condensed along with the steam. Some manufacturers have responded to this problem by equipping their distillers with venting systems. Some work, some don't. Those that do may vent toxic gases into your home. Laboratory-grade distillers are usually coupled with activated-carbon filters that remove chemical contaminants after the distillation process.

Because distillers use electricity for their heating elements, their operating costs are relatively high. A side-by-side comparison of home distillers and RO systems performed in 1985 by Rodale Press showed that distilled water cost about 24 to 30 cents a gallon (based on

Consumers should be wary of promotional claims. Contaminants are measured in parts per billion, so claims of 99.99 percent effectiveness are misleading.

the distiller's electrical use), while RO-treated water cost from 6 to 24 cents a gallon (based on the cost of replacing filters at the manufacturer's recommended intervals).

Distillers have a few drawbacks beyond their operating costs. When they're on, distillers produce as much heat as a small electric room heater does. For this reason — and because most distillers take up a fair amount of space — they are often kept in a basement or utility room rather than in the kitchen. (Some companies, like Sears, sell portable units that can produce up to about three gallons per day and take up about as much counter space as a large food processor.) Distilled water must be drained from the unit's storage

reservoir, usually into plastic or glass bottles, and then chilled in the refrigerator before being used. Most people find this much less convenient than having filtered water immediately available with a twist of a tap at the kitchen sink.

In cases where water testing reveals persistent microbiological contamination but no other significant contaminants, special ultraviolet lamps may be the most convenient and cost-effective form of treatment. Brief exposure to ultraviolet (UV) light kills bacteria, cysts and viruses, though it does not remove other contaminants.

Bacterial contamination is of special concern to homeowners with private water supplies. Municipal water systems chlorinate water to kill microor-

ganisms living in it, but owners of private wells must test and, if necessary, treat their own drinking water. Federal and state studies conservatively estimate that 40 percent of all private wells may exceed the public-health limit of one coliform bacterium per 100 millilitres of water. Small-scale chlorinators are available, but they are expensive to buy and operate. UV systems are a good alternative, particularly since they don't add chemicals to the water. (Chlorine can have an undesirable side effect. Free chlorine reacts with naturally decaying organic matter in water to form trihalomethanes — THM — a family of four chemicals, including chloroform, that are known or suspected carcinogens.)

Many UV units come with an activated-carbon prefilter. Such a hybrid system disinfects and removes organic chemical contaminants while leaving in the minerals responsible for the good taste traditionally associated with country wells.

Softeners, like UV systems, are not filters per se, though they remove potentially troublesome contaminants. The benefits softeners provide are more practical than health-related — they reduce scale buildup on water-heater elements and improve the sudsing action of soaps and detergents. But they also add potentially harmful amounts of sodium to the water they treat, so softeners are often plumbed only into hot-water lines.

Ion Exchange
Nitrates have been much publicized in recent years because of their appearance in rural groundwater supplies as a result of leaching from septic systems, livestock feedlots and overfertilized cropland. Nitrate in high concentrations is toxic, as it is transformed in the body to nitrite, which interferes with the blood's ability to carry oxygen.

Like calcium and magnesium, nitrates and nitrites are ions and can be removed by passing water through an ion-exchange resin. Nitrate-removing resins, called anion exchangers, can cost thousands of dollars. Homeowners with nitrate contamination of their wells might first consider getting a reverse-osmosis filter, which can reduce nitrate levels, or drilling a deep well, since nitrate contamination usually occurs in shallow, dug wells.

How much does a home water-treatment system cost? That depends, of course, on the nature of the problem and the complexity of its solution. A simple under-the-sink carbon filter costs as little as $25, including a filter cartridge. A decent under-the-sink RO/activated-carbon combination system can be purchased for $400 to $800. Distillation units run from $200 (for a portable model) to more than $800.

If testing reveals that your well contains unacceptable levels of pesticides or PCBs, you would be prudent to consider a whole-house filtration system.

Exposure to these chemicals occurs not only by ingestion but also by absorption through the skin and lungs. Bathing and showering in water containing some kinds of pesticides and PCBs is just as bad as drinking it. Whole-house carbon filters and RO systems are likely to cost from $1,000 (for a carbon filter) to $5,000 or more (for an RO system) .

When shopping for a water-treatment system for your home, beware of high-pressure sales pitches and exorbitant markups. "A lot of scare tactics and other shoddy sales tricks are being used," says Steve Wiley, who is a certified water specialist in Chalfont, Pennsylvania. "Watch out especially for telemarketing schemes. Someone who has responded to a 'Make-$5,000-a-month-in-your-spare-time' advertisement will call you up with a high-pressure sales pitch. Such unqualified people come into your home, perform an invalid test and then tell you that everything is wrong with your water. They say that their system, which usually consists of a softener and a reverse-osmosis filter, will solve all your problems, which may or may not be true. You may not need that much equipment, or you may need different equipment. Then they'll try to sell you the system for $5,000 to $6,000."

Randy Haring, owner of Hydro-Analysis Associates, a water-testing laboratory in Kutztown, Pennsylvania, adds, "Watch out for people selling water filters who say their products will provide 99.99 percent pure water. That may sound good to the layman, and it's probably a true statement, but 99.99 percent purity isn't very good. You could still have 100 parts per million of something in your water, which is way too much for lots of contaminants. The health limits for some chemicals are measured in parts per billion — that's eight places to the right of the decimal point — so two decimal places don't begin to tell the story."

In an effort to bring some standards of quality and ethics to its own industry, the Water Quality Association (WQA) has instituted a number of certification and testing programs for dealers and

manufacturers of home water-treatment equipment. Manufacturers participating in the association's Gold Seal program have their products tested by a third-party laboratory for conformance with industry standards, established by the WQA. The association has also established certification programs for sales representatives, installers and water-treatment specialists. A list of certified professionals in any state, as well as a listing of tested and approved treatment devices, is available free of charge from the association.

The only truly neutral standards for home water-treatment units have been established by the National Sanitation Foundation (NSF), which tests and certifies the sanitary soundness of everything from soda fountains and luncheonette equipment to trash compactors and hot-tub circulation pumps. The NSF's performance standards are high, and its testing programs are expensive — so expensive that only the largest and wealthiest manufacturers tend to carry the NSF's seal of approval on their products. Consequently, the NSF listing of drinking-water-treatment units is fairly short and does not necessarily include all respectable units.

If testing reveals that your well is polluted, don't stop at getting a home-treatment device. The ultimate solution is to eradicate the problem at its source rather than simply to treat its symptoms. Home water-treatment systems are only stopgap measures. Good equipment, properly maintained, offers families immediate and relatively low-cost protection from potentially harmful health effects.

But point-of-use treatment is no panacea. "The proliferation of in-home water-treatment devices is a smattering of Band-Aids on an environmental wound," says Lon Couliard, chief chemist of the municipal waterworks in Des Moines, Iowa. "If people don't like the quality of their drinking water, they should do more than clean it up at their tap. They should run to their politicians screaming."

Originally published in Harrowsmith Country Life *magazine (Charlotte, VT).*

Testing the waters before shopping

by Craig Canine

Buying a water filter without having your water tested is like getting a new pair of glasses without having your eyes examined. You may wind up with a filter that does a good job of removing pesticide residues when you really need something that can get rid of heavy metals. Or you may be spooked into buying a $2,000 hybrid treatment system when testing would have revealed that a $50 "polishing" filter would have been more than adequate.

Having your water tested requires a certain amount of knowledge about what might be wrong with it. If you get your drinking water from a public water supply serving 25 or more customers, chances are it is reasonably safe. In the United States, the Safe Drinking Water Act of 1974 requires water from public sources to meet primary drinking-water regulations set by the Environmental Protection Agency (EPA). Currently, these regulations establish maximum contaminant levels (MCLs) for 26 contaminants, including specific microbiological organisms, inorganic chemicals, organic chemicals and radionuclides. Amendments to the Safe Drinking Water Act passed in 1986 required the EPA to issue MCLs for 57 more contaminants in 1990, followed by an additional 25 by 1991.

The existence of federal MCLs does not necessarily guarantee the perpetual safety of all water from municipal sources, however. Each year, the standards are violated thousands of times across the country. Furthermore, even when the EPA completes the list of regulated contaminants in 1991, that list will still be small compared with the number of potentially hazardous substances that have been detected in drinking-water supplies. Nonetheless, laws do exist that require public water supplies to be tested, and violations of regulations must be made public.

But none of these rules apply to the 40 million Americans who rely on their own wells for drinking water. "It sounds callous," says Lon Coulliard, chief chemist for the Des Moines Municipal Waterworks, "but the federal authorities are willing to let farms go because, from a public-health standpoint, they don't count. There are no drinking-water standards for rural wells, because a rural well is a limited public-health risk."

Since no one else is looking out for the safety of their drinking water, owners of private wells would be wise to give their water supplies regular checkups. The most basic, which should be done once or twice a year, is a coliform bacteria test. County health departments and university extension services will often perform coliform tests free or for a nominal charge. Some county labs will also test for nitrates. Other indicators of basic water quality include pH (acidity), iron, manganese and TDS (total dissolved solids).

Beyond that, what you test for should depend on the history of your well, on its depth and age and on the potential sources of contamination in your area. Shallow wells near a feedlot or heavily fertilized cropland are more likely than deeper wells (more than 60 feet) to contain nitrates. PCBs, a group of toxic organic chemicals, have been detected in about 10 percent of private wells because they were once in widespread use as cooling fluid in well-water pumps. Any well with a pump installed before 1983 should be tested for PCBs.

Anyone living in an agricultural area would be wise to have any well, old or new, tested for several representative insecticides, herbicides and PCBs using the EPA 505 Gas Chromatography Method. Many private testing laboratories routinely use this newly developed test, which can identify and distinguish thousands of chemicals, even if they are present in extremely small quantities. Because of the expensive equipment that is required, testing by this procedure will cost at least $100, and probably more.

A company that is primarily in the business of testing water is likely to be more impartial than a company that is mainly in the business of selling home water-treatment equipment. Try to find a test lab that is certified by the EPA. Unfortunately, most such labs earn their money by handling large government and commercial contracts and are not necessarily good at dealing with the public. Some labs, in fact, may refuse to do individual water tests or else make it so difficult for the layperson to wade through technical jargon as to discourage business from homeowners.

A few laboratories have stepped into this void by offering "user-friendly" mail-order water testing. When I wanted to check the well water at my farm in Iowa, I dealt with WaterTest Corporation, the largest and most prominent of the mail-order labs. Their order form lists 12 tests, or batteries of tests, from a $30 bacteria test and a $32 lead test to a $245 "Supertest Plus," which checks for 101 items, including microbes, minerals, heavy metals, volatile solvents and trihalomethanes.

WaterTest and Hydro-Analysis Associates, a mail-order lab in Pennsylvania, include detailed information with test results to help homeowners interpret and act on the data. Both companies also offer consultation services for their customers. If there is not a competent independent laboratory near you, these mail-order companies are a good alternative.

(Canadian cottagers should check their local Yellow Pages for companies like Toronto's The Water Clinic.)

Originally published in Harrowsmith Country Life *magazine (Charlotte, VT).*

Winterizing the cottage pipes for a year-round water supply

Avoid That Old Winter Freeze-Up

by Charles Long

The beautiful places are at their best with nobody else around: the rustle and tang of an autumn walk, a ski trek over a pristine lake, a sky that tints a snow-drift blue. A winter weekend at the cottage can take your breath away — for which you may be truly grateful after working up a ski sweat that Jackrabbit Johannsen would envy, only to realize that the nearest shower is 60 miles and Sunday night away. Maybe that's why winter is the "off" season in cottage country. Maybe that's why nobody else is around.

Take heart, winter lovers. It is possible to have cottage water in winter without chopping a hole in the ice. But first, the bad news: Mortals have not yet devised the magic pill that will keep cold water from freezing or keep it from breaking pipes when it does. We still have to appease the plumbing gods by heating the water to keep it from freezing or by draining everything to keep the pipes from breaking. Those techno-gimmicks that claim to be winter beaters have not repealed the laws of science. They have merely simplified the chore of draining or whittled away at the cost of heating.

Consider the usual lakeside water-works: a pump by the cottage and a plastic supply pipe from the lake, with a foot valve at the nether end to keep the water in the pipe. You pull it out and drain it in the fall, put it back and prime it in the spring. It's part of a familiar ritual. But all prospects of pulling out and putting back are finished once the lake is locked in ice. Having winter water means, first of all, leaving the supply pipe in place and somehow protecting it.

Insulation might help protect the pipe, but practical difficulties undermine this well-known principle. Typically, the supply pipe lies tucked between the rocks at water's edge, an awkward spot to insulate. You could encase the pipe in foam insulation, but the foam would want to float to the surface; and, floating or not, the foam would be chewed to a litter of popcorn bits by the moving ice. You could bury the pipe below the frost, but not without dredging or blasting at the shoreline and then explaining the mess to environmental officials. It would be easier to drill a well.

The conventional answer has been electric heating cable. The simplest kind wraps around the pipe and heats it from the outside. It also heats the air, the ground and anything else it touches. Worse, exterior cable is open to the ravages of ice, gnawing animals and careless humans. The suppliers we spoke to would not recommend it for lakeside use. And, although the concept of exterior heating cable is simple, it isn't foolproof.

One cottager hired a contractor to install a cheap heating cable that had not been designed for water pipe. The contractor buried the pipe under the lawn, turned the bargain system on and watched water spouting through the grass. The wraparound heating cable had melted the plastic pipe in minutes and turned one man's false economy into a lawn sprinkler.

Heating cable is safer and more efficient inside the plastic pipe. Pyrotenax, of Trenton, Ontario, makes an internal cable for cottage use. You can buy it already installed inside 1¼-inch PVC pipe or ready for insertion in your existing pipe. The system has to be wired in rather than plugged in, which means hiring an electrician if your own skills aren't up to Hydro inspection. And do-it-yourself installers should read the instructions carefully; there are pitfalls for the unwary.

Pyrotenax technologist Karen Foley stresses that cottagers must protect the pipe against physical damage and ensure that it is full of water whenever the heater is on. The thermostat, attached to the outside of the pipe, senses the temperature only at that spot. It cannot tell if the pipe has emptied and is overheating from the inside. "If the prime is lost, I can guarantee the cable will melt the pipe," says Foley.

Bob Turnbull of Rideau Pipe, a Pyrotenax distributor, suggests that users check the foot valve once a year to ensure it will hold water in the pipe. That's not hard to remember if you're pulling the whole thing up every fall, but once the system is winterized, it becomes easier to forget about the foot valve at the bottom of the lake.

The thermostat is critical. One Rideau cottager mounted his new Pyrotenax control box at a convenient height on the inside wall and then extended the sensor as far as it would reach toward the outside, which happened to be just under the cottage. It wasn't in a heated space, but it was warmer than the unprotected part of the pipe at the edge of the lake. The sensor turned the heater off while the pipe froze solid farther down the line.

Any natural instinct to insulate the coldest sections of the supply pipe may be self-defeating. The heavily insulated spot can overheat and melt the pipe. The manufacturer tells installers to cover the line evenly with a few inches of soil. Exposed portions, where the pipe enters the water, for example, should be housed inside a larger pipe to protect them against the lake ice and chilling winds of midwinter.

Despite these potential pitfalls, the Pyrotenax users we spoke with expressed satisfaction, even those users who have experienced problems. Doug Clark had a Pyrotenax system at his Rideau home for 12 years. The pipe, which climbed a barren ledge and crossed a bedrock lawn, froze just once. "And that was because we hadn't turned the system on soon enough," says Clark. "We were away when the weather turned cold, and it was frozen by the time we got home. We just turned up the control to the highest setting, and in 5 or 10 minutes, the water was running again."

Clark wasn't so lucky when he installed another Pyrotenax heater after moving to the Little Mississippi River north of Mazinaw Lake. A splice in the pipe failed, the pump lost its prime, and Clark had to turn off the heater to avoid

Winterized plumbing requires money, careful planning and occasional maintenance, but an extended cottage season may be worth all the effort.

a burnout. The water that remained in the pipe froze solid, and Clark spent the rest of the winter without running water. "Still," he insists, "it is the simplest and most reliable system around. I'd definitely recommend it to anyone who has to move water any distance with poor soil cover."

Clark's long dry spell of plumbing-by-bucket underscores the importance of keeping water in the pipe. While Pyrotenax cable will thaw a frozen line, there is no guarantee that the freezing hasn't damaged the pipe or its joints. Any new leaks can result in a burnout or another freeze.

If Doug Clark considers Pyrotenax to

be the most reliable cable heater around, Lorne Heise means to change all that. The Minden-based contractor has spent the past three years developing a new heated water pipe that is just hitting the market. His Heat-Line system relies on "self-regulating" cable that, like the competition, is threaded through 1- or 1¼-inch supply pipe. Unlike the competition, according to Heise, Heat-Line cable can sense and adjust to temperature differences along the length of the pipe. Inch by inch, it cranks up the wattage in the cold sections and cuts back power in the warm sections, using less power to maintain the same minimum temperature. More importantly, temperature-sensitive cable is not susceptible to the same risks of burnout and freeze-up. You can insulate as unevenly as you like — no hot spots or cold spots. And if the pump loses its prime, the self-adjusting cable keeps the lower portion of the pipe thawed without burning out the dry top end of the line. The unit plugs into an ordinary outlet, which simplifies installation.

Heise is confident that lower installation and energy costs will compensate for Heat-Line's higher price. A 100-foot unit will sell for $1,000. The Retro-Line (cable and fittings to install in an existing pipe) will be about $950, compared with $490 for a Pyrotenax kit the same length.

Heat-Line may have another advantage in short applications, like an exposed pipe under the cottage. Here, or in any installation under 37 feet, Pyrotenax users are advised to step down the voltage by adding a transformer to the system. Heat-Line works on ordinary 120-volt house current and is self-adjusting for long or short runs.

It remains to be seen how the cottage market will respond to competing claims for heating cables. Not everyone is convinced, however, that an electrically heated pipe is the answer.

Sudden Risks

To avoid the risks of sudden freezes or power failures, some lakeside plumbers install self-draining systems with submersible pumps. The pump, left deep in the water, is safely below ice level. You have to remove the check valve from the pump or add a "bleeder" to let the water run out of the line. Then add a Schraeder valve at the upper end of the supply line to let air in as the water drains out. You'll need another check valve above the Schraeder valve to keep water in the pressure tank and inside plumbing. And you'll need an air eliminator in a loop above the pressure tank to let out the trapped air when the pump turns on again. In addition, the system requires a ground-fault circuit interrupter and also a flow inducer to ensure a continuous flow of water past the pump motor to keep it cool. Finally,

you may have to dig up the water-supply pipe and reposition it to eliminate any poorly sloped sections that would not drain quickly.

It's not a job for every do-it-yourselfer. One cottager neglected to include a proper air eliminator and became a local plumbing legend. Air compressed in his pipes until a simple flush blew the contents of the toilet over the walls and the flusher.

The real Achilles' heel of a self-draining system is the waterline, however. The pipe cannot drain lower than the lake surface. If it's not protected at that point, it freezes. You can't protect it with Pyrotenax, which would burn out the dry section of the pipe. You might, in the future, protect it with a self-regulating cable (a Heat-Line cable kept a self-draining system working at minus 34 degrees F last December). But, in the meantime, the submersible, self-draining system has to be heated externally, protected within a nonfreezing "well" or removed in the fall before the lake freezes.

The Ratko pump, a self-draining system used in Finland since 1951, is designed for a well but can be adapted for lakeside use by sinking a steel or concrete culvert vertically at the water's edge. The Ratko motor sits atop the culvert, connected to the submerged pump with a steel shaft. The motor stays high and dry, the pump is safe at the bottom of the well, and the self-draining pipe is safe against freezing from the tank to the waterline. Ratko advises users to fit a tight lid on the ersatz well and, if necessary, insulate it to prevent freezing at the waterline. Costs, not including well or culvert, range from $1,800 to $3,500, depending on the existing system.

Occasional Use

Lauri Toiviainen, Canadian correspondent for the Finnish daily newspaper *Helsingin Sanomat*, installed a Ratko pump at his Moira Lake cottage in 1989. "It's quite easy to use," he claims. "The cottage isn't fully winterized, but we had the plumbing on for three weekends of skiing last year." Toiviainen turned on the baseboard

heaters when he arrived and then switched on the 1½-horsepower pump. It pushed up clear water in about 30 seconds, with lots of volume and pressure. "The first night in the cottage was still cold," he recalls. "So we let the taps drip a little to keep water moving through the system. But when the cottage warmed up, it was fine."

Cable heaters, like Pyrotenax and Heat-Line, can protect the supply pipe from the lake to the pump; the rest, including the pump, still has to be heated or drained. Self-draining systems like Ratko put the pump safely under water, but you still have to protect the pressure tank, valves and inside plumbing from freezing temperatures. No commercial winter heater absolves the cottager from draining or heating the plumbing in the cottage. (You should not have to worry about the drainpipes, though; they're sloped to empty after every use between the traps and the buried septic system.)

The luxury route is to heat the whole building. New cottages, especially, are sometimes built to suburban standards, with lots of insulation and beefed-up Hydro services that can handle winter heating. Jean-Pierre Laflamme of Ottawa heats his cottage all winter long. Closing the cottage after a winter visit is no more complicated than shutting off the pump to avoid a deluge should something break, turning off the water softener and turning down the thermostat to 50 degrees F. Energy costs are high for part-time use ($1,200 a year) but would be much higher were it not for the house-quality insulation.

With a sharp eye to costs, Bob and Annette Edgington revamped their plumbing last year so that they could have running water in winter. Retired now, the Edgingtons travel during the coldest months but live on eastern Ontario's Lower Rideau Lake from April until December. Tired of chopping holes in the ice in between their sojourns to exotic warmer places, the Edgingtons moved pump, pressure tank and water heater into a compact cubbyhole in the bathroom. Then they insulated just that room to R20 standards: walls, ceiling, floor, even the bathroom door. A single

500-watt baseboard heater keeps the bath and basic plumbing warm while the rest of the rooms in the cottage are left to freeze.

Their autumn closing routine still includes draining the kitchen plumbing, sleeping cabin and outdoor taps. But the essential core of the system is left at the ready. Bob's well-lit little cubbyhole holds all the valves he needs to shut off the water to the unheated parts of the cottage. A Pyrotenax cable keeps the supply pipe open. Bob maintains that his winter water system makes no discernible difference in his Hydro bill.

Heating cottage plumbing involves more than energy costs, however. There is some risk in leaving any pressurized water system unattended in winter. A power failure, a fallen limb, a vandal who leaves the door open: such things can foil the best-laid plans. This is why most insurance policies won't cover the damage from ruptured plumbing unless you shut off the water or have someone check the place daily to make sure the heat is still on.

Freeze Alert

The Laflammes have a temperature alarm built into their electronic security system, so the remote monitor knows if the pipes are about to freeze. The Edgingtons have a year-round neighbour to keep an eye on things. But neighbours and electronic wizardry aren't options on every lake. For some, the risk (if not the cost) of keeping the plumbing heated for an occasional weekend visit outweighs the convenience of an après-ski shower.

The alternative is to drain the inside plumbing rather than heat it. That's easier in some cottages than in others. Some do-it-yourself tangles of splices, patches and roller-coaster pipe runs can take hours of tapping and blowing to empty completely. But if all pipes slope to a few well-planned discharge valves and if tanks can be emptied with the turn of a tap, the chore won't spoil a weekend visit. The pump itself is still a bother unless, like Lauri Toiviainen, you can leave the thing safely at the bottom of a nonfreezing "well."

"I have three valves to turn in order to drain the whole system and empty the tanks," says Toiviainen. "We put some antifreeze in the traps, and the whole procedure takes maybe two minutes."

Perhaps the only way to match Toiviainen's record for well-planned simplicity is to revert to original cottage plumbing: the outhouse and the old hand pump. Good hand pumps are self-draining and self-priming. They work all winter with no insulation, no Hydro and no maintenance. You might need a sauna instead of a shower, or a tin tub in front of the fireplace, but even those have their simple charms. If there were an equally charming alternative to the outhouse on a frosty night, the catalogue of winter beaters would be complete.

Originally published in Cottage Life *magazine (Toronto).*

Step-by-step fall plumbing shutdown

Without special provision for winter water, closing the cottage centres on the once-a-year ritual of shutting off power, opening up valves, draining and antifreezing. Forgetful cottagers, or optimists who perpetually hope the end-of-season guests will volunteer for the chore, keep a checklist of all the essential steps. The list won't be the same for every system. Cottage waterworks are, after all, unique stews of mix-and-match fixtures, where knowing the right swear words becomes part of the evolved Te Deum. The elements, however, are these:

☐ Turn off the water heater. If it's electric, shut it off at the panel; if it's gas, shut off the supply valve.

☐ Switch off and drain the pump. Don't forget that piston pumps have two pumping chambers to drain.

☐ Drain the hot-water tank, water softener, filter, purifier or anything else that holds water. Big tanks usually have a drain cock near the bottom. People who have wearied of mopping will have added a hose to the nearest drain.

☐ Water tanks can become plugged, especially if water is hard or is drawn from a lake. Make sure the tank is completely empty by observing the flow; if it stops too soon, it may be plugged.

☐ Open all faucets.

☐ Open all valves, and remove the small "bleeder" caps beneath them.

☐ Pull the intake pipe out of the water.

☐ Remove the screen from the foot valve and clean it.

☐ Open the foot valve, and drain the intake pipe.

☐ Remove and clean the intake filter (where the intake joins the pump).

☐ Remove all drain plugs from the pump.

☐ Blow into the primer hole to force out any remaining water. (If your lungs can't handle this, try a device called an Air Pig; it's basically a can of compressed air, useful for clearing all lines.)

☐ Grease the plugs and store them.

☐ Drain the pumps built into such appliances as washing machines. If they're too awkward to drain, put some antifreeze in the intake hose and switch on the machine just long enough to suck antifreeze into the pump. You can buy nontoxic antifreeze made for RV plumbing; just make sure to flush it out again in the spring.

☐ Flush the toilets to empty the tanks, then look into the tank to be certain the water is all gone. Dip out any that remains in tank or bowl.

☐ Put enough antifreeze in the bowl to fill it to normal level.

☐ Remove the plugs from the bottom of the traps (beneath every sink and tub). After they drain, replace the plugs and refill the traps with antifreeze or a nonfreezing, environmentally friendlier substance like mineral oil.

A cautious approach makes winter lake activities safe

Common Sense and Thick Ice

by Yvonne Cox

If ever there was a confirmed winter hater, it was me. My particular *bête noire* was ice. The traditional Canadian passion for skating held zero appeal for me, and I counted it a successful winter if the slippery stuff didn't make me fall even once. So it wasn't easy for my husband to persuade me to join him for a winter weekend at a friend's island cottage several years ago. ("What? There's an outhouse???!!")

There was another hurdle beyond the outdoor facilities: the island was about half a mile from shore, and I was terrified to make the crossing. What if the ice gave way? (I later learned my fears were groundless: this was February, and the ice was so thick, it could have held a truck.) But to everyone's surprise, that weekend turned me into a cottaging and winter convert. Now, after having spent a winter living full-time at our own cottage — one with indoor plumbing facilities, mind you — it's tough to decide which season I like best. Now that vast plain of ice in front of the cottage seems magical to me, making the impossible — walking on water — possible.

In 1989, when extreme cold came early to the lake, freeze-up literally happened overnight: on the last day on

November, I watched half a dozen mergansers bobbing in the water and wondered why they were still hanging around. As December 1 dawned, the sun glinted off the lake's thin, dark jacket of solid ice. Frigid nights of -13 degrees F and daytime temperatures at or below -15 degrees followed; by mid-December, the ice was strong enough to walk across the lake. The year before, however, the lake didn't even get a thin coating of ice until December 15. That's how variable ice can be.

Depending on temperature, wind, snowfall and current, the ice sheet will differ not only from year to year but even from day to day and from place to place on a given lake. "You can have 30 inches of ice on Lake Simcoe at Big Bay Point," says Alex Smith, fish and wildlife supervisor with the Ontario Ministry of Natural Resources (MNR) in Midhurst, "and the same day on the same lake, at a pressure crack near Orillia, you can have 2 inches of ice or even open water." On the Nottawasaga River, he adds, "you can have 12 inches one day, with people ice fishing, and if it warms up the next day, you'll have just 4 inches." Smith often fields telephone inquiries from city dwellers planning to come north, but because ice conditions vary so much, he is always reluctant to categorically declare an ice surface safe.

So how can *you* tell when and where the ice is safe? And how thick does it have to be to carry a person or snowmobile safely? There are no absolutes with ice, but assuming it is a uniform thickness without cracks, a minimum of 2 inches is necessary to support a person walking, and 7 inches is necessary to support a slow-moving snowmobile. But that's not just any type of ice.

"If you're measuring ice for strength and trying to decide whether it will support the weight of a snowmobile or person, you should measure the thickness of the white ice and the thickness of the black ice," says Craig Macdonald, outdoor recreational specialist at the MNR's Leslie M. Frost Centre in Dorset. He advises using an ice auger — $60 at Canadian Tire — to make a measurement hole. "Take half the thickness of the white ice, and add it to the thickness of the black ice, and that gives you the total equivalent in black ice, which is the thickness you should consider."

Black ice? White ice? Knowing the difference between types of ice is a first step in understanding where ice is safe.

Before the lake freezes, it first must lose a summer's worth of heat. That process begins with many days and nights of cold. As the mercury drops throughout the fall, surface water chills. Once cooled to 40 degrees F, the point

A family shares the brisk pleasure of a smooth, windswept patch of ice; safety demands at least two to four inches of black ice before setting out.

at which water is densest, water from the surface sinks and is replaced by less dense, warmer water from the bottom. This exchange continues until there is a layer of less dense cooler water on the surface. (Below 40 degrees, water actually becomes less dense.) When it gets cold enough, the lake freezes, the water molecules locking into a solid, hexagonal, crystalline structure. Because ice is less dense than the liquid form of water, it floats.

Once a lake has a solid coat, it conducts heat through the ice into the cold air above, causing the ice to thicken downward. This ice is known as "black ice," because that's how it appears when you look down into the water at it. (If you chop a piece out and hold it up to the light, it looks blue.) Black ice is formed directly from the water and thus contains few air bubbles; it's the strongest form of ice. Some people refer to the ice at break-up time as black ice, because that's how it looks

floating on the cold, dark water. But it's an improper use of the term; that kind of ice is actually very weak.

Where ice and water meet, the temperature is around 32 degrees F, but on the surface, it could be minus 15. This tremendous temperature difference creates extreme stress. One of winter's most enthralling sounds is the noise the frozen lake makes on clear, cold nights as the surface ice contracts in an attempt to equalize the pressure: violent crackings, deep muffled thunderbolts that reverberate from the opposite shore. Warmer temperatures can cause expansion of the ice sheet along these pressure cracks, resulting in ridges on the surface or even stretches of open water on bigger lakes.

Once snow begins to fall, the development of black ice is slowed because the snow acts as insulation. As it accumulates on a frozen lake, it depresses the ice sheet. The pressure of its weight forces water up through the cracks to

form a layer of slush. Since snow wicks the water up gradually, slush will often lie hidden under a white blanket, so you can't tell it's there unless you compress the top layer — throw a snowball, walk or ski on it. Given cold enough temperatures, the slush eventually forms a new layer of ice, called "white ice," which bonds to the black ice underneath. Opaque, granular and full of air bubbles, white ice isn't as dense and consistent as black ice and may be only half as strong.

If heavy snow comes early, before black ice has much of a chance to get established, it doesn't take as much weight to depress the ice and cause slushing; then the ice sheet will be composed mainly of weaker white ice. If ice forms on a lake during a snowstorm or windy conditions, you may also get mostly white ice.

Wind, of course, causes the snow to drift. Snow cover tends to be thicker in the direction prevailing winds blow; as a result, the black ice on that side of a lake (or island) tends to be thinner due to the snow's insulating properties, while the white ice will be thicker. Snow cover also tends to be heavier near shorelines than in the middle of the lake, where the wind has free rein to clear more snow off the ice. Thus white ice and slush are also more prominent near shore than farther out. "The deeper the snow and the less it's compressed, the less ice development overall," says Macdonald.

Wherever there is fast-flowing water on a lake — at a narrows or where a river or creek flows in or out — you'll find poor ice conditions. These parts of a lake are never safe for travel, although they may look deceptively solid when covered with snow or snowy slush. The tiny crystals of ice that form in very cold, fast-flowing water are full of air bubbles and therefore result in the weakest form of ice, called "frazil ice." On rivers that are too turbulent to freeze solid (because the water's constant movement keeps it warmer than 32 degrees F), you'll find heaps of frazil ice at shorelines.

As spring approaches, the big question for many cottagers is, When will the ice go out? On most inland lakes in cottage country, break-up occurs in April or early May, usually several weeks after the snow disappears: one day there is ice, and the next, open water. But just as it took many weeks of cold temperatures to freeze your lake, it takes weeks of spring warmth and rain showers to melt it away again. "Warm rain takes out ice much faster than strong sunlight," says Macdonald.

In the case of a black ice sheet, the disintegration of the ice is primarily the result of "candling": radiation melting the ice at the vertical crystal interfaces. As the heat gradually penetrates, pencil-shaped shafts of grainy ice with little or no bearing capacity are created.

Spring is a good time to study the ice on your lake (from the shore, of course). Since areas of current and weak ice open up first — along shorelines, for example, which collect rainfall and runoff — you can get a pretty good notion of the spots to be wary of during your subsequent winter excursions.

In the meantime, if you don't know the ice on your lake, check the conditions carefully with knowledgeable local people before venturing forth, advises the MNR's Alex Smith. "Don't assume that because the ice was safe last week, it will still be good today," he says. "People who have lived on the lake all their lives and know where the soft spots and pressure cracks are have a distinct advantage over the guy who comes up from the city occasionally." Talk to marina owners who live on your section of the lake year-round, to snowmobile shops, to local merchants. "If you don't know, don't go," says Bill Wicklund, manager of the Ontario Provincial Police Traffic and Marine Branch. Three people died going through the ice in Ontario in 1989, a number that seems to be increasing each year despite the warnings.

Check the weather forecast beforehand, travel with a buddy, tell people where you'll be going, and carry waterproof matches or a lighter so that you can make an emergency fire. Another good policy is to take along a 65-foot length of rope to help people get out if they fall through; a 6-foot pole or walking stick is handy for probing questionable ice and getting yourself out of a hole. In that nasty predicament, try to go out the same direction you went in — at least you know that a few seconds ago that ice supported you. Also, try to bring your legs to the surface and then kick your way onto the ice. (Woollen mittens make it easier to get a solid grip, since they stick to the ice.) Then roll away from the hole; don't stand up until you know the ice is solid underneath you.

Travel after dark is dangerous because it's easy to lose your bearings, especially in bad weather. Ice ridges pushed up by pressure cracks are hard to see at night — but finding one is like hitting a concrete wall.

Unless you're very sure of the ice conditions, don't automatically follow a snowmobile track assuming the ice is safe. Many new snow machines are so fast and powerful, they can easily make it over ice that's too thin to support a person on foot or driving a heavy, slower machine.

You might also want to get together with other cottagers to mark out a safe ice route. On Raven Lake, where most cottages have water access only, people who need to clear snow off their roofs or want to use their cottages must cross the ice. A group of them gets together in late December or early January to check the ice and mark out a "road" with wooden stakes to ensure better visibility at night and during snowfalls. Using the same trail over and over again packs down the snow, reinforcing and thickening the ice.

Although, in theory, 7 inches of ice is safe for a slow-moving snowmobile, as is 2 inches for a person walking (counting white ice as only half as thick as black ice), in real life, it's wise to double these numbers for good measure and stay off virgin ice. Cautious cottagers simply make it a policy to stay off the ice until it measures a good 10 to 12 inches thick — which, on many central Ontario lakes, means waiting until January.

Although many people do it — especially the farther north you go — driving a vehicle on ice is risky business. (Yes, I confess I've done it.) Because there are so many variables, no one endorses driving a car or truck on ice.

Those prepared to take the risk, however, usually wait until the ice is at least 26 inches thick and they are absolutely sure of its condition. Experts advise opening your window to ensure a quick escape, and if you park your vehicle in front of the cottage, keep in mind its weight can fatigue the ice over time, so don't leave it on the same spot day after day. If you have more than one car, never park them close together.

Driving on the ice causes a sag in the ice sheet, which creates a pressure wave (even snowmobiles are heavy enough for this). This wave bounces off the bottom and can magnify closer to the shoreline and actually crack the ice. That's why you should slow down as you approach the shore.

Originally published in Cottage Life *magazine (Toronto).*

Crafting the perfect porch accessory with a few basic tools

Build Your Own Adirondack Chair

by Tony Leighton

Fat, folksy and a little funny, Adirondack chairs are to enjoy the fireworks from, to watch the family grow up from, to read trashy fiction in, to doze in, to ponder life in.

The Adirondack chair has been around since before time, or so it seems. You know what it looks like even if you don't know its name. It is an archetypal folk design, with its slatted seat and back set in a position of permanent repose and wide, flat, often kidney-shaped arms that engulf you on both sides like an overweight lover. It is the all-time classic backyard chair, cottage chair or, as the Americans call it, "camp" chair.

Most of the world's homemade Adirondacks are overly friendly — so friendly, they hate to let go. Low-slung and deep-seated, they swallow your hips whole, like a toilet with the seat left up. When viewed from the front, a group of tall people sitting in Adirondacks look like creatures whose necks are attached to their lower legs.

Well-designed Adirondacks are widely available these days, thanks to that most remarkable of consumer miracles: Yuppie Love. The Adirondack is being discovered. And, in one refined form or another, it can be found in Bloom-ingdale's department store, L.L. Bean's mail-order catalogue and dozens of trendy little shops where humble pine Adirondacks sell for a decidedly unhumble $300. Some of the new Adirondacks are made from hardwood. Others adjust for the height of the occupant. Still others fold and fit neatly into European sedans. Like bronze sundials, computer-controlled sprinkler systems and injection-moulded composters, Adirondacks have become high-status backyard fixtures.

But purists would argue that it has become too beautiful; that a chair of such refinement has come too far from the original assemblages of found materials that constituted the first Adirondack; that an outdoor chair suitable for indoors cannot truly be called an Adirondack; that, like a wet dog, the Adirondack should never be allowed inside the house.

Hubert Yeoman's chairs are made for outside. A retired paper-mill worker who lives about a mile south of the *Harrowsmith* magazine offices in Camden East, Ontario, Yeomans builds gargantuan lawn swings, windmills, wooden wishing wells, bird apartment complexes and extremely sturdy, lightweight Adirondack chairs. Nothing fancy, mind you. His chairs achieve a nice balance between sensible design, decent craftsmanship, quality materials and fair price. They look good and feel good, but they aren't *too* good.

Hubert, who is in his late 60s, had a heart attack in 1976. While he was recovering, his wife Melissa bought him a table saw, thinking it might be therapeutic. A frugal man, Hubert tried to return the saw but couldn't because it had been out of the store for over 30 days. So Hubert started making lawn ornaments and chairs in his workshop behind the house. When he retired from the mill two years ago, his hobby became a modest business.

Although he knows the name, Hubert has never referred to his chairs as Adirondacks. His current model is a second-generation design that is an improvement upon the first chair he made in a number of ways: it has wider arms, a more comfortable seat and a higher back with a gentle vertical scoop. He knew he had a winner when he finished the prototype and allowed Melissa to test it. "That was it," says Hubert with a shake of his head. "She grabbed that one and said, 'Nobody's getting this chair.'"

The beauty of most Adirondacks is that there are few custom-cut pieces. The chair is made mostly from stan-

A crucial piece of furniture at any cottage, the Adirondack chair belongs outside, on deck or dock.

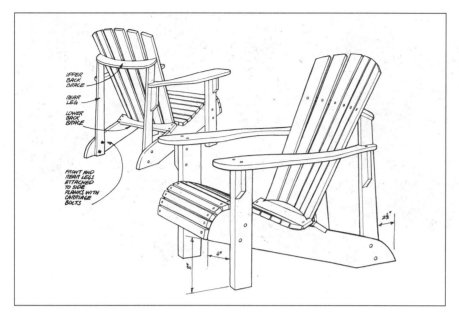

UPPER BACK BRACE

REAR LEG

LOWER BACK BRACE

FRONT AND REAR LEGS ATTACHED TO SIDE PLANKS WITH CARRIAGE BOLTS

dard-size lumber, putting it within reach of anyone with the time and inclination.

Hubert Yeomans gets his white cedar in ¾-inch thickness from a one-man sawmill near his home. The sawyer gets his cedar from the back woodlot. Lumberyard browsers may have less luck, but Hubert says 1-inch red cedar and pine (actual size: ¾ inch) are adequate substitutes. Cedar, which is more rot-resistant, is preferred for the legs and side planks — the parts that touch the ground.

Start by cutting all the pieces shown in the illustration, sawing the side planks, legs and arms in pairs to ensure uniformity. Use a table saw, radial-arm saw, circular saw or handsaw and mitre box for the straight cuts; and a band saw, scroll saw or jigsaw for curved cuts. Smooth all exposed faces, then chamfer any square edges with sandpaper or a router and ¼-inch-radius rounding bit.

Most important to the Yeomans chair and any like it are the side planks, which determine both the shape of the seat and the angle of the back. Start construction by attaching the front and rear legs to the side planks, front legs on the outside, rear legs on the inside.

The front of each front leg meets the bottom of the side plank 7 inches from the ground and 4 inches from the front of the side plank; the back of each rear leg meets the side plank at ground level

2½ inches from the end. Make sure the legs are all vertical, and clamp them in place. Drill two diagonally opposed ⅜-inch holes in each front assembly, and bolt them together. Begin with only one hole in each rear assembly so that you can adjust the other parts of the chair before committing yourself to the second hole.

Now fasten the four blocks that support the arms. The front pair lines up with the front and top edges of the front legs; the back pair is flush with the front of the rear legs 20 inches from the ground so that the arms will be level. Clamping the blocks in place, use 2½-inch No. 8 Robertson flathead screws for the front and 1¼-inch screws for the back, spaced about 3 inches apart. Predrill all screw holes to avoid splitting the wood.

Next, fasten the top back support to the top of the rear legs, using one 1¼-inch screw for each side. Fit the bottom back support into the notches on the side planks, using two screws per side and keeping in mind that the tops of the legs should be the same distance apart as the bottoms.

Some careful eyeballing must be exercised to position the back slats. To achieve a fanned effect, fasten the two outer slats to the bottom back support about ½ inch in from the start of the curve and to the top back support flush with the outer edge of the curve. With

these two slats in place, space the other four evenly between them, using one 1¼-inch screw at the bottom of each slat and another at the top.

More eyeballing comes into play when attaching the arms, for which a shallow ¾-inch-high notch must be cut out of the two outer back slats. The exact depth and shape of these notches is more art than science, so make them slowly with a coping saw, kerfing like a sculptor until each arm fits snugly onto the rear legs. Next, fasten each arm to the front legs and the front and back support blocks with 1¼-inch screws. Since the back of the chair is now firm enough, you can also install the second carriage bolt through the rear legs and side planks.

Finally, the seat slats: first screw one of the 1¾-inch-wide slats to the front of the side planks, giving the seat its width. Next, space the four 1-inch seat slats around the roll at the front of the chair, their bottom edges set about ⅛ inch apart. The remaining eight 1¾-inch slats are then spaced evenly toward the back. The last slat has to be cut in an unusual way to accommodate the bottom of the back. This cut, a sort of flared notch running almost the entire length of the slat, matches the curve of the back slats and is best made on a band saw. The same curve is extended into a half-moon wedge that fits between the last slat and the back. Attach the wedge to the last slat with a pair of 2-inch galvanized finishing nails before screwing the slat to the two side planks.

As for a finish, there are a number of options. Most of the world's Adirondacks are painted, usually with leftover house paint. Given the rough use most of the chairs receive — left out all summer in the sun and rain, banged by glasses and plates, stained with sweat and suntan oil — Hubert says that many of his customers fear chipped or flaking paint and choose a stain or protective oil finish. He recommends three initial coats of paint and another coat each spring.

Originally published in Harrowsmith *magazine (Camden East, Ont.).*

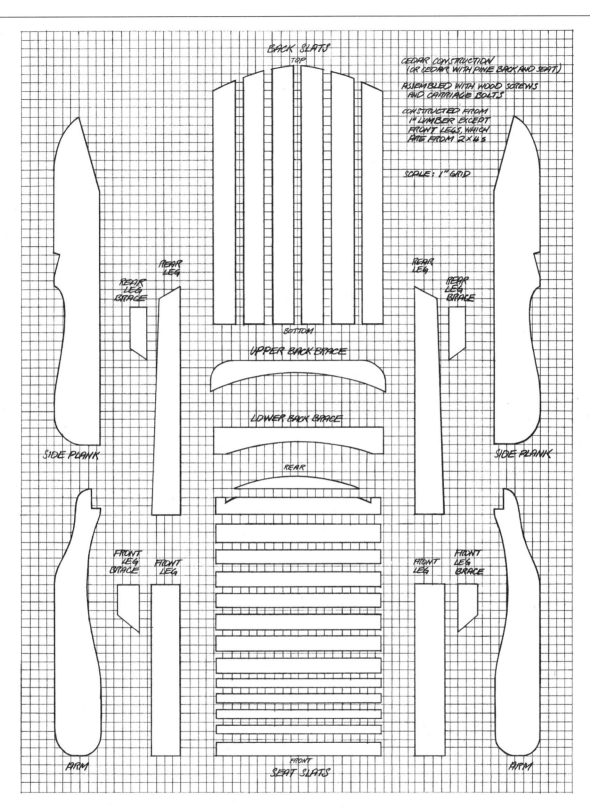

MATERIALS

side planks: 8' 1x6 cedar	*leg and back braces*: 6' 1x4 cedar or pine	*arms*: 6' 1x6 cedar or pine	*hardware*: eight ⅜x2" carriage bolts; six 2½" No. 8 Robertson
front legs: 4' 2x4 cedar		*seat slats*: 4' 1x2 cedar or pine	flathead screws; 5 dozen 1¼"
rear legs: 6' 1x4 cedar	*back slats*: two 8' 1x2 cedar or pine	two 10' 1x2 cedar or pine	No. 8 Robertson flathead screws; two 2" finishing nails

Building a driveway through the woods

Laneways That Really Work

by Jeremy Schmidt

Country lanes — the best ones — provide immense satisfaction to the owner. They are personal things. Your lane marks the beginning and the end of every journey you make. When you come home, it is the first thing you see that is truly yours, and over the years, you get to know it intimately: the location of birds' nests, the place where crocuses will come up in the spring, the individual trees, the hedge to which rabbits flee in the beam of your approaching headlights.

But a road can also be a yearlong headache. You come home to the same old ruts and bumps. You know where you will have trouble with drifting snow, where the mud hole will appear every March with the regularity of a migrating robin and where summer rains will work to turn the road into a ravine. Every year, you resolve to fix those places but then do little more than grit your teeth in frustrated expectation and make stopgap repairs.

Part of the problem is that property owners rarely build proper roads — surveyed, designed and engineered. Roads are expensive: a contractor may charge $10 to $15 per linear foot. That money somehow feels better used when invested in the house or cottage.

Besides that, many of us prefer a minimalist approach to what we see as a major alteration of our private landscape. We like to think of a country lane as a footpath for cars. After all, we walk where it makes good sense to walk, following the topography, paying attention to the view, avoiding places where our feet will do damage.

And so it can be with a lane. In some cases, no more construction is needed than to clear away some vegetation. The underlying soil provides the driving surface. Bushes and trees grow close. Grass brushes the undersides of vehicles. If conditions are right, the road serves adequately for many years.

Yet often, conditions are nowhere near right, and you find yourself thinking you have got to do something to remedy the situation or wishing you had planned things better at the start. What follows is a guide to design principles — many of them the same considerations used by engineers in constructing public roads. These principles apply to private lanes as easily as to highways, even if you do the work with a shovel instead of a bulldozer.

In planning initial construction, the first step is to define your needs. When will the road be used, by what vehicles and how often? These questions affect both design and location. For example, a road meant only for summer use

could be built over soil that turns to a quagmire during the spring melt. But if you need to use it all year, you'll have to consider ways to keep the road dry or find another route. The opposite extreme, lack of moisture, can also be a problem in places where soft sand can, in midsummer, trap a car as effectively as mud; but during wet seasons, the sand firms up and supports traffic.

When thinking about traffic, consider vehicles other than your personal car. If you plan to build a house or cabin, the road will need to handle concrete trucks, utility trucks (perhaps carrying large spools of underground cable), flatbed semis delivering lumber and cement blocks, and a few that might surprise you. While building my own house, I found that the only truck that had any difficulty was the one that brought the concrete septic tank.

Even after construction, you might have propane trucks, septic pumpers and others, including — much as you don't want to think about them — emergency vehicles. What a tragedy it would be to have a fire engine, during the moment of need, get stuck trying to make it around a tight curve 300 yards from the house. Plan the road to accom-

Every laneway has its own requirements based on the site, the traffic and the seasons it is to be used.

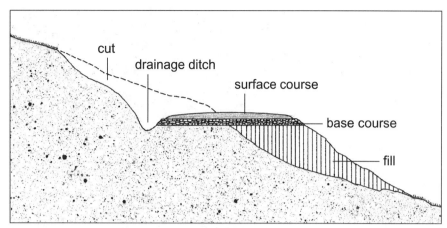

A hillside slope is cut away to build a roadway. A drainage ditch on the uphill side carries runoff away from the road. The surface is 4 inches of aggregate atop 8 inches of coarse stone which has been packed onto fill.

modate the largest vehicle that might use it. You can get advice from county planners or your fire department.

Unless easements restrict the roadway to a specific location, your next job is to find an appropriate route. This can be critical, because poor choice of location requires more construction, costs more money and usually makes a bigger scar. A good road fits the landscape, letting natural contours dictate, as much as possible, its shape and course. It should not run arrow-straight, nor should it stand out visibly for miles around. Beyond affecting aesthetics, proper location can often help with maintenance: a southern exposure will be drier than a northern one.

Most people want to avoid cutting trees, bulldozing hillsides or filling low areas. Yet some construction will be necessary, and deciding how much is the trick. For example, suppose you need to get around the base of a hill where it meets a wet area. You might feel reluctant to call in the heavy machinery and make a scar on the hill, but it is probably better to do that and get it over with than to contend forever with trying to fill the mud. Remember, the hill is already on a firm footing.

A good first step in planning is to walk the route, trying to picture how the road will look. Measure the critical places, pace out the curves, mark the route with stakes and plastic ribbon and then look at it from different angles. Consider the soils under your route,

and look closely at the way water moves at all seasons of the year. Of course, to do this properly, you need a grasp of design principles, which include dimensions, grade, soil types, drainage, surfacing and more.

Engineers for the U.S. Forest Service, who build and maintain thousands of miles of woodland roads, use specifications for what they call low-standard roads. These are built at minimum cost and with the least possible environmental impact — usually the main objectives of a private landowner. What follows is based largely on these low-standard-road specifications.

Dimensions

A minimum roadway is 12 feet wide, with a 16-foot side-to-side clearance. The road base itself should be 14 feet wide to allow for a 1-to-2-foot shoulder on each side. However, 10 feet of solid roadway will support a large truck, and if two-way traffic on such a narrow lane is a concern, you can build turnouts at comfortable intervals. If you are considering a narrow drive, you may get resistance from a contractor. The blade of a D7 bulldozer is 14 feet wide, and building narrower than that requires smaller machinery and extra care. Don Rivers, transportation planner for Wyoming's Bridger-Teton National Forest, says, "Sometimes you've got to ride these guys to keep them from thinking that bigger is better. They'll say, 'Hey, you've got 16 feet of road

for the price of 12. What are you complaining about?'"

The width of the road is a major consideration on sharp curves, and two factors should be kept in mind. First, long trucks can't turn as tightly as short cars. For example, a car with an 11-foot wheelbase can cut a turn inside a circle with about a 26-foot radius. That refers to the track of the outside front tire; the bumper needs a little more room than that. By comparison, a vehicle with a 20-foot wheelbase struggles to make turns in a radius of 44 feet. Second, the road should widen out on tight curves, especially for vehicles pulling trailers.

Grade

The steepness of a road is expressed as the percentage of rise to run; that is, a 10 percent grade climbs 1 foot for each 10 feet of horizontal travel. As a general rule, road steepness should not exceed 8 percent. In practice, however, a 12 to 14 percent grade is feasible for short distances, although erosion problems increase as the slope gets steeper. Pickup trucks and four-wheel-drive vehicles can handle 18 percent grades without difficulty — in summer — but winter driving is another matter, and local building standards might prohibit anything that steep (remember the fire truck). You can determine approximate grade with a builder's transit or a simple clinometer — a square board with a metal ruler attached so that it will hang freely when the board is held on edge.

As a rule of thumb for working in broken terrain, road designers keep the grade as much as 2 percent below maximum. That is because the final pitch of a road frequently works out to be steeper than the preliminary survey indicates. The errors inherent in taking many sightings and from variations when it comes to actual construction demand this built-in flexibility.

In general, slopes complicate road building. In mountainous areas, switchbacks become a necessity, and these are a special problem, requiring lots of room and bulldozer work. The grade leading into and out of switchbacks must be slackened to a maximum of 8 percent, with 4 percent preferred, to allow for acceleration when going uphill. Steeper hillsides require deeper cuts, until building a switchback becomes impractical; this maximum is reached on a 35 percent side slope.

The steepness of road banks can vary. Much depends on the depth of cut and the sort of soil in which it is made. Obviously, sand will slump to its angle of repose, and the cut should be somewhat less steep than that angle. But if the soil has more cohesion, you can cut a steeper bank. High banks are less stable than low ones. Where you might get away with a short vertical cut of 1 foot, a 5-foot cut may have to be angled back. A 66 percent slope is the recommended average on high cuts.

Other grade recommendations are that stream crossings should be level and perpendicular to the stream. Intersections with other roads should also be level, or one side will be higher than the other. In crossing a draw, the grade should be reduced — if it is not, the road can provide a new channel for continuing water erosion.

Soil Types

A rose may be a rose, but soil is not just dirt. It can be made of clay, silt, sand, cinders, pebbles and river cobbles. It can be filled with decomposing organic material or have virtually none. It can bake to concrete hardness in the sun and become a quagmire with a little rain. On the other hand, water firms up some kinds of soil that fall apart when they are dry.

In locating your road, pay close attention to existing soil. You might get away with not having to haul surfacing materials, and construction can be kept simple. But probably not. Monty Evans, a Wyoming contractor, says that to save money, "some guys don't even want me to put down a base course, but a year later, they're back, after they know they need it. You've just about got to have river gravel to get away without surfacing."

There are several ways of checking your soil. One, of course, is to go out with a shovel and look at it, but it takes an educated eye to connect what you see with how it will perform under a road. A better choice is to look at other roads in the vicinity. Find a neighbour, and ask the important questions. Does his drive drain well? Does it erode? Is it slippery in rain? What problems has he had, and how has he solved them? How much surfacing material has he put down? He doesn't need to be an expert; his road should tell the story.

Four-wheel-drive vehicles can handle 18 percent grades without difficulty in summer, but winter driving is another matter.

In the absence of a neighbour's example, you can get expert help from government agencies. Detailed soil surveys are available on a county-by-county basis all across the country and include detailed maps, aerial photographs and other charts on which you can locate your particular property and soil type. Other tables give information on soil uses and behaviour. These tell you how your soil rates as road fill, how well it drains, how steeply you can cut it before it collapses, and more. If you decide you need to haul fill from another location, the county soil map might help you find it.

Drainage

No matter where in the country you build, drainage is likely to be the most critical of all planning considerations. Water runs on the surface, seeps through the subsoil, expands upon freezing, pools in low areas and always seeks out the weakest point in your defences. If you plan well, your road will require little attention over the years. Planning is especially important on marginal soils, those containing a lot of clay or organic material. Plan poorly, and the results can be dramatic.

Here is the classic scenario, repeated in rural areas around the world: a country lane begins as a simple track across an open field. Gradually, it gets worn smooth and widened by traffic. As the soil compacts under the weight of tires and erodes under the influence of water and wind, the roadway sinks lower than the surrounding area. That makes it a natural collector of moisture. Before long, the road is a canal, a mud bog and an eyesore. Also, traffic goes around it rather than through it, resulting in even further damage.

Proper location can solve some problems. Try to keep the road on high, naturally dry ground. Avoid steep, erosion-prone side slopes. Stay out of ravines, and try not to run parallel to watercourses, or you may find that the stream prefers your road to its old bed, especially during floods or high water. Another consideration is exposure to sunshine. In shady places, the ground stays wet, snow melts more slowly, and ice gets thick. If that is likely to be a problem, avoid the north sides of hills. By the same token, a north-south road cut through dense forest gets less direct sunlight than an east-west road. One common recommendation is to clear the forest on either side of the road to a distance of 1 to 1½ times the average tree height.

But you can't always locate a road where it will drain naturally, and then you need some design work. Rather than let a sunken roadway turn itself into a canal during wet times of the year, it would be better at the outset to grade the road, pushing soil toward the centre and creating ditches on the sides. In some parts of the country, these ditches are called borrow pits, meaning that material for the road surface is borrowed from the ditches. It is a good commonsense term, because the road, encouraged by erosion and gravity, will eventually give the soil back unless you keep busy with a grader. I suppose that makes you a sort of soil-bank loan officer. This, by the way, is the most common and simplest system of road building in the world. In good soils, it can be done with nothing more than a grader. Rain and snowmelt drain off the raised surface into the borrow pits. At intervals, ditches graded into surrounding fields disperse the runoff.

On the sides of hills, standard construction practice gets more complicated, calling for a raised, more or less level road surface, with a ditch cut into the uphill side. Water runs down the hill above the road, collects in the ditch and flows to a culvert, where it is dumped below the roadway. This works well but requires elaborate construction and a considerably wider cut than most property owners would like to see. Happily, alternatives exist.

It is possible to use the road itself as a drainage structure. All it takes is some modification — shaping of the road and perhaps reinforcement in selected areas. For example, on a high-speed public road, engineers try to smooth out natural dips by cutting off the high spots and pushing the material into low areas. That makes a more level surface overall, but it disturbs existing drainage patterns and requires culverts in the low places. Not only do you need the bulldozer, but you must anticipate the volume of water the culvert will handle. A diameter of 18 inches is considered the minimum to prevent clogging with debris, but it might have to be a lot bigger than that.

A private lane meant for slow traffic, however, can rise and fall with the terrain and avoid disturbing natural drainage patterns. Where it crosses low areas, the road should be level and perpendicular to the flow of water (again, to prevent the road from becoming a watercourse itself). Rather than build culverts, you might be able to let water flow across the road; if that causes erosion, you may need surfacing materials, but you can start by reinforcing with rocks or gravel in only the vulnerable places. Or build a wooden culvert, which is nothing more than two boards set on edge and spaced several inches apart, into the road surface. The top is open, and the bottom is reinforced with stones or thick plastic.

In a similar manner, if you do without the uphill ditch on hillsides, you eliminate culverts and do far less digging. You also avoid a potential nightmare: the dreaded culvert domino effect. On an uphill grade, culverts are spaced according to anticipated water volume. The theory is to empty the uphill side ditch at appropriate, regular intervals. But if an engineer miscalculates or if a storm is severe, a culvert can wash out or become plugged. Water then surges past it, augmenting the flow at the next culvert, which in turn fails, sending destruction to the third and so forth on down the road. Bad news.

The alternative is to do away with that uphill drainage ditch. In this case, water comes off the hill, onto the road and down it — exactly what you wanted to avoid. You can handle this by building either drainage dips or water bars to shunt the runoff to the road's downhill side. A water bar is a ridge like a speed bump, often with a narrow ditch on its uphill side. It crosses the road at a slight downhill angle and substitutes for a culvert. You could build one with a spade simply by digging a shallow trench across the road and putting the soil on its downhill side. It will work as a drainage structure, but it has serious disadvantages. It is difficult to grade, erosion just makes it deeper, and every time you hit it in your car, you knock your teeth loose. The Forest Service uses water bars only when it wants to abandon a road, but homeowners might find them useful in some situations.

Drainage dips, on the other hand, are periodic breaks in the uphill pitch of a road. You could think of them as landings on a stairway or as expanded water bars; the principle is the same, but they are larger and less abrupt. In a car, they feel like the undulations of a roller coaster rather than speed bumps. Their disadvantage is that, like water bars, they can be hard to grade, so you need to watch them for erosion. If ruts appear, consider reinforcing the dip with stones or even concrete; you can go to a culvert as a last resort.

Without an uphill ditch, road tilt becomes an important thing to keep in mind. On concave side hills, the road

surface should tilt inward slightly — not more than 4 percent. On convex slopes, it should tilt outward. The idea here is that on a convex slope, drainage patterns naturally diverge and water runs off in small quantities; you can let it cross the road with little worry of damage. The reverse happens on a concave slope, which collects water toward its centre. Here is where you'll have to deal with the largest volumes of water. You can protect the road as well as the slope below it by keeping control of runoff until it reaches a suitable dumping place, such as an existing stream or a well-placed culvert.

If you have the misfortune of needing to locate a road across a wet area, such as a bog or a swamp, you will probably need help from an expert planner. Engineering manuals get theoretical at this point. Bill Conklin, forest engineer for Bridger-Teton National Forest, when asked for construction standards in wet areas, shakes his head. "That's where road building becomes an art." There appear to be no hard-and-fast rules. Basically, the situation calls for dumping fill — large stones and gravel — until you have a firm surface well above the saturated ground, but it is not just a matter of dumping in anything solid until it stops sinking out of sight. The water may look stagnant, but there is undoubtedly some flow to deal with, and you want a road, not a dam. Aside from the environmental damage caused by indiscriminate filling, the road itself is likely to fail. Large rocks may solve the problem by allowing water to flow through the spaces between them, but each particular situation demands its own solution.

Surfacing

Where native soils are insufficient to support a road, you need to add stronger material. A contractor will begin by shaping the roadway, then compacting the ground. On that surface, he will lay 8 to 12 inches of "pit run," consisting of stones and gravel 6 inches and less in diameter. This is the base course, and it, too, is compacted. Then he adds about 4 inches of surface course. He might call it crushed gravel, but what

Cottage road builders need not go to the expense of galvanized steel culverts when simpler wooden ones will solve the laneway's drainage problems. Two boards, set a few inches apart, create an open spillway across the road.

he means is aggregate, a material that meets rigid specifications.

To an engineer, gravel is crushed rock or stones between $\frac{1}{50}$ and $\frac{1}{3}$ inch in diameter, and by itself, it makes a poor road surface. Anyone who has dumped pure gravel on his road knows that most of it just rolls around and ends up loosely scattered everywhere but in the places it is needed most. For a road surface, you need aggregate. In some places, road builders call it "one-two-three," meaning a mixture of gravel and finer material like sand and clay. The smallest particles, called fines, serve as cement, filling voids between stones and adding strength and flexibility. Good aggregate contains 6 to 8 percent fines, which are defined as material small enough to pass through a sieve with 200 holes per square inch. The resulting road surface is relatively impermeable to water, but it is also capable of retaining a certain amount of internal moisture. (In some cases, calcium chloride, which attracts water, is added to the mix for that purpose.) Together, these properties resist erosion and create a dense, cohesive, long-lasting surface.

The right mix rarely occurs in nature; if you want perfect stuff, you may have to buy it from a construction company or a gravel pit.

Surfacing materials can cover the entire road or can be used selectively in trouble spots. On soft or wet soil, however, you risk having the new surface disappear as it is pushed downward under the weight of vehicles. Again, you are faced with a drainage problem and the need for expert help.

Construction

When it comes to actual construction, there are a few things you can do to limit damage and hasten recovery of scarred areas. First, try to schedule the work during the proper season. This depends on where you live. In desert areas, you want moisture to firm up the soil, but otherwise, mud is a big concern. Second, mark the roadway clearly with bright flags or paint to indicate trees you want to save. Protect them from damage by wrapping snow fence or tying vertical boards on the trunks, and cut obstructing branches off in advance of the machinery. If a favourite tree is on the downhill side of the road and in danger of being buried by fill, you might be able to save it by building a retaining wall on its uphill side. Many trees can tolerate 1 to 2 feet of fill on their roots.

Several techniques hasten recovery of cut slopes. You can reserve topsoil and spread it on scars after construction is completed. Rounding off the top of a slope makes it seem more natural, while cutting steps into it encourages the growth of vegetation. If rocks are plentiful, they can be piled on angled road banks; they look better than raw subsoil and provide shelter for seedlings. Given just a little care, the road can soon look less like an intrusive wound and more like the homeward path you intend it to be.

Finally, after listing all these standards and high objectives, I'd like to relate a personal story. My own country lane is about 1,000 feet long. It winds its way 100 vertical feet through piñon and juniper trees to the top of a small, presumably extinct, volcanic cinder cone. The cinders, which constitute most of the soil, are small, loose and impossible to drive on. When I began house construction on a shoestring, I couldn't afford to have a road built, so I looked hard for alternatives. What I eventually found was a large quantity of discarded 6-foot-high chain-link fence. Laid on the hillside and pegged in place with lengths of reinforcing rod, it served the purpose perfectly. The largest construction trucks had no problem with it. After a year's use, the edges began to curl up, so I pulled the pegs, flopped it over and staked it down again. Where I could see erosion beginning, I used a spade and a hoe to make small diversion ditches.

Every year for six years, I have made mental plans to replace the chain link with a proper road. Surely it wouldn't last another season. But it is still there, amazingly durable, thumbing its nose at all engineering principles. Come June, it will be time to flop it over again. Build a road? Maybe next year.

Originally published in Harrowsmith Country Life *magazine (Charlotte, VT).*

The secrets of hauling a trailer safely

by Tom Wilkinson

You don't have to be a trucker to enjoy the benefits of a good trailer. You can use it to tote wallboard, cement bags and other home remodelling supplies too large or too heavy to put in the trunk or in the back of a pickup. And come vacation time, a trailer can haul a boat or a camper.

Before you hitch any trailer to your car or truck, consult your owner's manual to find out the vehicle's maximum towing capacity. While larger, more powerful vehicles can tow more than smaller, less powerful ones, some sub-compact cars, particularly front-wheel-drive versions, can't tow at all. Typical family-sized cars can usually tow 1,000 to 2,000 pounds. Large cars and light trucks are rated from 2,000 pounds to nearly 10,000 pounds.

If you're buying a new car or truck with towing in mind, first check the towing guide available at many car dealers. It lists towing capacities for all car makes and models. As a rule of thumb, try to buy more towing capacity than you need. If possible, order the manufacturer's optional towing package, which has the heavy-duty mechanical components needed to handle the stress of towing and typically provides the connections for hitch installation.

Be sure the vehicle you choose is fit for the extra strain. Check its springs, shock absorbers, brakes, tires and wheel bearings for excessive wear. Since towing puts a strain on the engine and transmission by making them run hotter, change the engine oil and filter, and flush and refill the cooling system before a long tow. For a car with an automatic transmission, also change the fluid and filter. As extra insurance, add a cooling kit to help keep the transmission fluid from overheating.

Automakers define towing as "severe service." Consequently, it's important to follow the owner's manual's severe-service recommendations. Adhering to the typically more frequent maintenance schedule helps your vehicle last longer and helps you avoid a warranty dispute should something on your vehicle fail. Once you know your vehicle's towing capacity, stay safely within that limit by choosing the right trailer and loading it carefully. When buying or renting a trailer, make sure the trailer's gross-weight rating (GWR) doesn't exceed your vehicle's towing capacity. You'll find a trailer's GWR printed on or inside the trailer. Next, determine how much you can load into the trailer by subtracting its empty weight from its gross weight. A trailer's empty weight may be listed in its owner's manual. If it isn't, check with the trailer dealer or rental agent, or have the empty trailer weighed on a scale.

Next, load and secure the trailer's cargo properly. Emergency manoeuvres with a trailer are tricky enough without cargo shifting its weight from side to side. Put the heaviest items in the trailer first, loading them low and to the front. Try to pack items tightly, filling empty spaces with an old cushion or mattress.

As you load, arrange the items evenly from side to side, but put 60 percent of the weight at the trailer's front and 40 percent at the rear. U-Haul suggests counting about 7 pounds for each cubic foot of trailer space taken up by household items and about 21 pounds for canned goods and appliances. U-Haul advises that sand, dirt, gravel or other heavy items be put no more than four inches above the floor.

Using this 60/40 loading ratio, 10 percent of the trailer's weight should wind up on its front extension (the trailer tongue). This tongue weight is critical because it affects the tow vehicle's handling. If the tongue weight is too heavy, dling. If the tongue weight is too heavy, the tow vehicle will sag at the rear; if it's too light, fishtailing might occur during lane changes and in heavy winds. The best way to check a trailer's tongue weight is to put the loaded trailer on a scale.

Hitches are the vital link between the load and the tow vehicle. All hitches fall into two types and four weight classes. To choose the right hitch for your vehicle, find the hitch category with a weight capacity that matches the vehicle's towing capacity.

Weight-carrying hitches place the full load on the tow vehicle's rear axle; weight-distributing types place a share of the load on the front axle as well. Most hitches are the weight-carrying type. Least expensive and lightest duty of these hitches is the Class I fixed-tongue variety. These hitches cost about $50 and bolt onto the tow vehicle's rear bumper.

A hitch that bolts onto your tow vehicle's frame is a safer bet. Select one designed expressly for the year, make and model of your vehicle. This type of hitch features a beefy frame, or receiver, that attaches to your vehicle. The receiver accepts the hitch's tongue and ball, onto which you mount the trailer.

Weight-distributing hitches are for big towing jobs. In addition to their hefty receivers, these hitches include a long frame running beneath the tow vehicle. The frame distributes some of the trailer's tongue weight to the tow vehicle's front wheels, giving both trailer and tow vehicle a more level ride.

You can also buy hitch components separately. If you do, however, check with the hitch dealer to be sure each component is rated for your car's towing capacity. Hitch balls, for example, come in different sizes and load ratings. In addition to noting the rating stamped into the ball, be sure the ball's stud fits snugly into the hole in the hitch.

Even if you've done everything right, there's still the remote chance your trailer can come unhitched on the road. To avert a disaster should the hitch or ball fail, always attach safety chains between the trailer and the tow vehicle. Be sure each chain is anchored at both ends. Then cross the chains under the trailer's tongue. The crossed chains will catch and hold the trailer tongue if the hitch or ball fails, preventing it from hitting the pavement.

Brake lights and taillights for your trailer are safety necessities. The trailer lights link to your car's light circuit via wiring connectors. On some cars and trucks, a wiring connector for trailer lights is located in the trunk. On other vehicles, you can add an adapter box for trailer lights (about $25).

Many states require trailers weighing more than 1,000 pounds to have their own braking systems, which make it easier to bring both trailer and car to a stop. Trailer brakes come in two varieties: electric and hydraulic. They are activated along with your car brakes as you step on the brake pedal.

Some systems have a separate activator switch as well. The switch allows you to apply the trailer brakes separately — for added control on steep downhill grades, for example. Most hydraulic or electric trailer brakes also have a breakaway switch. It applies the brakes automatically if the trailer uncouples from the tow vehicle.

Once your trailer is connected to the tow vehicle, make some safety checks before hitting the highway. First, make sure the tow vehicle is sitting as level as possible. A dragging tail means the trailer is unbalanced or too heavy for the vehicle. A tail-up position indicates excess weight in the back of the trailer.

Now, take a walk around both car and trailer. Make sure hitch and safety chains are securely connected and that all brake and signal lights work. Also check the tire pressures on the tow vehicle and trailer when the tires are cold. Car and truck tires should be pumped up to the manufacturer's maximum suggested pressure. Tire pressures for trailers are often much higher than those for cars. You'll find the proper tire pressure on a sticker attached to the trailer or in the trailer's operating manual.

Always carry two spare trailer tires, as they come in odd sizes and may be difficult to find. (Also include a trailer jack and a wrench that fits the trailer's wheel lugs.)

Even a small trailer's added weight lengthens the tow vehicle's braking distance. It may also upset the vehicle's front-rear brake balance, making a skid more likely. Don't drive over 45 miles per hour when towing, and anticipate stops well in advance. When descending hills, shift into a lower gear to avoid overheating the brakes.

Your car or truck will accelerate slower than usual with a trailer in tow, so allow extra space when merging or passing. Also, don't forget the extra clearance necessary for a trailer that's wider and taller than your vehicle. Besides watching your clearance, be ready for side winds from passing trucks, which can cause the trailer to sway. If this occurs, ease off the accelerator, and brake only after the swaying stops. If the swaying continues, the load is probably unbalanced. Continue slowing down until you can stop safely. Then fix the problem.

Finally, remember that towing a trailer is a lot more work than driving a car. Be sure you're rested before you tow. When planning a long trip, schedule fewer miles per day than you normally would cover without a trailer.

Weighing a trailer can prevent an accident caused by an overweight or unbalanced load. The easiest way to do this is to drive the loaded trailer to a weigh station, lumberyard or other location with a platform scale.

First, manoeuvre the trailer so that everything from its tongue to the rear is squarely on the scale. With the trailer jack in place, uncouple the trailer from the tow vehicle, and rest its jack on the scale. The weight shouldn't exceed the trailer's gross-weight rating .

Next, reattach the trailer to the tow vehicle, and pull it far enough forward that its tongue and jack are resting off the scale. Uncouple the trailer, and weigh it again. If you've loaded the trailer properly, it should now weigh 10 percent less than before; otherwise, rearrange and remove items as needed.

To be sure the trailer is evenly balanced, alternately back its left and right sides onto the scale and compare readings. Each side should be at or near the same weight.

If your trailer has a GWR of 2,500 pounds or less, you can determine the tongue weight by resting its trailer-tongue jack on a bathroom scale. Again, the reading should be 10 percent of the trailer's GWR (250 pounds or less). There is, however, one problem with this setup: if the trailer isn't fully loaded, the scale reads will be only an approximate percentage of the trailer's total weight.

Backing up a trailer is like riding a bicycle: after a little practice, it becomes second nature. Most people find backing up a trailer confusing at first because the trailer moves in the direction opposite the car's. However, the trailer will move in the same direction as you move your hand on the steering wheel if you grip the wheel at the bottom. For instance, to back the trailer to the left, grip the wheel at the bottom and move your hand left (which actually turns the steering wheel clockwise). To back the trailer to the right, grip the wheel at the bottom once again and move your hand to the right.

Practise backing into parking spots and down long straight lines. Go slowly, and have a friend watch for trouble. If the trailer starts to jackknife, pull it ahead to straighten it. One other tip (from truck drivers): Use the vehicle's outside mirrors when backing up . The mirrors help you see exactly where the trailer is pointed and exactly how close it is to nearby objects.

Originally published in Home Mechanix *magazine (New York).*

A century-old
tabletop game
makes a welcome
comeback

Crokinole on a Saturday Night

by Michael Webster

"Better take the hard shot, Dan. You're missing the easy ones." An unsettling message of doubt beneath a gloss of trust-me sincerity.

Dan Battler, the recipient of this advice from a tablemate, leans intently over the crokinole board and cocks his index finger behind the end of his thumb. He lines up his shot, then fires a wooden disc across the board with a flick of his finger. The board is marked with concentric circles of ascending value: an outer 5-point ring, a smaller 10-point ring, an inner 15-point ring that is guarded by eight rubber-coated pegs and, in the very centre, a depression barely larger than the disc — the 20-point hole. Dan's disc passes between two pegs and strikes an opponent's disc, knocking it out of the 15 and off the board. From there, his disc deflects into another opposing disc, knocking it off the board as well. Then it bounces back, slithers around the 20 hole and settles neatly in the bottom. With one game-winning shot, he has erased a 30-point deficit and scored 20. His opponents groan.

"Now that," says Ira Zeller, Dan's great-uncle and partner in this game, "is a crokinole shot." Dan, Ira and the rest of the men in the basement of Ephraim

Hoffman's house are members of the Preston Crokinole Club, the oldest continuously operating crokinole organization in Canada — and therefore in the world. The Preston group was founded in 1932 by businessmen who competed in coats and ties. And although the ties have long since disappeared and Preston has been overrun by the galloping suburbs of Cambridge, Ontario, these men have kept the club name, many of its traditions and all of its records. According to secretary-treasurer Bob Mader, statistics keeping has always been a vital part of the game. "I can tell you the score of every game and who played in it on the night of" — he shrugs and picks a date — "April 17, 1939. Or whatever. It's all there."

The men in the Preston club take their crokinole seriously. Not so seriously that they forget to have a good time, but they recognize they are something of an anomaly, one of only a dozen such clubs across Canada. It was not always so. For decades, crokinole was a popular family pastime, especially in rural Canada, and groups gathered with differing degrees of formality in the kitchens and parlours of homes from coast to coast. It is odd, in fact, considering the widespread popularity of the game, that so little is known about its history. Crokinole appears to be a hybrid of two other board games: squails, an

English game descended from shove ha'penny, in which a coin is fired at a target by striking it with the palm of the hand as it overhangs the board; and carums, a game from India in which the pieces are shot with the distinctive flick of the finger but which includes netted pockets like a snooker table.

"The origin of crokinole is a mystery," says Wayne Kelly, who keeps the world's largest collection of crokinole boards — "Fifty-three, including the two I bought at a garage sale on Saturday" — at his home near Lucan, Ontario. "It's amazing, but nobody bothered to document the beginnings of the game." Intrigued by the paucity of information, Kelly spent two years researching the game in his spare time and has just published a book on the subject. "Crokinole is unheard-of in Europe, and the oldest existing board in North America was made near Stratford, Ontario, not 40 miles from here, in 1875. It seems the game developed in the Mennonite community of south-central Ontario." One of the few documented references says crokinole is as old as Canada itself and was popular here "from 1867 onward." By contrast, the first game played in the United States was on a board made in 1880 in New York State. Indeed, although boards were offered in the Sears, Roebuck and Co. catalogue as early as 1895, the game had virtually died out in the United States by about 1925.

Crokinole, then, appears to be Canadian in origin, and it is certainly Canadian by tradition. "I can't think of anything else that's so consistent across Canada," says Kelly. "I've talked to hundreds of people about the game, and the nostalgia it evokes is universal. It has really been an important social activity for Canadians, and not just for one generation either — there are very few Canadians over the age of 35 who have never played crokinole." The name of the game is derived from *croquignole,* a French word meaning a fillip, or flick of the finger, and, alternatively, a small, hard biscuit — crokinole discs are still called cookies in parts of western Canada. But it looks as if no one will ever know how it came about that German immigrants crossed a British pub game with an Indian board game, gave it a French name and then thought the story too uninteresting or too unimportant to record. In retrospect, though, it is hard to imagine a pedigree and an attitude more typically Canadian.

If the first game of crokinole has been lost to history, many more followed, and Kelly has documented the game's popularity, which peaked in the 1920s and 1930s and now seems to be on the rise again. "Crokinole was predominantly a rural phenomenon, and for the most part, it seems to have been a winter game," he notes. "In rural communities, when the harvest was done and farmers couldn't get on the land, they would bring out the crokinole board in the evening." The major distributors in those days were the big three catalogue companies (Eaton's, Simpsons and Hudson's Bay), reaching every privy in the Dominion. The T. Eaton Company winter catalogue of 1892 kicked off the marketing effort with boards offered at $2.25, $3 and $5 — pricey at the time, but competition and volume production knocked the price down to 60 cents before the turn of the century. Part of the appeal in those days was that crokinole was universally seen as a "clean" game. For whatever reasons, it was never associated with drinking or gambling, as were card games, and moralists who decried the sinfulness of other evening activities, such as dances and, later, picture shows, found no fault with the game of crokinole.

Still, the fact that it had, as an early catalogue euphemistically put it, "no objectionable features whatever" does not explain its enduring popularity. More than merely blameless, crokinole is also fun. "It's a family game," Kelly says. "Age doesn't matter — some of the best players I know are in their 70s — so adults and children can play together." In addition, he says, "crokinole is a very social activity. With other games, like euchre, for example, you have to concentrate on counting cards; but crokinole is a game you can talk over. Another thing is that you can advise your partner on what shot to make." And your opponent.

Varied Rules

The basic format of the game has remained remarkably static across decades and provincial borders, but according to Kelly, "the rules vary from neighbour to neighbour." Crokinole is usually played by two or four players, each of whom is given a quarter, or quadrant, of the board; with two players, they sit opposite each other, with four, partners sit opposite. They take turns in a clockwise direction, shooting one disc at a time until each player has shot six discs. A shot is taken by setting the disc on the 5/0 line within one's own quadrant and flicking it with the finger. Each player must shoot at an opposing player's disc, if there is one on the board, and any disc that does not hit an opposing player's disc is removed from play. At the beginning of the game or any time there are no opponents' discs on the board, a player may shoot for the 20-point hole.

Twenty-pointers are removed from the board immediately and set aside to be counted later. At the end of a round, when all the discs have been shot, each side tallies its score (discs touching the 15/10 or 10/5 line are valued at the lower score), and the difference in their scores is applied to a running total; that is, the losing side always gets zero, and the winning side gets the number of points it scores above the loser's score. The running total is also kept on a differential basis, and the first person or team to accumulate 100 points (100-0) wins. It will readily be seen that a closely matched game in which only 10 or 15 points are exchanged per round could be quite lengthy. Israel Bowman, now with the St. Jacobs (Ontario) Crokinole Club, remembers being allowed to stay up and watch a game in his father's store that was played three hours a night for five nights running. It was eventually decided by setting a time limit — the score after 15 hours of play was 20-0.

Club players avoid this situation by using a 2-point system: players receive 2 points for winning a round, 1 point for a tie and zero for a loss. In the Preston club, a game consists of four rounds, thus giving each player first and last shot once, and the best possible score in a game is 8-0. The Preston club, with 12 players, uses three boards at a time, and the members play 11 games a night, carefully scheduled so that each player is partnered with every other player once. Perfect score for the night is 88 points — in practice, few players exceed 60 points — and they play 12 times, once at each member's house, over a season that lasts from October to April. The statistician keeps a running average of each player's scores, much like a baseball player's batting average, and at the end of the season, the player with the highest average receives a trophy.

As for rule variations, the Preston club favours fun over formality, a philosophy exemplified by the rule that allows a player who misfires, or accidentally hits his disc, to retrieve it and shoot again, as long as the disc does not reach the 10/5 line. Also, players can turn the board to line up a shot — an accommodation considered scandalously slack by those who believe that neither the board nor the chairs should be moved. Another unique variation requires a disc to be off the playing surface before it is out of play. Under most rules, the disc has only to touch the 5/0 line, but according to Mader, their system prevents a lot of arguments. "This way," he says, "it's either in the gutter, or it's worth 5 points." Other rules are more conventional. A shot for the 20 hole must come to rest in the 15 circle, or it is removed from the board; this precludes the kind of defensive game in which players "hide" their discs behind the pegs. Combination shots — hitting your own disc in order to hit an opponent's disc — are allowed, but if neither of the discs hits an opponent's disc, they are both removed from the board. And any disc that is knocked off the board but bounces back on is removed, although the damage it does to the other pieces goes unrepaired.

One-Cheek Shots

The St. Jacobs club, which has been meeting in a room above the local fire hall since 1958, uses the same 2-point scoring system, except that they play "twice around the table" for a 16-point game. With a 24-player roster, they divide the membership into A, B and C rankings so that each group of eight plays seven games in a night — 112 points in all. They, too, keep a running average, establishing new rankings after each night's play and declaring a champion at the end of each season. Here, the rules are more conventional: no misfires, and neither the board nor the chairs can be moved. "We used to allow the chairs to be moved," Bowman remembers, "but we ruined a hardwood floor that way." Neither can their chairs be tipped, but players are allowed to slide from side to side on the chairs — the one-cheek rule.

As for the delicate question of how far one can go and still be shooting from one's own quadrant, Bowman demonstrates with discs he pulls from a briefcase full of paraphernalia. "Some people say you can't be more than halfway over the line," he explains, "but we decided that as long as you stay on the fence, you're not on your neighbour's property. So we say that as long as you are touching the dividing line, you're still in your quadrant."

Before repacking the briefcase, he points out the rest of its contents: scorecards; a spirit level and a bag of shims to level the playing tables; furniture polish, a piece of sheepskin and a shaker of shuffleboard grit to guarantee a slick playing surface; and several packages of black and natural-wood-grain playing discs, which he calls buttons.

"We used to be able to get red and black buttons," Bowman says, "and they were a lot more fair. With these, the black ones have a coat of paint, and the white ones don't. That extra weight makes a difference." Obviously, players for whom a coat of paint makes a noticeable weight difference are playing a different game than I remember from a youth misspent hammering opponents' discs off the table and into the next room. Indeed, a good crokinole player adopts a style that combines aggressive strategy with delicate shot making. Given a choice between removing another player's disc or bouncing off it gently enough to score a 20, club players take the 20.

The better players can do so unerringly, even if their opponent's disc is in the 5 circle, and every good shot finishes with a 20. Indeed, the discs seem drawn to the 20 hole the way the puck is drawn to Wayne Gretzky's hockey stick. To remove two of the opponent's discs and score 20 is a good shot. To remove three and score a 20 is not uncommon. Israel Bowman, a self-admitted middle-of-the-pack player, recalls the night he knocked off four opponents and scored a 20, and he has witnessed shots by master players that removed five opponents and scored 20.

Play like that is not achieved on just any old crokinole board, and club players look down their noses at the inexpensive boards made with synthetic materials found in toy stores today. They play only on carefully crafted wooden boards. Historically, crokinole boards were most often made by centring a circle of laminated hardwood on a square framework of four pine boards to which a low side rail was added. Before too long, the corners of the frame were cut off, leaving the traditional octagonal shape. In the 1950s, new materials — plywood, veneer, various pressboards and synthetics — were used for the playing surface and the backing; most all-wood boards were backed with eight pie-shaped wedges.

Kelly claims, however, that laminated (butcher-block) playing surfaces tend to become uneven over time and are susceptible to cracking or splitting, and the plethora of joints in the wedged boards make a weak backing. He welcomes the veneers and other modern products that permit woodworkers to make a long-lasting, high-quality board with relative ease. In his opinion and that of most club players, the best modern boards are round, with a birch plywood playing surface, a particleboard back and a plywood rim. The most popular model is made by Kraemer Woodcraft Ltd., a St. Jacobs firm that has been in the business for 35 years.

"The two important elements of a good board," says Kelly, "are a smooth playing surface and proper discs." Too often, discs that disappear down furnace vents and under furniture are replaced with checkers. Square-edged, embossed and made of lightweight pine, they are a poor second choice. Proper discs are made with hardwood — usually maple — are 1¼ inches in diameter by ⅜ inch thick and have rounded edges, the better to slide into the 20 hole.

Kelly's final advice is to those who have tried crokinole but found it hurt their finger to strike discs. "That's a common complaint," he says, "but one that is easy to correct. Just move your finger up so it is right behind the disc. You're actually pushing the disc rather than hitting it. Think of it as a wrist shot instead of a slap shot." In addition, players who adopt a strategic game on a properly waxed board will find they are making much softer shots than beginners who try to overpower each other. "How hard you hit your disc is everything in this game," says Bob Mader, watching his father Cecil remove an opponent's disc with a barely too soft shot that leaves his own disc hanging over the 20 hole.

"That's 19½," Dan commiserates, then knocks Cecil's disc off with a shot that settles smoothly into the 20.

Originally published in Harrowsmith *magazine (Camden East, Ont.).*

A few basic rules for cottage horseshoes

by A. Taede Rusty

The only problem with horseshoes is the fact that it is almost impossible to have a quiet, unobtrusive game. Within minutes of the first telltale clangs of the 2½ pound iron horseshoes hitting the steel stakes, a small clutch of onlookers will begin to gather, predicting shots and calling out suggestions.

If your cottage is on a sociable lake, the sound of crashing horseshoes could carry clearly enough across the water to turn your quiet game into a weekend tournament. Before starting any game, you had best check the supply of beer in the fridge — or consider a less conspicuous pastime, such as cribbage on the back deck.

Fortunately, horseshoes is not an expensive sport, and if you prefer solitude over small crowds, you can encourage your neighbours to build pits of their own. A set of shoes, two steel stakes and some lumber should not cost more than $50, and the space considerations are minimal. One only needs a playing lane about 14 feet wide and 46 feet long to accommodate the two pits. Best of all, given the nature of the game, it need not be well groomed or devoted exclusively to horseshoe tossing. Tree roots and uneven ground seldom influence the outcome of a game, and you can park cars, sunbathe or practise badminton on the pitch between games. Just try to avoid an east-west orientation so that the sun's glare will not become a problem at certain times of the day.

The stakes at either end of the pitch, spaced 40 feet apart, should be 1 inch in diameter but need not be fancy. Cold-rolled steel is recommended, but feel free to improvise. Scrap yards and welding shops should have something suitable — just remember that it has to be strong enough to withstand the impact of the heavy shoes being tossed against it. Those cottagers with little soil atop their slice of the Canadian Shield may have difficulty pounding the stakes in the recommended 18 inches or so, but serious adherents to the game will think nothing of using jackhammers or heavy-duty drills to open up a suitable hole — a dollop of cement will hold the stakes firmly.

Each stake should be in the centre of a sandbox 3 feet wide and 4 feet long. Two-by-sixes are ideal for framing the box, but use whatever is available. In doing the calculations, remember that when the boxes are filled with sand, the stake should stick out 14 to 15 inches. The stakes should also lean slightly toward one another to better absorb the shock of the tossed shoes. (If you are a perfectionist and have a plumb bob, the top of the stake should be 3 inches in front of its base.)

The rules of the game are simple enough: the opponents throw two horseshoes each at the distant stake, trying to bring their shoes to rest around the stake. Theoretically, players should be throwing from inside the sandbox (40 feet), but the shoes are heavy enough that a closer throw line can be established for kids and weak-armed desk jockeys (30 feet). When there are two players, each stands at the same end, throwing both their shoes consecutively. After all shoes are tossed, players switch ends and count their points, and the game proceeds from end to end. Foursomes have a member of each team at either stake, which eliminates the walking back and forth and speeds up the pace of the game. There is, however, an increased risk of getting hit by a shoe. (Beware, too, if your stakes are close to the forest's edge, as shoes that land on their edge can roll a long way.)

There are two basic ways to grip the shoe: one at the base of the U with the shoe held flat-side up; the other along the top prong of the shoe, which is thrown edge-side up. The stance is critical, and you should lead with the foot opposite your throwing arm. Also, position yourself so that your throwing arm is in line with the centre of the box. To maintain the pace of the game, both players should throw their shoes before inspecting the distant stake.

Points are awarded to the person whose shoe is closest to the stake: three points for ringers and one for non-ringers. Normally, only one team can score in an end, and games go to either 21, 40 or 50, but meals and long lines of waiting players may dictate otherwise. Most important is the definition of a ringer: a straight edge must be able to touch the tips of the shoe without touching the stake. Shoes that land outside the box and roll into the scoring zone are not counted.

The maximum number of points for an end is six (that is, if a player's two ringers are both closer to the stake than the opponent's). If opponents both have a ringer, the one closest to the stake scores. If no one has a ringer, only those shoes within 6 inches of the stake are counted. "Leaners" are only worth one point, no matter how unusual or ironic their lean. Ties can be counted as zero or both players can take their earned points.

One variation on scoring has both players counting all shoes within 6 inches of the stake. The score rises much higher and faster this way, although games are normally confined to 20 ends.

Usually, a coin toss determines who goes first, and then the lead can either be alternated or it goes to the winner of the last end — a key element given that the second player's tosses can knock the lead shoes out of scoring position.

Like all cottage sports, it is generally best to simply establish house rules that suit both the temperaments of the players and the realities of the playing field.

Pain and a little suffering in the name of fun

No Escape from Cottage Games

by Charles Gordon

Early on in the history of cottaging, someone decided that there should be games. People should not just sit there reading books. They should not just canoe around admiring rocks and trees. They should not just fish and lie in hammocks and stroll through the woods. They should play games and have fun.

Someone, very early on, decided that having fun and playing games was the same thing. This may have been a caveman. In cave days, games had just been invented, and their novelty had not worn off. People still liked to play games. Considering the alternatives, this made some sense. Since there were no hammocks or books, the alternatives to games, for the cave people, consisted of being chased by flying reptiles and trying to invent fire.

So we probably have the cavemen to blame for games. When they left the cave to go to the cottage, which consisted of another cave but closer to the river, they took the concept of games with them. For the types of cottage games we play, however, we have only ourselves, and a few more recent ancestors, to blame.

When the modern ground rules for cottage games were being laid down, someone decided that people who, because of age, infirmity or disposition,

would not dream of playing games in the city would play games at the cottage. They would take their bad backs, their trick knees, their arthritis and their rheumatism out to the badminton court, there to trip over roots, stumble and fall, pull muscles, twist knees and put backs out, all in the name of being a good sport, all in the name of fun.

Neither children nor adults train for the cottage. They do not begin a strict regimen of drills preceded by lengthy loosening-up exercises. They do not buy the proper footwear. They do not observe the proper diet. They just arrive, somebody gets out the badminton gear and away they go, charging back and forth, puffing audibly and sprawling in the dust or mud, depending upon weather conditions.

At the cottage, nobody says: "Sorry, I'm too old for that." At the cottage, nobody thinks he is too old for it. Nobody thinks he is too old for anything. As a consequence, within three days of their arrival, many sportsmen and sportswomen are nursing bruises, scrapes, pulled hamstrings, sore knees, aching backs and suspicious twinges here and there.

The Beauty of Badminton
Badminton is the ideal cottage game. It requires little space and almost no equipment. Theoretically, it involves no physical contact. In many games, the

ball will hurt a player if it hits him. In badminton, the ball — which is called a bird, is not round and has feathers — will not hurt. Distances to be run are not formidable. A badminton player can cover the entire court in a few quick strides. It is true that an older player, once having taken a few quick strides, often takes a few more than he should because of a difficulty in stopping. It is this that causes the tumbles into the bush that are fondly recalled every year, and it is this that causes the net to be knocked over at least once a game by some hard-charging veteran player.

Strategically, the game allows older players to keep up with younger players by being smarter about tactics. Later on, it allows the younger players to overcome the older players by being faster and stronger. It also allows the older players to convince themselves that the younger players only win because they are luckier.

Badminton comes with a range of built-in excuses for the loser. There is the sun, which is in the eyes of the losing player. Badminton is always played at sunset for reasons that must be clear to the inventors of the games but are obscure now. When players change sides midway through a game so as to neutralize the effects of the sun, the sun disappears behind a cloud to allow one player — usually the younger one — to be luckier than the other.

If it were not for the sun, the older player would win. The sun, however, is not the only factor in the losses suffered by deserving players. Wind is also important. Although it is thought by the uninitiated to have a predictable effect, always blowing in the face of one player or to the backhand of another, it in fact swirls unpredictably, often forcing the shots of one player to go long, then suddenly dying, just when the player has adjusted for the wind, causing his shots to fall into the net. Because of such environmental factors, badminton is an extremely difficult game to win. However, moral victories are quite easily obtained.

The Temptation of Targets

One year, somebody brought a BB gun. Another year, it was a powerful slingshot. A couple of years after that, it was a bow and arrow. The idea is to shoot at a target. The reality is that the pellets, the stones and the arrows hit trees, causing, in the minds of some of the tree fans around, irreparable damage and posing a threat to the ecology of the cottage.

Target shooters are always careful to avoid shooting at animals, but on rare occasions, someone accidentally hits a squirrel or a crow, thinking that squirrels and crows don't count. Thus endeth the target shooting.

Night Games

When more than one family uses a cottage, there is a rule that games must be played after dark. This has to do with the lack of television and with what some people see as the absolute necessity of being sociable. This, along with inferior lighting, precludes the reading of books.

The games to be played vary from cottage to cottage, from province to province. Often the game is a variant of rummy. Sometimes it is hearts. But each cottage has a game. It is The Cottage Game, and it is played because it has always been played. Sometimes people like The Game, which helps. It is not essential, however. Peer pressure

will ensure that there are always enough players.

"What do you mean, you're going to skip The Game? You *can't* skip The Game! *Nobody* skips The Game!"

So it is that a grown man finds himself, for the 15th night in a row, involved in the game of poker, in which the chips are black-eyed peas, in which threes are always wild, in which a flush beats a full house and two pairs beat three of a kind.

From time to time, an outsider participates in The Game and points out that two pairs do not, in real poker, beat three of a kind. It is pointed out to him that two pairs have always beaten three of a kind *here*. And when he tries to deal a game in which twos are wild, people look at him as if he is crazy.

The Morality of Monopoly

At such a time, he may be tempted to join the children, who are playing their fifth Monopoly game of the day. Parents rarely think about their children playing five Monopoly games a day when they look forward to the joys of the cottage. They think of a summer without television. They think of nature walks, fishing expeditions. They forget that it is the nature of children to beg off nature walks and fishing expeditions because they are in the middle of a Monopoly game.

The game has become cutthroat over the years, developing a set of under-the-table rules that would have amazed the Bros. Parker. Wheeling and dealing goes on at all times, regardless of whose turn it is. Get-out-of-jail cards are sold at cut-rate prices. Trading arrangements are arrived at, aimed at blocking certain players from ever owning Ventnor Boulevard and the other yellow properties. Railroads are traded for future considerations.

The children have a new board, which they are enjoying, barely noticing the fact that it is in French. A well-meaning relative, thinking to sneak in something that will help them improve themselves over the summer, bought the game, and the children thanked him profusely. Since they know the game so well, they continue to play with it in English, saying "St. James" instead of "St. Jacques"

and recognizing, without having to read it, the Community Chest card that says they have won second prize in a beauty contest, collect $10.

The Science of Scrabble

There is an uncle who always arrives with the latest games. Over the years, some of his gifts to the cottage involved various plastic devices that hurled plastic projectiles upwards or outwards. The projectiles eventually found their way into the forest, and the flinging devices are at the bottom of the closet. Others of the latest games were board games. Most of them are now on a low shelf, underneath the other ones. The kids looked at them, tried to read the rules and went back to Monopoly. Scrabble lasted, though.

It lasted with the adults, who turn to it when the rummy game gets too noisy. At a cottage, Scrabble is not an easy game to keep intact. There are cracks and holes, and letters keep falling into them. Every so often, someone notices that no one has made a word including the letter J all summer, and a new set is purchased. The discussions that highlight the game are not new:

"I thought italicized words were all right."

"It's *muddying,* not *mudding.* I don't think *mudding* is a word. And if it is, it only has one D."

"Q-A-Y. I'm sure that's how they spell it."

"It's a Greek letter. We always use Greek letters."

"I'm thinking."

"Eighteen points! You're going to take the triple word for 18 points?"

"Z-O-O-N. It's the singular of Z-O-A. Or the plural."

"Do you have to get a seven-letter word every time? You've been sitting there for 20 minutes."

"I'm thinking."

The beauty of Scrabble, aside from its inherent virtues, is that when nonplayers look over at the Scrabble table, they think something intellectual is going on.

Excerpted from At The Cottage. *Used by permission of the Canadian publishers McClelland & Stewart (Toronto).*

Our favourite family board games

by The Toy Testing Council of Canada

(Editor's note: Thoughts of cottage life would not be complete without consideration of time spent around an old kitchen table doing battle with siblings and parents in the time-honoured pursuit of some favourite board game. While games may have lost their earlier appeal at home where computers, televisions and telephones provide ample distraction, they somehow remain suitably popular at cottages. Perfect for passing time on a rainy day or bringing a family together after a day outdoors, games should be part of every cottager's basic equipment.

This list of games is an admittedly subjective abbreviation of a very thorough one produced by The Toy Testing Council of Canada in 1990.)

There are games for virtually everybody. Silly games, thinking games, games of chance, games of skill, word games, memory games, matching games, trivia games, group games and solitary games. Each has its own merits. Good games help to develop cooperation, sportsmanship, healthy competition and strategy. Games are fun, but they also exercise colour and shape matching, counting skills, memory and reasoning. They teach how to plan ahead and pay attention to detail. They also help children understand that rules are necessary and helpful. Many games encourage group play.

Several cooperative games are available. Parents may consider these games for variety or as an alternative particularly suited to young players just learning to enjoy game play. The rules of many games for preschoolers can be adapted to a cooperative approach.

When purchasing children's games, remember that they should be fun but challenging for the intended age group. Rules should be clear and easy to follow. Don't be afraid to establish house rules that accommodate younger or less skilled players or to set a shorter playing time. The game board should be durable and uncluttered, and the playing pieces should be of a suitable size and weight.

Fad games based on the latest popular licensed characters rarely have any lasting interest, although a well-conceived game may become a classic and be enjoyed for years to come.

ABALONE
Abalone Games
This strategy game for 2 players is easy to learn but can be endlessly challenging. Beautiful hexagonal board and large, heavy marbles. A potential new classic.
7 yrs + $35-40

AMAZING LABYRINTH
Ravensburger
Reaching your goal through the ever-changing maze on this unique board requires planning and logical thought. Can be played cooperatively. For 2 to 4 players or as a solitary activity.
8 yrs + $25-35

ANIMAL RUMMY
Whitman Golden
Simple, appealing version of the familiar card game played with animal cards. Well suited to youngsters not quite ready to deal with regular card games.
4-8 yrs   under $5

BALDERDASH
Canada Games
Try to bluff your opponents by inventing definitions for obscure words. Fast-paced fun that's best with a group of 6 or more. Particularly popular with teens.
10 yrs + $20-30

BATTLESHIP
Milton Bradley
This exciting naval game for 2 players combines strategy and luck. Each game lasts about 15 minutes.
7 yrs + $10-15

CANDY LAND
Milton Bradley
A good, lighthearted first game in which moves are determined by colour cards.
3-6 yrs $5-10

CAREERS
Parker
A new girls' version of the old classic in which players work at different occupations to achieve fame, fortune and happiness. Actions and stunts are involved.
8 yrs $15-25

CLUE
Parker
Intriguing, classic detective game for 3 to 6 players. A murder has been committed, and players must sift through the clues until they have solved it.
8 yrs + $10-20

COLOUR DOMINOES
Spear's
Fine set of wooden dominoes, colour-coded so that the very young can play.
3-6 yrs $5-10

CROSSFIRE
Milton Bradley
Played with ball bearings, this fast-paced, action-filled game is a new twist on table hockey. Good, noisy fun.
6 yrs + $30-40

DOUBLE TROUBLE
Milton Bradley
This fast-action game for 2 to 4 players has a strong element of chance but also calls for ruthless strategy. Matches take about 15 minutes. Very popular among older children and teens.
8 yrs + $10-20

GAME OF LIFE
Milton Bradley
Fast-paced classic board game of chance. Long rules can be streamlined for beginners. French version, Destins, (untested) available.
9 yrs + $10-20

HOTELS
Milton Bradley
"BEST BET 1988." A new classic for would-be land developers and tycoons. The spiffy 3-dimensional hotel models add a pleasing dimension to a great board game. A game takes over an hour, but the pace is brisk.
8 yrs + $20-30

LABYRINTH
Brio
It takes perseverance, concentration and a steady hand to guide the metal ball through a maze on the tilting wooden board.
9 yrs + $45-70

MASTERMIND
Chieftain
Compelling game of pure logic, in which you work out your opponent's chosen pattern of code pegs.
8 yrs + $5-10

MEMORY
Milton Bradley
Excellent family game of matching cards. Challenging with all 54 pairs but can be played with fewer.
4-8 yrs $5-10

MILLE BORNES
Parker
Fun card game in which 2 to 6 players overcome driving hazards.
9 yrs + $5-10

MONOPOLY
Parker
Interesting game about real estate buying and trading. Renowned the world over for 50 years.
8 yrs + $10-20

MONOPOLY JUNIOR
Parker
This fast-paced adaptation lets younger players use their allowance to ride the Ferris wheel or buy cotton candy at the amusement park. For 2 to 4 players. A game lasts 20 to 30 minutes.
5-8 yrs $15-20

PICTIONARY
The Games Gang
Fast-paced game of drawing charades stimulates innovative use of drawing skills and quick thinking. House rules can eliminate words unfamiliar to younger players. Frantic family fun that's best with 4 or more players.
12 yrs + $20-40

PICTIONARY JUNIOR
The Games Gang
Charades with a difference. This fast game for 3 or more players features reusable boards and different card sets for different ages and reading abilities.
7-11 yrs $10-20

REBOUND
Ideal
Amusing version of table hockey.
8 yrs + $10-20

SCRABBLE
Chieftain
Challenging family crossword game.
10 yrs + $10-20

SCRABBLE FOR JUNIORS
Chieftain
Introductory version of Scrabble. The two-sided board permits progress from simple letter matching to more advanced play.
5 yrs + $10-20

SOLITAIRE
Spear's
Classic solitary peg-jumping game in a compact format. Alternative version called Colourtaire adds interest and variety.
8 yrs + $5-10

SORRY!
Parker
This classic bilingual game for 2 to 4 players involves a little basic strategy and a lot of luck.
6 yrs + $15-25

STRATEGO
Chieftain
Outwit your opponent and capture his flag in this intriguing tactical game for 2 players.
8 yrs + $10-20

TRIVIAL PURSUIT
Parker
Pit your knowledge of trivia against that of your opponents. Requires both luck and memory. Great family game. French version (untested) available.
12 yrs + $20-40

UNDER COVER
Ravensburger
Board game for 2 to 7 players has an appealing secret-agent theme and effectively combines simplicity with challenge. The strategic implications increase with mastery of the game.
8 yrs + $20-30

UNO
Canada Games
Play "Crazy Eights" with 108 cards. Complex but clear rules. Good mix of challenge and luck. Poorly packaged.
7 yrs + $5-15

UPWORDS
Milton Bradley
Excellent 3-D word game. Challenging family fun.
10 yrs + $10-20

YAHTZEE
Milton Bradley
Excellent play value in this simple yet challenging family dice game.
8 yrs + $5-10

Adapted from a report by the Canadian Toy Testing Council (Ottawa).

Landscaping

Creating a backyard micro-sanctuary to attract birds

Giving Nature a Helping Hand

by Stephen Kress

Imagine, if you will, a phalanx of behemoth earth movers, towering steam shovels, massive bulldozers and road-paving machines starting at the southern border of Massachusetts and fanning out northward, leaving in its wake land cleared and flattened, networked with roads and streets and readied for an oncoming wave of transports, pickup trucks and utility vehicles carrying untold tons of building materials and millions of construction workers.

Imagine that when they finish with Massachusetts, they spread into Rhode Island, then north into New Hampshire and Vermont, stopping only when they reach the Canadian border. Looking back at their work, they see almost 20 million acres of former woods, meadows and farmland transformed into an instant suburbia.

Recent estimates predict that by the year 2000, approximately 3.5 million acres in the United States and Canada will be covered with pavement for highways and airports. In the last quarter of this century, an additional 19.7 million acres will be converted to sprawling residential developments — at a rate of 160 acres per hour, 24 hours a day, 7 days a week, year in and year out.

For those of us who cherish the presence of wildlife in general and wild birds in particular, this is a dismaying scenario. Even lands that are not lost to pavement and suburbia are becoming increasingly less attractive to many kinds of birds. The trend toward larger farms with fewer property lines has resulted in the loss of many brushy fencerows, farm woodlots and wetlands. Such varied habitats are vital to maintaining abundant and varied bird populations. Trackless horizons of single-crop plantings result in a similar monotony of bird life. In the same way, sprawling suburban areas often replace natural habitats with sterile lawns and miles of pavement.

It is true that some species have clearly benefited from the changes that we have brought to the land. Chimney swifts, barn owls and barn swallows even show their long association with humankind in their names, but these are largely incidental relationships in which birds have benefited without intentional management. More often, land development and modern agriculture tend to simplify plant and animal communities.

The trend toward a monotonous landscape has already claimed several North American birds, but the toll on plants is even greater. In 1978, the Smithsonian Institution listed close to 10 percent of the 22,200 plant species native to the continental United States as being "endangered" or "threatened." According to Peter H. Raven, director of the Missouri Botanical Garden, a disappearing plant can take with it 10 to 30 dependent species of insects, higher animals and even other plants. Clearly, protection and management of plant communities is essential if we are also to enjoy varied bird life.

Happily, however, it is well within the capabilities of most landowners to provide microsanctuaries for displaced wild bird populations by landscaping to encourage food and cover plants. Improving the quality of one's own property is the single most constructive step that anyone can take to assist wild bird populations and other wildlife. Those of us with large yards and rural acreage can play a vitally important role in creating substitutes for the frightening loss of natural landscapes in North America.

Consider the bluebird, which, as Thoreau said, carries the sky on its back. He might well have added that it carries the sunrise on its rusty breast and drags a reluctant spring just behind its tail feathers. Indeed, many northern pioneers regarded the bluebird as the true harbinger of spring and fondly called it the blue robin.

Attracted to a yard of bushes, cedar waxwings court each other by passing a chokecherry back and forth.

A young pileated woodpecker peers out from its nest in a tree cavity; dead trees provide valuable nesting sites but are often removed as eyesores.

Today, the average North American has probably never seen a bluebird, but half a century ago, it was one of our most common songbirds, nesting even in residential sections of large cities; since then, however, its population has been reduced by as much as 90 percent, and it has faced the very real possibility of extinction. This decimation can be traced to the increased use of insecticides, particularly in orchards — once a favourite bluebird haunt and now so heavily and persistently sprayed that few birds can survive in them.

Other new farming methods are also responsible: dead trees, which provided nesting cavities, have been cut down; fencerows where birds perched have been removed to accommodate larger farm machines; and the replacing of wooden fenceposts with metal stakes has eliminated another nesting habitat.

In the past decade, however, new hope for the survival of the bluebird has emerged, almost entirely because of the efforts of dedicated individuals and associations who have created new breeding habitats in the form of tens of thousands of bluebird nesting boxes.

An unplanned but equally dramatic example of human activity providing bird populations with a new foothold can be seen on an artificial sandspit on the shore of Lake Ontario in Toronto.

Created during the excavation of the city's subway system when the dumping of fill slowly formed a long peninsula into the lake, the opportunity was recognized by some 70 pairs of ring-billed gulls.

"Today," reports well-known naturalist Roger Tory Peterson, "the number of ring-bills is close to 80,000 pairs, each of which raises an average of 2.3 chicks per nest. This means that by the end of the summer, there are a third of a million birds. These multitudes of gulls give life and beauty not only to the Great Lakes but also to the beaches and bays along the entire Atlantic Coast during the colder months."

The opportunity to increase or restore wild bird populations rests on the remarkable ability of most species to replenish their numbers quickly where they find good habitat. Habitat improvement through manipulation of vegetation is often slow, but for those of us with patience and an interest in gardening, there will be a longer and sounder benefit than can be achieved by simply putting out food for birds. Many environmental problems may seem beyond our daily grasp, but the tendency toward monotonous landscapes is something that any property owner can do something about.

Well-conceived management projects meet the birds' needs for food, water, cover and nest sites by offering as much variety as possible. For the owner of a small property, increasing vegetation variety usually means replacing expansive, close-cropped lawns with trees, shrubs and flowers attractive to wildlife. Owners of large acreages, including farmers, have even more opportunities for improving habitat for wild birds, and improvements for wildlife can occur without losses in agricultural production. Regardless of a property's size, the same fundamental principle applies: Increase bird variety by encouraging plants that differ in size and texture and that bear their fruit or seeds at different times.

Encouraging these plants can be as simple as allowing nature to take its course, so that unmowed grass gives way first to weeds and then to a mix of shrubs and saplings. Or the property owner can consciously design habitat for birds, choosing trees and shrubs not only with the birds in mind but also with an eye toward aesthetics.

The first approach is inexpensive, but years will pass while a piece of ground naturally transforms itself. The managed approach will cost money for nursery stock and will require labour for planting, but the results can be both quick and attractive, with an array of plants greater than nature might have sent forth.

Life on the Edge

The terrain where two or more plant communities — such as woods and meadow — meet is known as edge. Because of the abundant mix of food, cover, nest sites and perches at these sites, bird variety is greatest there. This increase is known as edge effect.

Birds thrive at woodland borders, which are especially high in fruit-producing shrubs and insect populations. Many thicket plants, such as mesquite, juniper, hawthorn, raspberries and roses, have well-armed stems that deter browsing mammals like deer and rabbits. Prickly thickets also provide excellent predator-safe nesting places. Thicket-nesting birds and birds from adjoining habitats, such as meadows and forests, frequently find shelter and food in such hedgerows. When planting shrubby borders, it is best to mix several different species.

A small central patch of well-cropped grassy lawn is useful for viewing backyard birds. Birds that feed and nest in surrounding shrubs and trees will venture out onto the lawn — especially if lured there with feeders, baths and dusting areas. But lawn itself, especially expansive rolling fields of it, is one of the most destitute bird habitats in the whole world.

While some birds, such as robins, feed on earthworms and insects in grassy lawns, others, such as towhees, fox sparrows and white-throated sparrows, prefer feeding among fallen leaves, where they can scratch and look for hidden insects. Such habitats, however, are too often missing from manicured lawns. A good place to create the leaf litter preferred by such birds is under shrubs and trees where grasses already have a difficult time growing. Avoid raking these places clean, and even extend them several feet in front of the shrubs. Enrich these areas each autumn by adding several inches of leaves. Eventually, they will decompose into rich soil, with an abundance of earthworms and insects for ground-feeding spring migrants.

Even robins that so capably pull earthworms from grassy expanses may suffer if lawns are the only feeding habitat available. In West Newton, Massachusetts, a community with spacious lawns and many trees planted around the houses, a recent study found that robins were not producing enough young to balance losses to the adult population. Although West Newton seemed to be ideal robin habitat, closer examination found that the carefully groomed grounds around the homes had few brushy areas with available leaf litter. In April and May, the robins fed successfully; but in the drier months of June and July, when earthworms were not found in the lawns, the lack of moist leaf litter among the tended grounds left the robins with few alternative foods for their young.

Variety in ground cover can also be achieved by planting borders and patches of low-growing perennial plants like bearberry, coralberry and small-leaved cotoneasters, which can compete with invading grasses and yet produce large quantities of food for birds. These plants are more useful to birds than such known ground covers as Boston ivy, pachysandra and periwinkle. Although these popular plants are effective alternatives to grasses (especially in shady areas), they provide little food for wild birds.

Even within the same habitat, different birds show strong preferences for specific elevations at which they feed and nest. This is most apparent in forests, where characteristic species such as tanagers and grosbeaks sing and feed in the canopy level but nest in the subcanopy. Other birds, such as chipping sparrows, may feed on the ground, nest in shrubs and sing from the highest trees. Such up-and-down movement suggests that a multilevelled plan for wildlife plantings is especially important.

This principle is helpful in many different situations. Bird habitat in woodlots can be improved by planting shade-tolerant shrubs and vines at the bases of large trees to improve food supplies and nesting places. Isolated trees in pastures and backyards will attract more birds if shrubs are planted at their bases, creating vegetation of varied heights. First plant the tallest trees, such as pines and spruce; in front of these, plant a bank of subcanopy-level trees, such as dogwood and serviceberry, followed by a bank of tall shrubs, such as autumn olive and honeysuckle. Finally, plant some climbing vines, small shrubs and ground covers.

Changes in Grade

Ground-feeding birds, like sparrows, towhees and wrens, are attracted to abrupt changes in slope. In nature, birds frequently forage along stream banks, rock outcrops and tree roots, as these habitats have myriad tiny crevices and crannies in which to dig and probe for insects and worms.

On small properties, an artificial change in slope can be created by building a gently sloping soil mound with a steep rock face or by creating rock gardens or building stone walls. In northern habitats, the steep face of an artificial slope should look south so that the first spring thaw will reveal foraging places previously hidden by snow. On larger properties, the opportunities for creating varied slopes are even greater. Here, miniature cliffs landscaped with ground covers, rotting logs and shrubs will vary the terrain, creating warm south-facing slopes to attract early spring migrants and cool north-facing slopes where summer birds may forage. Changes in slope combined with rock-faced pools of water are especially attractive.

The seeds of many garden flowers are welcome additions to the diets of wild birds. When selecting flowers for your garden, keep birds in mind and choose some of their favourites. Most of the following garden flowers will grow in moist summer gardens throughout North America. The majority belongs to the sunflower family, which helps explain their attractiveness to songbirds like goldfinches and native sparrows. Most require an open, sunlit area. Be sure to let flower heads go to seed for fall and winter food.

Important Snags

Naturally developing forests have a high proportion of dead or partially dead trees, known as snags. Studies of upland forests show that 90 percent of the trees that reach an age of 20 years will die during the next 60 years. This abundance of snags gives cavity-nesting birds, ranging in size from the turkey vulture to the tiny prothonotary warbler, ample choice for both nesting and roosting.

The abundance of suitable snags has declined dramatically since colonial days. Lumbering operations during the 19th century eliminated old-age timber stands with high proportions of snags, and farmlands replaced forests throughout much of North America in the mid-1800s and early 1900s. The regrowth of forest on old farmlands since about 1940 is providing woods once again,

Bird Blooms

Asters	Love-lies-bleeding
Bachelor's buttons	Marigolds
Basket flower	Phlox
Blessed thistle	Portulaca
Calendula	Prince's feather
California poppy	Prince's plumes
Campanula	Rock purslane
China aster	Royal sweet sultan
Chrysanthemum	Silene
Coneflowers	Sunflower
Coreopsis	Sweet scabious
Cornflower	Tarweed
Cosmos	Verbena
Dayflowers	Zinnia
Dusty miller	

but even so, most of this woodland is still too young to produce an abundance of old snags.

Many cavity nesters, such as woodpeckers, require more than one cavity for each nesting pair. If all conditions are ideal, a pair of woodpeckers uses only one cavity for nesting. However, these woodpeckers require two additional roosting cavities in which to spend the night. Young woodpeckers need their own roosting cavities after they leave the parental nest.

Tree cavities may occur when limbs break off and heart rot fungus invades the tree's interior. But more frequently, woodpeckers create tree cavities as they excavate for insects and tunnel their nesting and roosting cavities. Preserving or creating ideal snags for woodpeckers is the best way to create nesting cavities for other birds, as woodpeckers are the principal developers of most nest cavities in trees.

Since most woodpeckers usually use the same tree cavity only once for nesting, they leave vacant sites for such cavity nesters as bluebirds, nuthatches, screech owls and other birds that are not capable of excavating their own cavities. Chickadees will enlarge woodpecker feeding holes into cavities big enough for their own use, and such small cavities may be further enlarged later by titmice, wrens, swallows, flickers and others until they become suitable for larger nesting birds.

The numbers and variety of cavity-nesting birds are usually limited by the availability of suitable nesting and roosting sites in snags. When snags are removed from a forest, the number of cavity-nesting birds will soon decline. Since most cavity-nesting birds are insect eaters, declines in such birds as woodpeckers, nuthatches, chickadees and swallows can set the stage for outbreaks of destructive insects. Many professional foresters now recognize the value of cavity-nesting birds in suppressing population explosions of forest insects, and scientific studies are beginning to describe the nesting requirements of these birds.

In the north-central and northeastern hardwood forests, the U.S. Forest Service

recommends that for each 20-acre woodlot, the following array of snags should be preserved: 4 to 5 snags over 18 inches in diameter at breast height (dbh: 4.5 feet above soil surface), 30 to 40 snags over 14 inches dbh, and 50 to 60 snags over 6 inches dbh. Generally, the bigger the snag, the greater attraction for cavity-nesting birds.

The most direct way to create tree cavities is to drill two-inch-diameter holes into the heartwood. This makes an excellent beginning for a cavity excavator like a chickadee, especially if the heartwood is already rotten. You should drill entrance holes about three inches below stout limbs on leaning trees so that openings point about 10 degrees below horizontal; the downward position of the opening provides some protection from rain. This slight sloping position may also be less conspicuous to predators.

You can also start cavities in trees by selecting a limb at least three inches in diameter and cutting it off about six inches from the main trunk. As the cut limb rots, the tree will heal around the edges, but it will probably not close over the hole.

To create additional snags in the forest, try girdling the trees, a common forestry practice sometimes used to thin woodlots. Select trees with at least a 12-inch dbh and with little value as a source of food for wildlife. To girdle a tree, simply use an axe to remove a three-to-four-inch band of bark around the entire circumference of the tree. To kill the tree, the cut should go at least one inch below the bark. This interrupts the flow of food and water between the roots and leaves. The tree will die soon, but it will bring new life to the forest by increasing the population of cavity-nesting birds and like-minded mammals.

Not long ago, widely held opinion said that the best thing one could do to improve large tracts of forest for birds was to create openings in the forest. While the technique remains a well-established and proven method for increasing the general variety of birds in stands of forested land, there is growing evidence that the clearings

A male yellow warbler perches on a cedar bough; hedges provide shelter and cover for birds while also serving as windbreaks and border fences.

to be a uniform habitat, it is actually a mosaic of slightly varied habitats, such as wet and dry forest and north and south slopes. Forest birds may require more than one habitat in their nesting cycle. By decreasing the size of forests, fragmentation can reduce the variety of habitats within the forest. Unfortunately, so little is known about the patterns of movement within the forest that it is impossible to determine exact habitat requirements for most species of birds.

Predators and Parasites

Another problem that occurs in small, fragmented forests is an increase in the number of nest predators and parasites. Fragmentation creates more edge and thus favours edge-nesting birds, like blue jays and grackles, that will often prey on eggs and nestlings of other species. Since neotropical migrants usually nest on or near the ground in open, cup-shaped nests, they are especially vulnerable to nest parasitism from the brown-headed cowbird. Recent studies demonstrate that birds nesting near the forest edge are more frequently parasitized by cowbirds than those nesting in forest interiors.

Brush piles, which are an important form of cover for birds, should be more than just a loose heap of brush. Building a useful foundation will greatly improve the value and life of the brush pile for both birds and mammals. Several approaches are commonly used to build brush-pile foundations, but all rest on the animals' need for a labyrinth of tunnels in which to hide from predators and gain shelter from weather extremes such as wind, rain and snow. You can create such tunnels by laying four six-foot-long logs (four to eight inches in diameter) directly on the ground and then laying another four logs of similar length and diameter perpendicular to the first set. With branch stems pointing toward the ground, pile brush on top of the log foundation to make a mound that has a tepee shape.

Another approach to building a foundation is to make three rock piles in a V formation or construct a brush pile over ceramic drainage tiles. Mound up large

created by this popular practice may actually reduce the population of certain forest-dwelling bird species.

Recent studies demonstrate that some forest birds require large tracts of continuous forest for nesting. One study found that in the heavily populated Baltimore-Washington, D.C., area, certain species required at least 200 acres of unbroken forest. Smaller areas apparently did not include enough habitat or protection from predators and nest parasites. This and other similar studies throughout forested regions of North America point to an alarming decline in forest-interior birds that appears to be linked to the increasing fragmentation and loss of woodlands caused by spreading suburbs.

The birds most sensitive to fragmented forest share the following characteristics: they migrate to tropical America annually, nest only in forest interiors, are primarily insectivorous, build open nests on or near the ground, have a low reproductive rate (usually only one brood per year) and are relatively short-lived. A few examples of sensitive species are worm-eating warblers, ovenbirds, red-eyed vireos, scarlet tanagers and great-crested flycatchers.

While these and many other species have seriously declined in some areas since 1940, other birds have either maintained stable populations or have shown increases. Most land birds with stable or increasing numbers usually share the following characteristics: they are resident or migrate only a short distance, inhabit the forest edge, have a varied diet, choose various nest sites and have a high reproductive rate (very often two or more broods a year). Some examples of birds in this more adaptable group include most sparrows, catbirds, mockingbirds, robins, jays, crows, wrens and blackbirds.

Although unbroken forest might seem

branches first, and add smaller branches to the top of the pile.

Living shelters can be constructed from a conifer such as spruce or pine with well-formed lower branches. Construct a tepeelike shelter by slicing partway through lower branches so that they fall to the ground, surrounding the tree trunk. Such shelters provide excellent cover for game birds such as grouse and quail. In winter, they also may serve as useful places to install supplemental grain-feeding stations. If sufficient connecting bark is left intact, the branches may survive in their new position for several years.

In the windy prairie states, planting windbreaks (also called shelterbelts) is well recognized as an important technique for protecting crops, soils, buildings and livestock from the force of the wind. By considering wildlife needs when constructing windbreaks, plantings can double as wind protection and wildlife habitat.

Although a two- or three-row windbreak will provide adequate shelter for crops and buildings, wildlife windbreaks should contain at least six rows. Where possible, they consist of up to 11 rows. Wide shelterbelts, with trees and shrubs of varying heights, can offer excellent cover and food for both birds and mammals on landscapes that otherwise could not support wildlife.

A six-row windbreak is approximately 60 feet wide and would cover 1.4 acres if it were 1,000 feet long. An 11-row windbreak would be approximately 200 feet wide and would cover 4.6 acres if it were 1,000 feet long. Such large amounts of agricultural land committed to wildlife windbreaks obviously means taking land from crop production, but the value of shelterbelts is so great that they usually more than pay for themselves. For example, a 1976 study in Nebraska found that agricultural lands adjacent to windbreaks produced an average of 55 bushels per acre, while unprotected cropland produced only 10 bushels per acre. The difference results from less water loss in the protected field and therefore greater water availability for crops. Windbreaks can also be money-makers if you plant valuable hardwoods such as black walnut or add a row of conifers that can be sold in a few years as Christmas trees.

The ideal wildlife shelterbelt should contain a central row of tall conifers edged by deciduous trees, with both tall and small shrubs at the edges. The conifers provide seed crops and shelter from the extremes of both summer and winter weather, the deciduous trees provide food and nesting cavities, and the shrubs provide additional nest sites and often abundant fruit crops. Establishment of a row of herbaceous cover on the outside edges of the windbreak provides additional feeding and nesting habitat for pheasant, quail and ground-feeding birds such as sparrows.

Rules of Windbreaks

To establish a wildlife windbreak, plant large trees 10 feet apart, small trees 8 feet apart and shrubs about 6 feet apart. You should keep the following considerations in mind as you select and plant the trees and shrubs that will make up your windbreak:

1. Plant the tallest trees in the centre and the lowest shrubs on the outside.

2. Within each row, vary the kinds of trees and shrubs.

3. Select trees and shrubs that fruit at different times of the year.

4. Plant the conifers in a weaving row to give a more natural appearance and to avoid an open parklike appearance under the conifers.

5. Mix fast-growing and slow-growing trees and shrubs in the shelterbelt to provide cover in both the near and distant future.

6. Plant a 10-to-15-foot-wide buffer strip of perennial cover (grass, alfalfa and clover) on the outside edge of the shelterbelt.

7. The length of windbreaks is even more important than the width. Sacrifice some width to increase length if space or money is a limiting factor on the number of trees to be planted.

8. Erect fencing to exclude cattle and other livestock until windbreak plantings become well established.

In eastern states and provinces, damage from wind may not be as great a problem, but shelterbelts are still a valuable addition to agricultural land. In more protected areas, shrubby fencerows may provide adequate cover for wildlife and offer great benefit to cropland by increasing the number of insectivorous birds and predacious insects. These help reduce agricultural pests. A comparative study in Ohio found 32 times as many songbirds in brushy fencerows as in open cropland and 60 times as many aphid-eating ladybird beetles as in open fencelines. To provide useful cover for birds, brushy fencerows should be at least 10 feet wide and 150 feet long.

Cultivated crops can provide abundant, concentrated food supplies for wild birds. They are also useful for attracting birds to preferred areas. Several small rectangular food patches within the 100-to-2,000-foot-square range located near water or good cover are best. A useful goal for density of food patches is one half-acre food patch for every 20 acres of land. The simplest way to establish a food patch is to till the soil thoroughly and then broadcast a mixed bag of millet and sunflower birdseed over the soil. Just 15 pounds of millet and sunflower mix is enough to seed about a half-acre plot.

Imaginative landscaping can turn unused areas in the backyard or back 40 into productive wildlife habitat. In smaller yards, the opportunities for bird-luring vegetation may be limited to secluded corners; on substantial rural properties, however, gullies, rock piles, corners of cropland, the shores of a pond, farm roads and hedgerows are all prime sites for plantings that attract birds. The more ambitious can spend a lifetime — and a fortune — developing a wildlife sanctuary; those with more modest ambitions can spend a mere few hours setting out some shrubs and thereby bless their lives for years to come with a flash of avian colour and the bright note of birdsong.

Excerpted from The Audubon Society Guide to Attracting Birds, *Charles Scribner's Sons, an imprint of Macmillan Publishing Co. (New York). Copyright © 1985 Stephen W. Kress.*

Plant blueberry bushes just outside the kitchen door

A Private Patch Close at Hand

by Lee Reich

Anyone who has ever sweated through a hot summer morning at a pick-your-own blueberry field or scrambled through woods and meadows collecting from the wild knows that those succulent morsels are sweeter and more fragrant than any berries available at the supermarket.

Why? Those fresh-picked berries have been sun-kissed to perfection, while market berries must be picked before they are ripe. Commercial growers harvest berries early — when they turn blue but before they have ripened — so the berries will stand up to the rigours of shipping and storage.

But you don't have to settle for less than the best. Acid soil is ideal for the plants, but your backyard doesn't have to be a bog in New Jersey or a rocky slope in Maine for you to have a successful crop. With attention to the plants' requirements — especially soil — and use of some of the new cultivars, blueberries can be grown almost anywhere in the temperate zone. They do not even need a great deal of space: small urban gardens with the right growing conditions can host blueberry bushes. Select a suitable range of cultivars, and you can pick fruit for six to seven weeks.

Blueberry bushes are easier to grow than apples and peaches, and they usually don't require spraying for pests or diseases. The few that do attack blueberries rarely get a foothold if all fruits are harvested.

Besides bearing fruit, these shrubs are also ornamental. In spring, the blueberry's branches are festooned with small bell-shaped flowers resembling those of lily-of-the-valley. Summer brings rich green foliage that turns fiery red like the leaves of sugar maples in fall. In winter, the stems of many cultivars also redden, a colourful contrast against the snow. The beauty of the blueberry is no surprise, considering that it's kin to mountain laurel, rhododendron and azalea. Blueberry bushes can be used in landscapes as featured shrubs or hedges with handsome results.

Numerous new cultivars have been introduced in the past 20 years, but the work has just begun. Blueberries are today where apples were hundreds of years ago. There are about 100 blueberry varieties compared with at least 2,000 apple varieties. The first wild selection was introduced in 1908 and the first hybrids in 1920. Work continues to increase the hybrids' tolerance to high-pH soil and drought.

So, with the varieties available now, you will have no trouble finding the right bushes for your particular growing conditions. There are four species of blueberries adapted to different parts of the continent, each with a number of cultivars that give an early-, mid- or late-season harvest and varying degrees of hardiness.

The type of blueberry most commonly sold in markets and offered for sale by nurseries is the highbush blueberry (*Vaccinium corymbosum*, sometimes designated *V. australe*). This species is native to the sandy, organic soils found along the Atlantic coastal plain running from Maine down through the Carolinas and in some inland areas as far west as Michigan. The highbush blueberry grows 6 to 10 feet high and will withstand cold to USDA hardiness zones 4 and 5. Most blueberry breeding has been done with the highbush; cultivars vary in hardiness, ripening season, size, colour and flavour.

A second type of blueberry, the rabbit-eye (*Vaccinium ashei*), finds a congenial home in the South, where summers are torrid and winters short. This species is native to the Piedmont and coastal-plain soils of the southeastern part of the United States. The rabbit-eye blueberry tolerates winter cold to just below 0 degrees F. But the early-spring blossoms are susceptible to frost, so the plants are best grown south of the Carolinas. Vigorous growers, the bushes often tower to 15 feet.

The ripening season for rabbit-eye blueberries begins after that of highbush blueberries. Rabbit-eye fruits are firmer and thicker-skinned than highbush fruits, which helps them keep longer in the refrigerator. To develop peak flavour, ripe rabbit-eye berries can be left on the bushes for a couple of weeks after they turn blue.

Rabbit-eyes have not been cultivated for very long; the species developed a bad reputation because early plantings had consisted of wild or poorly cultivated plants that consequently produced small, gritty fruits. The flavour of improved cultivars, however, rivals that of highbush blueberries.

The blueberries you find in cans on supermarket shelves represent yet another blueberry species, the lowbush (mostly *Vaccinium angustifolium*, although there are other lowbush species). This is the hardiest blueberry species, with some cultivars yielding fruit as far north as zone 3. Fresh fruits can be very sweet and have a waxy sheen that makes them appear sky-blue or even grey. These creeping plants, a foot or so high, spread by underground stems to blanket rocky upland soils of the northeastern states and adjacent portions of Canada. Lowbush blueberries can be grown as a fruiting ornamental ground cover.

Most lowbush-blueberry plantings consist of wild plants. On a commercial scale, fields are maintained by periodically burning wild stands to keep out competing plants. Nursery stock is usually seedlings or unnamed wild plants, rather than stock propagated from cuttings. The wild plants are variable: some have delectable fruit; some have leaves and stems that turn bright red with the onset of cold weather; and others are drab in fall and winter. Individual plants also vary in height. But recent work by researchers in the North has led to the selection and breeding of lowbush plants with superior fruiting and ornamental qualities.

The fourth and final class of blueberries is the "half-highs." These medium-sized bushes are hybrids of lowbush and highbush blueberries, although "half-high" is a somewhat arbitrary

As wild blueberry patches decline due to development and fewer forest fires, cultivated varieties have become attractive additions to cottage yards.

classification, since many highbush cultivars have some lowbush in their ancestry. The highbush contributes genes for aromatic fruit and nonrunning habit, and the lowbush contributes dwarfness, hardiness, drought resistance, sweetness and early ripening. Besides the hardiness that comes with genes of the lowbush blueberry, this class pushes the limits of blueberry culture north to wherever there is adequate snow to cover and insulate the low branches. Like the lowbush cultivars, half-highs come from northern breeding stations.

Location Requirements

All blueberries have similar needs when it comes to selecting a planting site. Blueberries need full sun for maximum production and quality, although the plants will grow and produce fruit in shaded woods (as they do in the wild). As for any fruit plant, choose a site with good air circulation, and, if possible, avoid low-lying areas where late-spring frosts are likely to damage blossoms. Blueberries are exacting in their soil requirements, and soil preparation can spell the difference between success and failure.

The highbush blueberry is native to hummocks, or raised areas, with bogs. These hummocks provide the ideal conditions for blueberries: acid soil, high organic matter, plenty of moisture and good aeration. Rabbit-eye and lowbush blueberries have the same needs.

Before planting blueberries, attempt to produce the same conditions by mixing a bucketful of peat moss or composted sawdust with the soil in the planting hole. If the planting site is not well drained, create a mound of sandy soil and peat — a hummock, if you will — on which to plant.

Test the soil to make sure the pH level is between 4.0 and 5.5 The peat moss or sawdust will help lower the pH, but additional material might be needed. Sulphur or aluminum sulphate can be mixed with the soil to lower the pH. Mix in evenly over the entire area where the bushes will be planted, as blueberries' shallow roots spread widely. Since sulphur takes time to react with the soil, it must be added a season prior to planting. Sandy soils with a pH higher than 4.5 require about ¾ pound of sulphur per 100 square feet; loamy soils need double that quantity. The amount of aluminum sulphate needed is six times that of sulphur. Test the soil pH every few years. Whenever the pH rises above 5.2, add another half-pound of sulphur per 100 square feet.

In areas where soils are highly alkaline, you can still grow blueberries by "making" soil. Sink into the ground a 50-gallon drum that has been cut in half and drilled with drainage holes. Fill this drum with a mixture of equal parts of sandy soil (or even sand) and peat moss.

If both soil and irrigation water are alkaline (in other words, if you have hard water), then you may also have to acidify your water or collect rainwater for irrigating. If you need to acidify water — by adding vinegar, for example — you can probably buy an injector for your garden hose at a garden-supply store. The trick will be calculating the right formula for the water in your area. An agricultural extension service may be able to advise you.

With their fine, shallow root systems, blueberries benefit from mulching — to help keep soil cool and moist, to suppress weed growth and to eliminate the need for hoeing, which can damage roots. One of the best mulches is a six-inch layer of sawdust at planting, replenished annually as needed. Other good mulches include wood shavings or bark, pine needles and straw. Perforated plastic mulches also can be used, but, unlike the above, they won't add organic matter to the soil.

You can plant in spring or fall. In the latter case, however, make sure plants are heavily mulched so that they don't heave out of the soil as it freezes and thaws. Plant more than one blueberry cultivar so that cross-pollination can occur. (Highbush blueberries are mostly self-fertile, but yields and fruit are increased with cross-pollination; the other types definitely need cross-pollination.) Two-year-old plants are the best size for planting. Some nurseries sell plants in containers, which reduces transplant shock. Set plants shallowly in prepared soil.

Space highbush plants 4 to 6 feet apart in the row, with 10 feet between rows. For a blueberry hedge, plants can be set as close as 3 feet apart in the row. Commercial growers set lowbush blueberry plants 2 feet apart each way. On the backyard scale, where rapid filling in of the area between plants is desired, set lowbush plants a foot or less apart. Plant rabbit-eye blueberries 15 feet apart.

Nitrogen Supplements

Blueberry plants need only moderate amounts of fertilizer to maintain annual production. Too much fertilizer or manure can kill them. Nitrogen is the element needed in largest quantities, ranging from just ½ ounce per year for young plants, gradually increasing to 3 ounces per year for mature plants. This amount of nitrogen can be supplied by ½ pound, increasing to 2½ pounds, of either soybean or cottonseed meal; or ¼ pound, increasing to 1½ pounds, of blood meal. Double these amounts for rabbit-eye blueberries. For lowbush plants, broadcast the equivalent of ⅒ pound of nitrogen per 100 square feet, supplied by 1½ pounds of seed meal or a pound of blood meal.

Blueberry plants, especially highbush species, will not tolerate dry soil. They need an inch or two of water each week during the growing season. An inch of water translates to a gallon per young plant and up to about eight gallons for a mature plant.

Although visions of cobbler and fresh "blues" on cereal will make you eager for that first crop of berries, it's advisable to delay harvest until the third year after planting. You'll encourage shoot growth on your plants if you pluck off blooms during the first two years.

When at last that third year rolls around, the green fruits take form and you can almost taste the berries. And that's when you're about to have competition for those fragrant fruits. Birds are the major pests that threaten backyard blueberries.

Small-scale growers have tried everything imaginable to foil birds — including foil, in the form of pie pans or strips dangling from branches. Gardeners have also experimented with plastic owls and snakes, black thread draped around bushes, portable radios playing in bushes and plastic lines that hum in the wind. But not one of these methods is wholly satisfactory for keeping birds at bay. The only sure cure for birds is a bird-tight net.

Lowbush berries are traditionally harvested with a blueberry "rake," which looks like a dustpan with tines attached along the front. The tines catch the fruit as the rake is combed through the plants. Yields will vary from plant to plant, but expect a quart or so per bush, or about a cup per square foot from a ground-cover planting. The harvest season begins in July.

Yields of highbush and rabbit-eye plants will vary with cultivar and growing conditions. Highbush season begins in mid-May in the South and in July in northernmost growing areas. Rabbit-eye harvest comes just after highbush harvest. At full production, which is reached after about six years, a highbush plant will produce about four quarts of fruit and a rabbit-eye plant about nine quarts. With good growing conditions, it's possible to double or even triple these averages.

Of course, the joy of backyard blueberries is the full flavour that comes from allowing the fruits not just to turn blue but truly to ripen on the bush. Peak flavour is reached a few days after the berries turn blue. How to tell which fruits are ripe? Tickle the fruits, and those that are ready will fall into your hand.

Reprinted by permission of Organic Gardening *magazine. Copyright 1991. Rodale Press, Inc. U.S.A. (Emmaus, PA). All rights reserved.*

Common sense and careful planning make healthy saplings

Planting Trees for the Future

by E.E. Vejore

With interest rates rising like young birches, it is timely to note that there are few investments in the world that compare with the cost and return of a tree. Not only do trees provide food, shade, beauty, living space for wild creatures and eventually warmth and building materials, but also there are no items around the house, save your kids, that expand so in value and size.

Compared with most appliances, for instance, trees cost less than the plugs, but in 20 years, they are worth more to one's realty than all appliances combined. On a national average, trees contribute 9.5 percent of the value of the house and land. Thus a hypothetical $100,000 property would contain $9,500 worth of trees that probably cost less than $95 to plant.

To quote from *Taylor's Gardening Encyclopedia*: "Many people think that because trees are big and permanent, they must be costly. There are ample facts to disprove such an illusion. A grouping of trees is the cheapest form of landscaping. They need a minimum of attention . . . and no garden of permanent value is possible without trees."

But to partake of any of these benefits, one must plant a tree properly. After eight years of selling nursery trees to the public, I tend occasionally to agree with H.L. Mencken's opinion that no one ever went broke underestimating the intelligence of the American public. Trees, after all, are to be planted root side down, they are not dug up in midsummer to be transplanted elsewhere in the garden, they are not to be stored in a heated house before they are planted, and they have a tendency to die when planted in rock piles or on raw manure.

From the time it leaves the nursery, the tree's first year is probably the most vulnerable period of its life. Trees are not used to getting up and moving about, so it is up to the gardener to make this relocation as free of trauma as possible.

The choice of the right tree is itself vital to the minimization of trauma for both the tree and its buyer. While the colour illustrations in the catalogue may be tempting, the shopper must first take an unbiased look at his situation — his desires and the limitations of his location — considering not only climate but also the quirks of his own place, its size and exposure to sun, the depth of the soil and the presence of swamps or rocky outcroppings.

Naturally, every situation will be different, but the climatic zones do group gardeners into broad areas of general similarity. Those coloured spaces interspersed between wiggly lines across the horticultural maps of North America, those demarcations of climate that blithely equate the seasons of Ottawa with those of Pierre, South Dakota, or a garden in Halifax with one in Pittsburgh, are a considered attempt to delineate the variances in the growing seasons of this continent. These zones are immensely important to tree purchasers, particularly in northern areas where a site a few miles inland from a heat-holding lake will kill a plant that flourishes by its shores.

Unfortunately, there are so many of these charts and such a bewildering numerology that one's residence may be in zone 5 on one and 6b on another. The only way to operate with them at present is to use the same number set as one's supplier.

Even so, some nurseries are inclined toward overoptimism in this regard. While one Canadian mail-order nursery recommends that their apricots can be grown in zone 4, the Ontario Ministry of Agriculture and Food says, "To ensure fruiting, apricots should only be grown in zones 7a, 7b and areas of 6b near the Great Lakes" — yet certain apricots are grown on the prairies. If in

A carefully planted, well-placed tree can provide shade and visual comfort to a family for generations.

doubt (which you should be if no one in your area is growing the tree you favour), contact the appropriate provincial or state department of agriculture.

One way you can at least be sure that a tree will survive in your area is to buy from a local grower (not simply a local importer). A local nursery offers the best opportunity for freshly dug root systems. With a little planning, you can dig a hole at home and move in a bare-root tree within an hour of purchase. This creates a minimum of shock and obviates the need for severe top pruning. Keeping the roots damp preserves their microorganisms, which is particularly important with evergreens. Since these microorganisms abet the absorption of nutrients, their protection means immediate tree growth, not mere survival in the year of purchase. Quick planting and dampness are the keys to preserving these organisms; although dryness will kill them, hosing or immersion in water will wash them off. Nevertheless, if there is a choice between drought or flood, choose flood as the least harmful.

Another reason to buy locally is that our postal and freight services seriously jeopardize any horticultural shipments and must make the reliable mail-order nurseries seethe with frustration. But this doesn't seem to cut down on the number of catalogues we receive every spring or the lushness of their prose and promise. Trees at local nurseries in April seldom look as colourful as they do in the catalogues, but you see what you get and you get what you see — stock that has grown and survived in your area.

Many large nurseries dig much of their stock in the comparatively quiet autumn season, then store it in huge insulated quonsets at a constant temperature and humidity, misting the bared roots several times a day. It's probably not the trees' idea of a fabulous winter, but it means the elimination of frost damage as well as easy access to the trees in the spring rush. If consistently maintained, stock comes through this rather radical cold storage quite well. Mail-order trees that arrive with their roots bound in a bit of damp sphagnum and a plastic bag have probably gone through the winter in this manner.

Increasingly, nurseries are turning to planting trees in pots so that the planting season is extended and the roots are protected from excessive shock. Sometimes, small containerized evergreens are stored indoors over winter, usually in polyethylene huts, which helps maintain the sparkling leaf that sells so well in shopping malls, where the leaf faces reality and may lose a bit of its sheen.

Proper Packaging

A percentage of the trees and shrubs sold in eastern Canada and the northeastern United States are shipped en masse from the midsouthern states or from the dulcet West Coast, where even snail-slow 'Crimson King' maples shoot up. Northern recipients of these goods are not always well served because, for example, even a stout-hearted native like black cherry will die back in eastern Ontario if the seed comes from southern Pennsylvania. On the other hand, West Coast 'Crimson Kings' gain a beautiful straight trunk unobtainable in our harsh winters.

Modern tree packaging, as dictated by shopping-mall outlets and all the interconnections of big business and trucking, makes for very neat-looking, beautifully packaged plants which all too often stand on only the number of roots that could fit in the pot. Shade and fruit trees are particularly affected by this reversal of priorities. On the other hand, the local grower does not have to package plants for distant shipment or long shelf life, and chances are he knows a bit more about horticulture and can answer your questions better than the average mall employee.

If the tree is containerized and looks overcrowded, ask the salesperson to remove the pot so that you can check the roots. If they grow round and round inside the container and look dead, they probably are. Healthy roots have a white growing tip and, if scratched with a thumbnail, will appear white to cream-coloured under the outer skin.

As a rule, the bigger the roots, the bet-

ter the buy. In a natural setting, the root system of a tree is often double the circumference of its crown; and consequently, wild or forest trees are often difficult to transplant, because only a fraction of their "foundation" makes it into the lawn. Nursery trees, by contrast, have been (or should have been) root-pruned in their presale life or, better yet, transplanted several times. This causes their root systems to grow more densely inward, in much the same way that a hedge thickens with shearing. The nursery tree thus stands on a root system often equal in length — if laid out and measured — to the sparse but very long roots of a wild tree of the same dimensions.

While you cannot always check the roots of a possible purchase, you can be fairly sure of getting a healthy tree by checking for a plump, fresh-looking trunk, green willowy branches (not dry and brittle) and plump, not shrivelled, buds. The needles on evergreens should be green and spring back when bent; yellow or brown needles and those that snap when they are bent indicate a dried-out plant which may be impossible to revive.

The Importance of Rootlets

A sure sign of proper root management in a bare-root nursery tree is the numerous fibred rootlets that grow like a beard from the stouter anchor roots. If the tree has only thumb-thick roots, it will likely be two years before serious growth resumes.

Root damage or poor root growth will especially affect the successful transplanting of older trees. In fact, it is usually worthwhile to buy younger, smaller trees if given the choice. Not only do smaller trees usually suffer less damage in transplanting, but they are less expensive in both the short and long terms; the Ontario Ministry of Agriculture and Food estimates that a six-foot tree planted beside an eight-foot one will be almost the same size in four or five years.

When transporting the tree home, take care that its bare roots are protected from the wind and sun. Wrapping it in burlap or temporarily "planting" it in a pot of peat or damp sand will help if the trip is long. Buyers with pickups should bring their own tarps.

At home, plant the tree as soon as possible. Always make the hole bigger than you think it should be; the tree will soon fill it. Even if the soil is superb, work it up at the bottom of the hole, crumbling the lumps; the more friable the soil, the easier it is for the roots to feed and expand.

The planting hole for bare-root trees and shrubs should be wide enough that the roots can be spread in their natural position and deep enough that the plant can be placed at its original depth. If the tree has been grafted, be sure that the grafting point is above the soil line.

Generally, the soil removed from the hole is the best planting medium for the tree. As Bob Fleming of the Ontario Ministry of Agriculture and Food says, "Recommendations for planting trees and shrubs have changed as a result of research, which now indicates that it is better to use the existing soil from the planting hole than to add purchased soil or organic material." Many nurserymen, however, still disagree with this advice and prefer new soil.

If the soil is really poor, dig out as much junk as possible and then invest in quality topsoil, dumping half of it into the hole and leaving the rest to fill in around the tree. In fast-draining, sandy soil, add up to one-half peat moss to the removed soil, as peat will increase water retention and aeration. Before planting the tree, moisten the hole thoroughly, but do not drench it. In large holes, water a portion at a time; it is surprising how slowly water penetrates deep soil.

For balled-and-burlapped or container trees, dig the planting hole about twice as wide as the diameter of the rootball or container and deep enough so that the tree will be the same depth as before. Remove the container from the tree, trying to retain as much soil around the roots as possible. With balled-and-burlapped stock, keep the burlap intact as the tree is placed in the hole, then cut away as much of it as possible around the roots before filling in the hole.

Holding the tree straight up (this is usually a two-person job), fill in the soil around the roots, tamping it down gently but firmly as it is replaced. Air spaces are dangerous at all times but particularly so with fall plantings. The new soil level should be just slightly lower than that of the surrounding yard. Now water the tree. University of Idaho

---

It has been our unhappy finding that fertilizers should be avoided entirely by the inexperienced tree planter the year following planting.

---

ornamentalist and fruit specialist Tony Horn advises: "Water the tree or shrub when you plant, even if the soil is moist. The water will help settle the soil around the roots and eliminate air pockets." It is important to water after tamping down the soil; firming wet soil can produce an impenetrable mass.

While balled-and-burlapped or container-grown trees generally need no pruning directly after transplanting, bare-root trees often do to compensate for root loss during transplanting. If root loss has occurred, remove about one-third of the branches. The aim is to keep the tree from losing more water through its foliage than its roots can take up through the soil. Also, always prune away broken branches or any dead growth.

If the tree is planted in a windy place, or if it has a very small root base in comparison with its height, it should be supported for at least its first year. The best system for large trees involves three guy wires secured equidistantly around the tree, while a single stake

placed in the direction from which the wind usually blows will support a small tree. Place the stake in the planting hole before filling it with soil. Tie the tree to its support with lengths of old garden hose, bicycle tire or rags, anything that will not rub away bark as the tree blows.

Give most standard-sized trees about 20 feet of free space in all directions; birch, however, look best in a closely planted grove. Dwarf fruit trees can be as close as 10 feet, and trees raised for lumber, such as white pine, may be as close as 5 feet and row-culled in later life. Be sure not to plant too close to septic tanks, sewers or wells: tree roots can crack through them in the quest for water and nutrients. When you plant the tree, visualize its full-grown size, breadth of trunk and root spread. That decorative little maple may shade all the home's south windows in 10 years.

It has been our unhappy finding that fertilizers should be avoided entirely by the inexperienced tree planter during the year following planting. All too often, the "worked compost" or "old manure" described by a customer is not quite worked or old enough. The ensuing heat and acid can then easily attack the roots through the newly worked soil. Ironically, compost or even turf that is placed at the bottom of a planting hole can sometimes interfere with the capillary action of water ascending — the real source of survival in dry weather — by absorbing an inordinate amount of this flow. Instead, flip the turf over, and place it upside down over the filled-in hole, which should be shaped into a holding bowl around the tree for catching water.

Admittedly, this is a conservative opinion expressly for amateurs, but we have seen damage done even with the "safe" (and often extremely expensive) inorganic fertilizers, either because of excessive application, which causes burning, or because of late application, which causes tender growth that lacks the time to harden off before winter and dies back when the cold weather comes. Early July is about as late as any fertilizer should be applied — but not until the second summer in the yard. Remember, the higher the analysis numbers on the package, the more fertilizing potential and the greater risk of burn or of a toxic buildup of insoluble salts.

Lack of fertility is seldom a problem with newly planted trees. The largest single cause of tree loss in the year of planting is lack of water or, more specifically, lack of consistent watering. Many of our customers get their plants started brilliantly, but when the pagan joys of spring wear off, the tree tends to be taken for granted; it seems so much more self-reliant than a tomato or a geranium, so green and healthy even during the three-week June drought or the pounding sun of late July. Why water it?

A week or so after a big heat, the problem may show up: a tree's leaves curl and brown, or an insect or fungal inroad may take advantage of its lowered health. Maples, oaks, ashes, elms and fruit trees are particularly hard hit by drought.

During the critical first year, think of your tree or shrub as a patient fresh from the hospital — after all, it has been amputated. Give it an inch of water every 10 days to two weeks when rain is lacking, even into late autumn, when the roots, especially of evergreens, need a reservoir of inner moisture to get them through the drying winds of winter. Check the soil around evergreens before the ground freezes, and add water if it is dry — but adding water to moist soil at any time may do more harm than good.

Overwatering is far less usual than underwatering, but it can occur if, say, a lawn is being established around the newly planted tree and watering is taking place daily. Often a problem on clay soils, waterlogging can be avoided with provisions for good drainage under and around the tree. Waterlogging causes the tree to appear much like a drought-stricken one.

The second major cause of planting-year failure is weed and grass competition. An area around the trunk as wide as the roots extend (which corresponds approximately to the width of the top growth) should be kept clear of all com-

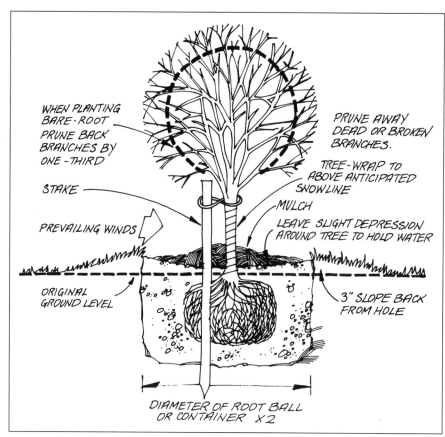

WHEN PLANTING BARE-ROOT PRUNE BACK BRANCHES BY ONE-THIRD

STAKE

PREVAILING WINDS

ORIGINAL GROUND LEVEL

PRUNE AWAY DEAD OR BROKEN BRANCHES.

TREE-WRAP TO ABOVE ANTICIPATED SNOWLINE

MULCH

LEAVE SLIGHT DEPRESSION AROUND TREE TO HOLD WATER

3" SLOPE BACK FROM HOLE

DIAMETER OF ROOT BALL OR CONTAINER X 2

If using a stake, avoid root damage by placing it in the hole before backfilling.

petition. In the race for water and food, the grasses win easily, their aggressive root systems filtering out the goodies that really should be headed down to the tree roots.

For mulch, use straw, hay, leaves or grass clippings in preference to sawdust or bark, which can leach nitrogen. Spread the mulch in a thick layer around the trunk. As mulch attracts rodents, wrap a tree guard against or even under the ground; this is especially important in winter, when young tree bark is a delicacy for rodents. While tree guards may be bought at nurseries, aluminum foil or a heavy mat of burlap tied with strong twine, wrapped higher than the anticipated snow line, will suffice. The combination of mulch and judicious hoeing — avoiding the tree's roots — will double a plant's chances for growth and survival. But be consistent, and try to stay a step ahead of the problems the tree feels but cannot express until it is too late.

Trees that die from midseason neglect or overfertilization pose a dilemma for

nurseries. The tree leafed out, it looked fine, and then, mysteriously, it died. Who is responsible? Should the nursery replace the tree free, or should the cost be split, or should the customer — who often fails to realize that the fault could be his — take his lumps? No one answer suffices, but any reputable nursery should give at least a 50 percent rebate on dead stock if it is returned with the receipt during the subsequent planting season.

Generally, spring-sold stock is at least guaranteed to leaf out, while fall-sold stock is guaranteed to leaf out the following spring. The only other general nursery guarantee is that stock be true to name: if your maple sprouts beans, you can take it back.

Insecticide Advice

Our opinion concerning insecticide use is once again conservative: spray for bugs only when absolutely necessary. Not only does this keep money out of petrochemical pockets, but it avoids possible health risks. Besides, chemicals do eliminate pests with a marvellous if unnatural efficiency, but the bugs usually return, next month or next year, and the problem resumes, with the pests just that little bit more resistant.

In modern orchards, spraying occurs as often as 20 times a year, because consumers, it seems, want a totally unblemished apple and because no engineer of chemicals can keep up with the genetic development of a bug. The evolutionary turnovers available to insect populations — even during one season — mean that they can potentially mutate. Sooner or later, the chemicals lose, but they take a great many innocents with them. If Rachel Carson, one of the true heroes of this century, had not written the classic *Silent Spring*, it is quite possible that many of our natural allies would now be extinct.

Chemicals, then, despite their rosy packaging, are not playthings. Accept your apple or your tree with a few spots on it. If general health is sound enough, most trees can grow right through disease or insects the same way a healthy human gets through the flu. There's nothing like a caterpillar patrol as a way to keep an eye on both the young trees and the pests — and don't burn off the bugs, just squish them between the leaves and move on.

That said, it must be admitted that a growing number of species are susceptible to new blights which might be thought of as nearly symptomatic of our times. The wretched Dutch elm disease is probably the worst, though there may be some surviving elms capable of producing disease-resistant seedlings. Several varieties of fruit trees and mountain ashes suffer a fast and random killer called fire blight. Birches are increasingly infested with leaf miner. Sugar maples are mysteriously dying back, with scarcely a ripple of government research . . . and on and on the sad litany goes.

Do we spray them all à la spruce budworm? Personally, I prefer to cultivate ladybugs and build bird houses (with an opening of 1¼ inches to keep out starlings). But in a pinch, yes, our nursery uses malathion or cygon, but as seldom and as discreetly as possible. Meanwhile,

in our first eight years, our farm's bird population tripled, and it has continued to grow ever since.

Transplant Seasons

If there is enough soil surrounding the roots, trees can be moved any time of the year, but it is an age-old practice to dig most stock in the spring before leaf bud or in the autumn after leaf fall, when winter preparation has shut down the plant's complex chemical circuitry. The tree is then dormant and can be operated on like a patient under anaesthetic. On the other hand, the roots are vibrantly alive during the growing season, and to dig them then not only cuts off food and water but often creates fatal shock.

A few species — birch, poplar, sycamore, stone fruits — do not transplant well in autumn, but I feel that there is no general rule that spring is best. A University of Idaho agricultural-information release recommends early spring as the best time to plant deciduous, bare-root trees, "while they are still dormant and when danger of severe winter temperatures is past and the ground is no longer frozen." Even balled-and-burlapped or container-grown trees and shrubs can be transplanted nearly any time of the year, but they will become established better if transplanted in the spring or early summer. This gives them a chance to grow a strong root system before severe cold temperatures set in. The Ontario Ministry of Agriculture and Food advises: "Plant deciduous trees, sold bare root, before mid-May to provide the best growing conditions. Container-grown deciduous trees can be transplanted safely until the end of May or early June."

Conifers, however, are often best planted in fall, but any tree's success will be partially dependent on the particular season that follows its planting. A moist autumn followed by a good snow cover is just about optimum, but let a series of thaws ice up your stock, and losses will be very heavy. Unfortunately, only the *Farmer's Almanac* would hazard a guess about the approaching season.

Whether the tree is planted in spring

or fall, one rule always applies: the sooner it is planted, the better. The soil will then have more time to settle properly before frost or growth begins. In spring, buy your trees as soon as you can get a shovel in the earth — every day's wait works against you.

As a last bit of advice, be aware that there is no such thing as a perfect tree. Each one has both good and bad points. A customer may love the shape and flowers of mountain ash but find that the fruit messes up the sidewalk because the transport trucks have driven away the birds that used to feed on it. A blue spruce may seem too expensive, but it is a diamond investment. A green spruce, on the other hand, may seem too common, but green spruce have superb, clean lines and form a cheap, hardy hedge. A poplar is often criticized as short-lived, but it jets up, and only white pine has a better wind sound. An oak is too slow? But then, so is a Rolls Royce.

No matter how much planning you have done, keep an open mind at the nursery. Best, visit once before doing any purchasing, just for advice and to take a look at the stock. Some nurseries have done breeding work on their own or may have brought in several unusual trees and can offer species and strains that you might never have considered but that are especially well-suited to your area. If the local expertise is there, it pays to make use of it.

High-arching, fast-growing black locust, a wonderful "bee tree," for example, is seldom sold now because patented varieties that conform to shape, usually suburban shapes, have dominated the market. In the brutish climate of eastern Ontario, our tiny tree nursery has already introduced a few species that flourish here with unexpected vigour and may, a century hence, be the only mark we leave on Earth. Fair enough.

(The author operates the Golden Bough Tree Farm, whose mail-order catalogue is available for $1.00, General Delivery, Marlbank, Ontario K0K 2L0.)

Originally published in Harrowsmith *magazine (Camden East, Ont.).*

Fixing up the waterfront might just mean leaving it alone

Naturally Kept Shorelines

by Suzanne Kingsmill

On the Ontario side of the Ottawa River, water laps gently on a miniature man-made beach, drawing rivulets of soil back on each wave. Above the waterline, the land lies gouged by ice and wind. Deep channels snake out into the sand from under the exposed roots of the only two trees left standing amidst a sea of groomed grass.

On the next lot, the shoreline changes abruptly. Water pushes against a towering wall that keeps the imprisoned land from falling into the river. At the end of the wall is one of many access roads that litter the shoreline; it cuts through the sandy soil that once underlay a vast pine forest. Beyond that, another retaining wall.

And so it goes: Every 15 metres, the waterfront changes to reflect the owner's taste. However, one thing remains the same. There is very little sign of life here. This community could be any of thousands that dot the Ontario landscape wherever there is water. "The public perceives industry as the destroyer of our waters," says Lindsay Penney, fish and wildlife supervisor at the Brockville district office of the Ministry of Natural Resources (MNR). "But when we look at many of our recreational waters, we find no indus-

try. The public has difficulty realizing that individual landowners can damage lakes and rivers, often unwittingly, in their bid to urbanize their residential and cottage shorelines."

Although it is mostly cottagers who contribute to the problem, Penney notes that year-round residents are also responsible. Many people have bought property on lakes and rivers, willing to commute long distances to their workplace. The result is that most of southern Ontario's shorelines have already been developed, and as the trend toward commuting grows, people are settling for less desirable properties that have escaped development up until now, with the intention of "cleaning up the waterfront."

So what's wrong with that? For one thing, the province has made it illegal to tamper with shoreline habitat without express permission from MNR. But more important, every alteration of shoreline, repeated thousands of times on lakes and rivers throughout Ontario, has a huge cumulative impact on the health of our waterways and the flora and fauna that live there.

"Some of these lakes have been so sterilized that they are, in effect, just like a bathtub," says Mike Buss, MNR's regional ecologist in Algonquin region. Ironically, landowners are destroying the very values that they sought when

they purchased their waterfront property.

A shoreline is not an impermeable border but a transition zone between land and water. The health of a shoreline affects — and is affected by — the health of both the backshore and the inshore. A landowner who tampers with one zone will inadvertently do damage elsewhere too.

Problem I: Clearing the Backshore

On a large property on Lake Ontario's Bay of Quinte, a lush city-bred lawn sweeps down to the water's edge. The owners have cleared most of the trees and shrubs to provide a view of the lake. They have planted flowerbeds, fertilized the lawn and used herbicides to control weeds. It looks beautiful, in a tame sort of way, but the beauty is only skin-deep. Hidden problems await the owners.

Natural vegetation, with its maze of roots, provides a buffer zone between land and water, soaking up nutrients and contaminants and binding the soil. When vegetation is cleared, soil and nutrients spill unchallenged into the lake during rainstorms. The result is disastrous.

Says Pat Ferris of Mutual Associa-

A family of mallard ducks paddles through a patch of water lilies left intact by a conscientious cottager.

tions for the Protection of the Lake Environment in Ontario (MAPLE), a volunteer organization that helps waterfront landowners rehabilitate their shorelines, "The vegetation around a whole lake is like the skin on your body. If you have one cut, it's not really serious, but imagine if you had a hundred cuts. It's the same with a lake. You start cleaning out the protective natural living barrier, and your lake is going to change. It's too much stress for the lake to handle at once."

Tremendous blooms of growth begin to appear in the water because of the infusion of nutrients. Then, says Penney, "some of the larger water weeds begin to grow and choke out the lake or river. This is nature trying to cope by sucking the nutrients out of the water. Next, the weeds die off. When they sink to the bottom and rot, undesirable side products such as hydrogen sulphide and methane result, and the process of decay eats up the dissolved oxygen in the lake."

When shoreline trees and shrubs are cut down, the creatures that once fed, bred and sheltered there — shorebirds, ducks, nesting sparrows and warblers, mice, voles, muskrats, otters and beavers — must try to find alternative habitat. Fish also vanish with the overhanging vegetation, which provided shade, cover from predatory birds and a haven for the insects that they eat.

If your property is still in a natural state, don't alter it by clearing brush and trees. As Ferris says, "It's better to have a partial view of a healthy lake than a totally unobstructed view of a sick lake."

If your property has been cleared, consider the route taken by the landowners on highly developed Mississippi Lake, near Carleton Place. Some years ago, they began noticing severe erosion and a sharp drop in the number of bass spawning in the shallows. Their lake association decided to join MAPLE, which coordinated a mass planting of native shrubs by the cottagers themselves along the 35-mile shoreline. Although the lake has not yet completely recovered, shoreline vegetation is making inroads thanks to the group's

efforts. In many areas, erosion has been halted, and shrubs provide shade for bass, which have returned to spawn.

Problem II: Getting Rid of Weeds

In a private bay on a northern Ontario lake, landowners used herbicides and mechanical harvesters to clear the aquatic plants on the lee shore. They then covered the area with sand. With the leftover sand, they also covered the gravel shore on the windward side to make one long beach.

Now, every spring, the cottagers must haul in more sand to bury the vegetation again and replace the soil taken out by the ice. They give up precious leisure time to wrestle with a problem of their own creation. They are also noticing that much of the wildlife that gave them pleasure has vanished from the bay.

Aquatic vegetation is of critical importance to a body of water. Yet, says Penney, "if you ask anybody what type of plants grow in a lake or a river, they say weeds, and to them, a weed is an undesirable plant. Nothing could be further from the truth."

Aquatic vegetation takes in both contaminants and excess nutrients, maintaining the health of the body of water. Aquatic plants temper the effect of wind and wave action on the shore, slowing erosion. These plants are also a major source of food and shelter for fish and other fauna.

"They incubate the lower level of the food chain — the insect larvae and the smaller minnows," says Penney. "So when we turn our shorelines into a barren desert, we lose this productivity zone."

Raymond Biette, habitat protection and rehabilitation biologist with MNR in Toronto, adds that "by covering natural habitat with sand, you destroy all the nursery areas and much of the diversity that is essential for fish and for the organisms that they depend upon. You eliminate the nooks and crannies and rough structures that most aquatic organisms need. It's like converting a productive grassland into a parking lot."

In Ontario, any work done on the shoreline below the high-water mark re-

quires a permit from MNR. "As soon as landowners go beyond the water's edge, they are doing things off their property," says Penney. "They're on the Crown lands or waters of Ontario. People have a hard time grasping that.

"When a person comes to us with the infamous phrase, 'I'm going to clean up my frontage,' we must tell them we no longer authorize wholesale cleanups of the offshore," adds Penney. Instead, MNR tries to limit the cleaning to a functional size. "If the landowner has 100 feet of waterfront," says Mike Buss, "we suggest that, instead of making it all look like it's Wasaga Beach, they just develop 20 feet and leave the rest as is."

If you've bought a property where aquatic plants have been cut and gravel covered, don't try to undo the damage. Let nature heal itself.

If you are in the unusual situation that your property is undeveloped, don't alter it to suit your needs. Learn to put up with walking on gravel. Clear a small path through the aquatic vegetation if you must, but remember that the cut or uprooted plants can propagate, effectively foiling your efforts to eliminate the problem.

In general, try to overcome an aversion to so-called "weeds" by educating yourself and your family about aquatic life. Says Penney, "It took me years to convince my children that snorkelling over aquatic plants and watching insect larvae and panfish flit and dart in the shadows was more fun than diving for quarters in a cement swimming pool."

Problem III: Docks and Boathouses

On Lake Couchiching, a two-storey boathouse sits over the water. A crib dock runs along one side and snakes out in front in a massive L. In the dock-sheltered waters, weeds now grow, beaten back with herbicides every year. Sickly fish swim into the shallows, seeking the only shade available — inside the covered boathouse. They die there amidst the debris that gets trapped in the backwater created by the large dock.

In old-style crib docks, rocks are scavenged from the water and piled into the crib. Not only is habitat stolen from the offshore, where larval fish thrive among the rubble, but habitat in the inshore is then buried under tons of rock. This immovable structure also affects water currents and wave refraction, leading to weed and erosion problems. Boathouses sitting over the water or solid ramps and wharves sitting in the water also destroy habitat.

Crib docks being approved by MNR today must be built with stones brought from somewhere other than the lake bottom. Much preferred are floating docks or docks that are built on I-beams or pipe stilts. These designs minimize the intrusion on the lake bottom and allow waves to move underneath them.

One boathouse design that MNR recommends has open sides and a roof supported by I-beams. "The currents can move up and down your frontage, flotsam doesn't collect, and muskrats and beavers will not build their homes inside them," says Penney.

Municipal bylaws differ on setback allowances for other buildings, such as houses; some are so lax that owners can build virtually right on the shore regardless of the consequences to wildlife. MNR advises that houses, cottages and other intrusive buildings be set back at least 50 to 100 feet from the water.

Problem IV: Retaining Walls

On the Ottawa River, a landowner extended his lot by erecting a gigantic three-sided retaining wall, filling it in and then building his house 10 feet above the water. Wedged into a gaping crack at the base of the wall are several small boulders. A sign reads, "Do not move these stones. They protect the stone wall" — a testament to the owner's maintenance problems.

By erecting a retaining wall, you're fighting a losing battle against erosion, which was usually caused by altering the natural shoreline. A man-made shoreline "doesn't have the living component or the give-and-take that natural vegetation does," says Ferris.

Retaining walls also destroy wildlife habitat. Says Ross Ferguson, an engineering technician with the Mississippi Valley Conservation Authority, "Retaining walls don't provide any shade. You get rapid warming of the shallows, and minnows and crayfish have problems. The walls also change the velocity of the wave at the shoreline. When the wave crashes onto the wall, the energy has to be transmitted up and down and into it, resulting in turbulence in front.

As cottager Pat Ferris says, "It's better to have a partial view of a healthy lake than a totally unobstructed view of a sick lake."

There is no habitat left for the little fish, because they can't live in that kind of turbulence."

If a retaining wall is absolutely necessary, it should be built at least five feet from the water's edge and on the owner's property, keeping it back from the high-water mark. Instead of the old-style wall built of cement or railway ties and set at right angles to the water, MNR suggests building a gently sloping loose-rock wall, which is more flexible and better able to withstand the forces of nature.

But in most cases, you should forget a retaining wall. Ferris tells the story of one landowner on Christie Lake, near Perth, who runs a campground built on reclaimed land. "He spent a good part of his time rebuilding his retaining walls every year. He was getting tired of it, so I suggested an easier solution. I said, 'Let's do what Mother Nature is doing. Let's go natural.'"

They determined what species grew in undisturbed areas around the lake and then planted a border along the old retaining wall — shrubs like sweetgale, dogwood, Virginia creeper, willow and alder. "These are all indigenous species," says Ferris. "Mother Nature's shrubs can take a beating and come back kicking. They have a dense root system that locks the soil along the shoreline and provides a living, flexible retaining wall that can take the ice and wave damage and flooding in springtime."

The old retaining wall was left to rot away rather than being torn out, because "you can do more damage to the lake environment by removing walls than by putting them in," says Penney.

Today, a healthy, tangled mat of shrubs and bushes hides the old wall as nature slowly returns the land to its natural state. The landowner has barely had to lift a finger to maintain the planting, and his erosion problems are a thing of the past.

The Good Old Days

Shoreline residents like to talk about how things used to be — when the waters were clear, with no scum on the rocks; fish and other wildlife were plentiful; and the night air sang with the chorusing of frogs. They recognize that the quality of their shorelines has deteriorated, yet most fail to see that by taming their waterfront, they have contributed to its degradation.

"Most shoreline owners aren't really aware of what they've done, whether it be good or bad," says Mike Shields, co-chairman of the environmental committee of the Lake of Bays Association, near Huntsville. "I see it as an ecological chain — every link has a reason for being there. If you break a link, there are going to be repercussions. Some of the problems we're seeing today are due to a link that was broken 20 or 30 years ago," says Shields.

While most of the shoreline on his lake has been left fairly natural, Shields knows that only informed landowners can keep it that way. "The qualities that attracted us and keep us at our lake are in jeopardy," he says. "We've got to pay attention from here on in."

Originally published in Seasons *magazine (Toronto).*

Fighting the weed war with few casualties

by Gordon Graham

Slippery strands of submarine squish; gooey gush that gums up your prop. Most cottagers consider weeds in their water one of the unpleasant aspects of cottage life. But finding an environmentally sound method of getting rid of them is as difficult as grasping an underwater handful of the slimy plants.

"There is no simple or single answer to aquatic-vegetation control," admits an information kit prepared jointly by Ontario's Ministries of the Environment (MOE) and Natural Resources (MNR). It lists possible tactics such as chemical herbicides, mechanical harvesting, habitat manipulation and biological agents. But no single method works in every setting, and each has its own drawbacks. In fact, once you start fighting water weeds, you are probably in for a complex, never-ending battle.

Whether you like it or not, native aquatic plants such as Canada water weed, muskgrass and stonewort play a key role in the drama of lake life. They are an important component of fish habitat, serving as spawning, nursery and feeding areas for many species; they also provide nesting sites and protective cover for waterfowl. In addition, their roots hold down sediment, thus helping to keep the water clear, and some species prevent shoreline erosion.

"Lakeshore plants are important to the whole chain of life," says Jean Anthon, past president of the Federation of Ontario Cottagers' Associations. "If every owner thinks he should sterilize his whole lakeshore, we're going to have lakes that can't sustain any life."

True enough, but on some lakes, weeds reach epidemic proportions, and excessive amounts of aquatic plants can be as detrimental as no plants at all. They can suffocate fish (by using up oxygen), as well as make swimming and boating unpleasant and, in some cases, impossible.

The culprit in many cases is a foreign invader rather than a native plant: Eurasian water milfoil, which apparently found its way to North America on freighters travelling to New York in the early 1900s. It was first spotted in Canada in 1961 and had already become troublesome in the Kawarthas by the early '70s. Now it infests hundreds of lakes in Ontario, where it aggressively crowds out every other water plant.

Milfoil, which can be recognized by its sets of four symmetrical, feathery leaves coming off a central stem, is extraordinarily tenacious. Gord Harse, vice president of Aquamate, an Oakville company that specializes in weed harvesting, speaks of it with the kind of admiration you reserve for a formidable opponent. "It will grow in anything: silt, sand, rocky bottoms, warm water, cold water," he says. "Even a little piece an inch or two long can reroot and become a whole new plant. It's just devastating." A tiny shred of milfoil can survive for weeks in a puddle in the bottom of a boat, on its propeller or on the undercarriage of a trailer. If you travel to another lake and that snippet gets into the water, a whole new invasion can begin.

Whether the problem is milfoil or a combination of aquatic species, what steps can a cottager take? "There are no guidelines, no document you can turn to that says 'Under these conditions, do this,' " explains Ken Nicholls, supervisor of the aquatic-plant unit of the MOE's water-resources branch in Toronto. The key, he says, is keeping the water useful for everyone: swimmers, boaters, plants and fish. And the way to achieve this is by "getting rid of some plants in just a limited area."

Clear out only the channels you absolutely need for swimming and boating, he explains. "Cutting zigzag channels and opening up little pockets also really enhances fish habitat. Any angler will tell you the best place to catch largemouth bass is along the edge of a weed bed." By the way, any Ontario cottager planning to do something about weeds needs to get permission from the district office of the MNR first: it's against the law to harmfully alter, disrupt or destroy fish habitat, and aquatic plants are a component of fish habitat.

Nicholls' branch most often advocates mechanical removal rather than chemicals. As the plants are killed by waterborne herbicides, they die and sink to the bottom, where they become food for the next crop. Meanwhile, both the chemicals and the decaying plants deplete the water's dissolved oxygen, which will kill fish that can't escape to an untreated part of the lake.

Although herbicides are not an ideal solution, in some circumstances, they seem to be the only answer. For example, the Trent-Severn Waterway (TSW), which links Lake Ontario to Georgian Bay, is kept clear of weeds with ministry-approved chemicals. "Quite frankly, it's very successful if done at a certain time," says John Lewis, the waterway's superintendent. He points out that the TSW guarantees boaters a depth of at least six feet in the waterway, and without chemicals, there's no practical way to do it. (The chemicals are not applied throughout the whole system but only in specific navigation channels where weeds are a problem.)

Like others who know Ontario's lakes, Lewis says that weeds run in cycles and every lake is a little different, depending on its water temperature, nutrient supply and sediment. Northern lakes on the Canadian Shield suffer less from weeds but more from acid rain, he says. In fact, use of herbicides has been prohibited by the MNR in the Algonquin region, as the aquatic plants there are essential to the lakes' ecological balance. Southern lakes may have a limestone base that buffers them against acid rain, but they also have heavy development that encourages more weeds. And what some cottagers consider "the attack of the weeds" may be simply part of the natural ageing process of their lake. "Cottagers never like to hear this, but in some areas, it's a natural phenomenon where the lake is filling in from the bottom. It may take 50, 75 or even 100 years," says Lewis, but in time, those lakes will become marsh and perhaps even dry land. "All lakes have weeds, and they're there for a reason," says Patrick Ferris, a former lake planner with the MNR. "If you're living on an older lake, you can't suddenly change it back to a young, pristine condition. The solution is to learn to accept it."

Acknowledging that their problem is part of an ecological cycle is small consolation to cottagers such as those in the shallow inlets off Stony Lake. Their channels were first dredged 20 years ago and now seem to be reverting to their original swampy condition. Six to eight inches of decaying plants litter the bottom, and by midsummer, the weeds are so thick that they prevent swimmers and boaters from getting to the lake. "And people spend hours scooping weeds and algae out of their water," says Jo-Anne Darnbrough, president of the local Juniper Point Cottage Owners' Association.

So every year, her association applies to the MOE for a "multiple-property water-extermination permit." And every June around Father's Day, volunteers post warning signs before dumping the herbicide Reglone A (diquat) into the waters of each inlet. Cottagers then wait 24 to 48 hours after treatment before swimming in or drinking from the lake. Darnbrough, who works as a hospital administrator, says nobody likes the idea, but they have no other choice. "I'm not too pleased about this

chemical going into the bay," she says, "but we want to have usable water in our little inlet."

Darnbrough's group tried another method as well last summer: it hired Gord Harse's Aquamate to bring in a huge mechanical weed harvester. For a group rate of $2,000, Aquamate used one of the dozen such rigs in the country to pull up and truck away weeds from four inlets and two bays. The harvester, which looks something like a combine, didn't clear the entire lake bottom but, rather, cut channels (the widest about 20 feet) to provide access for boats. Harse did a good job clearing the channels, says Darnbrough, although the cottagers plan to see how bad the weeds get this year before calling him back.

Harse prides himself on his firm's environmental awareness — he even steam-cleans his equipment after each job — and says he won't harvest plants that belong in a lake, no matter how much money he's offered. But there's a practical side to his position: the MNR can confiscate his $250,000 worth of equipment if he removes the wrong plants from the wrong places.

Other cottagers take things into their own hands. Some drag logs, chains or bedsprings along the lake bottom to chew up their enemies. But this can do more harm than good: the floating plant fragments left behind simply sink to the bottom and reroot, or they decay and fertilize the next crop.

Another approach entails using an underwater version of a lawn mower to cut down weeds in their own beds. New York's Waterside Products reports selling "hundreds" of its $350 (U.S.) models into Canada since they went on sale last summer. The same rule applies to the pieces, though, and it's often a case of the more you mow, the more you have to mow.

Then there's the possibility of putting down plastic sheets and covering them with sand to suffocate the weeds. Most accounts say it's hardly worth the time

and expense; within a couple of summers, holes usually poke through the plastic, while weeds once more take root on top of it.

In the end, the most sensible advice is probably to handpick weeds by their roots if you can or to use a mechanical cutter or harvester of some sort. But make absolutely certain to remove all the pieces (the natural spot to discard the weeds you remove is on your compost heap), and clear just the channels that you absolutely have to have for boating and swimming.

Biological agents may offer a long-term option for weed control: finding some organism that eats the weeds, then introducing it into problem lakes. Several insects and snails, for instance, have been seen feeding voraciously on Eurasian milfoil, but researchers investigating this area are cautious about predicting any breakthroughs. There is always the risk that any outside species brought into a new area can have unpredictable results.

Remember that many cottage activities encourage the growth of weeds; for instance, cottagers who fertilize their lawns, use high-phosphate dishwashing detergents or don't replace worn-out septic systems are aiding aquatic-plant growth. So, too, are boaters who dump greywater overboard. These sources all add phosphorus, a plant nutrient, to the lake. Runoff from farms, construction sites and logging operations is also a terrible offender. According to Ferris, cottagers should try to prevent such pollution from going into the lake. This will help control the weed problem, he says, or at least keep it from getting any worse than it already is.

But, adds Ken Nicholls, "at some point, there just isn't anything left to do. Once you've got them, it's almost impossible to get rid of them for good." Learning to live and let live is probably the best answer.

Originally published in Cottage Life *magazine (Toronto).*

Boating

A short guide to outboard motors for boats

Making Wise Use of Power

by Derek Stevenson

"There is nothing," wrote Kenneth Grahame in his popular children's novel *The Wind in the Willows*, "absolutely *nothing* in all this world is half so much worth doing as simply messing about in boats." Millions of Canadians would agree. With oceans on three sides of the country and thousands of miles of inland lakes, rivers and streams, we're among the most avid boaters in the world. This summer, more than half of us will be involved in some kind of pleasure boating.

A good deal of that "messing about" will be done in boats fitted with small outboard motors. Small outboards offer boaters a number of advantages. They provide plenty of power. You can propel a large boat at slow "trolling" speeds for fishing, scoot along at a respectable speed in a small boat, even water-ski under the right conditions. Yet they're portable and easy to operate. And at prices from about $700 to $3,000, these light outboard motors are relatively affordable. There are also a lot of them to choose from. We surveyed 138 models, from 1.2 to 15 horsepower (hp).

The first thing to decide when you are shopping for an outboard is the kind of power you need. Outboard motors are measured in horsepower, rated by the power that is produced by the engine at full throttle. Although motors of up to 300 hp are available, we confined our survey to more modest units of 15 hp or less, probably the most popular category among casual boaters. Motors in this range are suitable for small boats such as rowboats, canoes and inflatables. They are also ideal as backup propulsion for small sailboats or as trolling motors for fishing boats whose large motors may be difficult to control at slow speeds.

But power has its price — the more powerful motors are more expensive. The average suggested list price in Canada for a 5-hp motor is about $1,200. Doubling the horsepower almost doubles the price: 10-hp motors sell for around $2,100, while a 15-hp unit will set you back about $2,400.

Don't clamp on the most powerful motor you can afford, however. The motor has to match the boat, and a too-powerful motor is dangerous — the boat could be swamped by its own wake if the engine is suddenly shut off. To avoid giving your boat more kick than it can handle, consult your dealer or check the boat for a plate indicating the maximum horsepower recommended by the manufacturer. In Canada, boats that are designed for motors over 10 hp and are under 16 feet in length are required to have such plates. If your motor exceeds 10 hp, you'll also need a small-craft licence for your boat (see "Learning to Stay Afloat," page 110).

On the other hand, don't worry if you can't afford all the power you crave. Minor differences in power ratings are not always significant. And because different manufacturers measure power output in slightly different ways — at the propeller rather than the crankshaft, for example — their ratings are not always directly comparable.

The power rating will tell you how a motor operates at full throttle but not necessarily how it performs at lower speeds — that is, at fewer revolutions per minute (rpm). When you throttle back the motor to slow down, the engine's power output will decrease. How much it declines depends on the design of the engine: one motor that produces 9.9 hp at 5,500 rpm might produce 5 hp at 2,000 rpm; another might deliver only 2 hp at that speed and might stall or be unable to move your boat. A motor with similar power ratings but with a larger displacement (the volume of the cylinders in the engine) generally provides more power at lower rpm.

An engine's power output depends not only on its speed in rpm but also on the torque, or turning force, it generates. In theory, if two outboards have similar power ratings but one operates at a lower rpm range, the outboard with the slower engine will produce more torque. In practice, most outboard motors with similar power ratings operate at about the same rpm range, so the torque they produce is similar.

Within the same rpm range, however, a motor with slightly more torque can propel a boat faster and push a heavier load. If your boat is small and light, you are likely to be able to move fast. A 9.9-hp motor, for example, can drive a 14-foot boat at speeds of up to 15 miles per hour — a respectable clip for a small, open craft. With a lightweight skier and boat, the larger models in our survey may even allow you to water-ski. Smaller outboards won't get larger boats up to that kind of speed. But they can provide the slow and steady push needed to move, say, a heavy fishing boat at trolling speeds.

Fine-tuning an outboard motor's thrust to suit your boat is as simple as changing the propeller, or prop. Props are classified by the diameter of their blades and by their "pitch" — the distance in inches that one rotation of the propeller would move the boat under ideal conditions. In theory, a high-pitched prop will mean a faster boat, because the boat will move that much farther ahead every time the prop completes one revolution.

That doesn't mean attaching a high-pitched prop will turn any boat into a speedboat. The propeller must be matched to both the motor and the boat to allow the engine to run properly. If a high-pitched prop is used with a very large boat, for example, the inertia of the heavy load will cause resistance to the prop's pushing efforts. That can overload the motor, causing overheating and carbon deposits in its cylinders. A low-pitched prop, which will propel the boat more slowly but cause less strain on the motor, should be used with a larger boat.

Combining a low-pitched prop, a high-powered motor and a lightweight boat isn't a good idea, either. The propeller will experience little or no resistance, causing the engine to "race" or to operate at excessive rpm. That can lead

Budget alone should not dictate the size of outboard motor a family buys; boats and motors must be carefully matched to avoid dangerous pairings.

to the problem of increased engine wear. In most cases, the propeller supplied with your motor will be suitable for most boats; check with your dealer if you aren't sure.

A motor's performance can also be affected by its combustion method. Most of the motors we surveyed had two-stroke engines, similar to those in some gas-powered lawn mowers. In a two-stroke engine, fuel is ignited in the engine cylinders with every stroke of the piston. In a four-stroke engine,

found in Honda motors and some Yamaha models, ignition takes place with every other stroke. Two-stroke engines are generally lighter and easier to maintain and repair. Four-stroke engines are more complicated but more fuel-efficient and may be more powerful at low speeds.

Engines of either type may have one or two engine cylinders. Two-cylinder engines are usually heavier — something to consider if you'll have to carry the motor — but run more smoothly

Small outboard motors can provide good fuel economy, reasonable power and reliability; consumption is usually a half-litre per horsepower per hour.

the gasoline, saving boaters the trouble of premixing fuel.

Suzuki goes a step further; rather than using a constant oil-gas mixture, its oil-injection system varies the amount according to the speed of the engine, adding less oil when the engine is idling but more when it's running at full throttle. It's a standard feature on a few models. Similar variable-injection systems are available on larger motors from other manufacturers.

Finding fuel for a hungry outboard shouldn't be a problem: most motors are happy with a diet of regular-grade leaded or unleaded gasoline. The smallest have a built-in (integral) fuel tank of three litres or less. Larger motors have a separate fuel tank. That keeps the motor's size and weight down and makes for more convenient fill-ups, because you can simply bring the tank to the pump. Look for a tank with a long hose that can be stowed in the front of the boat, under a seat or somewhere else out of the way.

Small outboards don't have a big appetite for fuel. The tiny integral tanks will hold enough to keep you going for two or three hours at medium speed; slightly larger ones should provide for a day's trolling plus transportation to and from the fishing grounds. Even going flat out, most outboards consume less than a half-litre of gasoline per horsepower per hour. Still, it's a good idea to have extra fuel along just in case.

Alternatives to gasoline-run motors are available, although they're much less common. You can get a motor that runs on kerosene, paraffin or diesel fuel, for example. Like diesel cars, these outboards tend to be noisier and dirtier than conventional gas-powered models, but they do offer better fuel economy. Another alternative, at least for trolling, is the electric outboard. These battery-powered mini-motors don't have the speed or the power of a gasoline motor, but they're quiet, reliable and easy to control at low speeds.

Starting your outboard motor may seem like starting a lawn mower. The simplest outboard motors have manual starters; to get them going, you pull once or twice on the starting rope. Electric-start

and produce less vibration. That may be important for anglers, since small, light boats vibrate easily, causing loose objects to rattle inside the boat and scare the fish.

You will need specially formulated marine engine oils for both two- and four-stroke engines. Unlike the latter type, two-strokers don't have a separate oil reservoir, or sump. That means you'll have to premix the oil with the fuel. The oil is then circulated and

burned with the gasoline. As a result, spark plugs tend to foul more quickly in two-stroke engines than in four-strokers, and their exhaust is often dirtier. Motors that use less oil in the mixture are usually cleaner operating motors and are much more convenient.

To save you the trouble of premixing, some manufacturers offer oil injection as an extra-cost option for their two-stroke motors. A small oil reservoir built into the fuel tank releases oil into motors, like cars, can get you on your way with the turn of a key. That convenience will add about $400 to the cost of the motor, however. You'll also need to buy a battery, which will be just one more thing to carry to and from the boat. Fortunately, a dead battery won't necessarily leave you stranded, since most electric-start models can also still be started manually.

The battery is charged by an alternator. Since batteries can also be used to power lights or electronic equipment (depth finders, for example), an alternator is often available as an option on manual-start motors. Some motors may also have a lighting or charging coil, which provides similar power as long as the engine is running.

Keeping the engine running smoothly is the job of the ignition system. Most motors under 3 hp have magneto ignition. As in conventional automobile ignition, the electric current that goes to the spark plugs is controlled by points

that open and close mechanically. The points require occasional servicing and replacement and may be troublesome if they or the spark plugs are dirty.

The more sophisticated motors have transistor or capacitor discharge (CD) ignition. Both types are usually more reliable, because there are no moving parts and they deliver a higher voltage, making even cold, oily spark plugs more likely to fire. Plugs may also last longer and require less maintenance. If these types of ignition do break down, however, they will require a dealer's help to repair.

Before you choose a motor, you'd better measure your boat. For efficient propulsion, the shaft, or leg, of the motor should put the motor's propeller below the boat into a clear flow of water. Most motors above 4 hp are available in at least two sizes: a regular shaft length, usually 15 inches, and a longer version (20 inches) for deeper-hulled boats. Special "sail" versions of

some motors are also available; these have extra-long shafts to fit sailboats, which have deeper keels.

Propulsion is also more efficient if you can adjust the trim of the motor, making minor changes to its angle in the water and thus raising or lowering the bow of the boat. That can help you compensate for a heavy load at one end or make it easier to plane. Larger, heavier units have more power-trim mechanisms that can be operated with the touch of a button, but these lightweight motors don't need them. All you need to do is release the locking mechanism — usually a rod that fits into a slot — and push up or down on the tiller handle until you achieve the desired angle.

The motor should also be easy to tilt so that it can be lifted out of the water for a check of the propeller or to reduce drag when sailing. Some motors have one or more special "shallow water drive" tilt positions. That holds the propeller just under the surface of the

Preserving the cry of the wild

Not everyone who enjoys the great outdoors is a fan of outboard motors. Lakeside cottagers sometimes complain of the noise from high-powered motors. And any boat owner is familiar with the film of oil that often floats on the water around a busy marina.

The boating industry argues that boating's environmental effects are minimal. For example, outboard motors are designed to reduce noise pollution. According to one industry representative, smaller outboards should (from shore) be barely audible over the slap of the waves. And because the outboards' fuel consumption is so low, industry people say emissions of pollutants in the motors' exhaust should be low as well.

Still, one Toronto company thinks it's come up with an environment-friendly

alternative: an engine that's powered by compressed carbon dioxide. Experts we talked to said the new engine could help reduce pollution to some extent, but they doubted it would be practical for widespread use.

The Viro was developed by Environmarine Corporation. A 9.9-hp version of the engine is available in Canada and the United States for about $2,500.

The motor's power comes from the energy released by the escaping carbon dioxide, rather like a balloon that's inflated and then released. Its only emission is carbon dioxide.

Critics point out that the gas is a major contributor to the greenhouse effect believed to be causing a gradual increase in temperature around the world. However, the Viro's inventors claim the motor won't add to the problem. The carbon dioxide it uses, a by-product of industrial processes such as fertilizer manufacturing, would be released into the atmosphere anyway. And if it's used instead of gasoline-

burning engines, which also produce carbon dioxide as a by-product, the Viro may actually prevent more of the gas from being generated.

Kai Millyard, policy director for Friends of the Earth, an environmental research and lobby group, said the engine makes sense if it can reduce the use of fossil fuels such as gasoline. François Lavallee, a program engineer with Environment Canada, agreed. But Lavallee noted the Viro's use would be limited by the amount of carbon dioxide available. Carbon dioxide is plentiful now but could become less so if companies take the desirable step of limiting their emission levels to stave off the greenhouse effect.

And producing the energy required to pressurize the engine's carbon-dioxide "fuel" may not prove to be very environment-friendly. Millyard noted that the electricity required could come from coal-fired plants, whose emissions produce acid rain, or from nuclear generators, which produce nuclear waste.

water, keeping it away from weeds, sandbars or rocks while still providing a certain amount of thrust.

If underwater obstacles do damage the propeller, it should be replaced. A damaged prop will reduce your speed and increase your fuel consumption. Most motors are designed to protect the propeller from minor impacts, using a special hub that absorbs the shock or lets the propeller slip. The propeller on a motor under 5 hp is usually protected by a shear pin that breaks on impact. Once that happens, the prop won't turn until the pin has been replaced. That's easy but a nuisance if it has to be done too often.

A damaged prop is not difficult to replace. Replacement propellers are available in a variety of sizes and materials. Generally, the more powerful the outboard, the more types of replacement props available. The propeller supplied with the motor is usually aluminum or, in the case of the smaller motors, plastic. Both types are inexpensive, but they are often easy to damage. Stainless-steel propellers, on the other hand, are more durable but also considerably more expensive.

Most engines of 5 hp or more can be started and operated in neutral. That allows you to idle without shutting off the engine. It also makes for safer starts: a motor that starts in gear could take off suddenly, leaving you in the drink. Many motors won't let you start in any gear but neutral. Most outboards with neutral also have a reverse gear. Those without can be rotated as much as 360 degrees, allowing you to back up by simply pivoting the motor half-way around.

Whatever direction you're travelling in, you'll want the motor's controls within easy reach. The starting and throttle controls for most motors are located on the top or the front of the engine or on the tiller handle, allowing you to operate the motor with one hand. Remote controls that can be installed at the front of the boat are available for many of these outboards. That convenience will cost you extra, of course; remote-control Nissans, for example, are $50 to $140 more expensive than their regular counterparts.

Normally, you have to hold the throttle control open to keep the engine running, just as you keep your foot on the gas pedal of your car. If you're fishing, however, you may want to have both hands free, yet keep the boat moving slowly forward. That takes an idle-stop or idle-speed control, which keeps the engine running at a selected speed — a handy feature. (Consider it the marine equivalent of cruise control.) Most of the larger engines have one.

Most outboards have a stop button to shut off the engine in a hurry. An emergency engine cutoff lanyard is a safety feature: this cord (which you can clip to your belt) connects you to the motor and kills the engine if you fall out of the boat.

If you plan to carry the motor up rocky slopes or load it into your car, consider its weight. Motors can range from a 5 hp at 40 pounds to a 15 hp at 90 pounds. Long-shaft motors generally weigh a couple of pounds more than the regular models; electric starting may add an additional two pounds; and don't forget the weight of the fuel. Be sure to lift a few engines in the store to check their balance and the comfort of the handle. If you leave your motor on the boat, be sure it is locked to the craft. If it's left out in the open, a cover to protect the engine from the weather may also be a good idea.

Most outboards are used for about 100 hours a year. At that rate, a motor should last at least as long as a car. The Japanese-made outboard motors — Honda, Nissan, Suzuki and Yamaha — come with two-year warranties; the rest usually are covered for one year. All include parts and labour. Mercury and Mariner motors are also protected against corrosion for three years; the manufacturer of both Evinrude and Johnson motors offers an optional two-year extended warranty.

The best outboard motor for you will depend on your boat and what you use it for. If your needs are purely utilitarian — shuttling people and supplies to and from an island cottage, for example — one of the simpler, smaller motors may be the perfect one for you. Pleasure boaters and fisherfolk, on the other hand, may want something larger and fancier. Hopefully, the features we have described should make the choice much easier.

Adapted from a report in Canadian Consumer *magazine (Ottawa).*

Learning to stay afloat

You've got your boat, you've got your motor. What more do you need? For a start, perhaps a licence.

In Canada, boats powered by motors of more than 10 hp are required to have a small-craft licence. That shouldn't be a big factor in your choice of motors, however. The licences are free and available on request from Revenue Canada Customs and Excise offices (check under "Customs" in the blue pages of your phone book). Once you have a licence, your only obligations are to paint the licence number on the hull of the boat and to notify Revenue Canada of any change in ownership. You're also required to carry some basic safety equipment such as life jackets or personal flotation devices.

A basic knowledge of the rules of safe boating wouldn't hurt, either. The Canadian Coast Guard's *Safe Boating Guide* is available free from Coast Guard and Transport Canada offices. For information on boating and water-safety courses, contact your local office of the Canadian Red Cross or the Canadian Power and Sail Squadrons, a national volunteer organization. You can write to them at 26 Golden Gate Court, Scarborough, Ontario M1P 3A5. Both organizations offer courses across Canada.

A bit of basic outboard-motor maintenance goes a long way

Achieving the One-Pull Start

by Max Burns

Ted MacDonald stands tall and proud on the dock, his short wisps of thinning grey hair framing a face tailored by time and weather. For 42 years, outboards have been an integral part of his life and livelihood. In the summer of 1946, he and his British bride Gwen opened Whip-Poor-Will Lodge for business. It was a 28-mile boat ride from Port Loring to their isolated rocky island on Dollars Lake, about 25 miles southwest of Lake Nipissing in Ontario. MacDonald boasted three cedar-strip boats, each powered by a 5-horsepower Viking. Electricity, telephones and showers were yet to come. Now a new road cuts the water ride down to about two miles, and the lodge has all the amenities of a city hotel except traffic noise — plus 18 boats, 24 motors and a son-in-law, Bruce Davies, to help keep the works running. For MacDonald and Davies, proper outboard care and maintenance are second nature.

The technology hidden beneath the cover of a modern outboard tends to come in hermetically sealed modules of silicon mystery: unfathomable, sometimes unrepairable yet, as MacDonald and Davies both point out, amazingly reliable. Today's outboards, especially the 7½-to-30-horsepower workhorse varieties, are abuser-friendly. If an engine is not running right in May, then odds are the owner did not have the necessary work done before storage last fall or before putting it in the water this spring. "If you're planning on keeping it for a long time, read the owner's manual for the proper storage procedure," advises Davies. As far as midseason maintenance goes, there is very little to do — which means that what little there is usually gets neglected.

The best defence against outboard failure is a good marine dealer. Because you depend on your outboard to get you safely back to shore, a dealer's ability with a wrench is far more important than his or her ability with a calculator. When engine problems transcend basic tools to the digital world of electronic instruments, even the pros at Whip-Poor-Will Lodge take their outboards to a trusted dealer. Invest the time to seek out the best in your area — there is no better form of preventive maintenance.

Another often-overlooked aid to happy boating is the owner's manual, a quarter-pounder of dull facts garnished with an overdose of litigation-lawyer-inspired warnings. Fuel grades, engine and gearcase oil types and quantities, storage procedures, spark-plug gaps — the manual holds a wealth of information for your particular machine. Be a nonconformist and read it very carefully, at least once.

Contrary to brochure hyperbole, most outboards do have a lot in common. Esoteric devices with impressive names such as Thunderbust Ignition and Nasalburst Fuel Injection sound great and may have some impact on engine performance, but the average owner need not be concerned about the function of these gizmos beyond keeping the corresponding decals on the engine cover clean. And regardless of your outboard's brand or cover décor, whether it's got a fuel-injection system or a plain old carburetor, it will benefit from a little midseason attention.

Before delving into this hour or two of cool drinks and grease, a few owner-manual-style warnings are necessary. Whenever you work on engines, you are in close proximity to acids and flammable fluids. Exercise reasonable caution when handling them: do not smoke, carry an Olympic torch or allow any other form of open flame within the vicinity.

None of what needs to be done in the way of midseason maintenance is difficult, but if you feel intimidated by the prospect of working on your own motor, stick with the cool drinks and leave the grease part for your dealer, using the following as a guide for when to see him again.

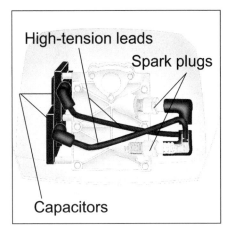

High-tension leads
Spark plugs
Capacitors

Always disconnect the high-tension leads (above) before working on the motor or removing the spark plugs.

"When you take a motor off a boat," warns Davies, "do not allow the bottom end to come up higher than the head. Any water in the exhaust system will very likely run down into the cylinder."

"It could rust your bearings," adds MacDonald, "and then that's the end of your motor. This is very important, because at some point or other, cottagers are going to take the motor off and hoist it up to put it into their trunk, and the first thing you know, the motor's no good." So always remember to keep the propeller end down when carrying your motor.

When parking or storing your outboard, keep in mind that if you do cover it up (a practice customarily indulged in only by the fanatics), no motor enjoys being tucked under plastic, even for the night. The condensation that results can cause component damage; to prevent this, cover your motor with something that breathes, like canvas.

The first item on a midseason checkup, if your boat is equipped with a battery, is to check fluid levels and top up if necessary, using only distilled water. The fluid should just cover the lead plates inside. Spills are best tended to with a sprinkling of baking soda, which neutralizes the battery acid. Remove any corrosion on the battery terminals with a stiff wire brush, then coat the terminals with a light film of grease or petroleum jelly.

Using a water-resistant grease or a

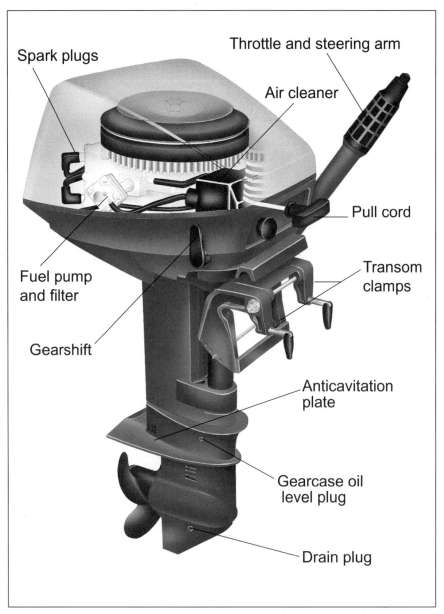

Spark plugs
Throttle and steering arm
Air cleaner
Pull cord
Fuel pump and filter
Gearshift
Transom clamps
Anticavitation plate
Gearcase oil level plug
Drain plug

Although boaters need not become mechanics, they should at least be familiar with the basic components of an outboard motor and learn a few maintenance routines. Help is often some distance away when it's needed.

shot of anticorrosive oil for hard-to-reach places, lubricate the engine-cover lever, throttle-gearshift arm, throttle linkages, throttle-handle stopper, transom-clamp screws, tilt-angle adjusting rod and tilt mechanism. Use a grease gun on any grease nipples.

A simple check can alert you to a worn propeller-shaft seal. The majority of motors have a gearcase drain plug located just below the propeller shaft and a level plug located above it, next to the anticavitation plate. After the motor has been sitting idle for at least a

night, undo the lower plug. Any water in the case will usually have settled to the bottom and will readily drain out. Quickly replace the lower plug as soon as the oil starts to seep out. The presence of water points to a worn propeller-shaft seal, which should be replaced immediately to prevent expensive gearcase damage. Special tools are sometimes required for this task, which relegates it to a function best performed by your dealer.

MacDonald recommends performing this check about once every month. "If there's any water in it, definitely have it looked at." Davies adds, "If the oil is milky-coloured, then it has emulsified with the water, which probably means there is a slow leak. Again, it should be resealed."

If no water is present, go on to check the gearcase oil level — a check that need only be done once during the average season. Remove the upper plug. The oil should barely trickle out of the hole. If it does not, top it up. You will need the type of oil specified for your make and model of outboard (see your owner's manual or ask your dealer). Adding oil to the gearcase can be a messy process. The only way I know to keep your hands clean is to talk someone else into doing the job for you. Failing that, the following method is the least of all slimy evils.

Loosen the drain plug, and with a thumb pressed over the level plug hole, remove the drain plug, quickly inserting the oil container's nozzle tightly into the hole. Your thumb's contribution slows the oil's tendency to run out the bottom hole. Uncover the level hole, and gently squeeze the oil tube until you see that trickle dribbling out from the level hole up top. Cover the level hole with your thumb again, squeeze just a tiny bit more oil in, then zip out the nozzle and quickly screw in the bottom drain plug (remembering to replace the gasket as well). Retrieve your thumb, let any excess oil drain out the level hole and then screw in its plug. It is time to wipe your hands and have a cool drink.

If your outboard is pre-'70s vintage, there could be a plethora of ignition and carburetor adjustments to attend to, but if the motor is that old, you likely are already well aware of what needs to be done, or it would not have got you this far. If you have recently bought the old beast, invest in a comprehensive repair manual of the type published by Chilton, Clymer or the manufacturer, plus a good set of tools. You will inevitably need a greater quantity of cool drinks too.

Virtually all gasoline-powered outboards are now water-cooled. Periodic *(continued on page 115)*

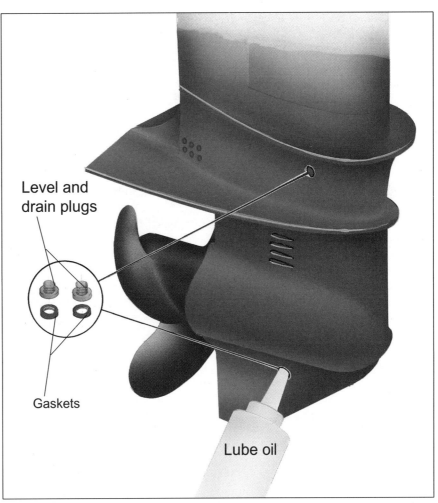

Level and drain plugs

Gaskets

Lube oil

It is wise to check for water in the gearcase about once a month; open the lower drain plug to see if any water escapes before the oil starts to flow out.

On-board tools

At the very minimum, a tool kit for your boat should contain:
- ☐ spark-plug wrench
- ☐ adjustable wrench
- ☐ insulated pliers
- ☐ variety pack of screwdrivers
- ☐ waterproof flashlight
- ☐ electrical tape
- ☐ wire
- ☐ duct tape

The wire is dandy for temporarily securing loose bits, while the duct tape is good for silencing nagging advisers stranded out on the lake with you.

On-board spares should include:
- ☐ 1 spark plug for each cylinder
- ☐ shear pins (unless your propeller is of the rubber-bush type)
- ☐ cotter pins
- ☐ fuses of the correct type and amperage (if your motor has fuses)
- ☐ rope (for emergency starting if the electric starter should fail)
- ☐ 2 oars or paddles (when all else fails)

The oars or paddles are part of the minimum on-board equipment required by the Canadian Coast Guard. Also required on pleasure craft up to 18 feet are one approved life jacket, personal flotation device or life-saving cushion for each person on board; one hand-held bailer or manual pump; and some type of sound-signalling device. You might also want to have an anchor.

Mid-trip troubleshooting

When I asked Davies what he does when far from the lodge and his outboard fails him, MacDonald quickly answered, "He calls me on the CB."

A mechanical breakdown at sea (or lake) need not be accompanied by a nervous breakdown. Fortunately, most of what will go wrong is reasonably basic — sometimes embarrassingly so once you've been towed back to the cottage dock. Mechanical aptitude is not a prerequisite here, as long as the captain of the ship is properly prepared.

If the engine was purring along fine prior to the problem, then odds are very good some minor gremlin lies at the root of the power failure. The secret of a successful diagnosis is to follow through a logical sequence of potential spanners in the works.

Does the motor fail to turn over? If you've got an electric start, check the battery terminals (sometimes giving them a light tap helps dislodge corrosion) and connections to the engine. For both electric and pull starts, check that the propeller is free of restrictions, such as weeds, rocks and anchor rope. Is the fuse blown?

Out of Gas

Is there fuel in the tank? If it's equipped with a vent valve or fuel tap, are they in the "on" position? Is the fuel pumped up, using the squeeze bulb? If the motor or fuel line is equipped with a fuel filter (see owner's manual), check to see if it is clogged. There is usually one fuel filter in the tank and another in or before the fuel pump. Sometimes a screen-type filter in the tank can be unscrewed and blown out, but in many cases, as Davies points out, the ones on the motor are "a little involved to get at." The paper variety has to be replaced.

Is the fuel line pinched by the tank or some other heavy object? Is the choke lever in the correct position for engine and ambient temperature? Is the shift lever in neutral? (This can be particularly embarrassing.)

If the stubborn engine still refuses to start, it could be suffering from not enough spark or too much fuel. Assuming the engine does not reek of raw gas, indicating that it is flooded by an overdose of fuel, a mechanic's next step would be to test the plugs for a healthy spark, a task the novice should bypass. Modern outboard ignition systems can self-destruct if not properly grounded. They contain enough voltage to spark a parliamentary backbencher into action, and they often are beyond simple repair. But an easy response to either flooding or fouling is to replace the spark plug(s) with the new one(s) from your spare kit.

Disconnect the high-tension lead from each plug, wipe all grease and oil away from the base of the plug, and then remove the plug. By far the best tool for this job is a plug wrench of the correct size, as the porcelain portion of the spark plug can be quite fragile and of little value broken. Thread the new plug in, tightening it by hand, and then give it a final one-eighth to one-quarter twist home with the plug wrench.

If you have systematically gone through these steps and your outboard still refuses to cooperate, it is time to admit defeat and hand out the rations and paddles.

Sometimes, of course, the outboard doesn't completely die. "Missing" is a term used to describe an engine's intermittent inability to ignite the fuel-air mixture. The engine still runs, but not without sputtering and coughing. Tracing the cause of this dilemma can be an extremely frustrating experience, with umpteen different suspect gremlins to investigate. However, the most common fault is a fouled or worn spark plug — particularly if the sputtering is isolated to one cylinder. The easy solution, once again, is to replace the plug.

If that does not cure the problem, sputter along to your dealer.

Fortunately, some causes of breakdown are going the way of the dinosaur — snapped pull cords, for instance. Actually, the cords were never really at fault, except that they were sometimes attached to motors born with a noncommittal attitude toward starting. "People got frustrated when they were trying to start them, and they'd stand up and pull harder and harder," recalls Davies. "The next thing they'd know, the cord had come out in their hands."

Easier Starts

Times have changed with the advent of electronic ignition and lean fuel mixtures. "They start a lot better. You can count on one hand the number of cords we now have pulled out in a season, whereas 10 years back, we'd have one a week. Unless you're talking about motors of 40 horsepower or larger (electric-start motors usually have provision for a cord to be attached to the flywheel up top), there's nothing you can do. It's all enclosed."

The age-old worry of getting the right fuel-to-oil ratio is another problem slowly being consigned to history as a result of the oil-injection and automatic-mix systems in new outboards. But there are still owners who have to cope with who put what and how much into the tank when. Because so little oil is added to the gasoline, it is virtually impossible to tell by looking just how much, if any, oil is in your tank. The engine's behaviour, though, will let you know soon enough.

"If you're over on your oil, the engine is going to smoke; if you're under, it will likely seize. So if you're uncertain," Davies suggests, "add some more oil. The worst that could happen is you'll have to replace your plugs a little sooner." Of course, the best policy of all is not to guess but to mix it right the first time, following the manufacturer's recommendations in your owner's guide.

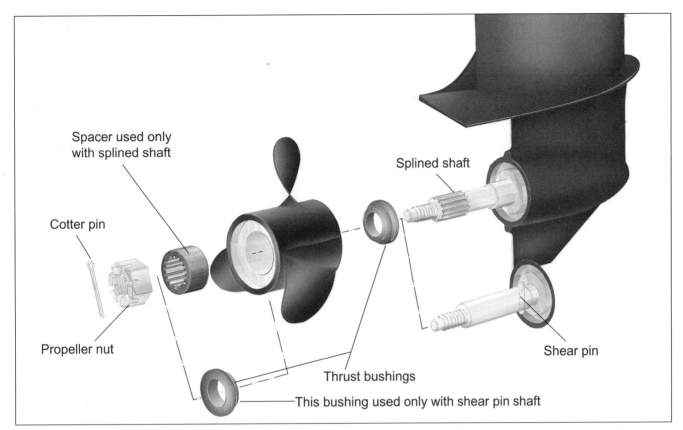

Spacer used only
with splined shaft

Splined shaft

Cotter pin

Propeller nut

Shear pin

Thrust bushings

This bushing used only with shear pin shaft

A monthly inspection and cleanup of the propeller will assure smooth running. After removing fishing line and weed tangles, check the prop for nicks and bends.

checks while the motor is running to ensure the water exits freely from the cooling system could catch a motor meltdown before it begins. Every outboard has a hole in its leg to allow the water to flow out, appropriately called the telltale and most often found just beneath the head. If no water flow is evident, shut the motor off and check to ensure the water inlet port (usually located down near the propeller) is not clogged with debris. If the telltale continues to report dry when running, shut the motor down again and head for your dealer. Operating a motor without a functioning cooling system will cause the motor to seize, which can put a severe strain on your vacation, not to mention your bank account. (For the same reason, never run a water-cooled motor out of water.)

A regular check of your fuel connections and their ubiquitous O-rings is good preventive maintenance, since they are some of the weak links in the system. Damaged O-rings can allow the engine to suck in air instead of fuel

through the lines, creating a starvation crisis and stranding boaters. (If the engine starts, then immediately stops, it is likely starving for fuel.) "If the O-rings are chipped around the inside edge, replace them; otherwise, they're probably all right," advises MacDonald. "The end that gets plugged into the motor all the time gets the greatest wear." O-ring replacement varies from outboard to outboard, each boasting a better system than the other brands, so consult your owner's manual. Replacement kits are sometimes available, but it is often much easier to pass the job to your dealer.

One of the most abused and neglected parts of the outboard is the propeller. "Every one of our props is banged up," claims MacDonald. "They're all carved up at least a little bit, but we don't completely replace them unless they're banged up badly." Not only will an out-of-balance propeller cut performance and increase fuel consumption, but it will also damage the prop-shaft seal, letting water seep in. Neglect it, and

"you'll chew the gears and shaft all up and seize up everything in there," a calamity that could cost you close to a thousand dollars, warns MacDonald.

Reliable outboards are obviously not the only product of modern technology. There is also monofilament fishing line, for instance — great stuff if you are reeling in an award-winning pickerel but a curse for prop-shaft seals. According to MacDonald, it is so tough that it can tear seals and even gouge the shaft, a silent menace nearly impossible to detect when tangled around the shaft. Although propellers are removed and checked more than once a week at his lodge, once a month should do the trick for the average cottage owner. "If you're out trolling and you get a line in the propeller, you can carry on for the day. But when you get home, you should definitely take the propeller off and take out any line in there. For that, you need a pair of pliers and a wrench."

Before you begin, disconnect the high-tension leads from the spark plugs — the big thick wires, usually black, with insulating caps at the plug end — since rotating the propeller could accidentally start the motor. With the pliers, pull out the cotter pin at the end of the shaft, undo the nut or cone, and slide the propeller off. There may also be a washer in there. Getting the propeller off is a piece of cake — as long as you don't drop any of the pieces into the lake. Often a spark-plug wrench will fit the prop-shaft nut; if it doesn't, an owner's manual is probably the fastest way to find out what will.

After extracting the fishing line from the outboard, examine the propeller for nicks and scrapes. If they're small, it's wise to clean them up with a file, being careful not to alter the original taper of the edges. Using water-resistant grease, lubricate the prop shaft before replacing the propeller, and if the cotter pin has had the biscuit, use a new one. Pins are less expensive than lost propellers. The same propeller removal and replacement technique applies if you are replacing a shear pin.

Davies starts to laugh, calling out to MacDonald, "Remember the time when Gerry took your new Yamaha out? Ted just got it, put it on the boat, Gerry took it out, and KABOOM" — he laughs again — "hit a rock and came back with a big chunk out of the side of the prop." Davies stops laughing when he notices MacDonald is not enjoying the joke as much as he is. "You can have them rebuilt," he adds seriously. And if a propeller is beyond rebuilding, it is false economy not to buy a new one.

Because of prolonged hard use, most of the outboards at Whip-Poor-Will Lodge are replaced every three years, but a few — such as those that run the barges — are kept longer. One 15-horsepower Evinrude, which was bought new in 1968, accumulated more that 10,000 hours before it was sold in 1975, and it still sees regular use.

For more than four decades, MacDonald has been proving to himself and his customers just how far a little maintenance will go. Whether your outboard is a classic 1946 5-horsepower Viking or one of today's hermetically sealed mysterious wonders, it, too, will benefit from a midsummer moment of cool drinks and grease.

Originally published in Cottage Life *magazine (Toronto).*

Salvaging drowned motors

Strange things happen in the North, most of them involving my good friend Paul, it seems. This one is an exception — it is about his brother Pidge and his sidekick Guysie (these are genuine nicknames, their origins best left to magazines such as *Psychology Today*). It was a beautiful day, about 90 degrees F, when Pidge and Guysie decided to go fishing. They managed to get six or seven miles down the lake before the engine quit.

Naturally, it did not take long before the conversation became as heated as the air. Guysie, who was rowing, became increasingly upset with Pidge, the owner and neglectful caretaker of their cankerous engine. Fortunately, this argument between friends ended abruptly and before things came to blows, when Guysie laid down his oars, unscrewed the motor's transom clamps and dropped Pidge's motor into the lake, proudly announcing, "We don't have to worry about that piece of junk anymore," which leads me to the topic of what to do should your outboard become submerged.

It is very important to get a motor out of the water as quickly as possible. Once it's out, unscrew the drain plug at the bottom of each carburetor float bowl, letting the contents drain out into an appropriate container. A float bowl is attached to the bottom of each carburetor and looks a lot like a little metal bowl. The drain screw is usually located at the bottom or to the side of the bowl. If your outboard is one of the new ones with fuel injection (see your owner's manual or the engine-cover stickers), ignore this step and proceed to the spark plugs.

Remove the spark plugs, and with the stop button depressed or the plugs grounded, spin the engine over several times until all the water is cleared out. If oil is handy, squirt a small quantity into the cylinders, spin the engine over some more and then mount it back onto the boat. Dry off the plugs and reinstall them, or use new ones, and try to start the engine. If you succeed, run the engine for about an hour to dry everything out. Newer ignitions are not seriously affected by water; if it's an older machine and won't start, try drying out the ignition system with an electric hair dryer. And, when all else fails, or the motor has been submerged for more than an hour, get it to a dealer as quickly as possible.

If your motor fell into the drink while it was running and the engine now binds when using the pull cord, take it to your dealer along with your chequebook. Chances are, there's internal damage — which is expensive. If you own a four-stroke outboard, like a Honda, the crankcase oil will have to be drained and replaced with new oil before attempting to start it. Again, consult your manual.

Outboards generally become overboards as a result of not having the clamps tight enough or through careless handling. Dropping them into the drink while installing them and removing them from the boat while it is in the water seem to be popular ways to go about it, but a lot of people prefer just to knock them off the dock — all of which can be avoided simply by exercising a little caution. Of course, if you are really serious about not soiling your fingers in the intricacies of motor resuscitation, don't take anyone by the name of Guysie fishing.

An aluminum-boat buying primer

by Penny Caldwell

You see them everywhere: trolling around promising shoals at twilight, zipping across sparkling water with a couple of happy adolescents in control, putting slowly across the bay with a boatload of visitors and a weekend's worth of gear. Aluminum runabouts are a way of life at the cottage.

Versatile and almost indestructible, these rugged craft are as popular now as when they were first mass-produced in Canada in the early 1950s. But today, there are so many models of runabouts on the market, you'll want to give some thought to your needs and budget before making a purchase.

Aluminum runabouts usually range from about 9 feet to 18 feet in length, although a couple of 22-footers are made; they can weigh as little as just over 100 pounds, with load capacity near 500 pounds, to as much as 1,000 pounds, with load capacity closer to 2,000 pounds. So your first consideration has to be how many people will use the boat at the same time.

The location of your cottage is also important. For rough, open water, you'll need a bigger, deeper boat with a thicker-gauge aluminum hull than for a smaller, landlocked lake, advises Bruce Cleland, a former boat seller who now markets floating dock systems through WDA Products of Keswick, Ontario. Cottagers without docks who haul their boats up on shore and people whose boats will be subjected to rocky landings during picnics and other excursions should also opt for a thicker hull. Hull and side-panel thicknesses range from about 0.051 to 0.098 inches.

Generally, lighter-gauge hulls are less expensive; this isn't always the case, as there are many other factors, such as the engineering and structural integrity of the boat, involved in hull strength. Sometimes even a heavier-gauge runabout can be inadequate and experience hull deflection (the tendency of the aluminum to pop in and out) if the heavier hull is not combined with proper structural support — including horizontal ribs, stiffeners and seats that go through the bottom of the boat to become a structural member.

For extra strength if your boat is subjected to rough terrain, look for a model with multiple keels (the ridges or strakes that run along the length of the boat's bottom). Some manufacturers, such as Genmar Boats Canada Inc. of Steinbach, Manitoba, increase strength by adding a second row of rivets to hold the aluminum panels together.

The boat's structural qualities are also matched to a horsepower rating. Do not purchase an engine over the maximum rated horsepower for your boat. The boat will easily become airborne if it's overpowered, you run the risk of structural damage, and you will void the boat's warranty as well as your insurance policy.

However, the best horsepower for your boat isn't always the engine rating in the brochure. One boat seller says he tries to "sell people down" to smaller engines. "Maximum horsepower isn't necessary to get maximum performance out of a boat," he advises.

Cleland agrees, adding that a 9.9-horsepower engine is usually ample for youngsters. He owns a 14-foot aluminum boat with a 7½-horsepower motor, "because it's a secondary boat and I have young people driving it." It is also a sturdy workhorse that hauls garbage to the mainland and loads of wood around the island.

Allowing children to drive larger engines is like giving a 14-year-old the keys to a Corvette, cautions Marcel Dubois, of Altra Marine Products in Quebec.

On the other hand, if your 14-footer must carry adults or heavy loads, you'll get better speed and planing ability by upgrading to a 15-horsepower engine, Cleland says. A family using the boat as its primary means of transportation and for water-skiing would likely be looking for a 16-footer with wheel steering and a 70-horsepower engine capable of towing adult skiers.

Your dealer is the best source of advice when matching an engine to your boat and may offer a discount on the boat-and-motor package. If you already own an engine and are replacing an older boat, however, you'll need to choose one that won't be over- or underpowered and to make sure its transom weight is right for your motor. Engines come with short, long or extra-long shafts. Boats over 16 feet generally have deep transoms, and on these, an engine with a short, 15-inch shaft would be inadequate. Pairing long shafts with short transoms, on the other hand, will put the engine too deep, Cleland warns. It will run inefficiently, and the boat will tend to plough.

Wheel steering and an electric start on the engine — usually optional on smaller engines — can be a safety feature for children and older adults who don't have enough strength to start a pull-cord engine while sitting down.

In spite of all the other uses of aluminum boats, Cleland says, most cottagers buy them to go fishing, and this is where the greatest development has taken place in new runabouts. Avid anglers will find models 14 feet and up with a wealth of fishing enhancements, such as flooring, livewells, rod holders, locking storage compartments, swivel seats, casting platforms and pads that accommodate bow-mounted trolling motors. But the price goes up with every new feature, and the difference between a 16-footer fully outfitted for fishing and a standard 16-foot runabout can be several thousand dollars.

Originally published in Cottage Life *magazine (Toronto).*

Experience the quiet joy of kayaking across tranquil lakes

A Sleek Craft for Silent Paddling

by Sue Lebrecht

Kayaks glide through the water and go like the wind, and they're catching on as a new cottage sport. Getting started is a breeze — here is what you need to know.

If two words could describe kayaking, they would be "intimate" and "playful." Swift and silent, a kayak allows you to streak across the morning glass and watch nature awakening without disturbance. Stable and manoeuvrable, it also lets you ride the afternoon waves.

But kayaking is much more, and cottagers who have paddled one — after a few quick lessons — hardly look back at their canoes. Susan Buckley, a mother of five ranging in age from 6 to 17, found kayaking so addictive that she got the whole family involved. At their island cottage in Georgian Bay, the Buckleys have two sea kayaks and four river kayaks. "We feel perfectly comfortable letting our kids go out by themselves," she explains. "They're self-sufficient, they can launch on their own, and it's the easiest way for them to visit their aunt and uncle across the bay. You don't get as tired in a kayak as you do in a canoe — my 6-year-old can paddle more than four miles."

At the beginning of the season and throughout the summer, her children do dunk drills — tipping and getting out — and they always wear life jackets. However, it's not just the practice that gives Buckley confidence when her kids are on the water; it's the very nature of the craft. Kayaks are more stable than they look because of their low centre of gravity. "You sit in a moulded seat only an inch or so from the bottom of the craft, so you're at water level or slightly below — not top-heavy or vulnerable in six- or eight-foot waves," Buckley says. "I can feel comfortable when boaters pass."

Skimming through marshes, flitting over rocks and coasting up to the shore, you probably can't get any closer to nature than while on the water in a kayak. Dave Scott, travel editor of the *London Free Press*, discovered that when he made the transition from canoe to kayak several years ago. (He didn't feel confident soloing a canoe but wanted a boat he could paddle alone so that he wouldn't be dependent on someone else.) A bird watcher, Scott saw his first green heron on his inaugural kayak outing. "There it was on a branch, looking down at me. Another time, I came across a raccoon so close, I could have touched it with my paddle. The look on its face as I passed by!" A man who likes his comforts, Scott had a custom-built cup holder and ice bucket added to his boat.

Kayaking can be physically relaxing or demanding, depending on your temperament. You can lean back and take in the setting sun with the occasional dip of your paddle, or you can steam along with full-bodied strokes. "I know of few better upper-body builders than kayaking," says Maks Zupan, a member of the national kayak team and a World Masters champion. "With the double-bladed paddle, you power both sides of the body." Proper technique, he explains, provides a total workout: with your feet on the footrest and knees bent, the whole body twists as you reach and pull, incorporating leg, abdominal and large chest and back muscles — not just those in the arms.

Zupan started kayaking in 1972 at his island cottage on Lake Tomiko, near North Bay, because he needed a craft more stable than a canoe in which to carry supplies. He fell in love with the sport, feeling so close to the water: "The kayak becomes an extension of yourself," he says. He and his wife Dawn Williams — a Canadian champion and U.S. Open champion — now run Huron Kayak Adventures in Port Elgin, which offers trips, tours and weekend clinics. Beginners take to kayaking

Lightweight kayaks are quiet craft with a low profile that provide easy access to northern lakes and rivers.

from the very outset, Zupan says. "It's as easy as walking — much easier to learn than wind-surfing, for example, so they like it from day one."

The centuries-old kayak, traditionally made of sealskin or other animal skin, wood and bone, only came to life in cottage country a couple of years ago. It has been a slow dawning for two reasons: the availability of kayaks and the image of the sport as the preserve of daredevils with a passion for roaring through white water.

In 1975, when Gary Barton first came to Toronto from England, he couldn't find a kayak to buy and consequently built his own. Now, as co-owner of Rockwood Outfitters in Guelph, Ontario, which manufactures kayaks and canoes, he has witnessed the sport's tremendous growth — not just among white-water enthusiasts but also on lakes and along ocean coasts. What helped the sport take off, Barton explains, was mass production of polyethylene plastic kayaks (called "Tupperware" in serious kayaking circles), starting in the early '70s.

Polyethylene kayaks are less expensive than fibreglass or Kevlar designs, which are more labour-intensive to produce. They are also heavier and very durable. The lightest, best-performing and most expensive kayaks are made of Kevlar. Fibreglass falls neatly in the middle — cheaper than Kevlar and lighter than plastic.

There are two basic categories of kayak: river, or white-water; and sea, or touring. Designed for easy turning, river kayaks ($500 to $900, depending on the material) are agile and responsive to your strokes. They are built with more rocker (the curvature along the keel line) than a sea kayak, the raised bow and stern creating a half-moon shape; the pivot point is you, the paddler. About 12 feet long, with some models weighing as little as 24 pounds, river kayaks are shorter and lighter (about half the weight) than sea kayaks made of the same material.

Sea kayaks ($1,200 to $3,000) are more stable than river kayaks and track a straight line well, but they don't turn as easily. Most have a retractable rudder controlled from the cockpit, which aids in steering and allows you to maintain course regardless of crosswinds. (To move diagonally through waves without a rudder, you will have to paddle harder on one side.) Ideal for touring and overnight trips, sea kayaks have hatches and bulkheads for storing gear, as well as deck lines and bungee cords for holding down things you need at hand (a plastic water bottle, for instance, or your waterproof camera). And unlike river kayaks, some sea kayaks are built for two.

Crossover models that combine aspects of both river and sea kayaks are now being manufactured. Some river kayaks, for instance, have a skeg attachment — a fixed rudder — which can be put on prior to launching. Although most skegs are neither retractable from the cockpit nor adjustable while under way, they do help the boat track well. A river kayak with a skeg is a great choice for a cottager — versatile, fairly inexpensive and easy to control.

There are crossover kayaks that are longer than river kayaks and have less rocker, which Tim Dyer of White Squall Wilderness Shop in Parry Sound also recommends for cottagers. They are more stable than river kayaks and consequently are excellent for lake paddling. But since they aren't as long and don't have all the rigging and hatches of a true touring kayak, they sell for less ($500 to $1,000).

Folding kayaks and inflatables are also on the market now. Fitting snugly into two carry bags, a folding kayak can easily be transported in a small plane. Also very expensive (about $2,500), it is not recommended unless you have an isolated cottage somewhere like Baffin Island. Inflatables are fine toys for the beach but have no place on open water.

Any good manufacturer — and there are many, including Rockwood Outfitters, River Runner, Loki Boats, Current Designs, Aquaterra and Camp Lake Kayak Company — will put a footrest in its kayaks. This is imperative for developing proper paddling technique and avoiding back fatigue. Kayaks should also have built-in flotation devices such as foam pillars, air bags or watertight compartments.

Paddles come in a wide range of designs and prices (from $50 to $300). For the beginner, the basic choice is between feathered and unfeathered. With blades at right angles to each other, the feathered paddle requires a twist of the wrist; while one blade pulls the water, the other end slices through the air, keeping wind resistance to a minimum. The unfeathered paddle — straight on both sides — has no twist, and as a result, some beginners find it easier. If you're undecided, collapsible paddles are available, which can be switched from feathered to unfeathered.

A skirt is one accessory you may also want. Available in nylon or neoprene, it fits over the cockpit and hugs you at the waist, creating a near-watertight seal for wavy days. Neoprene traps your body's warmth and is important if you plan on extending your season into the beautiful but crisp days of fall.

Other accessories include a paddle leash, which will keep your paddle from straying if you stop to fish or have a picnic on board. Drip rings attach around the paddle's shaft and will stop water from running down the blade and along your arm.

While kayaking is not difficult to learn, it's advisable to take an initial lesson to develop good technique — the relaxing form that allows the most return for your muscle power. Safety precautions, self-rescue and how to help others should be learned immediately, and it's also a good idea to practise "wet exits" so you won't panic if the kayak tips.

Your kayak should be comfortable right away, so if possible, you should water-test it before you decide to purchase. Good stores won't sell what you don't need, because it's in their interest to make you a happy and returning customer. "I'm almost at the point where I can promise customers they'll enjoy the sport," concludes Tim Dyer. "I've never had anyone come back dissatisfied with the experience."

Originally published in Cottage Life *magazine (Toronto).*

A homemade rowboat that's perfect for kids

The Miniature Dreamboat

by Craig Canine

I once read that a disproportionate number of officers in the U.S. Navy come from landlocked states of the Midwest. At the time I encountered this bit of trivia, I was a boy growing up in Iowa, but I had no great urge to go to sea. Now, having passed the age of enlistment, I've started to feel the tug of the water. It happened a few winters ago: the desire to skipper my own boat struck me with a mysterious urgency.

I find it difficult to account for this nautical yearning. Could it be that native Midwesterners have an innate love for flat, wide-open landscapes, like fields of corn and soybeans, stretching from horizon to horizon? Maybe for those of us who grew up in such country, the sight of rippling waves, whether of water or of grain, evokes a comforting sense of familiarity. Perhaps it is not so strange after all that a great many boys who leave prairie farms wind up on the ocean.

Friends and colleagues offered a different explanation for the lure of the sea. My wife was pregnant with our first child; about the time I started talking about boats, in fact, she was entering the advanced stages. My friends reasoned that the burst of energy that many women feel before giving birth had leapt the gender gap and stricken me, the expectant (and nervous) father. When I announced, near the middle of the third trimester, that I had purchased construction plans for a 15-foot sailing skiff, these same friends suggested that I was devoting my burst of prenatal energy to devising a vehicle of escape.

I assured them, and my wife, that escape was not my motive. There's simply no accounting for taste when you are pregnant, I said. Some people develop a craving for chocolate-covered pickles; others get the urge to build a boat.

The boat plans, when they arrived in the mail, cooled my ardour. They bandied about words like "scarfing," "lofting," "scantlings" and "gains" as though I knew what they meant. The design was a simple one by boatbuilding standards; even so, my lapstrake skiff would require woodworking skills more advanced than those I possessed. I had yet to perfect my ability to execute a 90-degree angle in wood, let alone the compound bevels, graceful curves and precise joinery demanded by a boat.

My hopes languished for a while until, in a moment of profound escapism, I was reading a newsletter published by a manufacturer of marine epoxy resin. In it, there appeared some plans for a 7-foot rowboat designed for a child.

Building the scaled-down skiff required only one sheet of plywood and some scrap lumber, along with epoxy glue and fibreglass tape to join the edges. Best of all, the skills required to make the boat were well within my modest range. As I imagined the child-sized craft, I recalled that a friend's son would be turning 5 this summer. I decided that he would get a rowboat for his birthday — just the thing for exploring the new pond his parents had excavated last fall — and I would get some practice before building my alleged escape vessel.

While the snow cover was getting deeper and nightly temperatures were exploring their winter lows, I managed to start our old pickup and drove it down to the local lumberyard. The basic ingredient of my "baby boat" is a single 4-by-8-foot sheet of ¼-inch plywood. My plans specified lauan plywood, which is easy to work with, is inexpensive and possesses a moderate degree of natural water resistance. I bought a sheet for $8.50. Belatedly, however, I realized that lauan is a type of mahogany, which is harvested from tropical rainforests. A good alternative would be Douglas fir plywood (a sheet of ¼-inch AC fir plywood, which has one finish-grade side, costs about $10). While at the lumberyard, I also picked up several sheets of 80-, 100- and 200-

Built for 40-to-80-pound skippers, the author's birthday boat provides children with a shallow-water sense of seamanship and several seasons of fun.

grit sandpaper, along with two dozen flathead brass wood screws. I imagined I would need to hold various parts of the boat together, which proved true — but only until the epoxy glue set up. Excluding the oarlock hardware, the finished boat contains two screws, and even those are not absolutely necessary.

A 7-foot-long boat made of ¼-inch plywood would be structurally impossible without modern epoxies. They form bonds that are far stronger than the wood they join together, and they can be mixed with fillers that give the epoxy various properties. At a nearby marine-supply store, I bought a quart of Gougeon Brothers West System epoxy resin and the corresponding small container of "fast hardener," which, along

with a set of "mini-pumps," cost about $28. The reusable small pumps are calibrated so that a stroke of each dispenses the resin and hardener in the proper ratio. I also bought a bag of the same manufacturer's Filleting Compound. When added to a small quantity of mixed epoxy, this fine brown dust turns the runny glue into a puttylike mixture, useful for filling cracks and rounding joints. At the same store, I purchased 40 feet of 3-inch-wide fibreglass tape, of which I eventually used about 35 feet. Several small glue brushes and some latex rubber gloves rounded out my shopping list. Their products are also available through the mail: Gougeon Brothers, Box X908, Bay City, Michigan 48707 U.S.A.

Armed with these materials, I was ready to lay out my sheet of plywood for cutting. Marking the lines for the sides was easy enough, since they are all straight. Drawing the shape of the bottom was trickier, since its sides are curved. Cutting the shape of this curve exactly is less critical than making sure both sides of the bottom are identical in contour. On the plywood, I marked a point for the boat's bow, then the two points that define its stern and, finally, the point of each side where the bottom is the widest. Then I took a long, slender scrap of wood and clamped it to the sheet of plywood so that it connected the points at the bow, beam and stern on one side of the bottom. Using the curved piece of scrap as a guide, I marked a line representing one side of the bottom. After cutting along this line with a jigsaw, I flipped over the resulting plywood scrap to transfer a mirror image of this contour to the other side of the plywood, yielding a symmetrical, boat-shaped bottom.

Once the bottom, sides and transom (the piece that forms the stem end of the boat) were cut out, I made a stem piece out of a 1½-foot long scrap of 2-by-4. The stem provides structural rigidity and a fastening surface for the sides of the boat where they meet at the bow. The sides converge at the front of the boat at a 45-degree angle. I cut one edge of the 2-by-4 to this angle with a circular saw, leaving me with a piece of wood 18 inches long that vaguely resembled an airfoil.

To provide a surface on the transom to which the sides could be fastened, I glued and screwed two pieces of 1-by-2 lumber, each about 14 inches long, flush with the sides of the plywood transom piece. I left some extra length protruding from the bottom of the transom; that way, I could later bevel the ends of the 1-by-2s so that they would be flush with the bottom of the boat. The directions I was working from suggested putting an additional piece of 1-by-2 framing across the inside bottom of the transom, but it seemed to me unnecessary, so I left it off. With this detail, as with many others, I followed

the sketchy plans in the Gougeon Brothers newsletter quite loosely, improvising along the way. Fortunately for me, the design proved to be more or less foolproof.

Finally I cut out a "spreader" from a piece of ¾-inch plywood that was lying in my scrap heap in the garage. The spreader measures 7 inches wide, 30½ inches along one edge and 26 inches along the other edge. It would eventually become the seat, but its first purpose in life was to hold the boat's sides apart at the proper angle and by the desired distance after they had been fastened to the stem and transom.

Assembling these pieces was the next step. To do it, I first "dry-fit" the sides to the stem piece and transom frame, drilling pilot holes and temporarily fastening the pieces together with #8 x 1-inch screws. At this stage, the assemblage was floppy and misshapen. But I persevered, removing all the screws, mixing a small batch of epoxy and re-assembling the thing, brushing epoxy on all the joined surfaces before screwing them together again (here, as elsewhere, the screws functioned as temporary clamps; they were removed after the glue had set up). Then I jammed the spreader between the sides at a point 45 inches from the bow, 39 inches from the stern, with the long side of the spreader at the top, flush with the top of the sides ("gunwales" to old salts, who

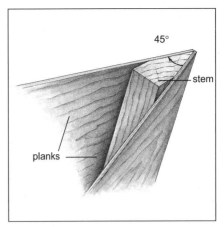

Cross-section view shows the stem (above); plywood layout (below).

pronounce it "gunnels"). I was expecting the boat's shape to be square and bargelike. But with the addition of the spreader, the sides snapped into classic nautical curves. I fastened the spreader in place temporarily with a few long finishing nails pounded into the sides. Suddenly, I was beginning to feel like a boatbuilder.

But my boat still had no bottom. Before test-fitting the bottom piece, I set the structure upside down on a pair of sawhorses and cut off the stem and the transom frames flush with the bottom of the boat's sides. Then, with a block plane, I bevelled the bottom edges of the sides so that they would fit flat against the plywood bottom piece. I tacked on the bottom, starting at the bow and doing my best not to let the small nails I used split through the thin plywood sides. The bottom didn't fit exactly: it protruded an inch and a half beyond the transom and bulged beyond the sides here and there. (I planed the bottom later, after it was securely glued in place.)

Once the bottom was tacked on, I turned the whole thing over. I mixed another batch of epoxy, thickening it this time with some filleting compound, and applied it with my gloved finger to the joint between the boat's sides and the bottom. I also used the brown putty to fill gaps between the transom and the 1-by-2 framing pieces.

The next day, I discovered that the filleting compound had dried with a slightly rough surface, which was not

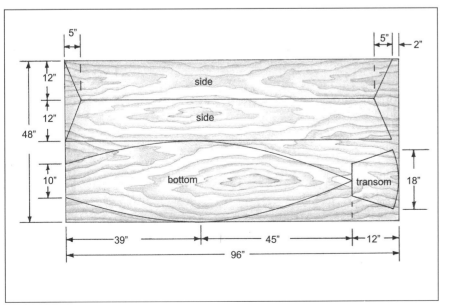

Detail of the seat (above); view of the keel after installation (below).

easily sanded smooth. The people at Gougeon Brothers told me later that their low-density filler would have been a better choice for this application, since it is easier to apply smoothly and to sand.

My four pieces of plywood now looked like a boat with remarkably graceful lines. It was, however, a long way from seaworthiness. It was time to seal and reinforce the edges with fibreglass, another procedure that was entirely new to me. So I improvised, first brushing a coat of epoxy along the seams, laying the fibreglass tape down on top of it, then slathering more epoxy on top of the tape to saturate it completely. I let this cure, then brushed on another coat of epoxy. Although this procedure created strong joints, they leave something to be desired cosmetically: even after several coats of paint, the edges of the fibreglass tape still show through.

Later, I learned the right way to apply fibreglass tape. Ted Hugger, a technical expert at Gougeon Brothers and the editor of the company's newsletter, *The Boatbuilder*, filled me in. "Embed the tape in a layer of epoxy," he told me over the phone, "then squeegee out the excess, taking care to smooth out all the bubbles and wrinkles in the tape. The fibreglass fabric shouldn't look wet; it should have a mattelike appearance. After allowing this to cure, apply more coats of epoxy to fill in and smooth the tape's woven texture. Then feather the edges of the tape using low-density

filler." My next boat will benefit from Hugger's advice.

Taping all the edges with fibreglass, inside and out, added considerably to the boat's strength and rigidity. Still, the top edge of the sides — the gunwales — obviously needed reinforcing. A strip of oak about 8 feet long, ½ inch thick and ¾ inch wide, glued to the outside of each gunwale, solved the problem. I glued another strip of oak, this one about 19 inches long, to the outside top edge of the transom. Gluing on the long strips (outwales) required all the wood clamps in the house (about a dozen), and I could have used a few more. I secured the outwales at the bow with two #8 x 1-inch brass screws driven through the sides and into the stern. These two screws — one on each side — are countersunk into the oak and covered with ⅜-inch wooden plugs, obtained from a hardware store. With my plane, I tapered the oak outwales down to nothing at the tip of the bow. While I was fooling around with the bow, I trimmed off the top of the stem with a curved cut, leaving 1½ inches protruding above the boat's sides at the front edge of the stem. A ¼-inch hole drilled through the stem would later serve as the point of attachment for a hemp painter.

The boat's bottom, curved now to conform with the "rocker" shape the sides had assumed, seemed fairly solid, despite its mere ¼-inch thickness. Gluing on a keel provided even more rigidity (though torquing the keel down on the boat's curved bottom with temporary screw fasteners took some doing). The keel is made of ¾-inch oak and runs down the centreline of the entire bottom, gradually tapering in height from 2½ inches at the stern to about ¼ inch at the bow.

Now the boat was ready for a seat. I fashioned seat brackets out of four blocks cut from a 2-by-4. Their exact shape isn't important, as long as they hold the seat securely in its proper spot. The placement of the seat is crucial to the boat's stability, comfort and manoeuvrability: it should be mounted so that its bottom surface is 6 inches from the floor of the boat and so that the middle of the seat is 34 inches from the bottom of the transom. The most important of these dimensions is the 6-inch seat height. If the seat is any higher, the boat may become unstable with a person aboard.

As mentioned earlier, the boat's seat can be fashioned from the same piece of ¾-inch plywood that was used as the temporary spreader. I had to cut the

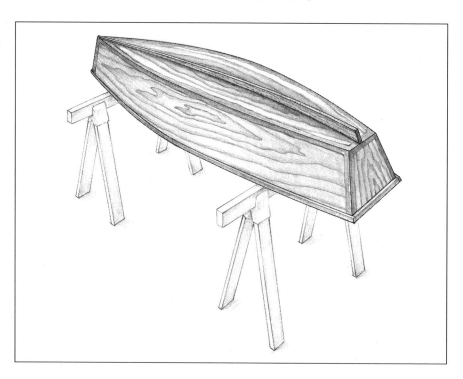

spreader down a little to fit it between my brackets, which were held to the boat's sides with screws until a generous coating of epoxy had cured.

The final step before painting was to mount two oarlock pads to the inside of the gunwales. These were cut from a scrap of ¾-inch oak, procured for a dollar from a local hardwood dealer. They are rectangles measuring 2½ inches wide by 5 inches long. The blocks were glued onto the inside of the boat flush with the top of the gunwales, centred on a line marked 8 inches from the back edge of the seat.

Painting is a task best saved for warm weather, as I learned when my first few coats of glossy marine paint sagged and dripped uncontrollably in the 50-degree-F temperatures of my workshop in midwinter. (That's with the woodstove going full blast.) Subsequent coats, applied in the spring, behaved much better. But it was too late: even though I had sanded down the worst of the drips and wrinkles, the fourth and final coat showed the dimples beneath. I can only hope that the boat's snappy colours distract somewhat from its imperfect complexion. The inside is painted sky blue, the outside is royal blue, and the gunwales and seat are white. I primed the whole thing with a primer/sealer before applying the paint.

Then there was the matter of oars. A pair of new ones would cost at least $40 — too much, I thought, for a boat whose wooden parts had cost half of that. So I found a used pair of 5½-foot oars for $15 and cut them down to about 4½ feet. Bronze oarlocks — the only ones I could find, though a galvanized pair would have been cheaper — cost $6.50 each and added a dash of elegance when they were mounted on the oarlock pads.

On totting up my receipts when the boat was finished, I was surprised to see they added up to $135, since the wood itself had been so inexpensive. But hey — this boat got me through pregnancy. Our baby (a boy) was born somewhere between the second and third coats of paint. Maybe the pint-sized skiff will be handed down to him. By the time he celebrates his fifth birth-

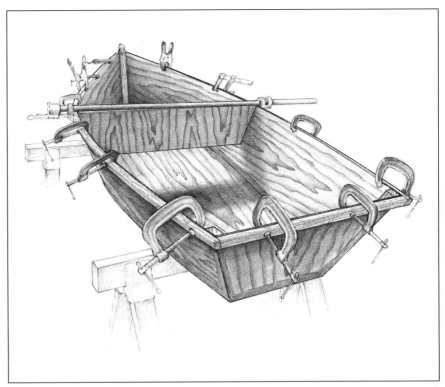

After a test run with dry pieces, the boat parts are joined with epoxy and screws and held tightly together with strategically located clamps.

day, the boat's intended recipient will no doubt have graduated to bigger and better means of navigation.

But before the boat's official launching on my young friend's birthday, I was eager to give it a preliminary trial. My neighbour's 5-year-old daughter said she was game to be my guinea pig — but only, she said, "if the water is low." Her father arranged to borrow a life jacket, and the three of us went to a small local pond one chilly spring morning to launch the boat. It floated high and dry — an encouraging sign — so my young test subject stepped aboard and took her place on the seat. With the end of the boat's 30-foot painter in one hand, I shoved her off with the other, and she glided gracefully to the middle of the pond.

Although she had only been in a boat once before and had never been in command of a pair of oars, our young sailor was up to the task at hand and was soon making headway and having a good time of it. The boat was quite stable and still riding high in the water, with plenty of hull showing above the waterline.

The situation changed drastically when it was my turn to be shoved out onto the pond. With a much higher centre of gravity and only a few inches to spare above the waterline, the boat tipped precariously with my smallest movement. It was only with great concentration that I avoided tipping the rowboat over. I didn't dare try to use the oars, and the painter was coiled up in the bow. I was hopelessly, embarrassingly, adrift. Fortunately, the wind soon blew me ashore. This, I concluded, is a boat strictly for kids in the 40-to-80-pound range.

Once I was safely back on terra firma, my 50-pound friend was eager for another turn at the oars. She explored the pond's far bank for a while before we all declared the trial a success. Recounting the morning's adventure later over a cup of hot chocolate, she gave the boat what I considered the ultimate vote of confidence. "Next time," she said, "I want to go when the water is high."

Originally published in Harrowsmith Country Life *magzine (Charlotte, VT).*

Boat hull shapes make the difference

Riding the Waves in Comfort

by Jan Mundy

Choosing a family runabout these days is as complicated as buying stereo components. The array of choices in design, styling and options is so bewildering, it can leave you making a very expensive decision ($15,000 to $40,000) based solely on aesthetics. The shape of the hull seems almost incidental when you're confronted with plush interiors, dazzling dashboards, ski lockers and digital depth sounders. But it's crucial in determining a boat's handling, ride and response. A little knowledge of hull design can help you narrow the choices and could make the difference between a comfortable ride and a teeth-jarring one, between a boat that serves your needs and one that is all wrong for your lake and weather conditions.

To understand how hull shape affects performance, it helps to remember a basic principle of physics: water is resistant to compression. Therefore, boats in motion must either push it — a displacement hull — or rise above it — a planing hull. Almost all runabouts in the 15-to-22-foot range have planing hulls, but variations in their shape determine cornering ability, rough-water handling and quickness to plane. The designs most prevalent are deep-V, modified-V, tunnel and cathedral. Of these, V-bottoms of one kind or another are the most popular. "They offer the best combination of comfort in rough water, quick planing, speed and stability," says John Blair, president of Lackie's Marina in Toronto.

The major distinction between all V-bottom boats is the amount of deadrise (the angle at which a boat's bottom slants up from the horizontal). A deadrise of less than 12 degrees produces a flattish bottom suited for speed in calm, sheltered waters; such hulls will pound mercilessly, however, in any sort of chop. More than 18 degrees — steep deadrise — is typical of boats designed for rough water such as you'd find on the Great Lakes or Georgian Bay; the V shape cuts into the waves, helps the hull grip the water and thus reduces pounding.

The deep-V hull, originally built for the big swell of coastal waters, has a constant deadrise of about 20 degrees or more from the middle of the boat to the stern, with flat planing sections and strakes (ridges running the length of the bottom of the hull) that give it increased lift. These qualities have been adapted for smaller runabouts, producing a good family boat, with a couple of minor drawbacks. At high speeds, the deep-V travels well in a straight line and "corners like a train on a track," says Blair, whose company sells Sea Ray boats. But at idle, it snakes, requiring constant steering correction to maintain course. "Any kind of inboard/outboard will do this to some extent," says boat designer Mark Ellis, "because the boat tends to pivot around the driving force — the propeller. The snaking is worse if the engine is in the stern, as opposed to the centre, because the pivoting arm is longer."

Ellis' Tadenac 22 — at about $40,000, it's the high end of runabouts — is an example of a deep-V with a centre engine. The placement of the engine improves the performance in rough water and enables the boat to stay on plane at lower speeds, according to the designer. The down side is that it won't go as fast as a sterndrive.

Another factor to consider with the deep-V is gas consumption. As the angle of the V increases — and hence the deadrise — so does the amount of horsepower required to push the hull. Although fuel efficiency also depends on the size and placement of lift strakes, more power generally means greater gas consumption.

Most of the 16-to-20-foot Grews, Dorals, Peterboroughs, Thundercrafts and Sea Rays you see on the lakes in cottage country, however, have modified-V hulls, which combine a pronounced V in the bow with wide, flat sections in the stern. One advantage of this shape is that you can build more seats and storage compartments into it, and thus it can carry larger loads than a deep-V. It can also be powered by a smaller engine. At low speeds and in choppy water, the sharp forward section slices through the waves; at higher speeds and in flat water, the boat planes on its wide stern sections.

"They're all fairly similar," says Andy Adams, one of Canada's leading boat testers and a Lake Rosseau cottager. "Normally, they have 12 to 20 degrees of deadrise, a wide chine (the sharp intersection of a boat's topsides and bottom) and strakes that give them a lot of lift and get them planing faster and at lower speeds."

Larson Boats' Delta-Conic hull is an example of a modified-V. Designed by marine-architect Harry School of Fort Lauderdale, it has a deep-V entry (30 degrees of deadrise), a wide-lipped chine that deflects spray, and a relatively flat planing surface in the stern. It's designed to present a convex surface to the water from virtually any direction. "In rough water, when it's idled slowly or anchored, a Delta-Conic hull will roll from side to side rather than pitch," says Adams. "As a result, it's often a preferred choice for fishermen, but it also performs very well as a general cottage runabout."

When you're looking at boats, you may come across some tunnel hulls (also called air-trap hulls), which are designed to be very stable at high speeds. "It's like a V-bottom with training wheels," says Mike Canzano of Charger Boats, which manufactures several runabouts of modified-tunnel design. As the name itself suggests, the hull is in the shape of an inverted U, with small Vs, called sponsons, on either side. "At high speeds — in excess of 75 miles per hour — it's more efficient and easier to drive than a V-bottom because you're riding on a cushion of air," explains Canzano. "But for all-round cottage use, a V-bottom is better. It's much more comfortable in rough or choppy water."

Another design that has found a real niche among cottagers is the cathedral hull, typified by the Boston Whaler. In

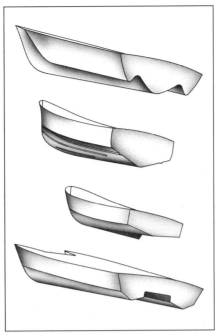

Cathedral hull, deep-V hull, modified-V, and tunnel hull (top to bottom).

cross section, this hull resembles an inverted W with a deep-V centre pod and two sponsons. Boats of this design are extremely stable — you can stand on the gunwale without the boat listing — and very fleet and manoeuvrable. Boston Whaler also boasts that its boats are unsinkable. "The hull consists of two layers of fibreglass with a foam core," explains Charles Brown of Sea Mark Industries, the Whaler's eastern Canadian distributor. "If you hit a rock and rip a hole in the bottom, chances are you're not going to puncture both layers. And even if you do, the hull will float when it's full of water."

Cathedral hulls are very quick to plane and extremely stable (thus great ski boats), but one often hears complaints that they pound in rough water and give a very wet ride. While this is true of the 9- and 13-foot models, says Brown, the hulls of the larger boats (15 to 31 feet) have more of a deep-V and give a much smoother ride. They also come with a full top for boaters who like to stay dry on the water.

Although hull shape plays a large part in a boat's overall performance, length is also important. According to Adams, there are wave conditions when an extra three feet would make the differ-

ence between a passable ride and a queasy one. On the smaller inland lakes, where waves and wake are modest, a 16-to-18-foot boat is fine; but on Lake Simcoe, "you'd be better off with a 20-foot boat," says John Blair. "And on the exposed waters of Georgian Bay, Lake Ontario and the St. Lawrence, where you're dealing with the swell of tankers, you need something from 22 to 24 feet in length."

Once you've figured out the shape and length of the hull that are best for you, the next consideration is the boat's configuration above the waterline: should you get a closed-deck, bowrider or a centre-console model? Closed-deck runabouts, with no seating forward of the wheel, are all-purpose boats, usually with back-to-back sleeper seats for the driver and companion and two jump seats if the boat is equipped with a sterndrive.

But if you need more room for the kids, dog and groceries, the bowrider is a good option. With its open-bench seating forward (wet and uncomfortable in any sort of chop, but the kids probably won't mind at all) and additional storage underneath the seats, it offers more usable space than a closed deck. An added bonus is that bowriders are in great demand and offer excellent resale value at trade-in time. "They represent 96 percent of the market in runabouts now," says Blair.

Centre-console models such as Boston Whalers, KMV's Pro 528 or Altra's Super Pro 225 have a steering console in the centre, with limited bench seating forward. With their walk-around decks, these boats are great for fishing or skiing, but comfortable seating is limited. Some models are not equipped with a windshield and top and thus offer very little protection from spray and wind.

When you finally decide on the boat you want, don't forget to take it out for a water test (not on Lake Ontario if you plan to use it on a smaller inland lake). Nothing beats a ride on rough water for measuring a hull's true performance.

Originally published in Cottage Life *magazine (Toronto).*

Trailers and techniques that work

by Sue Lebrecht

When John Burch hooked a borrowed trailer onto his truck and noticed a slight looseness in the fit of the hitch and ball, he didn't think twice about it.

But later, on the highway, he hit a dip in the road, and the truck jolted, causing the trailer to come off the hitch. Attached only by the chains, it began to fishtail, and Burch braked to regain control. "Just as I was almost stopped, the trailer yanked to the left," he recalls. "The safety chains broke, and it headed into oncoming traffic, hitting a pickup truck square in the side and flipping it over two or three times."

Miraculously, the other driver suffered only minor bruises. But for Burch, it was a hard lesson in towing: by failing to make sure the trailer hitch was the right size for the ball, he almost caused a fatal accident.

Although you may only use it to tow the boat to the lake at the beginning of the season and bring it back home in the fall, a good trailer — properly maintained, hooked up and driven — protects your family and your boat.

Often, boat dealers include a trailer as part of a boat package; custom-made to fit the boats they come with, these trailers are usually completely welded and not adjustable. While the price may be right, it's worthwhile to look at other trailer options before you jump in.

The size of trailer you need is determined by the length of your boat (the centreline length, excluding bow pulpit and swim platform) and its weight — that is, the weight of the boat including the motor, fuel, gear and all the stuff you'll toss in at the last minute rather than cram into your car, plus an addi-tional recommended 10 percent safety margin. "An extra 10 to 15 percent is just right," says Gene Quinn, general sales manager of EZ Loader Canada Ltd. "Anything more than that, and you're buying too big a trailer."

Trailer capacity generally starts at 600 pounds; a 14-foot fibreglass runabout with a 50-horsepower outboard requires a trailer with a capacity of anywhere from 1,200 to 1,500 pounds, according to Larry Moore, president of Northtrail. (The price could range from about $950 to $1,700.) For loads greater than 3,000 pounds, the trailer must be equipped with its own brakes. However, it's sometimes a good idea to have brakes even on lighter trailers for the additional safety they provide, especially if you tow with a smaller car.

When trailer shopping, bring a brochure or the owner's manual for your boat so that you'll have the pertinent statistics at hand. Also keep in mind the trailering capacity of your car: a four-cylinder won't pull 2,000 pounds very far. As a rule of thumb, the weight of the trailer and its load should never exceed that of the towing vehicle.

There are two basic types of trailers for powerboats: roller and bunk. By far the most popular is the roller trailer, where the boat slides on and off sets of rollers, making handling very easy. This type of trailer does not have to be immersed very far to launch the boat — an advantage on steep, poorly main-tained launch ramps. Another big plus is that the rollers "automatically centre the boat when you winch it in," explains Quinn. Different manufacturers offer different types of rollers — big, small, hard, soft, ribbed, smooth — but the most important thing to specify is the number: make sure there are enough rollers to support the boat properly.

While there's no denying rollers are pressure points, if they're positioned correctly, they shouldn't damage the hull. "Only very thin-skinned boats may be damaged by rollers," says Quinn. "Even aluminum-boat manufac-turers put their boats on roller trailers these days."

Bunk trailers support the hull on lengthwise carpet-covered planks, alle-viating hull-warping concerns, as they support the weight evenly. "You can use bunk trailers for any hull shape, because they flex and allow the hull to make its own niche," says Quinn. Since they usually start at a lower capacity than roller trailers, they're often chosen for small, light boats. A bunk trailer uses the water's buoyancy to load and launch the boat, so it must be immersed — a disadvantage on shallow ramps. (If you can't completely submerge the bunks, wet them first, and the boat will slide on much easier, advises Quinn.)

Most bunk trailers also have a keel roller at the back that helps centre the boat and reduce friction when loading and launching. On the down side, the carpeting tends to collect particles that can scrape the hull. And if your boat's bottom isn't spanking clean, you may have a slimy time trying to slide it onto carpeted planks.

Whichever type you decide on, before you invest in a trailer, it's important to look for an extensive dealer network, warns Quinn. "When you break down, you generally can't afford to wait around by the side of the highway four or five days for parts."

"The biggest mistake people make is cheaping out and buying an undersized trailer," says Douglas Ogilvie, manager of Leisure Marine in Woodbridge, Ontario, which carries EZ-Tow and Heritage Custom trailers. Be wary of trailers with 12-inch or smaller tires, he advises; small tires rotate faster, creat-ing more heat. And every sunny day bears witness to more than one sorry cottager on the side of the road, miles from the lake, staring at the remains of a small trailer tire gone poof.

"For longevity in a trailer," adds Ogilvie, "look for a proper steel frame-work, and make sure it's adequate for the load you're carrying."

The dropped axle, available on most

trailers, enables the boat to be carried two to three inches lower and thus improves the aerodynamics of the car-and-trailer combination, but they don't make launching any easier.

This brings us to another recommended feature: bearing protectors. A grease fitting on the axle hub — standard on most 2,000-pound trailers and larger, optional on smaller models — allows easy application of grease and prevents water and dirt from getting into the bearings. (They are especially valuable on bunk trailers, which require a deeper launch.) For about $15, they are an inexpensive way to protect your trailer. "Just get them," says Quinn. "Don't even consider them an option."

The tongue jack is another recommended add-on. It's a small wheel attached by a stationary or folding leg to the tongue (the front part of the trailer that links to your car). The jack has a handle crank to raise and lower the tongue to the desired height; it provides extra support and makes it easier to move a loaded but unhitched trailer. The winch strap can be made of rope, galvanized wire or webbed material (similar to a seat belt). Some manufacturers recommend the webbed strap because it handles well, looks neater and is less inclined to scratch the boat.

Some trailers have plastic fenders rather than steel. While they won't be chipped by stones, they're not strong enough to be stepped on — a use they are often put to, as they make a convenient ladder for entering the boat.

Balancing your trailer with the boat is essential. If the tongue weight is too light, the trailer will fishtail; if it's too heavy, your shocks and springs will age quickly and stopping will be difficult. As the rear of the car is pulled down, forcing the front end up, your headlights will blind oncoming drivers, mirrors will be out of whack and steering may be affected. To alter the tongue weight, the dealer will shift the wheel axles. There's no hard-and-fast rule for optimal tongue weight — some people

recommend about 150 to 200 pounds, others say 5 to 20 percent of the gross weight — but you (or you and a friend) should be able to pick up the tongue with both hands.

Are you ready to go? Before every trip, check the tire pressure — of both the trailer and the car — as underinflated tires develop excessive heat. Connect the electrical system, and test all the lights (including trailer turn signals and brake lights). Make sure that the boat is adequately secured to the trailer and that all hold-down straps are fastened. Make sure any gear you've stowed in the boat is evenly distributed. For a final test, climb aboard, jump and wriggle — the boat shouldn't shift at all. If your boat has an outboard, be sure the engine is in a vertical position or, at most, a slight angle. A horizontal engine puts a great deal of stress on the boat's transom. Also, keep the engine in neutral so the propeller can spin.

Do you have a spare wheel and tire, a jack that fits the trailer and a lug wrench for trailer wheel nuts? Check that the bearings are packed with grease; a dry bearing will quickly seize, forcing you off the road — or worse. They should be lubricated twice a year if you're trailering often; once a year, it's best to take the wheels right off to clean the bearings and grease them thoroughly. When repacking the bearings with grease, be sure not to tighten the spindle nut too much. This could cause the bearings to fail, which could result in a seize-up.

If you have hydraulic brakes, check the lines for cracks and cuts and make sure you're not leaking any fluid. Safety chains should be hooked up (and crossed to keep them from dragging), and the coupler should be locked and secured with a cotter pin. And to avoid an accident like John Burch's, make sure the coupler fits snugly on the ball.

When you take to the road, make your motto "no hurry, no worry." Slow down before a turn, take corners wider than you normally would, and keep a

greater distance from the car ahead — if the trailer doesn't have a separate set of brakes, it's going to take you considerably longer to stop. If you must pass, give yourself lots of time and lots of space; remember, the added weight will reduce acceleration. Shortly after setting out (and occasionally thereafter), stop to check the hitch and the hold-downs, and feel the wheel hubs. "If they're not hot enough to burn your fingers, there's something wrong," says Quinn.

Now the fun part: Zen and the art of backing up. With a car, of course, you steer in the direction you want to back in: right for right. (That's your right when sitting in the car facing forward.) With a trailer, you do the opposite: left for right. Steering the car to the left will make the trailer go right. Just to make it more confusing, you'll see the opposite in the mirrors.

Patience is required. Go very slowly, turn the wheel slightly, then straighten. Catch deviations as soon as they start.

Before you launch your boat, replace the drain plug(s) and disconnect the wiring coupler between car and trailer. If you don't, as you apply the brakes when backing up, the bulbs will heat up — and hot bulbs in water can burst. You may have heard it's best to allow time for the wheel bearings to cool down before backing the trailer into the water, on the premise that hot wheel hubs will draw water into the bearings. However, many manufacturers maintain that this is unnecessary if you have bearing protectors. "If you have bearing buddies, you'll be just fine," says Hank van Baden of EZ Trail.

One final piece of advice: Remember to secure a long rope to the boat and to hold the end as you push the boat off the trailer. Although spectators may find it highly amusing, swimming for your boat is no way to end a long drive to the cottage.

Originally published in Cottage Life *magazine (Toronto).*

Fishing

A guide to the uncanny senses of game fish

Who Is Really the Smartest?

by Tiny Bennett

Fish tend to dominate most life in the waters not only because they are bigger and more powerful than most other forms but also because they have a highly developed range of senses, coupled with a reasonably large brain and a well-ordered central nervous system. It is essential that we understand these capabilities in order to successfully pursue fish by angling.

Even highly skilled anglers sometimes have rather mixed-up ideas of the important senses possessed by fish, often giving top marks to a limited sense while tending to ignore highly developed senses. Fish can see, hear, feel, taste, scent and judge distances. They also have a colour awareness, as most experienced fly fishermen know through years of using specific shades in artificial flies. Science has also recently revealed that colour sightedness is quite an important sense. The sense ability between one species and another often varies, but what we shall deal with here plays a part in most types of angling.

Sight

The eye of a fish resembles the human eye, as they both consist of a transparent lens focusing on a sheet of nerve cells that are sensitive to light. Unlike the human eye, however, the eye of the fish changes the distance between lens and retina to alter focus, while the human eye changes the lens curvature .

The eyes of fish are large in proportion to their size, and even the deep-dwelling species appear to use the sense of sight in a number of circumstances. Some species, such as pike and bass, rely on their eyesight to feed during normal daylight conditions. But the walleye, for example, has what scientists term a *Tapetum lucidum* in the retina of its eyes, which actually allows it to see better under dark or dim-light conditions. As a result, walleye avoid bright sunlight by burrowing under cover or migrating to deep water. It is usually only in the evening that they move into shallow waters to feed under the cover of darkness.

Fish also detect and react to colours in various ways. Pike and bass, for example, are much better able to distinguish between different hues than walleye. Also, pike appear to be positively attracted to the colour red, while walleye seem to respond to chartreuse and orange.

Not only can fish see through water, but they can also see through water and air, and many species are quite capable of spotting danger in the form of an unusual movement made by a human being walking close to the water.

It is my experience that a visual warning of danger is more developed in heavily fished waters.

I was walking with a friend once along a riverbank where carp were busily spawning, when he suddenly threw up his arm to point out a lone duck winging down the river. This quick movement startled a huge carp lying unnoticed by us in the margin of the river beneath our feet. In sheer panic, it thrust away, and a huge scoop-like tail came out of the water, lifting about a gallon of river water and mud, and showered us from head to foot. This is not a rare occurrence, and I believe it is the sudden move that has the greatest effect upon the vision of a fish. Certainly, we should always take the greatest care to keep as well hidden from view as possible and, wherever practical, conduct an angling approach to the water as we would stalk a wild animal on a hunt.

Many a stream that is well stocked with good fish has gained the reputation of being fished out, because clumsy or unskilled anglers walk the bank in full view of their quarry. I see this happening all the time, with people wading in small clear streams where it is quite unnecessary to get into the water. Ob-

No one would call the pumpkinseed fish a genius, but it does have a good sense of sight and "touch."

Long ignored by fishermen, the lateral line that runs down each side of a fish is the key to its ability to detect movement and vibrations in the water.

viously, a keen-sighted fish will go down at this gross disturbance, while a more cautious approach from behind bushes or trees might well reveal some fine lunkers.

The Lateral Line

Running down each side of all fish is a curious and faint line that appears, at first glance, to be nothing more than part of the pattern of the scales or the coloration of the fish. This is the lateral line, a keenly sensitive organ that plays a crucial role in survival.

Found only in fish and some amphibians, the lateral-line sensory equipment consists of a tube running the length of the body on each side and joining together at the head. These tubes are filled with mucus and are open to the water through minute canals that pierce through the scales.

Exactly how this sense system works is still being argued, but clearly, some form of nerve cell here records vital data for the fish, such as water temperature, currents and, especially, vibrations and the movement of objects through the water.

The significance of this sensory system cannot be overemphasized, for experiments suggest that it is often more critical to the fish than the sense of sight. In one experiment, a batch of fish were blinded yet still swam confidently through a maze of obstacles, and when minnows were moved close to them, they turned quickly and managed to snap the prey up. So the lateral-line system must play a critical role in the balance and, by extension, the very survival of the fish.

For anglers, the important factor in our study of the lateral line is that it

acts as a sort of sonar system by picking up vibrations that can be interpreted as a warning of danger or the presence of prey. A good hefty stomp on the bank will probably send the fish scurrying to safety, while the strum of a vibrating lure will bring the predator forward in an attack.

Primitive fishermen the world over are aware of this and make up lures to vibrate and produce strikes. In recent years, there have been a number of gimmicky off-beat vibrating lures put on the market, with scads of publicity on what they will do. Some of the new lures are very good, but some are silly. Vibrating lures have been around for a long time, and a great many old baits have been successful over the years simply because they were made on this principle of movement.

The long, slim Canoe Spoons used for

lake trout strum and flicker through the green half-world deep beneath the surface, bringing in a great trout to the attack. A red and white spoon fluttering through a shallow, weedy bay lures a pike out of hiding, and the superb Mepps tap and shiver across a rainbow creek, bringing a scarlet-sided fresh-run fish forward with a rush to engulf the bait. On the troll line for walleyes, the almost purring action of a Flatfish or an Arbo-gaster puts fillets in the skillet.

Predatory fish are attracted and drawn by all vibrations seeming to come from a creature struggling in the water. This effect is less known in fresh water than in the sea, probably because of the greater size and numbers of saltwater predators.

Once, when we were fishing off Bermuda with light spinning gear, we got the attention of a big school of false albacore by pouring quantities of bait off the stern. False albacore resemble overgrown mackerel; they are speedy, strong and grand fun on light tackle. Indeed, my first two fish on this occasion stripped all the line from my spool in furious rushes down deep. The third fish took off down the tide, and I was sure I was going to be stripped again, when he turned and came flying back, closely pursued by a motley bunch of sharks, a glorious wahoo and assorted barracuda. There was a snick at the end of the line, and all I brought in was the head of what had been a fish of about seven pounds.

Apparently, the frightened flight of the first two fish I hooked and lost had sent out struggle vibrations that had drawn the predators. So when I hooked the third fish, they were ready for action. Note that although there were many more false albacore around, they chased the one emitting unusual vibrations — the one on my hook.

I have experienced similar incidents with pike and muskie, and it is common for one of them to take a hooked panfish. Only once did I get into a situation where attack after attack was made on the fish I had hooked. This occurred on a wild trail in Ontario on the way to Pickle Lake, a mining complex almost level with the south end of James Bay.

Normal speech above water and even singing and loud shouts seem to leave fish unmoved, and I don't care if a companion sings operatic arias at the top of his voice.

Arriving at Rat Rapids, we pitched camp, I clipped a red and white spoon to my big baitcasting outfit, stepped to the edge of a churning white-water chute and took a cast. A long, lean pike of about seven pounds took the bait almost as it hit the water, and as cast after cast took similar fish, my two companions hurried down to join in the game.

In a two-hour session during which we must have hooked about 100 hungry pike, giant pike came boiling in seven times to grab fish of six to seven pounds while they were on the hook. Yet these big pike simply wouldn't look at our lures themselves.

Most anglers today are aware of the value of the vibrating lures, even if a few fail to understand the way they work; but less known and less observed by fishermen is the warning effect on the lateral-line system of some loud shock or noise. Water transmits sound far more efficiently than does air. So the careless anchor heaved over to drop with a thud on a rocky bottom, the tackle box clanking against the hull of the boat, the incautious foot stomping against a rock, all send out waves of sound to create an area of disturbance that is quickly sensed by the fish.

Some fish, such as sharks, are attracted to underwater noise, and it is well known that any explosion will quickly bring these giant predators to the scene. But for most freshwater fish, there is a point where vibration ceases to excite predatory instincts and instead becomes a signal of danger.

Hearing

Fish have ears and a sense of hearing. For some reason that I have never been able to fathom, however, most anglers pay more attention to this sense than to the fish's other far more highly refined sensory factors.

The classic example of this attitude is when some oaf comes stomping happily into the pool where you are trying for a particular trout. He sends a great bow wave ahead of his waders, takes a couple of slashes at nearby weeds with his landing net, kicks mud off his boot on a rock at the edge of the water and then begins to talk to you in a sibilant whisper — because he doesn't want to scare off the fish.

This drives me into a hysterical rage, and I usually turn and ask in a loud voice why he is whispering, as there now isn't a fish for miles that will look at a bait or lure.

Fish simply do not have as refined a sense of hearing as mammals do. Fish have an inner ear but lack the complicated snail-shaped cochlea found in mammals, which gives land predators and victims their vital sound sensitivity. Ears in fish, however, play a role in balance and are probably tied in with the lateral line and gas bladders for detecting low-frequency sounds.

Normal speech above water and even singing and loud shouts seem to leave fish unmoved, and I don't care if a companion sings operatic arias at the top of his voice, as long as he refrains from stomping on the bank or kicking things around the boat. As a matter of fact, a friend and I were once taken to task by some disapproving anglers who heard us singing at full tilt all the old favourite hymns while enjoying a float-fishing trip down a northern river. One man came over to our boat as we docked and said in a most reproachful voice, "You fellows will never catch fish making all that row while you are fishing." His eyes bulged when our guide lifted stringers of very nice fish from our stern.

Taste and Scent

It is wrong to lump taste and scent together, because these are separate senses, even in fish. But they are so closely associated in our minds when we think of fish senses that I have joined them for better explanation.

In both humans and fish, the sense of taste covers limited situations, whereas the power of scent has a great impact in our daily living. Scents are highly stimulating to the human mind, to the point where a particular one can revive memories of things that happened many years previously.

Freshwater fish vary a great deal in their taste abilities, some having quite inferior taste senses and others, usually bottom feeders, having them to a higher degree. The taste buds are located in different places, according to need. The pike and muskie, who pursue their food, have little opportunity to taste before grabbing, so their taste buds are located in their throats, where they can select before sending the food down into the gullet. But make no mistake, these fish will reject an item of food if it has qualities of flavour that they find unacceptable.

Fish that locate food by grubbing on the bottom often have taste buds in their mouths or, in the case of catfish and sturgeon, in the barbels that hang from their mouths and are used as outside tasting feelers to locate food. Carp, one of the most selective fish when it comes to accepting a bait, have taste organs located all over their body surface. For this species, the taste of the bait is a factor of capture, and anyone with experience in carp fishing knows all too well that tobacco taint or the careless contamination of doughballs with insect repellent is a sure-fire way to get properly skunked.

The scenting capability of fish varies and yet may be of such power as to be almost incomprehensible to a human being. The salmon, it is thought, can detect the odour of its birth stream even when miles out to sea, where the scent

> I have made a habit of wiping my lure down with cod-liver oil before it goes over the side. This scent clings to the lure for long periods.

is incredibly diluted. Catfish find most of their food by scent, and it is always rather eerie to me when a channel catfish picks up my dead bait from the bottom of a deep and fast channel in the middle of the darkest of nights.

Fish actually have noses, in the form of two pouches, one on each side of the head, although there is no connection to the mouth as there is in mammals. Water flows through these nostrils, meeting ultrasensitive cells that fully line these orifices. It is these cells that are able to detect microscopic amounts of matter dissolved in the water.

Unlike taste, which plays a lesser part in the feeding pattern of predators, scent is important, far more so than most freshwater anglers imagine. I had a shattering experience of this once while fishing for lake trout, and it left me much wiser. For years, I had rejected the idea of placing dead minnows on the hooks of lures designed for fishing for lakers. It always struck me that this was nothing more than superstition, and moreover, I felt it interfered with the wobbling action of the spoon. I always refused to have minnows put on the hook, usually arguing that predators don't come along and take a sniff; they home in and hit. Since I generally got a good share of the catch, I never felt there was a loophole in my argument.

Then out on a northern lake in Ontario with a highly skilled lake-trout fisherman who knew the water inside

out, I met with a big debate. "Okay," said the old fellow at last, with a disgusted snort, "you fish a bare bait, and I'll use a fish-head mount at the root of my gang hook."

At the end of the day, we had 10 beautiful lakers nicely laid out for pictures, two limits of five fish each. But the old man had taken every fish! Not only had I not caught one, I hadn't had even a solitary hit. Since we had swapped tackle several times during the day and the only difference was that I always had a bare lure while he had a fish head mounted, it did appear that he had a point worth considering.

The following day, I, too, used the head of a river chub mounted on the root of the lure's gang hook. And that day, the score was even — five fish each — and I was sold, even though this could not be called a serious test by any method of comparison. But since then, I have made a habit of wiping my lure down with cod-liver oil before it goes over the side. This scent clings to the lure even after it has been trolled for long periods. I would hesitate to suggest that this makes a difference in the number of strikes, but it only takes a second to do and does remove the taint of human odour from the lures.

For bottom-feeding fish, such as carp and catfish, the preparation of the bait can be important when it is realized that these fish have highly developed powers of scent. As some fish are frightened by unnatural odours, I feel it is important that hands that have touched tobacco should never touch bait. To keep my doughballs fresh, I make a point of carefully washing my hands between smoking and baiting up. As well, additives of a highly scented nature can at times improve baits intended for bottom-feeding fish.

Amid a tremendous amount of hype and hoopla, a number of fishing-tackle companies recently have developed and introduced scent products that the angler can spray or dab onto his or her lures. Generally speaking, these concoctions can be grouped into two quite distinct classes: concentrated extracts and organic compounds.

The concentrated extracts are produced by freeze-drying natural fishing baits such as minnows, night crawlers, leeches and crayfish, while the ingredients on the tube of an organic compound often reads like a witch's brew. Here, amino acids, fish sex pheromones, baitfish fear pheromones and special kairomone attractants are blended together in vats to produce elixirs for the most popular game fish. But do they work?

I have rubbed many of these scents onto my fishing lures, and frankly, I believe that they do produce the desired results. In particular, they appear to be most effective in cold-water situations, such as early spring, late fall and during the winter, when sport fish are at their most sluggish.

Touch

To many people, the act of sticking a hook into a fish is an act of cruelty. Approaching this from the point of human perception, they argue, "How would you like a sharp hook stuck in your mouth or throat?" They have a point that we should examine carefully, for if I felt that fish suffered the kind of pain that I would if I were hooked, then I would never fish again.

Fish are supplied with touch nerves in the form of small pits found all over their body. Nudge a fish with a stick, and he will respond by moving off or possibly by turning and snapping at it. In addition to these touch-cell-pits, some species have touch nerves located in feelers, like the barbels of the catfish and the carp.

However, a sense of touch is one thing, pain is another. It is certain that fish do not experience pain in any way that relates to human experience. I honestly don't know why. All I have to go on is a great deal of personal observation that tends to prove that this is true.

In terms of freshwater fish, it is quite common for pike or muskie to feel the sting of a hook, shake loose and then hit the lure again. I have even caught perch on their own eyes (used as bait after I foul-hooked them earlier); the mutilated fish just took the eyes as food.

When we deal with pain and fish, we are in a field in which our own emotional outlook on the subject bears very little connection with how fish really react to mutilation.

From this ramble through the various sensory powers possessed by fish, we should have learned that they are not exactly defenceless in terms of survival mechanisms rooted in their nervous system. But what of the brain? Are fish "intelligent" creatures?

Fish Intelligence

The fish brain, which is a specialized enlargement of the spinal cord, varies tremendously from one species to another not only in size but in the uses to which it is put.

Fish that feed mostly by scent will have one section of the brain enlarged to accommodate this needed sense, while other species, each according to specialized situations, have other portions of their brains more dominant to aid in the daily business of feeding and avoiding danger. In some fish, therefore, we might expect the midsection of the brain — which deals with vision — to be much more highly developed if that species uses optic power in the pursuit of its food.

Pike and muskies have binocular vision, with both eyes front and centre to allow them a greater degree of distance-judging efficiency in tackling prey. Both these fish species attack rather like a fighter pilot making a deflection shot at an enemy aircraft, and it can be fascinating to watch their approach pattern. I was once casting spoons in a shallow, weedy and crystal-clear lake that was filled with medium-sized pike, and it was usually easy to see the pike hit the lure. They seemed to scull along, finning fairly easily, and then, their minds made up, they would slightly curl their bodies and launch themselves in one sudden thrust. This action was so speedy that they turned into a blur as they headed for the spoon. Still, I noticed with deep interest that they never hit the lure from the rear but came out and slammed into the bait slightly from one side.

I am told (although I have never seen it happen) that very young pike and muskie appear to have to learn and indeed practise this sudden final attack. At first, the young fish often miss and can be seen to be at a loss as to where the chosen minnow has gone.

On the question of intelligence, there is much nonsense bandied about, and anglers credit fish with a greater degree of brain power than they actually possess. Also, it is not uncommon for some species to be talked about in terms of human characteristics, such as the "brutal" shark, the "vicious" pike, the "dainty" trout and the "lordly" salmon. All these descriptions are human and have no true value in the evaluation of a group so low on the evolutionary totem pole. Fish are not vicious or brutal but are merely performing in a natural way according to what part they occupy in the scale of marine life.

You may have noticed my use of the words "wily" or "smart" in connection with carp. I make no apology for this, because I know from experience that large, old carp are extremely difficult to hook. They do have big brains and for my money are the most intelligent in terms of survival capacity.

Many fish can be conditioned to distinguish colours and to associate certain sounds with rewards and punishment. I believe that some species have the ability to inherit wariness, especially those produced from stock that has been subject to constant angling pressure for a number of centuries. Possibly, such fish, dwelling in heavily fished waters, are the product of parent stock that has escaped capture by sharpened senses, in which case, we could expect to find the progeny owning many of the superior traits of the parent stock.

But one thing is clear in my mind. While it is not at all scientific to credit game fish with advanced powers of reasoning, it makes good sense for us to be aware that we are dealing with creatures having an excellent range of senses, and we should govern our approach accordingly. It is better to overestimate the intelligence of our quarry than to barrel in flat-footed and scare all the lunkers within casting distance.

Excepted from The Art of Angling, *Prentice-Hall Canada (Toronto).*

Finding fish in the hottest months of summer

A Midsummer's Fishing Scheme

by Ken Schultz

Where are the fish on a hot summer day? They are deep, shallow or somewhere in between.

That may be a flip answer, but it's a truthful one, for depending on the type of fish, the section of the country and the type of water and habitat, they can be anywhere at all. And they still have to eat to survive — which means that they can be caught.

So to answer the question of where and how, let's look at midsummer strategies for a variety of fish.

Largemouth Bass

An intensively sought summer fish, largemouth bass pose the most where-do-I-go questions because they are found in so many different environments. That's part of the charm of fishing for them. In big reservoirs with little cover, largemouths will be deep in midsummer, especially on structures along submerged drop-offs, ledges, points and creek or river channels. In lakes with timber and vegetative cover, try fishing that cover, especially where it is near deeper and cooler water. Cover means shade, protection and opportunity to ambush.

Aquatic vegetation may be loathed by many anglers because it is harder to cast in and around, lures get hung and fouled with debris and working a boat through it can be a nuisance. But that is where the largemouths hang out. Especially work the pockets, edges, cuts and channels, both deep and shallow, the latter if the cover is thick. Plastic worms are the best bet, weedless spoons and weedless surface lures a second choice.

Look to small waters, if possible, because they are easier to figure out in a day or several days. Fishing at dawn and dusk and in the evening is popular with many midsummer bass anglers, partly for their own comfort and partly because lake activity during the day from skiers, cruisers and the like makes fishing difficult.

Smallmouth Bass

Rocky reefs, shoals and drop-offs are the places to seek smallmouths in most lakes in midsummer. The tailrace areas of dams are also good.

As with largemouths, you can catch some smallmouths on surface lures early and late in the day in midsummer, but your very best bet overall is a jig, worked in and around the deeper rocks. "Deep" may mean only 8 to 12 feet, perhaps, in cooler northern waters or 20 to 25 feet in warmer lakes.

Smallmouths don't hang out in the midst of vegetation as largemouths do, although sometimes they can be found along the weed-bed edges. They are not as comfortable in bathtublike water, so look for them in the shallows very early in the day or at night but deeper during the rest of the day.

In rivers, smallmouths hold close to bottom, and most midday presentations should be deep. Here, too, jigs often tipped with a night crawler or piece of worm are a hot ticket, but a spinner or diving plug that mimics a crayfish also catches fish. Focus efforts on natural objects that interrupt the flow, such as boulders or mid-to-large-sized rocks, as well as fallen trees, uprooted stumps, bridge supports and other structures that might provide a holding spot.

Striped Bass

Stripers are found in open water in the summer, where they often move and chase schools of baitfish, primarily shad. In some waters, the stripers school and chase pods of baitfish on midsummer days, providing exciting action. This usually occurs late in the afternoon until dusk. Anglers search for stripers that are busting bait on the surface, then race to the spot and cast surface plugs, jigs or shallow-running vibrating lures into the commotion. This continues as long as the fish are up and can be followed.

Most of the time, however, midsummer striper fishing is a searching game.

I'm partial to trolling to cover ground and look for stripers, but many anglers prefer to jig or drift live bait down to fish in appropriate places. That includes over old creek beds and channels, near sunken islands, along ridges with drop-offs, at the deep end of points, near bridges and adjacent causeways and on or over humps. Stripers will visit these areas to feed and then depart, and they will also suspend in or near the tops of submerged trees. They are frequently found in 25 to 50 feet of water in mid-summer.

Salmon

Salmon are a migratory fish, and they, too, wander in pursuit of bait, which is mainly alewives or smelt. Chinook and coho salmon stay for the most part in a preferred temperature range of 48 to 55 degrees F, although they will venture "out of temperature" as August pro-gresses and then wander closer to shore as the urge to head toward natal tribu-taries is heeded. Much the same is true of landlocked Atlantic salmon, but they are more likely to remain in water of the preferred temperature.

You have to search intensively and aggressively for midsummer salmon, almost exclusively trolling with down-riggers and diving planers and using spoons and some wide-wobbling plugs. Salmon are caught suspended, often over deep water, and they wander con-siderably, so one has to be ready to cover a lot of ground, change lures (and colours) frequently, search for bait and for salmon and pay attention to the depth being trolled and the depth of cooler water.

Trout

Like salmon, temperature and bait also govern the location of these fish, al-though brown trout and steelhead are found in slightly warmer water than salmon, and lake trout are usually found in slightly colder water. Scour the thermocline for browns and steel-head, especially where it intersects with the lake bottom.

Lake trout orient toward structures and toward the bottom and are found in most American lakes on or near the

Midsummer fishing is best approached with a plan; each species tends to have its own way of dealing with warm temperatures and long days.

bottom and around deep open-water reefs in midsummer. Slow trolling is necessary for these fish, while a faster speed is more conducive to other trout and to salmon. Lakers in cold northern waters will not be as deep, they fre-quently wander along steep, rocky shorelines, and they visit reefs to feed. Spoons are the primary lure, but large diving plugs work; casters can score with large, bright jigs.

Fishing for trout in streams is an alto-gether different matter than in lakes. Late afternoon and evening in midsum-mer will often produce some surface feeding activities for dry-fly angling, and the night can be a good time to find big stream or river trout on the prowl.

During the day, however, look to deep pools and slicks, undercut banks and locations that afford shade. Remember

that small creeks, especially if they flow through thickly shaded woods, will bring cooler water into larger flows and that trout can often be found directly downstream of such mergings. Use light line and tippets in the clear and shallow water, make accurate casts, and fish with small lures or flies.

Walleyes

The midsummer walleye game is gen-erally thought to be a matter of fishing at low-light hours, especially just be-fore dark. While that may be produc-tive and is certainly traditional, these fish can be caught during the day as well. In lakes, look for weed edges, weed protrusions, deep-water weeds, thicker clumps of weeds and even the overlooked water between weed beds and shore. Jigs tipped with live bait work well but are hard for the average angler to get used to (it's tough to feel strikes in the weeds). Other good lures include crankbaits along the edges and sometimes a jig-and-bait combo on a bobber or slip-sinker rig.

In lakes with little or no vegetation, look to long bars or points, reefs, shoals and island edges, using jigs, bottom-walking rigs and spinner-and-bait combos. In large lakes where baitfish are suspended and roaming, look for suspended fish, and troll plugs and spoons, off either downriggers or sideplaners.

In rivers, the midsummer walleye game is quite a bit different. They are exclusively bottom feeders here, and you should look for them below an eddy, along the edge created by merging currents, in slick water and pools, directly behind bottom rocks, below and behind islands and behind rock wing dams and gravel bars. The best offerings are plain jigs, jigs tipped with bait or used in tandem with spinners, and in-line spinner-and-bait rigs.

Northern Pike
Pike are another fish species that orient toward weeds, which are usually plentiful in most places where the fish are found. So-called cabbage, or pike, weeds, which are broad and extend almost to the surface, are particularly favoured by summer pike. These exist along shorelines in bays, off points and around islands and shoals.

In midsummer, pike, especially large ones, will be deeply ensconced in these spots because of the good ambush opportunities. Look to the deeper edge, which is usually in 10 to 15 feet of water, for the larger fish. Flashy lures, including bucktail spinners, spinnerbaits and minnow-imitating plugs, plus noisy surface lures and swimming plugs, are good pike candidates here.

In rivers, look for places where there is a merging of currents, still water near a back eddy, shallow backwaters, the shoreline below points or wing dams, water below islands and in weeds.

Muskellunge
Muskies are such quirky fish that you can't give any definite advice for summer fishing. The regular muskie spots are the regular muskie spots regardless of the season. The only question is, Will this be the day they strike or not? The one point to note is that in some places, the fish are actually shallower in midsummer than you might suppose. I've seen this at Lake of the Woods on the Minnesota/Ontario border in August, where muskies were mostly found shallow, close to small islands and shoals, and caught primarily on bucktails, with large, shallow-running minnow-style plugs and jerk baits also taking fish. So in the summer, you basically continue to work weed beds, shoals, points and drop-offs, whether trolling or casting, just as you would in the other seasons.

Crappies
Not as readily caught in midsummer as in spring, crappies are nonetheless still clustered at this time. When you get one, you should be able to catch a few or a lot in a lake with a good crappie population. The trouble is that you have to do some hunting to find these fish, unless you have planted, or know of, brush piles or other fish attractors.

Summer crappies often string out horizontally and just a bit off the bottom, so you have to get your offering at the right level. This is quite often the case in lakes where flooded timber is found or along old river-channel drop-offs, ledge drops, steep, rocky shorelines or riprap shores, bridge supports and other places that offer shade, sometimes as deep as 25 feet. Small marabou jigs or grubs on light line are probably the best bet, but such bait as worms, small minnows and crickets get a lot of play too.

You'll note that I've used the word "deep" often here, but realize that this is relative. Pike in 12 to 14 feet of water are deep for pike. Walleyes along the deep edges of weeds may only be in 10 feet of water. And so forth. Generally speaking, fish are deeper in midsummer than they were in spring.

But, with a keen eye and common sense, they are still within your reach.

Originally published in Field & Stream *magazine (New York).*

Catching fish at home is the key to success

by James Rudnick

Warm breezes and little waves tapping on the hull, the boat slowly rocking as I almost doze off and miss that bobbing bobber near the lily pads. Slow trolling in the sunshine past the point, hoping to entice that big pike I just know is there into hitting my old, beat-up lure. Maybe casting a few over the top of the weeds in the bay, trying to get a walleye to strike.

No matter what style of fishing you like, cottage fishing is simply the best — the best to savour and the best to remember, especially if you catch something. There's the rub: actually catching something.

Understanding Habitat
Most people know their cottage waters like the backs of their hands: the rocks and the rapids, the shoals and the sandy points, the islands and the back bays. The trick to successful cottage fishing is making the link between knowledge of the lake itself and the fish you're after. That link is an understanding of fish habitat.

Simply put, find the proper habitat — or home — of the fish you're after, and sure enough, they'll be there when you come knocking. On most cottage lakes, there are a few basic fish habitats; we'll look at the big four and then consider one more "secret" home for many top game fish.

Weed patches are the number-one spot, usually lying in shallower waters of less than 12 feet, with a bottom that is muddy to sandy. Yes, I know, you hate water-skiing anywhere near them, so think of fishing them instead.

Why? Some fish just like weeds.

Walleye, for example, have very sensitive eyes and prefer the shadows weeds provide. Perch hide among the stems and leaves, hunting minnows while trying not to get hunted themselves. So do other species, such as sunfish, crappies, bluegills, carp, suckers, largemouth bass and catfish. Pike and muskie also head for weeds; with their size and savagery, they go where other fish already are to get a meal.

Since all these fish love weeds, there's plenty of opportunity at weed patches if you use the right bait or lures. Try fishing lively minnows on a bobber near the very edge of the weed line, hoping to pull out some hungry fish looking for dinner. Or cast a long, minnow-looking plug over the top of the weeds to try to pull a fish up to hit this imitation bait. Fishing right in the weeds is a little tougher, but it can be done using jigs and tipping them with a worm or minnow for an attractive sight-and-smell bait. Each of these techniques can attract any of the weed fish at any time, although some times of the day — such as dawn and dusk — are best for all species.

The second excellent habitat for fish comprises rocky shoals, reefs and boulder piles. The summer's sweltering sunlight on the rocks warms the water, and the warmer water attracts more microscopic life. This in turn attracts tiny minnows, which attract bigger minnows, which attract bigger panfish, which attract bigger sport fish, right up to the top of the food chain — big pike, muskie and those aggressive jumpers, the smallmouth bass.

To successfully fish these habitats, try trolling parallel to the drop-off between shallow and deep water. Here, fish will tend to suspend, hoping to catch a smaller fish for dinner. When they see your lure come by, they'll give it the once-over, as if they're looking at a menu. Try spoons with a big wobble for pike and muskie, diving plugs for smallmouth and walleye or big spinners for almost anything. And if trolling is

just too much work, anchor and cast a weighted hook and worm to the bottom. Reel in just enough line to make it taut, and put the rod down. Now look over that new magazine, or savour the view around the lake. The bang, bang, bang of the rod will let you know you've got one.

Third on my list of fish habitats is what is called a current break. Think about your lake. Is there a spot where there is current? Perhaps a river or a stream empties into it, or water is channelled through a culvert that passes under an island causeway dividing the lake. Maybe there is a narrows where high rock cliffs tell you what the bottom must be like or an old beaver dam where water rushes by. No matter what creates the current, it makes things flow, including fish themselves — especially those which are smaller in size or injured and can't fight it. They are swept along, right into the mouths of waiting game fish.

These fish haunt the downside of current flows, right at a "break," or spot where they don't have to fight the current at all. They hide behind a rock, downed log, ledge or shoal and wait for dinner to come to them. In this way, they catch a meal without expending much energy. When you fish a current break, you have to be able to imitate that injured minnow or other food item in the current.

Begin by putting on high-quality line and tackle, such as ball-bearing snap swivels and premium hooks. Rig up a fat night crawler, or lip-hook a lively minnow with enough weight to go almost to the bottom. Cast into the heaviest current flow, and watch carefully where your line goes. Then use this information to cast the next time just a little upstream of where the line ended after the first cast. What you're doing is trying to float your bait by the fish waiting at the current break.

Enticing fish at current breaks is a little easier than most other types of live-bait fishing, as the waiting fish know

they either take the bait right away or it floats on by. As a result, they tend to hit swiftly. Try casting over and over to many other nearby spots too, as fish may often cruise current flows looking for dinner if they're hungry enough.

The fourth place you can usually find fish is near any other boat on the lake. This method usually works for those who don't know the lake too well. Think about catching fish, then get out and join the fellows who are doing just that. Check them all out with a good pair of binoculars: watch just what they're doing and right where they're doing it, and mentally mark the spot for future fishing expeditions. Then move over slowly and anchor near (not next to) them. Watch carefully for any tips you might be able to pick up, and don't pass on any of your own. After all, fishing is still something that can be shared by family and friends — but never with the guy across the lake.

Beneath Your Feet

Now the last "secret" tip — and perhaps the best of all. If you want to catch fish — big ones — think docks. Fish often come into shallow water near dawn to feed and remain after first light, tucked up under low-lying docks. So check out your own dock by casting a bobber and a big, frisky minnow. Or lob a little spinner to come back beside the dock. Or pitch a plastic worm right on the surface, then hop it along till it barely falls in. Usually, it's at dockside that you'll find the best early-morning action.

Nothing can be finer than returning to the cottage in midmorning and hauling up your stringer right in front of the neighbours. And nothing brings a bigger smile to my face than letting go the biggest fish they've ever seen and commenting, "Things are a little slow in midsummer." Let me tell you, that grin lasts just about all day.

Originally published in Cottage Life *magazine (Toronto).*

Catching up with cottage country's favourite fish

What It Takes to Win a Walleye

by Jake MacDonald

Scientists call them *Stizostedion vitreum*. But in northern Manitoba, they're better known as "yellows" and are considered not so much a game fish as a foodstuff, like flour or pork. In Quebec, anglers won't know what you are talking about unless you refer to them as "*doré*," in reference to their golden scales. American tourists and Canadian fishing guides call them "walleyes," which is generally accepted as their proper name. But in Ontario, calling this fish anything but "pickerel" is downright un-Canadian.

Under any alias, *Stizostedion* is one of the most sought-after game fish in North America. It's a dogged fighter, and there's no better critter in the frying pan. Found in lakes and rivers from the Arctic to the Deep South, this fish reaches a good average size (two to five pounds) and adapts well to a variety of habitats.

The countless lakes of the Canadian Shield are ideal walleye habitat, although cottage owners sometimes complain that their lakes are "fished out." Biologists and scuba divers, however, report large schools of walleyes in even the most overdeveloped cottage lakes. If that is the case, then why are they so hard to catch?

Part of the problem, perhaps, is that we're using outdated fishing methods. Many of us learned to fish on semi-wilderness lakes, where predatory-fish populations were at a peak and any bait was avidly attacked not long after it entered the water. Grampa would take us out, and we'd catch a mess of pickerel right around the corner from the cottage. We grew up believing that catching walleyes was simply a matter of trolling a lure behind the boat.

But times have changed. Lakes are under increased angling pressure, developments encroach on spawning areas, and the supply of baitfish is greater than the supply of predators. Cottage-country lakes have become buyers' markets, and any angler who wants to sell regularly to today's well-fed, twice-shy walleyes should discard any notion that fishing is a matter of "luck" and study up on a few basics.

Walleye fishing can be very complicated, but it boils down to a handful of essentials. Anglers should learn something about the walleye's life and build an approach based on that. In simple terms, it means building a fishing strategy around the walleye's preferences rather than the angler's. To guess at what the fish "wants," an angler should be familiar with its seasonal movements, habitat, preferred foods, habits and daily patterns.

Walleyes migrate annually, moving between deep water and their spawning grounds. As soon as the ice goes out in the spring, they congregate in creeks, shallow bays and river outlets to spawn. After spawning, they disperse and migrate to their summer hunting grounds in deep water, where they remain through fall and winter. When the angling season opens in late May, their journey from the spawning grounds back to deep water is usually just beginning. Anglers should look for walleyes along the shoreline stretches near likely spawning areas. A quiet, moosey-looking bay with a creek running in and maybe a beaver house would be a good place to start.

By mid-June, walleyes have moved to their summer habitat, which is often an area of shoals with deep water nearby. During midday, they rest in the deep water or, if that's not available, in weed beds. However, they're not seeking cold water so much as avoiding the sun. At this time of day, they aren't actively feeding, and a bait must be dropped right in their laps to be effective.

Conventional wisdom holds that in summertime, walleyes are "sluggish from the heat." In fact, they are at their metabolic peak in the warm waters of summer and feed more actively than ever. What makes fishing sometimes difficult is the abundance of forage. By midsummer, the population of small fish and minnows explodes, and the angler, with his pathetic offering, is up against a range of foodstuffs that, from a walleye's point of view, is equal to the spread at a Roman orgy.

Walleyes feed on perch, shiners, ciscos and other small minnows. None of these can see in the dark as well as the walleye, and that's one of the reasons the walleye has evolved into a night hunter. Baitfish seek shelter around weeds, underwater structures and in the shallows. In the evening, when walleyes are hunting, they move into the areas where baitfish live. Anglers should try to intercept walleyes in those places and present a lure or bait that matches the prey.

Since walleyes congregate in schools, if you catch one, it means others are probably nearby. Concentrate on the area, but avoid spooking the school. This is particularly important in clearwater lakes. Walleyes have good vision and hearing, and they will shy away from sudden movement or noise. Shut off your motor, and anchor to one side. Cast a minnow-and-jig combination toward the area where you caught the first fish, and retrieve the bait slowly so that it skips slowly along the bottom. The idea is to imitate a minnow that darts forward a couple of feet, stops, rests on the bottom, then skips forward again. Most novices use heavy jigs. A light ⅛-ounce jig has better action and won't get snagged as easily.

Walleyes have a daily schedule, but it's the opposite of yours. Think of them as college students with fins: they sleep all day, stay out all night. Scientists have confirmed this by radio-tagging them and studying their movements. All conditions being equal, walleyes are active during two peak periods: one that begins just after sundown and lasts until approximately 11 p.m., and another that kicks in about 3 a.m. and continues until sunrise.

However, many of us don't get out walleye fishing until a quiet afternoon when the sun is beating down on a flat lake, the kids are out water-skiing and the relatives are making gentle hints about how much they would enjoy a

Walleyes prefer late nights and early mornings to the heat of midday.

meal of fresh-caught pickerel. Instead of spending a fruitless afternoon convincing your relatives (and yourself) that your little corner of paradise is "fished out," you should just relax and thaw out a package of hamburger. Bide your time, and watch the weather.

A few days later, when there's a mean wind blowing at daybreak and rain squalls blackening the lake, put on your rain gear and head for your favourite shoal. The overcast morning will encourage walleyes to feed late, as will the wind, which breaks up the surface of the water and reduces light penetration. The walleyes may well be active until 10 or 11 in the morning, and with a bit of Grampa's luck, you will have fresh fillets in the fridge the next time the relatives show up.

Walleyes usually don't smash the bait — they announce their presence with a gentle tap — so a light, sensitive rod is extremely helpful. The old heavy baitcasting rod in your closet was designed for trolling and won't really deliver the sort of finesse required for successful walleye fishing; invest in a superlight, ultrasensitive graphite rod and a matched spinning reel. You should also use the lightest fishing rod you can manage; especially in clear water, light line is a

must for wary walleyes. A gentle angler can subdue the biggest walleye that swims with a light spinning outfit and four-pound-test line.

When choosing lures and bait, the idea is to present a close imitation of whatever the walleyes are hunting at the moment. A small jig tipped with a bit of night crawler or a minnow is a good year-round lure that combines the best aspects of an artificial lure (provocative motion) with those of live bait (attractive smell). Artificial lures like an orange Flatfish or a black-and-silver Rapala are good for attracting large walleyes, which prefer a hefty mouthful. The ideal size is three to six inches long, although hungry walleyes will strike lures up to eight inches. Artificial lures, however, work in poor light conditions or murky water. Bait, particularly a lively minnow, is the best bet with fussy midday walleyes. Hook it through the nose, and use a slip-sinker rig. When the walleye takes the minnow, let the line run out. After several seconds of taking line, the walleye will stop. The fish is now turning the minnow to swallow it. Set the hook.

Originally published in Cottage Life *magazine (Toronto).*

Are sunfish kids' stuff, or can they please adult anglers too?

A Fish Made for Tossing Back?

by Jim Bashline

Words used to describe North America's most glamorous fish are familiar to most anglers. Brown trout are "crafty" and "leader-shy" and are often referred to as the Einsteins of the piscatorial world. The strike of a muskellunge is "violent" or "savage," and smallmouth bass invariably "leap with abandon," "fling themselves skyward" or perform some other aerial antic. Books and articles about fishing for sunfish, however, usually contain no glowing superlatives. The most frequently used accolade is "gamey," and of course, there's always the mandatory mention of fried bluegill fillets.

The various trouts may be the glamour species of the world and the largemouth bass the favourite game fish, but sunfish, which include bluegills (or bream), red breasts, redears, longear sunfish and others, would have to win the most-fished-for title. Consider these facts: Sunfish exist in healthy numbers in every state except Alaska (and I wouldn't bet the farm that they aren't there too); can be caught at any time of the year on all kinds of bait, lures and flies; are in no danger of being overfished; and yes, I've got to say it, taste great as well.

The sunfish's most outstanding attribute is its distinction of being the number-one training fish for future anglers. Fly-rodders have known for years that learning how to handle tackle properly comes quicker when there are a lot of willing bream waiting to snap at bugs and flies. Other types of tackle, however, are often overlooked where the sunfish is concerned. The catchall term "ultralight," usually used in conjunction with spinning tackle, is the preferred bluegill gear in many locales. What about baitcasting outfits? The would-be plug chucker can't always find bass ready to devour his lures. Sunnies to the rescue!

Slowly and quietly, the tackle manufacturers have been offering anglers better ways of catching small fish on more sophisticated gear. Low-profile casting reels with magnetic spools and finely honed drag systems allow light-line casting without too many mechanical failures (translation: backlash) if you are careful. Today's high-tech graphite rods, with their sensitive "tip-hand feeling," provide a wonderful assist in tossing tiny poppers and crankbaits. I'll confess that in spite of a half-century love affair with the fly rod, I find few fish and few techniques offer more pure fun than casting to sunfish with scaled-down lures on spinning or casting tackle. Besides, it can't help making you a better bass angler too.

As water temperatures climb in spring, fishing for sunfish with lures is at its peak. Depending on latitude, they spawn in April, May and June. If you don't hit the nearby water at precisely the right time, however, there's no cause for alarm. A month before female sunfish are ready to drop their eggs, the males are itching to do battle. They remain in an aggressive state for a month after as well, and lures passing over or through their bailiwicks rarely fail to attract attention.

If you find a pod of sunfish nests along the shoreline near spawning time, a battle will quickly follow. The males of the species are the most jealous husbands in the world, and any and all intruders are quickly tested. In fact, sunfish will literally fight an egg-eating bass to the "finish" and will do the same with a lure. They will smack it several times before they are hooked and have even been known to come back and do it again immediately after they have been released.

For the most exciting strikes, try tossing a surface lure four feet away from a nest-guarding sunfish, and bring it quickly across his post. His fins flutter momentarily and then, pow, a high-speed dash for the collision.

Because sunnies prefer to spawn in shallow spots, it is easy to locate their beds in clear water. Just look for a saucer-shaped depression, 18 inches to 3 feet in diameter, and the man of the house will be hovering close by. There will probably be several more nests in the near vicinity, so your lure may be attacked by a squad of sunfish. Somehow, the fish know which nest is theirs and return to it unerringly.

In these clear, shallow-water spawning areas, lighter lines are more desirable. Most pocket-sized baitcasting reels will handle light lines better if they are spooled first with a padding of braided line. You'll never need more than 75 feet of monofilament for sunfish, and the cushion of braided line will prevent the small-diameter mono from cutting into itself. If a revolving baitcasting reel doesn't suit you, the newer spincast reels will also handle light line.

It's difficult to manage really long casts with light lures, but with a bit of practice, a 30-footer is long enough. What is light? Quarter-ounce models are about the maximum size for good hooking success due to the sunfish's small mouth opening. Oh, they'll hit larger lures and occasionally get stuck on them, but smaller lures are preferred. Any lure longer than 2 inches is a giant for sunnies, but there are dandies in this range. Among them are Bagley's Kill'r "B," 1¼ inches; Arbogast's Hula Popper, 2 inches; Bomber's Model A, only ⅕ ounce; Cordell's Jointed-Spot, 1½ inches; Gaine's Baby Crippled Killer, 2 inches; Rapala's Little Rainbow, 2 inches and ³⁄₁₆ ounce; and a fine performer in deeper water, Heddon's old Sonic, 1½ inches. Some of these lures weigh more than ¼ ounce, but length is more important than weight. Sunfish are seldom fussy about the colour of a lure when they are in shallow water.

The good selection of tiny plugs for small fish now available notwithstanding, I'd like to see more old favourites made in vest-pocket form. Rattling plugs and propeller-equipped lures, for instance, would also be fun to try; I'd certainly use them on bluegills and bet that not a few larger species would go for them too. The soft entry of a tiny lure could also help if a big bass were

Sunfish, a perennial childhood catch, are also an excellent-tasting panfish.

hanging around watching the bluegill battalion. Talk about a thrill — think about landing a 5-pound bass on 2-pound-test line.

Sunfish may not be glamorous, but what better fish is there to practise casting skills or lure-dancing tricks on? What else is so plentiful and fights with such heart? And what freshwater fish tastes better when their almost transparent wedge-shaped fillets turn the colour of whole wheat toast in the skillet?

In the current catch-and-release climate, you may want to start letting your sunfish go once you have enough fish for the frying pan. There are several ways to do this that prevent injury to both the fish and yourself. Sunnies are toothless, yet they have sharp spines on the dorsal, anal and ventral fins. To avoid pricking yourself, first grasp the fish behind the head, and then slide your hand down over the gillplates as you fold the dorsal fins back with your palm. Your thumb and forefingers should hold the fish near the fins alongside the

fish's belly, your palm resting over the folded-down fins. If the spines do stick you, wash the puncture and apply antiseptic. The spines are not toxic, but bacteria can enter the wound and cause a painful infection.

If your hand is large enough, you can also hold the fish by grasping it around the belly with your thumb and folding the dorsal fins down with your fingers.

Often, bluegills struggle so violently as the hook is being removed that anglers drop them on the hard bottom of a boat or a rocky bank. One way to avoid injuring a fish this way is to have a wet towel handy to fold over the fish, covering its eyes to calm it down (this works much the same as blinders on a racehorse). It's very important to keep the towel clean and wet, since a dry, dirty rag removes moisture from the sunfish's skin and leaves it vulnerable to infection.

Originally published in Field & Stream *magazine (New York).*

Remember that fishing with kids can be fun

by James Rudnick

Kids say the darndest things — and fish in the darndest ways. I've had to cut line from around my own hat, as well as from the anchor line, prop and cooler — all the result of a single cast. The wind "must have come up," suggested the culprit, my 6-year-old son Kyle. I just nodded and continued to cut the snarled line that evening near dusk, until all that was left was just enough for him to dunk between the lily pads with a fat worm on the end. (Kyle proceeded to catch a three-pound largemouth. Beginner's luck — probably.)

Kids can accomplish the most intricate and impossible manoeuvres with fishing tackle. And nothing can better the odds of them tangling, muddling, snarling and snagging their lines than giving them the wrong equipment. There's also no better way to increase the speed with which they decide that fishing simply isn't fun.

No rod and reel are entirely snafu-proof, mind you. (For some kids, like Kyle, nothing is impossible.) Parents, however, often go astray when they're outfitting their kids for fishing, falling prey to one of three schools of thought. First, there's the nothing's-too-good-for-my-kid contingent, who head for the $200 baitcasting reel with matching rod (that's matching in price too). I can guarantee those parents will soon have that rig in their own hands. Their kid will be so frustrated trying to use what is obviously adult equipment that any excitement he or she has for trying to catch fish will quickly evaporate. (My mom said that when Dad did this kind of buying "for the kids, hon," she always knew he was just trying to expand his own selection of tackle.)

On the other end of the spectrum are parents who give the kids their old stuff. After all, hand-me-downs worked when it came to clothes from older siblings, so why not fishing tackle from Mom or Dad?

The answer is simple, really: kids are shorter and lighter. They have small hands, and they don't have the same sense of balance as an adult does. A rod and reel may not seem heavy, but it probably weighs in at more than a pound. To hold and cast it — properly, that is — means a tired kid after one short half-hour. Hand-me-down equipment is too big and too heavy — and consequently more awkward for them to achieve any reasonable success. (What's reasonable success? When I was starting to take Kyle fishing at our cottage a few years ago, the ability to cast more than 10 feet away from the dock or boat without the rod following the bobber into the water would have elicited praise.)

After trying the hand-me-down route, I got smart — or so I thought, as I fell into the third mistake many parents make. I bought cute.

I went for an outfit from one of the successful manufacturers. "These guys make great long-lasting toys for kids," I reasoned, "so their fishing tackle for kids should work great too." Believe me, a big mistake. The companies that make those long-lasting toys do so by building in as few moving parts as possible and by using no engineering principles beyond friction and gravity. This approach has little to do with the design and manufacture of fishing rods and reels.

Have you ever seen what sand can do to plastic gears and pulleys? Or the look on Junior's face as that nibbling fish wraps the bobber around a lily-pad stem and the line breaks as if made of gossamer and a used-car salesman's promises? Or handles made of foam so cheap, it wears off after three fish (two if they were perch), and line guides that pull clean off the rod when you try to set the hook?

I made the same "cute" move twice: My daughter is two years younger than my son, so I figured the toy companies might have read my letters and re-designed their fishing outfits — but no such luck.

I finally found the solution in a Canadian Tire store, but any other large, mass-merchandise store will do: K-Mart, The Bay, Eaton's, Zellers or Towers, for example. While such stores often don't have the expertise or inclination to buy even a fraction of the tackle many experienced adult anglers would want, they do stock the parent's best friend — the combo package.

Simply put, manufacturers combine a rod and reel suited to each other in one package for a price cheaper than that of the two pieces bought separately. The Big Five tackle manufacturers — Abu-Garcia, Berkley, Daiwa, Shakespeare and Shimano — as well as a host of smaller companies, all put together well-engineered, easy-to-handle combo packages. The components are lightweight, balanced (no mismatched jumble of equipment here) and difficult to jam. Such combos come in a wide range of prices (approximately $15 to $100), but you should be able to pick up a good one for the kids for $20 to $30. And if you are planning to attend a spring sportsmen's show, such as the one in Toronto each March, keep in mind that it's a good place to check out and compare the options.

Some companies market combos particularly for kids, and you can identify them by their packaging — brightly coloured graphics with stylized fish — or their names; for instance, Berkley's Tadpole and First Catch combos. Some packages are designed for the very young, while others are for older children who have a bit more dexterity and skill. Daiwa, for example, markets both a package for tiny tots, the Strikekit (which runs $15 to $20), and one for kids aged 8 to10, the Stinger (which

Early fishing experiences should match fun and success with adult patience.

costs about $40). Other manufacturers put out combos not designed or marketed specifically for youngsters but a good choice for them nonetheless.

What characteristics make a rod-and-reel package ideal for children? First of all, the rods are short so as not to tire those little arms that cast all day (or until lunch at least). The best ones are made of strong, stiff fibreglass that reacts well to a fish strike yet won't break when wedged between two dock boards or jammed into the gunwales of the boat (as they often are). Some companies, such as Shimano, offer great graphite rods suitable for kids, although they cost more.

The reels are of lightweight aluminum and have heavy-duty gears, so they will take a season or two of regular abuse (water and sand won't hurt them either). The most popular combos available have spincast reels — with the button on top and the line completely enclosed — which are the easiest to teach your youngster to use and

the least likely to tangle. Wait till Junior hits about 8 or 10 before you introduce a spinning reel, and a few years more before you bring on the complexities of a baitcasting rig.

Most of the big tackle companies have already learned to provide handles that switch from right- to left-hand side on their reels for adult anglers, and this feature is often carried through on their combos for kids. (Although this is your best bet, if you choose a package without a switchable handle, you'll probably want a right-hand retrieve for a right-handed child and the reverse for a left-handed one.)

Some of these combos have line already spooled on the reel, while others require you to add your own. In either case, make sure you've got the proper test for the fishing — and not for the abuse the line is sure to take (8-to-10-pound test, for instance, if the kids are after bass or panfish). Teaching new anglers to respect their line is a chore, but one any parent

should expect to deal with early on.

Don't forget the lesson learned when you brought home only one chocolate bar or handed out one felt-tip marker when there was more than one kid in the house: buy one combo per little person. To teach responsibility and care of tackle — no laying it down on the dock to be stepped on, no using it to hit the family dog — it's important for each child to have his or her own equipment. Recognizing this, Abu-Garcia sells its combo for the very young with different-coloured rods: you can buy a blue rod for one child, an orange one for another and a silver one for a third.

While it's true these combos will be outgrown one day if your youngsters really take to fishing and want more sophisticated equipment, they can then be relegated to the boathouse tackle pool. You can provide a combo set to cottage guests you wouldn't trust with your own tackle or to visitors, young and old, who have never fished before.

So pick up one combo per kid, and buy lots of bobbers; single, small live-bait hooks; medium split-shot sinkers; and a pile of worms. Live-bait fishing with worms will attract every known game fish in the province — and almost everything else too. But as any angler knows, the sport requires skill, patience, expertise gathered through decades and a modicum of luck. To try to teach anything like that to the kids in an afternoon is well-nigh impossible. To get them even to enjoy the sport is going to require some adjustment in your fishing style. Forget about trolling around the lake for 10 hours or casting big muskie-sized plugs at dawn. Instead, take the kids where you know there will be quarry and they are likely to get at least some bites. Try for bass in the lily pads or walleye on the bottom, if you think that will work. But never forget a panfish on the end of the line is as good to a kid as a sport fish.

Originally published in Cottage Life *magazine (Toronto).*

Knowing what you are doing will increase your catch

Developing Eyes for Big Bass

by Cliff Hauptman

Lots of people catch bass, often without even knowing what they're doing. I was once trying to seduce the bass population in a small lake by showing it just about every lure in my tackle box, including flies, with such consistent failure that my ears began to hurt from frustration. Meanwhile, about 25 yards down the bank, a youngster was hauling in bass after bass by baiting his hook with bread. The infuriating thing about it was that he was actually trying to catch bluegills.

That kind of occurrence often leads anglers to the erroneous conclusion that bass are easy to catch and that they can habitually expect bass-fishing success without spending much time on subtlety, finesse, patience and a thorough understanding of the species. The fact is, though, that the difference between enjoying routine bass-fishing success and occasional good luck is often an angler's ability to pinpoint subtle elements of the bass's environment.

A bass gets large by being good at being a bass. As a result, it falls into a self-sustaining cycle of dominance that works like this: for one reason or other (possibly genetic), a particular fish catches more food than its fellows. It gains weight and size faster than the rest. Because of its larger bulk, it can dominate the best feeding areas, driving smaller fish away, thereby reducing competition, which in turn allows it to feed without expending much energy. That happy circumstance lets it increase its size even faster. Before long, it is the uncontested lord of all it surveys, and it can choose as its lair the best spot available. To catch big bass, then, a fisherman has to know how to find that spot.

Here is where a little knowledge of natural history and a lot of common sense come into play. It helps to know, for example, that the creatures bass love to feed on do not all live in the same aquatic environment. Insects eat plants and other insects, so they are most abundant among weeds and decaying wood. Baitfish eat insects and so are drawn to areas of particularly high insect activity, especially submerged weed beds thick enough to offer some protection from larger predators — like the bass you are hoping to catch. Frogs eat insects too, but they need to breathe air while keeping their skin wet; that makes emergent weeds in shallow water the most attractive place for them. Crayfish, generally, are scavengers that frequent rocky areas where they can hide in the crevices and crannies to dine on the food that conveniently gathers there.

Although that overview is something of a simplification, it leads to an enlightening conclusion: there is more food in greater variety at the edge where two environments meet than in the midst of a single environment.

Armed with this knowledge, any angler can understand the value of working a lure where an acre of coontail abuts a few thousand square feet of cabbage, and doing so, he will likely draw the attention of some accommodating bass. But anglers who consistently find the lairs of monster largemouths are playing a game of subtlety and finesse; they know that an entire environment can consist of nothing more than a solitary sodden log.

It does not take much in the way of a rotting piece of deadwood to serve as the basis for a whole aquatic universe of complex interrelationships among small organisms. Something the size of a fallen birch can be a veritable organic gold mine. Not only does it serve to attract and hold a smorgasbord of goodies for a bass's banquet, but it also gives the guest of honour an ambush point right under the table. If that log happens to be lying in a bed of lily pads, you are looking at the meeting of two distinct environments, a place that's tailor-made for big bass.

A small rock pile in the middle of a bed of cabbage can be another promising spot that too many fishermen view

Bass thrive on the baitfish that feed on the insects found in weedy areas and around decaying wood. Rocky ledges and shallow water also attract bass.

merely as a boating hazard. Here, a bass can find cover and baitfish in the vegetation while picking crayfish and hellgrammites out of the rocks. Big-bass hunters treasure these areas and fish them with care and persistence.

This fine-tuned attention to detail is what separates the successful angler from the frustrated fisherman. Just as the development of your eye is critical to noticing potential big-bass haunts, so is the development of your technique to fishing them.

I have a friend who will no longer fish with me. He subscribes to the school of bass angling that is born of tournament fishing. That method presupposes a time limit and a race against the clock. Al likes to hit and run. He works a fast-moving lure through an area that holds potential, and if he gets no response after a shotgun coverage of the general territory, he moves on. When he does find takers, he favours only the most aggressive in the area and then heads out to seek new terrain at top speed.

You can't argue with his results if it is numbers of bass you seek. But generally, the fish are small to average. The bass that go after Al's lure are those which are forced to chase just about anything because they have been driven out of the better feeding spots by bigger fish. The day Al forswore fishing with me was the day I spent a half-hour casting to a lone stump in a patch of pads without finally producing a fish. I sense no need to hurry.

I don't know if he would have seen

things differently if a six-pounder had finally come bursting out from beneath that stump, but one didn't on that particular occasion. Still, there have been so many similar occurrences when one has that I have learned an essential lesson: if you have developed a sharp eye for those perfect and subtle big-bass spots and that well-trained eye locks onto one while your knees go soft, the butterflies riot in your gut and the adrenaline surges through your sinuses, work that spot until you catch that big bass or are certain you've spooked it into leaving the area.

When you find an edge where two environments meet, fish it with the confidence that there is something nearby worth catching. Let the specific circumstances determine your lure choice, and work the spot with the faith of your convictions. The successful big-bass catchers operate on the simple premise that if they spot a prime bass lie, a prime bass lies there. If you should happen to find three environments coming together, say a rocky shoreline with a growth of pads into which some timber has fallen, you may want to apprise your family and friends of your new address.

Your road to success begins with your eyes. Watch not only for those elite edges but for other subtle signs as well. An area of particularly abundant insect life should set your nostrils twitching. So should a particular profusion of frogs or wading birds. Watch, too, for any movement of the water, and never fail to cast to swirls, because you don't know if the disturbance was caused by a bluegill chasing minnows or a 10-pound bass chasing a bluegill through the weeds. In either case, however, the commotion indicates current feeding activity and the presence of bass food. And that very likely means bass too.

The speedy angler who likes to cover water can raise plenty of bass, but he will rarely develop an eye for, nor take the time to carefully work, those magic spots which produce the kinds of bass that raise eyebrows.

Originally published in Field & Stream *magazine (New York).*

Mastering the basics of a good tackle box

by John Partridge

What does "Dylite Creepy Nitwit" mean to you?

If it sounds like an epithet to hurl at the fellow in the muscle boat down the lake, hang about. But if you know it's the name of an exotic fishing lure from bygone days — "the amazing Nitwit with the live-action legs" — you should be out flogging the water, not inside reading this.

For those still with me, I'll admit I lured you in with a slightly red herring. You don't need a tackle box bulging with Nitwits or other erotica to boost your — and your kids' — chances of catching more than sunstroke in the few hours you spend fishing during cottage weekends. That's because the experts agree that the best bet for casual anglers after pickerel, bass and other panfish is live bait — dew worms and minnows. And this means life really can be as simple and inexpensive as hook, line and sinker.

The most critical of these three elements is the line, and there's one irritating little ritual you should follow every year before heading out for the first time: change it. Chances are, you've got monofilament on your reel, which deteriorates over the winter. Take it from a lazy past master, there's nothing quite so frustrating as losing the season's first and inevitably largest lunker when hook and stale line part company just as you reach out with your net. As for line strength, a happy medium is 8-to-10-pound test — lighter is too risky, heavier is overkill. Look for well-known brands such as Stern and Trilene. A couple of 250-yard spools should keep you going for a season and

not set you back much more than $8 or $10 apiece.

Next into the tackle box should go hooks, and lots of them, because you should change them at the first hint of dullness. The rule of thumb here is the smaller the better. You won't go wrong if you opt for sizes 4 to 6 and for premium brands such as Eagle Claw and Mustad, which will cost about $3 to $5 for packets of 50 or 100. If you're planning to fish with worms in particular, go for a style called "bait-holder": they feature a couple of little barbs on the shank designed to stop the slippery critters from wriggling off. (Remember that live bait should wriggle. Demand space in the fridge for your worms, and keep your minnow bucket in the lake. Bait won't survive long otherwise on a hot summer day.)

You'll do better if you tie the hook directly onto your line — the theory being that you are less likely to spook fish that way. However, if you want to avoid the other rule of thumb that has to do with the powerful attraction between hooks and human flesh, go for the "snelled" varieties. They come attached to the steeper prices but also to a short length of monofilament with a loop in the end. You attach them using a "snap swivel," a kind of stylized safety pin that you tie to your line. Snap swivels are inexpensive — $2 to $3 for a packet of a couple of dozen in the 20-to-25-pound-test size — and they make it, well, a snap to change the offering on the end of your line.

That's handy, especially if you're bored by live bait — or tired of constantly being called on to equip the other fisherfolks' hooks with fresh worms — and want to switch to artificial lures. Building a small inventory of lures for your tackle box doesn't require taking out a second mortgage on the house or cottage; you should be able to kit yourself out with a minimal assortment of half a dozen or so for about $20 to $25.

Go for a selection of small metal

spoons and spinners, which sink and look like what their names suggest. They're good for both casting and trolling, you can generally pick them up for $2 or $3 apiece, and they've been known to catch just about any kind of fish from perch to muskie. For instance, with spinners, which are ideal for shallower waters, you might try the classic Mepps Aglia brand (or its numerous imitators) in sizes 2 and 3 with brass or silver finish. You're likely to pick up a nice pickerel or bass.

Then there's another species of inexpensive lure called the jig that costs from 75 cents to $1 or $2 apiece. Some anglers, such as Canada's best-known professional tournament fisherman Bob Izumi, won't go anywhere without them. Essentially little more than hooks with lead heads, they come either naked or dressed in skirts or bodies or wiggly tails of an enormous variety of styles and colours. You can fish the fancy-dressed ones on their own or, as you must do with the naked variety, with a worm or a minnow. They work best in deeper water — 8 to 10 feet or more. Pick up a handful of different varieties in weights ranging from ⅛ to ⅜ of an ounce. Ask your local bait shop which kinds are best for your lake.

If you feel like spending a bit more (around $5 to $6 apiece and up), you might throw in a couple of plugs, which are plastic or wood lures that imitate live bait — everything from minnows to frogs to muskrats. The Beno, particularly in a frog finish, is a good all-purpose bet. So, too, are minnow imitations such as the Rapala Shad Rap or Wally Diver, which both come in models designed to run at different water depths. Start with just a couple that are three or four inches long, in a silver and black or "perch" finish.

There's also a murderous species of lure known as the spinnerbait, a hybrid that features a spinner or pair of spinners on one leg of a V of steel wire and a fancy-dressed jig on the other. These lures cost $3 to $4 and are good for

A new tackle box should fill up over several seasons; when starting off, add line, lots of hooks and sinkers and a selection of spoons and spinners.

landing pike, bass, muskie and pickerel.

You'll also need to have some sinkers in your tackle box for when you switch back to plain old hooks. Here again, think small, and go for split shot — sizes 5 through 7, say — which come in packages of 40 or 50 for about $1. Simply crimp a couple onto your line 15 or 18 inches above the hook (no closer) with that pair of needlenose pliers you should also have in your tackle box.

You might throw in a few of those red-and-white plastic bobbers (about 50 cents), which will signal to young or particularly lazy fisherfolk when they have got a bite. Add a stringer ($2 to $6) for holding your catch and a filleting knife ($12 and up), and you are in business.

Oh yes, there is one more item you've

got to have: a fishing licence. Since January 1987, every angler in Ontario — resident or nonresident, guest or cottage owner, anyone between the ages of 18 and 65 — must have one. Any self-respecting tackle shop or marina will be able to sell you one. Check with the locals about fishing regulations in whatever province or state you happen to be in, as fines and penalties are usually high.

Indeed, about the only other thing you need to take out on the lake with you is faith. And that is critical, for as veteran Mississauga tackle dealer Sandy Aikman eloquently sums up, "It all depends on the vibes you send down the line."

Originally published in Cottage Life *magazine (Toronto).*

The care and collection of a favourite bait

by Joseph Bates

The common earthworm, which comprises more than a thousand varieties, is found almost everywhere, is easy to keep on hand and is a favourite food for most species of fish. Since it is the most popular bait from coast to coast, too many fishermen think all one has to do is to put it on a hook and drop it into the water to get results. Fishermen who get the best results know there's a lot more to it than that, so let's see what successful ones know that others don't.

Freshly dug worms are dark (because of the earth in them), soft and slimy. They should be prepared for fishing by scouring, which means leaving them in sandy, mossy soil or in a combination of sand and leaf mould for a few days. In such a preparation, they expel the dark earth from their tracts and become a brighter shade of red. Their bodies toughen and are relatively free of slime. Thus they become livelier, easier to handle and more attractive to fish.

The quick way to partially cleanse and scour them is to keep them in a can of damp moss or pulverized damp leaf mould for a few hours before going fishing. A better way is to have a scoured supply always on hand in a worm box sunk in damp (but not wet) ground or perhaps kept in the barn, garage or cellar. A supply can be dug from fertile soil by using a spading fork (which is less inclined to cut the worms than a shovel is). Once dug, worms will propagate in a suitable box, from which a day's supply for fishing can be obtained quickly.

A fairly large and sturdy wooden packing crate — about two by three feet square and two feet deep — makes an excellent box if there are no holes or crevices through which worms can escape. A rectangle of wire screening can be laid on the bottom to cover small holes made for drainage. While the number of layers of material in the box and their composition can be varied, there should be a minimum of soil so that the worms can scour themselves in alternate layers of sand and leaf mould or moss. Before filling, sink the box in cool, damp ground in a shady place, leaving a few inches of box above ground. The bottom layer should be of sand and the top layer of leaf mould or moss. Commercial bedding preparations, available at sporting-goods stores, can also be used.

When the box has been prepared, the worms are dropped on top so that the lively ones can burrow in. The others should be picked out and discarded. A quart or so of food — coffee grounds, vegetable cuttings, bread crumbs, cornmeal, chicken mash or a combination of such materials — should be placed on top as well. Enough water should be added to dampen the contents. The box can be covered with canvas or burlap, held in place by boards. When a supply of worms is removed for fishing, the layers will be disturbed, but that is unimportant. If the box remains outdoors in freezing weather, leaves or other debris should be piled over it for protection. If small worms are found, it means that the box is functioning efficiently because a new crop is coming along.

A flat tobacco can makes a good container for carrying worms because it will fit in a pocket. Air holes should be punched into the cover, and the can should be partially filled with damp moss or leaf mould. A difficulty with this is that the worms burrow to the bottom, so the contents may need to be dumped out to find a few. An alternative is to obtain a small, round can that comes with a plastic cover; cocktail peanuts come in such cans. Cut out the bottom, and put another plastic cover from a similar can on it. The worms can be seen through one cover or the other and easily removed. They should be kept in a shady, cool place, out of the sun. Special cans for carrying worms can be purchased in tackle stores. These strap to the belt and keep the worms fresh.

When using worms as bait, there is one basic rule: use small worms for small fish and large worms for large ones. If the worms are too big for the fish, the fish will steal the bait.

For trout, a single worm hooked through the collar is usually best. Trout like worms that wriggle naturally, and they rarely will take them when they have been impaled on the hook more than once or twice. I like to have the worm cover the barb; otherwise, the fish feel the barb and won't swallow the bait. This also prevents the hook from catching in weeds.

When fishing for large fish, two small worms can be used or a single large worm can be strung up the hook's shank.

Because panfish are notorious bait stealers, put half a worm, or a small end of one, on a small, light-wire hook. In quiet water, let the worm sink slowly to the bottom under its own weight.

Large bass, catfish and some other species prefer several worms on a No. 2 or larger hook, strung up the shank and down onto the barb.

In places where more than one hook is allowed, a tandem rig of two or three hooks keeps the worm more securely on the hook for casting. Such a rig is also used for slow trolling, usually with a spinner or two ahead of it. Worm rigs are also popular for bobber fishing.

Important rules in worm fishing are that the worm(s) should be bright and lively; hooked so it can wriggle naturally; be allowed to drift with the current (instead of being towed through it); and fished where the fish are — which generally means on the bottom or very close to it. To get down there, you may need to use a sinker or one or two split

Worms make excellent bait that is often free; just ensure that they remain healthy and lively enough during storage to attract fish when needed.

shot. If lead is necessary, the smallest amount that will do the job is the best, and it should be placed well up on the monofilament rather than too close to the hook. Many beginners use hooks that are too large or too heavy; smaller ones of light wire are usually better.

Beginners use night crawlers too often, evidently on the theory that if a smaller worm will do well, a bigger one will do better. Night crawlers are typically so big as to prevent hooking fish of reasonable size that could be caught readily with a worm or two. Favour night crawlers for big fish or for smaller ones with bigger mouths, such as bullheads, large bass and catfish, and hook them as you would other worms. The best time to use them is during a rise of water after a rain.

There are several ways of obtaining night crawlers (and earthworms) in addition to digging them with a spading fork. Some fishermen shock them to the surface with electrodes pushed into the ground; others produce underground vibrations by raking a driven stake with a board, as one would use a bow on a violin, or throw solutions of one thing or another on the ground so the liquid will drain into their burrows and drive them up. The simplest way is to gather them on the lawn after dark, just after a rain or after heavily watering the lawn with a garden hose.

Some sort of illumination is needed to see the night crawlers, but since they are sensitive to light, it should not be shone on them directly. A piece of red balloon rubber stretched over a flash-

light lens with a rubber band provides enough light to see the quarry without frightening it.

While night crawlers lie on the surface in the grass, their tails are inside the neck of the burrow so that they can slip into it instantly. The trick to gathering them is to crawl slowly and quietly over the lawn until you spot a crawler and grab its tail end. The crawler will hold on to its grasp in the burrow. Hold on to the rest of it until it relaxes enough to be pulled out. Some crawlers may be entirely out of their burrows, but it's hard to tell for sure. They can be dropped into a container, then be kept in the worm box with the worms.

Excerpted from Fishing, *Crown (New York).*

Pests

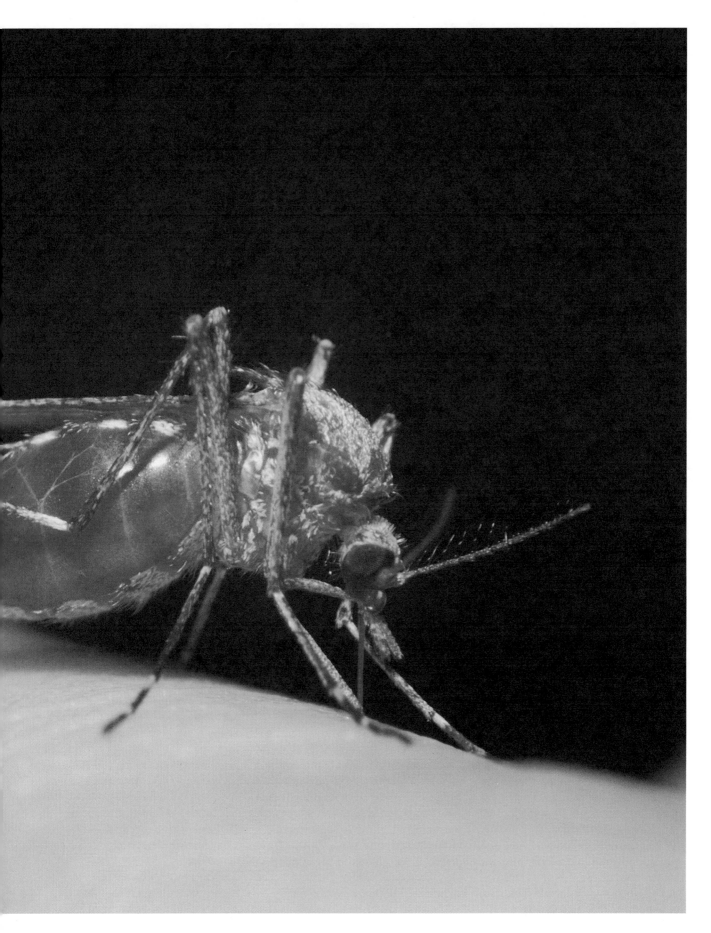

The scientific essentials of insect attacks

Some Are Biters, Others Just Sting

by Bev Smallman and Allan West

Ask a beekeeper if he ever gets "bit," and his smart-ass answer will be, "Never! But I am occasionally stung." The difference is valid: bugs bite with their front ends and sting with their rear ends. You should understand the difference between these two ends, because bites and stings are the commonest afflictions of those who love the outdoors, and they are capable of ruining great summer weekends more often than anything else.

The basic function of each end will be familiar. The front end is for the intake of food and drink; the rear end is for the eventual elimination of same and for reproduction. But the equipment for performing these functions in the bugs differs from us humans to the point of the bizarre.

The Biting Equipment

By human standards, the mouthparts of a cockroach or a grasshopper are fairly normal. There are recognizable jaws, or mandibles, operating between a front and a hind lip that enclose a mouth cavity. Familiar also is the provision of a duct for introducing saliva into the mouth cavity. True, the jaws close on each other from side to side instead of up and down. True also that the mouthparts include Martianlike jointed appendages for stuffing things into the mouth. Nevertheless, the front-end assembly is clearly a mouth that is equipped for biting and chewing substantial, solid food.

But now, look at a mosquito. No trace of the roach's understandable lips and jaws is apparent. Instead, a long, slender snout, called a proboscis, extends from the base of the head. Although you can't easily see it, all of the biting machinery is still there, but it is wondrously transformed to accommodate a liquid diet. The proboscis is actually the hind lip, greatly elongated and curved to form a sheath that embraces the jaws, similarly transfigured into long, needlelike lancets. Other bits and pieces of the roach's mouthparts are remodelled in the mosquito to form ducts for the transport of blood upward and of saliva downward.

When a mosquito "bites," the proboscis is pressed against your skin and the lancets are activated to pierce it and to enter or tear the blood capillaries. As if this outrage were not enough, neat little pumps in the head and thorax now transfer your blood to the mosquito's stomach. All the time, saliva from glands in the thorax is being pumped into the wound. More later about the significance of this saliva for you.

Of course, all of that marvellous machinery would be useless without some means for guiding it. After all, a mosquito must be able to locate you in total darkness, then decide at hovering distance whether you merit risking a closer encounter and, finally, whether she should land to obtain the nutrient she needs. All this information is received by tiny sensors on the proboscis and scattered over her body. They are acutely sensitive to warmth, water vapour and carbon dioxide — all telltale emissions from the bodies of warm-blooded animals, and that includes you. These are the signals that guide the mosquito to her target and give her clearance to land. As you will learn, methods for jamming or confusing these signals provide some of your best defence measures.

A tempting analogy to the mosquito's proboscis is that triumph of Canadian technology — the Canadarm of U.S. space-shuttle fame. Both are attenuated appendages of a flying platform. Both are tubular for strength and flexible for manoeuvrability. And both are guided by precision sensors capable of directing minute mechanical responses. But the proboscis exceeds in miniaturization even the electronic chips of the

Looking much like an extra leg, the mosquito's slender, feathery proboscis extends down from its head.

An unpleasant summer beachmate, the horsefly delivers its painful bite with a pair of short, stout mandibles that slash, rather than pierce, the skin.

Canadarm computers. It seems perfectly adapted to the size and function of its flying platform. Perhaps it is. However, other effective versions exist in the insect world.

Within our area of concern, the familiar blackfly provides such an alternative. It is, in fact, shared to some extent by those other vicious biters, the horseflies and deerflies.

Unlike the long, slender proboscis of the mosquito, the snout of the blackfly is short and stout. As before, the outer sheath consists of the front and hind lips, but with the innovation that the tip of the hind lip is expanded to form a fleshy pad with minute channels sculpted into its surface. Between the lips are the mandibles—flat, scissorlike blades. When a blackfly bites, the mandibles snip through the skin while other structures with recurved hooks abrade the puncture to produce a ragged wound. At the same time, the fleshy, channelled tip of the hind lip is pressed against the wound and acts as a surface seal, confining the blood as it is sucked into the mouth. As with the mosquito, saliva is introduced into the wound during feeding. And again, there are many sensors to inform the blackfly that it is on target.

The biting apparatus of the horsefly and deerfly are modelled on similar lines except that the mandibles are stout, sharp blades for slashing a relatively wide wound. In contrast to the delicate rapier thrust of the mosquito, the horsefly's attack is a vicious sabre slash. As we will explain later, this biting equipment accounts for the oozing wounds left by the bites of blackflies, horseflies and deerflies.

The Stinging Equipment

For insects, it can properly be said that the female of the species is deadlier than the male — only the females can sting. This is because the stinger is derived from the egg-laying apparatus located on the end of the abdomen. In some insects, this benign instrument of reproduction has been modified to serve also as a poison-emitting lance for defence.

The stinger consists of two parallel lancets encased in a stout sheath. The lancets extend beyond the sheath and are alternately driven by muscles to penetrate the skin. Internally, a diabolical bit of chemistry produces venom, which is stored in a poison sac. On receipt of the appropriate signal, the muscles surrounding the poison sac begin spasmodic contractions, forcing the venom into the hollow lancets and from them into the wound.

This whole process can be beautifully illustrated by persuading a honeybee to sting you. The demonstration is possible because the lancets of the honeybee's stinger are equipped with retrobarbs, like a fishhook, so that once they have penetrated your skin, she cannot withdraw them. In this predicament, she eventually tears out the end of her abdomen and flies away to die; however, to satisfy your scientific curiosity, she leaves behind the embedded stinger complete with the poison sac and associated muscles — all easily visible to the naked eye. Thus, for your calm contemplation, you can observe how the lancets are alternately driven deeper into your skin and see the pulsations of the poison sac as it injects its venom into the deepening wound. Whether you wish to experience this scientific exercise or take it as given, the knowledge of how bees sting suggests some simple measures for reducing the painful reactions. Don't try this experiment until you have read about the sting reaction.

The honeybee, on the other hand, is least likely among stinging insects to be met in the bush or at the cottage. Much more likely are hornets, wasps and bumblebees. While their stinging apparatus is basically the same, there is an exception: the stinging lancets of these insects are smooth and without retrobarbs. So, unlike the honeybee, they can sting repeatedly. As we will warn

> For insects, it can properly be said that the female of the species is deadlier than the male, as only the females can sting.

you, the multiple stings can be particularly dangerous in the relative isolation of camp and cottage.

The Bite Reaction

The initial irritation of being stabbed by a mosquito or slashed by a blackfly is understandable and expected. But not so the subsequent reactions. Why does the bite leave a legacy of burning weal and intense itching that can persist over an uncomfortable day and a restless night or longer? This question was not answered until fairly recently, and even now, there remain uncertainties.

Many studies have shown that you must be bitten at least once before any reaction occurs; similarly, prior exposure to certain offending pollens must occur before hay fever symptoms develop. This observation suggests that the bite reaction is an allergic one. That is, the body's normal defence system is activated to combat an introduced foreign substance just as it is against an invasion of bacteria. No reaction occurs with the first bites because the defence or immune system must first learn to recognize the injected foreign substance by producing specific substances called antibodies. After that, these antibodies are present and initiate the body's bite reaction.

In our laboratory some years ago, we looked for evidence that the offending substances are in the saliva of biting insects. To test the idea, we challenged a student assistant to develop a technique for cutting the salivary duct of a mosquito without impairing its ability to feed. This was a challenge of daunting microproportions. After the demise of many mosquitoes, a successful operation was performed. The violated mosquito was then persuaded to feed on a person susceptible to the bite reaction. Dutifully, it drank its fill of blood, as was apparent from the distended, ruby-red abdomen. Its victim, however, showed no reaction whatever. The suspected source of the allergic reaction was confirmed, then, to be the saliva of the insect, introduced into the wound during feeding. We should add to this anecdote that the student assistant with the steady hands later became a highly respected neurosurgeon.

Except for newborn infants and perhaps a few individuals who have never ventured from large urban centres, most of us have been bitten by one or more kinds of blood-seeking bugs. As a consequence, we have been sensitized to their bites. Most people, when bitten by a mosquito, for example, experience an almost immediate reaction characterized by a raised whitish weal surrounded by a reddened area and accompanied by itching. This reaction generally disappears within an hour. Less common is a delayed reaction, which may not appear for several hours. When this happens, a small, hard lump forms, with reddening and usually intense itching that may come or go over a period of days.

Actually, a well-established sequence of reactions occurs with successive bites and may proceed over weeks, months or years. After the first few bites, which produce no reaction, succeeding bites over time will cause the delayed reaction, followed by both the immediate and delayed reactions and terminating with the immediate reaction only. A complete reversion to the desensitized state has been produced in the laboratory with experimental animals but occurs rarely, if at all, in humans.

But why do you suffer severe and sustained reactions to bug bites while your co-worker or your neighbour in the next cottage experiences only minor irritation? The answer seems to lie on the human side of the interface with the bugs. With continued exposure to bites, one person may show a rapid change in type of reaction, whereas another will change slowly, if at all. Those who proceed rapidly through the sequence of reactions will acquire a degree of desensitization over the summer. Although this happy state may diminish over the winter, it will usually be regained with a fresh onslaught of bites during the next summer. Better still, you may be able to retain your immunity by spending the winter on some bug-infested tropical island.

These observations lead us to rather callous advice: Be bitten. Although it probably is no advice at all to the outdoorsperson who is going to be bitten anyway, at least it will support your Spartan stance that these hurts are ultimately helpful. But don't be overenthusiastic. We have seen men hospitalized in a state of shock after being lost in the bush and subjected to massive attacks by mosquitoes and blackflies. Just comfort yourself with the thought that a slow, steady drip of bug saliva is your best bet for building resistance to the bite reaction.

As most of you know, you can be desensitized to many allergic reactions by a series of injections of the offending substance, such as ragweed pollen or bee venom. So why not to insect bites? Theoretically, this should be possible, but the present state of the allergist's art extends only to a procedure for desensitization to flea bites. So at least for the present, you will have to tolerate the reaction to bug bites.

The Sting Reaction

The cause of the sting reaction is basically the same as that of the bite reaction. In both cases, your body's immune system is alerted to take defensive action against an intrusion of a foreign protein. An obvious difference is that the vehicle for introducing the foreign protein is the venom, not the saliva, of the stinging insects. Another difference is that the venom contains toxins which produce an instant, painful response even to the first sting, as distinct from

---

With continued exposure to bites, one person may show a rapid change in type of reaction. Another will change slowly, if at all.

---

the allergic reaction which develops later. And there is a more ominous difference. Most people have been exposed to insect bites since childhood; but few people except beekeepers have experienced more than a few episodes with stinging insects. So your chemistry has had little opportunity to develop the relative tolerance that you have to bites and that beekeepers have to stings. This may be one of the reasons for the often severe and sometimes serious reactions people have to stings.

On being stung, most of you will experience what is known as the normal local reaction. You may be surprised by the broad interpretation of the term "local." A sting on the back of the hand can result in the coalescence of your fingers into a boxing glove and a swelling halfway up your arm. A sting on the cheek can close one eye and produce a grossly lopsided face. The term "local" is justified only to distinguish it from the dangerous systemic reaction.

As its name implies, the systemic reaction involves the whole body system. In a few people, a single sting can initiate a swift and sweeping reaction throughout the body. The bronchial tubes contract, causing breathlessness similar to a severe asthmatic attack. A feverlike flush sweeps over the body. Dizziness, disorientation, intestinal cramps and other symptoms of stress quickly multiply. One of us had just such a reaction.

"I had kept bees for about five years with pleasure and profit and without untoward incident. Of course, I had been stung, and in retrospect, I can see that my reaction had recently become more pronounced. But I thought nothing of it. That is, until the night I was stung helping a friend Jim capture a swarm that had settled on my mini-farm in eastern Ontario.

"I wasn't stung badly — perhaps half a dozen stings on my hands and wrists. We got on with the job. But less than 10 minutes later, I began to feel very strange indeed. My ears began to ring, and Jim's voice seemed to recede. I felt my lips and the area around my eyes begin to stiffen. A feverlike warmth spread over me, and I felt dizzy and slightly sick. I decided to go back to the house with the vague idea that a cup of coffee might help.

"My wife Susan met me at the back door. She took one look at me and abruptly said she was taking me to the hospital. She stuffed me into the car, dashed back into the house and returned with something in her hand. As she started to drive, she told me she had the hypodermic of adrenaline.

"By the time we reached the nearby village, I was starting to hyperventilate and I could feel my throat constricting. Susan pulled in under the lights of the deserted gas station, pushed me out of the car and told me to drop my pants. But instead of giving me the shot of adrenaline, she stood there swearing—she had forgotten her glasses and was desperately trying to read the instructions. A police car slid through the intersection and pulled up beside us. Without hesitation, Susan handed the hypodermic through the open window of the cruiser and commanded, 'Please read me these instructions!' The young policeman was good for it. He coolly read her the instructions as though the sight of a senior gentleman with his pants down and a lady brandishing a hypodermic needle were commonplace. Susan administered the adrenaline, and the policeman said, 'I'll clear you through to the hospital.'

"Two hours later, and after another injection of adrenaline at the hospital, I was back home enjoying a mild adrenaline high and was drowsy from antihistamine pills."

The personal administration of adrenaline was crucial in that case and preparedness for similiar occurrences can be a lifesaver.

You need not be hypersensitive to suffer the symptoms of anaphylactic shock from a concerted attack by multiple-stinging insects such as wasps. And cottagers are at some risk because of their separation from medical aid. For these reasons, a syringe of adrenaline (epinephrine) should be *de rigueur* for those of you who have experienced a pronounced reaction to stings of any kind. It can be obtained on prescription, together with antihistamine tablets, from an allergist, allergy departments of hospitals or drugstores.

Fortunately, only a small fraction of the population is hypersensitive — that is, likely to suffer the systemic reaction to insect stings. You can determine your sensitivity status by consulting an allergist who will test you in the same way that asthmatics are tested for their sensitivity to pollens, cat dander and house dust. You will be tested for your reaction to a variety of insect stings, because you can be sensitive to the venom of yellow jackets, for instance, and not to that of bumblebees. If such tests confirm that you are indeed at hazard, you can be desensitized at least to the level of the normal local reaction. The therapy uses preparations of insect venoms administered by injection of a graded series of doses over a period of time. This repeated challenge stimulates the production of substances that combine with the venom proteins and reduce their potential for exciting your immune system to overreact.

Like the vast majority of people, you will probably suffer no more than the

Protective clothing is the best defence against blackflies; a head net may be necessary during peak season if repellents and other devices fail.

normal local reaction to stings. Your reaction can change with time, however, and there is always the possibility of the more severe reaction. Short of the syringe of adrenaline, your best precaution against emergencies is a supply of antihistamine tablets. These can be obtained, without prescription, at any drugstore. They should be included in the first-aid kits of every cottager, camper and gardener.

Despite the combative tone of this narrative, you should not regard the bugs as malevolent. Those that bite you are simply trying to make a living by exploiting a plentiful supply of suitable food. Those that sting you do so only in defence of themselves, their young and their stores. The hazards of bug bites and stings take their place beside those other hazards of living in the great outdoors — the axe, the wood fire, the poison ivy and the skunk. As with these others, with some basic knowledge and practical know-how, you can relegate them to the background of your enjoyment, knowing you are prepared.

Excerpted from Goodbye Bugs, *Grosvenor House (Montreal, PQ).*

Some popular insect repellents do a better job than others

Forcing Pests to "Bug Off!"

by Richard A. Casagrande

In my neighbourhood in southern Rhode Island, we don't normally schedule outdoor parties during the summer months; there are too many mosquitoes. But in the late summer of 1989, we threw a party at which these bloodsucking insects were the guests of honour. Purpose of the party: to evaluate the effectiveness of so-called natural mosquito repellents. With proper incentive (lobsters on the grill worked nicely), my fellow faculty members and students from the entomology department of the University of Rhode Island (URI) assembled. Among entomologists (those who study insects), we at URI apparently have a reputation for being even crazier than most, and we proved it by subjecting our bodies to the ravages of hungry mosquitoes in the interest of science.

For our test, we gathered six "natural" (let's call them alternative) products reputed to repel mosquitoes and compared them with Off!, the standard of mosquito repellents. Marketed by Johnson Wax for more than 30 years, Off! contains N, N-diethyl-meta-toluamide (deet), an effective, synthetically formulated repellent whose safety has recently been questioned. Deet is the primary active ingredient of several other well-known

repellents, including Ben's and the line from Cutter Laboratories. In this test, we wanted to avoid highly concentrated deet products; therefore, we selected the standard Off! formulation containing only 14 percent deet instead of other products that range up to 100 percent deet.

Among the alternative repellents we tested was Jaico Mosquito Milk, an interesting product whose advertising speaks of insect-repelling plants from the south of France and emphasizes the cosmetic appeal of its roll-on applicator. Close inspection revealed its active ingredients to be 22 percent deet and 2.4 percent plant oils. With a price on the order of $20 per 50-millilitre bottle, its cost per ounce of deet is nearly four times higher than other deet products. (But it is an attractive bottle.)

We also included Natrapel, whose active ingredient is 10 percent citronella, an oil derived from a grass native to southern Asia known for its repellent qualities. Natrapel is the only non-deet repellent registered with the Environmental Protection Agency (EPA).

Another herbal contender was Bug-Off, a product advertised as "The Natural Alternative," containing pennyroyal, citronella, cedarwood and eucalyptus. Bug-Off sounds a lot like an insect repellent, but the label states prominently that it is "NOT a chemical

insect repellent," and it has no EPA registration number on its label.

We tried Skin-So-Soft, an Avon bath oil whose ingredient list includes mineral oil, isopropyl palmitate, dicapryl adipate and dioctyl sodium sulfosuccinate. Skin-So-Soft comes with a list of 31 uses, including, in addition to repelling mosquitoes, removing chewing gum from hair, cleaning greasy hands, removing tar from cars and eliminating "ring around the collar."

Cedar-äl — an extract of western red cedar — and I&M Natural Skincare's Sesame Sun Oil and Olive Sunscreen Lotion filled out the bill. Like Skin-So-Soft, these products are not specifically sold as insect repellents, but they had been recommended for use for their mosquito-repelling abilities. The sample of Cedar-äl we received was labelled as a room deodorizer. I&M's products consist of extracts of various fruits and vegetables (peanuts, carrots, avocados, olives and others) and some other plant products, such as horsetail and lemon balm.

Sitting on my deck one evening a few days before the scheduled cookout, I did some preliminary tests. I put Natrapel on my exposed right arm and used my left arm as an untreated control. Between 7:00 and 7:05, I had 13 landings and several bites on the treated arm compared with 39 landings — and even more bites — on the untreated arm. Two hours later, when the strong smell of Natrapel had diminished and the mosquitoes were less active, I had 5 landings on the treated arm and 7 on the control arm. These results were consistent with scientific literature indicating that citronella, the active ingredient in Natrapel, is a somewhat effective short-term repellent.

The next evening, with a few neighbours and fewer mosquitoes, we evaluated Cedar-äl (5 landings versus 8 on the control arm) and I&M Sunscreen (treated, 7; control, 2). Could I&M's product be an attractant?

Repellents don't actually repel mosquitoes. Instead, some of them, particularly deet, seem to mask the factors that attract mosquitoes. Female mosquitoes need to feed on blood in order to develop a batch of eggs. They are attracted to animal (including human) hosts by the carbon dioxide, moisture, warmth and lactic acid that hosts emit through their skin. Some people seem to emit more of these signals — or emit them more appealingly — than others, which is why some people are more attractive to mosquitoes. In the presence of repellents, mosquitoes may not be able to receive or recognize these signals.

The party day's forecast called for warm temperatures, low winds and high humidity — a great mosquito day. That evening, 23 of my colleagues gathered in my backyard for a cookout. Shortly before 7:00, we applied the products to be tested. Each of seven repellents was tested by a group of three people, with three people serving as untreated controls. Between 7:05 and 7:15, everyone counted the mosquitoes that landed on their arms and chests. Later, while the rest of us ate dessert, Janne Cookman, Rhode Island's mosquito-abatement specialist, captured a sampling of mosquitoes to identify them. It turns out that *Aedes vexans* and *A. canadensis*, two woodland-pool species common throughout Rhode Island during the summer, had joined us at the cookout.

In this backyard test, the product rankings came out as expected. Off! outperformed the rest with only one

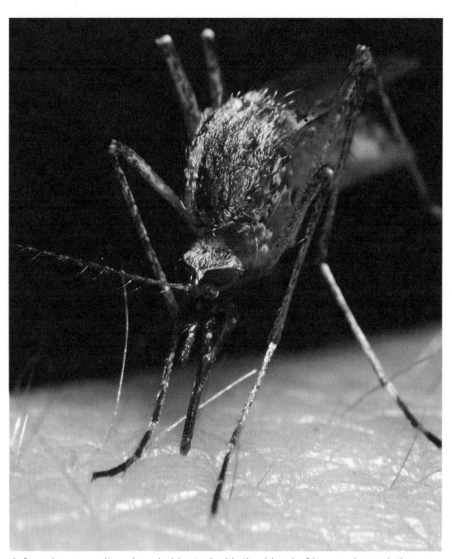

A female mosquito, already bloated with the blood of its previous victims, inserts its stinger into the skin of its human prey.

landing on three people, a 98 percent reduction from the controls, who reported an average of 13 landings each. Mosquito Milk came in second with an 85 percent reduction. With the same primary active ingredient (deet) as Off!, Mosquito Milk probably would have performed as well as Off! if people had applied it in the same manner, but the roll-on applicator does not give the same coverage as the aerosol can of Off!. (Among the products tested, only Off!, Natrapel and Cedar-äl could be sprayed on clothing, giving them a relative advantage in this test over the oils and creams that were applied only to exposed skin.) But even though we were able to get good coverage with the spray cans of Cedar-äl and Natrapel,

they were considerably less effective than Off!.

Two other products, Bug-Off and Skin-So-Soft, have some repellency. Bug-Off contains the known repellent citronella, and I had subjected Skin-So-Soft to the party test the previous summer and had found that it reduced mosquito attacks by 50 percent shortly after application. But both initially showed up poorly in this test because two of the three testers proved to be particularly attractive to mosquitoes, averaging 31.5 landings. In the interest of a fair comparison, their counts were dropped from the analysis. Without their data, these products performed about the same as Cedar-äl and Natrapel. As in the preliminary test, the

I&M Skincare products did not repel mosquitoes.

We were a bit disappointed by the field performance of the alternative mosquito repellents, so two days later, Janne Cookman and I did some lab tests on these products. We put about 150 mosquitoes, again primarily *Aedes vexans* and *A. canadensis*, into each of two cages, and we put our untreated arms into each cage for four minutes, counting landings. We then repeated this procedure using each of the products, carefully washing our arms with soap and rinsing with alcohol between treatments. During the trials, we ran four sets of control experiments with our untreated arms, averaging about 45 landings per test.

In these tests, deet products again performed best, but there was less discrepancy between deet and the other products than we saw in the field. Cedar-äl showed marked improvement in the laboratory test relative to both field trials. Natrapel and Bug-Off also looked much better in the lab.

On the arms treated with I&M's Sesame Sun Oil, we counted twice as many landings as on the untreated arms. And we recorded 30 percent more landings on arms treated with the company's Olive Sunscreen Lotion. Based upon both our field and laboratory tests, it might be fair to call I&M's two products mosquito attractants rather than repellents.

There are two reasons why the alternative repellents looked relatively good in the lab. First, we got much better coverage on our hands and arms than was possible in the field test. Second, the laboratory tests were conducted immediately after application. In the field, the highly volatile oils in the alternative repellents were partly dissipated during the 30 to 45 minutes between application and the end of the test. By contrast, an application of deet lasts several hours.

Given the clear superiority of deet products, one might question why there is any demand for the alternative repellents. The answer is that many people are concerned about health risks associated with deet. For years, I've wondered about its safeness. I used to apply a great deal of it when I went trout fishing a few years ago. But I quickly learned not to get it on my plastic fishing reels (it dissolves them) or to get it in my eyes (it hurts a lot) or on my lips (it numbs them).

The EPA hasn't done too much to allay fears about deet. Despite more

---

> The EPA argues that "natural" would be interpreted by many to mean relatively safe, although many of our worst toxins are also natural.

---

than 30 years of widespread use and direct application to skin, the EPA still says it has "data gaps" in its information on this chemical's ability to cause cancers, birth defects and reproductive problems. The agency is just now analyzing data submitted in 1989 on these possible chronic effects. The results won't be known for a few years.

In August 1990, the EPA issued a consumer bulletin in which it noted that a small segment of the population may be sensitive to deet. Repeated applications, particularly to small children, may sometimes cause headaches, mood changes, confusion, nausea, muscle spasms, convulsions or unconsciousness. EPA scientists have told me that there are only a dozen or so documented cases of deet-induced problems of this type. Nonetheless, they recommend that people use the least concentrated formulations of deet and wash it off soon after returning indoors — especially in the case of children.

But are other products safe to use? If you are concerned about the data gaps on the health effects of deet, you may be interested to know that there are even more data gaps with alternative repellents — if there are any data at all. Any product sold as an insect repellent must be registered with the EPA, but many of the alternative products that appear to be advertised or suggested as mosquito repellents do not have EPA registration. And although EPA registration is no guarantee that a product is safe to use, it does mean tests have shown it to be effective. Furthermore, EPA registration requires testing for significant health and environmental effects. If the manufacturers of a product simply avoid calling it a repellent, they can dodge EPA regulations.

The EPA generally will not allow labels that include words like "natural," "safe," "nontoxic" and "harmless." The agency argues that "natural" would be interpreted by many people to mean relatively safe, although many of our worst toxins are also natural products. Mosquito repellents that make these claims are being sold illegally and should be carefully scrutinized.

Of a whole boxful of alternative mosquito repellents on my desk (I tested only a fraction of my collection), only one product, Natrapel, has an EPA label. One repellent containing citronella and pennyroyal, like Bug-Off, claims to have a "powerful natural formula" that is "safe and pleasant" to use. Another product claims that it is "safe for children and pregnant women" and that it "contains no citronella or pennyroyal." Since neither company bothered to file for EPA registration, I'm willing to bet that neither tested its products on mice, rats or rabbits, let alone children and pregnant women.

So what will I use this summer? Deet on myself. Skin-So-Soft on my young children. When the mosquitoes are too troublesome, I'll add a bit of deet to the Skin-So-Soft. I find that a few drops of diluted deet added to a small handful of Skin-So-Soft is generally adequate to repel mosquitoes even when they are thick. If not, I'll take the kids inside.

Originally published in Harrowsmith Country Living *magazine (Charlotte, VT).*

Coping with the recurring curse of blackflies

Spring's Clouds of Discomfort

by Allan West and Bev Smallman

Blackflies are well named, most species being both black in colour and black by reputation. Their bad reputation is based on their stealthy method of attack and the vicious bites they inflict. Together with mosquitoes, they constitute the major bug problem for most outdoorspeople.

A comparison of these two principal pests is useful. With a few exceptions, the females of both groups require a blood meal to develop their eggs — and human blood is a favourite source for some species of both groups. Similarly, the larvae of both groups require watery places to grow and develop. But there the similarities end.

An important difference is that larvae of most species of blackflies require fast-running water, in contrast to mosquitoes, which breed only in stagnant water. Just about any geographical area where blackflies occur will also have stagnant waters that produce mosquitoes. However, in regions without fast water, such as coastal plains, blackflies do not occur, although mosquitoes may be abundant.

Compared with mosquitoes, blackflies have one virtue: they will not disturb your slumber. When darkness falls, blackflies pack it in until the next mor-

ning. Furthermore, unlike mosquitoes, they will not invade your tent or cottage with bloodthirsty intent, even during their daytime activity. They seem to be claustrophobic, avoiding enclosed spaces. If they do accidentally blunder into your living quarters, they will not bite you but will crawl on windows or screens trying to escape back outdoors.

The blackfly also approaches its target much differently than the mosquito. You have probably watched a mosquito land on your arm, take a few tentative steps, constantly testing with its proboscis before selecting a suitably delectable spot to insert its hypodermic. At this point, you may decide to terminate your scientific study with a resounding slap. The blackfly, on the other hand, is sneaky. After landing, it scurries around seeking a protected spot — along the hairline, under the shirt-sleeve cuffs, up the pant legs or on the chest or waist after gaining access through a gap in the shirt front. Having slipped past your first defences, its success is practically guaranteed, because you are usually unaware of its painless bite at the time.

In appearance, the blackfly is a robust little insect compared with the delicate mosquito, an impression that comes mainly from its stout little thorax, which is strongly arched upward to accommodate the motor centre for the

wings and legs. Because of this characteristic, it is sometimes called the humpbacked fly. Most species are uniformly black, but one kind that commonly attacks people is distinguished by white legs, giving it the ludicrous appearance of wearing white stockings.

Blackflies are widely distributed throughout Canada and the northern United States but with some gaps due to the absence of fast water needed for the development of the larvae. There are many different species, but you may take some comfort from the fact that only a few of them, perhaps six or seven, feed on people. The other kinds prefer animals or birds for the blood feed essential to mature their eggs.

Blackfly eggs are usually deposited in masses on partially submerged rocks, sticks or trailing vegetation, most commonly at the beginning of a stretch of fast-running water — just below a beaver dam or just above a natural rill of rapids, for example. Most blackfly eggs are laid and develop in permanent streams or rivers, although those of a few species can stop development and survive when, for instance, a drainage ditch dries up.

Running water is essential for the survival and growth of blackfly larvae. The main reason is that it contains the abundant supply of dissolved oxygen that they require, which they obtain by means of their so-called blood gills.

The need for running water poses the problem of how to stay put in the current. The larvae solve this problem by using silken threads and a sucker with a circlet of hooks at the tail end of their bodies to anchor themselves to underwater objects such as stones. Just back of the head, on the ventral surface, there is a stumpy "proleg," also provided with a sucker and a circlet of hooks. By means of the anterior and posterior hooks and suckers, the larvae can walk in a looping fashion, not unlike the gait of an inchworm.

The running water along with an ingenious pair of mouth brushes enable the larvae to obtain food: the running water carries a continuous suspension of small particles of suitable food, and the fan-shaped brushes filter and collect the particles (mostly one-celled plants) from the flowing water. This filter-feeding method offers humans the greatest possibilities for the reduction of larval populations of blackflies, a subject for later discussion.

Although a larval population begins in a concentrated mass where the eggs are laid, it gradually becomes dispersed downstream. This dispersal is initiated when individual larvae are disturbed — when buffeted by floating debris, for instance. They then detach their anchoring hooks and float downstream, using a silken thread as a safety line, until they attach themselves to another submerged object. This behaviour serves to spread their chances against being eaten by fish. Divided, they win!

Checking for Bugs

If you want to determine whether your babbling brook harbours a potential population of blackflies, look for rocks or other submerged objects that have a moss-coated appearance when populations are dense. Closer inspection will show you the separate slipper-shaped larvae, which, when feeding, stand upright, shoulder to shoulder, and wave with the water current from which they obtain their food and oxygen supply. In colour, they will vary from off-white to greenish brown. You may still have a potential problem even if you find only

a few larvae on each stone you examine.

When the larva reaches its full-grown size of just under half an inch in length, it spins a cocoon, still attached to an underwater object. Within this cocoon, the larva transforms into a pupa; its only need is for oxygen, which it is able to obtain by means of a pair of threadlike tufts on its head. Finally, the adult flies emerge, congregating on stream-side vegetation and drying themselves in preparation for flight and the search for food.

Can you avoid blackflies by staying away from their breeding sites? A few years ago, we tried to find an answer by using newly emerged blackflies and a radioactive-tag technique. After five days, tagged blackflies were recovered more than 22 miles from the dispersal point; to go that distance, they had flown through largely wooded country. In addition, they were able to cross a river that is more than one mile wide. Although the experiment was done with only one species of blackfly, the general answer to our question seems to be — no. Avoiding close proximity to running water is probably not going to free you from blackflies.

Some species of blackflies produce only one generation of offspring each year; others may produce several, depending on environmental conditions. Most species overwinter in the egg stage, but a few pass the winter as larvae. And as a final comment on the ways of blackflies, in contrast to mosquitoes whose populations fluctuate between "good" and "bad" years, it is generally agreed that blackflies are always bad — just worse in some years than in others.

Your wardrobe requires special attention to thwart the cunning blackfly's ability to find and crawl into or under any opening to get at you. Trousers should be tucked into boot tops, or better still, pull your socks up over the trouser cuffs. Tuck your shirt in firmly; a gap around your shirt can leave you with a band of bites as uncomfortable as a case of hives. Shirt cuffs should fit snugly to the wrists. A zippered-front shirt is much better than a buttoned one. If wearing the latter, an undershirt

or T-shirt is advisable. And remember to avoid those attractive colours such as dark blues. When blackflies are really bad, a head net is essential; it is uncomfortable in hot weather and interferes with vision to some extent, but it can save you from a bloodied face and the possibility of a severe reaction.

Lust for Blood

Blackflies are strongly attracted to fresh blood. An accident, such as cutting yourself when cleaning fish, can have consequences beyond the injury itself. We know this from painful personal experience. Some years ago, one of us was involved in a field study that required collecting blood from various birds — with permission and for scientific purposes. A syringe malfunctioned, and blood covered the investigator's bare hands. Blackflies immediately descended in hordes, literally covering his hands. Devotion to duty prevented him or his assistant from brushing the flies off until the operation was complete. The result was traumatic. The victim became flushed and fevered, and the hands became so swollen and stiff that they were incapable of holding even a spoon for several days. So it is with some feeling that we make our final recommendation about protective clothing: if you venture beyond the immediate area of your camp or cottage, always wear or have available a pair of gloves.

Unfortunately, protective clothing is the best defence against blackflies, as the possibilities for eliminating blackfly breeding sites are very limited. Your best bet is to invite a couple of beavers to set up shop. The trick is to convert running water into still water, and beavers are good at that. In fact, we once lost a useful experimental site when beavers dammed a river, reducing its downstream flow to a mere trickle and thereby wiping out the population of blackflies we had planned to study. Lacking cooperative beavers, you might be tempted to try a little damming yourself. But before you do, you should be advised that tampering with a stream can run you afoul of the law. In any case, your effort would pay off only if

Blackfly pupae, drawing oxygen from moving water, cling to a plant as they develop toward adulthood. They grasp the plant with a sucker and silken thread.

you had the sole stretch of fast water for miles around. Otherwise, your little oasis would quickly be reinvaded — nature abhors a vacuum.

In some blessed places, such as southeastern Ontario, the blackfly season lasts no more than two weeks, and cottagers can simply bide their time because the resident species has only a single spring generation. But seasonal avoidance is scarcely possible in many areas where a variety of species produces several generations over the entire season from spring to fall. We have experienced annoying blackfly attacks in central Labrador during mid-September.

When truly exasperated by the inadequacy of your preventive measures against blackflies, you may decide to take offensive action. If you do, you are again faced with the choice between attacking the larvae or the adults — except that in this case, the choice is more theoretical than real.

Populations of blackfly larvae can be effectively reduced for considerable distances downstream by introducing a synthetic insecticide into the upper reaches of a stream. But this method is not a viable option for an individual cottager or camper. Your interest is in pre-serving the natural environment, which is protected by legislation prohibiting such introductions into waterways, except by special permit. A permit for a cooperative effort by a cottage association might be approved, but probably only with the rider that the operation be supervised by a licensed professional.

However, an environmentally acceptable method for the control of blackfly larvae is on the immediate horizon. This is the biological insecticide *Bacillus thuringiensis*, which is harmless to most organisms other than blackfly and mosquito larvae. Moreover, dispersed into running water in the form of small particles, it is beautifully suited to be selectively picked up by the filter-feeding fans of blackfly larvae. When it is approved, this should be the larvicide of your choice.

The space and surrounding vegetation you wish to free from adult blackflies must be treated with an airborne insecticide. A portable or vehicle-carried fogger will provide the best protection. And again, we emphasize that if you are going to use a fog, a cooperative effort spread over a considerable area will be more effective than a limited individual one.

We are often asked whether repeated fogging might lead to a buildup of an insecticidal residue, persistent and harmful to other components of the environment. Within current knowledge, we can only say that the dosages applied by fogging are minute and, more importantly, that the approved insecticides rapidly lose their toxicity when exposed to the environment. Moreover, insecticides approved for this purpose are harmless to most beneficial bugs, such as pollinators.

Because you may have a choice of several insecticides for fogging, remember to read the labels. Don't let a salesperson tell you that a particular formulation is good against blackflies unless the label says so. As far as we know, all insecticides that are effective against blackflies are also effective against mosquitoes. The reverse is not true. A number of insecticides that are effective against adult mosquitoes are almost useless against adult blackflies.

A fluid mix of preventive methods with a supplementary dash of offensive methods, as required, will best serve your needs.

Inevitably, a few of you avid outdoorspersons will find yourselves lost. Such fecklessness suggests that you may also have left camp without adequate protective clothing or a supply of repellent. And you have blundered into a swamp humming with mosquitoes and blackflies. This is a potentially dangerous situation, but there are a few emergency measures you can take.

To protect your face and neck, attach leafy twigs to your hat so that they dangle and move. From your lunch, smear anything greasy on your exposed skin — butter, dairy or peanut, will do fine. If you decide to stay in one place to await help or dawn, build a fire using damp wood or green foliage to produce a goodly cloud of smoke and stay within this smoke screen. It may also serve to attract those searching for you. Distasteful as these measures may be, they will ease the panic and prevent you from being hospitalized with an anaphylactic reaction to bites.

Excerpted from Goodbye Bugs, *Grosvenor House (Montreal, PQ).*

Defending your family against Lyme disease

Invasion of the Deadly Ticks

by Jean Wallace

You won't see Betty Gross outdoors in shorts and sandals this summer. A resident of Westchester County, New York, she lives in a hot spot for Lyme disease. To ward off ticks, she covers herself up in a long-sleeved shirt, slacks, socks and shoes before walking in grass or woods.

"When I go out, I'm extremely cautious," says Gross, who had Lyme disease but who has since recovered and formed a support group for sufferers. "I'm not the least enchanted with the outdoors anymore."

Summer is here, and so is Lyme season. A bacterial illness spread by infected immature deer ticks, Lyme disease has become the nation's most common tick-borne ailment. The parasites, which range in size from that of a poppy seed to that of a pinhead, are active in warm weather. Most cases occur between May and October, with the peak in July. Children are most susceptible because they're outdoors so much, but any member of the household — including the family dog — can contract the illness.

With all the publicity about this disease, you may wonder whether it's safe to enjoy the outdoors this summer. How serious is the threat in your area?

Should you think twice about sending your kids to camp? Should you, like Betty Gross, worry about venturing into your own backyard?

Medical experts agree that there's no need to panic or to lock your family indoors. Here's the reason: You can prevent Lyme disease by taking precautions to avoid bites. And even if you are bitten, you may not develop the illness. Also, the disease is usually curable with antibiotic treatment, especially if caught early. Summer camps and scouting organizations are helping to minimize the risk by widening trails, mowing tall grass and brush and teaching camp counsellors and campers about the illness.

The disease, named for Lyme, Connecticut, where the first cases were discovered in 1975, poses a serious threat in four regions of the United States: the wooded coastal areas of the Northeast and upper mid-Atlantic states; Wisconsin and Minnesota; the West Coast from Washington to California; and Texas. Last year, New York State had 3,239 cases, up nearly 30 percent from 1988, when the state accounted for about half of the country's approximately 5,000 cases. It appears that over the past few years, the disease has slowly spread to new areas, and Canadian authorities feel that Lyme disease is a growing threat across

the country. The many reasons for this may include the ticks' hitching rides on the fur of animals.

The earliest symptoms are a flulike illness and a rash in the vicinity of the tick bite, occurring two days to a month after the bloodletting. Typically, the rash surrounds the bite like a bull's-eye, with a clear centre inside a red ring. However, the rash may take other forms or not appear at all. Other symptoms include fever, chills, malaise, a sore throat, a stiff neck and muscle aches. Because deer ticks are so small, many people don't realize they have been bitten until symptoms appear, and then they may mistake the early symptoms for the flu.

If you have suspicious symptoms, see your doctor right away. "If Lyme disease is diagnosed in the early stages, there is an excellent chance that oral antibiotics will cure it," says Hans Liu, M.D., acting director of the division of infectious disease at Thomas Jefferson University Hospital, in Philadelphia.

Without treatment, the early symptoms disappear, but new and more serious complications may emerge even years later. The most common problem is arthritis, especially in the knees. Some people develop a slow or irregular heartbeat and need a temporary pacemaker. A few develop problems such as memory loss, poor concentration and recurrent headaches. "Once the disease enters its later stages, many, but not all, patients can be successfully treated with oral or intravenous antibiotics," says Liu.

Diagnosing Lyme disease can be tricky, especially in areas where doctors are unfamiliar with it. Its symptoms can masquerade as those of many other diseases, especially juvenile rheumatoid arthritis and meningitis. Jane Benjamin, 18, suffered for more than a year from extreme fatigue, headaches and blurred vision before Lyme disease was finally diagnosed. "We took her to a number of doctors and specialists," recalls her mother Barbara. "They tested her for multiple sclerosis, mononucleosis and a brain tumour. Everything came back negative. At one point, we were ready to go to a faith healer," she says jokingly.

Unfortunately, there is no foolproof test to confirm or rule out the illness. About 60 percent of people in the early stages of the disease test negative. More accurate tests are on the horizon. Some currently in research are expected to be used in conjunction with other tests to confirm questionable cases. Until these tests become available, the diagnosis will depend on an individual's symptoms and medical history.

If you are pregnant, it's wise to take extra care to avoid ticks. Recent studies have shown that the corkscrew-shaped organism that causes Lyme disease, called a spirochete, can cross the placenta and infect the fetus. Researchers suspect (but have not proved) that the spirochete may cause birth defects.

If a pregnant woman develops Lyme disease, prompt treatment with antibiotics may prevent her fetus from becoming infected, says Christine Williams, M.D., associate professor of pediatrics and medicine at New York Medical College, in Valhalla. A pregnant woman who knows she has been bitten by a deer tick should be treated by her physician with oral antibiotics before symptoms of Lyme disease emerge, Williams explains.

On the other hand, there's reassuring news for parents: Lyme disease tends to have a milder course in young children.

Unfortunately, there is no foolproof test to confirm the illness. About 60 percent of people in the early stages of the disease test negative. More accurate tests are on the horizon.

Ilona S. Szer, M.D., associate director of pediatric rheumatology at the Floating Hospital for Infants and Children, in Boston, studied 48 youngsters who had the illness before the standard antibiotic regimen was developed. Even without proper treatment, all but four recovered spontaneously. With antibiotic treatment, "the overwhelming majority of children never go on to develop later problems," she says.

Researchers are testing a vaccine in laboratory animals that one day may eradicate the disease. But for now, the best defence is a good offence against ticks. Here's how to protect your family if you happen to be in an affected area:

☐ When you're outdoors, wear a long-sleeved shirt and tuck your pants into your socks. Wear light colours so that you can easily spot the dark ticks. Don't go outside in bare feet or sandals.

☐ If you've been walking in woods or grass, check carefully for ticks when you return home. Don't overlook such areas as your groin, scalp, ears, inside the navel and the back of your calves. Remember, you are looking for a tick so small it could pass for a freckle. Young children who play outside should be checked every night at bath time, and older kids should be reminded to check themselves for ticks.

☐ Before you go out, spray clothing with an insect repellent containing deet (that's short for N, N-diethyl-meta-toluamide). Deet may be applied sparingly to exposed skin, but choose a product with a low concentration of the pesticide (30 percent or less). Some doctors advise against using deet directly on children's skin, because in rare instances, it has caused seizures and severe skin reactions.

☐ If the family dog or cat goes outside, a tick collar may help. Not only can pets get Lyme disease themselves, but they may also bring ticks indoors that can infect family members. Locating ticks on a dog or cat can be very difficult. It may be best simply to keep the family pet either indoors or outside during the tick season.

☐ If you find an attached tick on the skin, remove it with a pair of blunt tweezers. If you must use your fingers, wear tight-fitting gloves. Grasp the tick as closely as possible to the skin surface, and pull straight upward with gentle, even pressure. Disinfect the site with soap and water, and then wash your hands. Never try to remove the tick by smothering it in petroleum jelly or pressing a glowing match against it.

☐ Just because you have been bitten by a tick doesn't mean you will develop the disease. Only the deer tick carries the infection; the larger dog tick does not. Also, not every deer tick harbours the spirochetes.

☐ Most important: If you find an attached tick, remove it quickly. A feeding tick may take several hours, and possibly a day, to transmit the infection, so time should not be wasted. "If you spot the tick and remove it, you've gone a long way toward preventing the disease," says Liu.

☐ After removing the tick, watch for a rash or any unusual symptoms for several weeks. Call your doctor if you notice anything suspicious. If you're pregnant, tell your doctor about a tick bite right away, even if you don't have symptoms. It is always best to err on the side of caution.

Originally published in Parents *magaine (New York, NY).*

Poison ivy and people seldom mix well on vacation

Bad Reactions to a Pretty Plant

by David Seburn

Every kid who has ever set foot in a Canadian forest knows about the lurking danger of poison ivy. It's one of the bogeymen that parents love to warn about, and from the time we're 4 years old, we keep a wary eye out for a plant with three leaves. It's become a national tradition, passed on from generation to generation.

So maybe we should learn some more about it. It is a fairly common plant, after all. You find it everywhere in Canada except Newfoundland, the Yukon and the Northwest Territories. But despite its importance — in the woods and in our minds — there's a lot about poison ivy we don't know. Can you get a poison ivy rash from someone who has it? Is poison ivy dangerous in winter? Does the rash last seven years? Can you treat yourself after touching the plant but before developing the symptoms? Will eating its berries make you immune? Don't be too sure you know all the answers. Even some supposedly authoritative books give misleading information.

Poison ivy belongs to the cashew family and is also related to the mango and the pistachio. Its only close relative in Canada is the sumac, and one type of sumac — the poison, or swamp, variety — gives humans a reaction similar to that from poison ivy.

Poison ivy has many names, including markweed, poison creeper and climbing sumac. But my favourite is French Canadian — *bois de puce,* meaning flea-wood, and it's bang on for anyone who has ever squirmed through an itchy dose of poison ivy.

Obviously, the first step in avoiding poison ivy is identifying the plant. And poison ivy should be easy to identify. It has three leaflets, the middle one is on a longer stem than the other two, and the leaflets tend to droop down from the main stem. "Leaves of three, let it be," goes the old rhyme. Unfortunately, there's nothing beyond the three leaves that you can use for positive identification. Poison ivy is what botanists call a plastic organism. That means there are often huge variations from plant to plant. Its leaves, for example, can be anything from three to six inches long. They can be shiny or dull. They can be slender, broad or stubby. The edges can be smooth or toothed. In spring, the leaves are often reddish. In summer, they are usually green. In fall, they may turn orange, red or yellow.

The plant itself can be a vine or a shrub. As a vine, it can grow over rocks and logs and climb cliffs or trees. It has climbed 50 feet up trees on a main stem that is five inches thick. As a shrub, it is usually less than three feet high and often grows in patches.

Poison ivy's shifting shape sometimes baffles both amateurs and experts. According to Alan Foster, a biologist from Kleinburg, Ontario, officials at Killbear Provincial Park once tried to control poison ivy but had a hard time identifying it. "They sprayed eight plants that weren't poison ivy, including strawberries and dogbane," says Foster. Strawberry plants have three leaves, and dogbane has drooping ones.

He also recalls how one lady he knows grubbed poison ivy out of her garden for years without realizing it. Only after 10 years did she finally get a rash. Then she knew.

The key to understanding how poison ivy affects us and how to deal with it is to realize that the active ingredient is a kind of oil. Like any oil, if it gets on your skin, it can be hard to get off. Almost every part of the plant contains the whitish oil. And yes, you can get infected at any time of the year, even from a leafless vine in the middle of winter. One of the most common ways to pick it up is by petting your dog after it has romped around in the woods. Poison ivy does not seem to affect ani-

Often a pretty plant, poison ivy comes in many sizes and shapes, but it always has three leaves.

mals, just people. So the dog goes scot-free, and you won't.

Poison ivy doesn't affect everyone. About 70 percent of us are susceptible to it. We develop a rash from poison ivy because we are having an allergic reaction to the plant's oil. As with any allergy, some people react more violently than others. Light-skinned people seem more sensitive than dark-skinned people. Also typical of allergies, everyone starts out immune to poison ivy. A first exposure never causes a rash. But for most of us, one exposure is all we need to lose our immunity. Forever after, we're vulnerable. Even the lucky few who seem immune can fall prey any time. Just a few more contacts with the plant oil might do it.

Victims of poison ivy often insist they've had no other exposure, but the truth is that the first time they passed through a patch, they weren't aware of it. Maybe it was years ago. Or maybe they became sensitive to poison ivy indirectly. Ralph Florence, a Toronto dermatologist, says he has heard of people who became sensitive by handling an old fishing rod painted with a Japanese lacquer containing oil from poison ivy's cousin, the cashew nut. (Roasted cashews are delicious and harmless, but the potent fumes from the raw plant have even blinded people.)

Likewise, you can get a rash by burning poison ivy, since the smoke contains tiny unburned particles of the oil. Also, if you get poison ivy on your clothes, the oil will remain active for at least a week — so you can get it on your skin just by undressing. Needless to say, you should wash your clothes thoroughly before wearing them again. And make sure whoever does the laundry knows that the clothes have poison ivy on them.

Some people wonder whether you can get a rash by touching an unbroken leaf or whether the oil escapes only when the leaf has been damaged in some way — partly eaten by insects or stepped on, for example. The answer is that even a flawless poison ivy leaf can give a rash. That's because the oil can rise to the surface by what scientists call capillary action — the same way water

seeps through a wet canvas tent roof if you put your finger on it.

It is not true, however, that the rash will last seven years or keep recurring indefinitely, like herpes. Alan Foster has a friend who got the rash one June and still had it in September. That's a long time. The same friend gets recurrences every year, but only because he keeps going into the woods where there is poison ivy. When you've had the rash once, your body becomes extra sensitive to the oil and it is much easier to get again.

Once you contact poison ivy, you have at most an hour to get the oil off your skin before it gets to work. Simply wash with soap and water as soon as possible. Wash several times, and be sure to do between the fingers and under rings and watches. If you don't have any soap handy, use alcohol, kerosene or gasoline. But I wouldn't recommend that treatment on any parts of the body except your hands and legs.

The sap from the jewelweed, or touch-me-not, plant is a popular folk remedy. I remember my father telling me about his father telling him about it. Alan Foster also agrees that the sap of the jewelweed seems to neutralize the oil of the poison ivy plant.

If you know you're going to be around poison ivy, one trick is to rub soap on your legs and arms beforehand. Let the soap dry on your skin, then wash it off when you come back.

Despite all your precautions, you might still develop the symptoms, which generally appear within one to two days of contact. It starts with a slight itching and redness. The skin may swell and sometimes have raised streaks. Next, blisters filled with fluid appear, often in short rows. In severe cases, the blisters grow quite large and may run together. A fever may develop, as well as swollen glands and aching muscles. The rash is usually uncomfortable but not serious, although one college student I know of nearly died when he had to roll naked in poison ivy at a fraternity initiation.

Most of the time, medical treatment is not necessary, if you are sure it's poison ivy. When I get poison ivy, for

example, it rarely itches at all. But some people find the itching almost drives them crazy. Then a doctor can help by prescribing a lotion or medication. In extreme cases, they may treat it with cortisone.

There are also some home remedies to fight the itching. Running cold water over the infected area tends to dull the nerve endings and soothe the itching temporarily. Many sufferers find calamine lotion or a paste made from baking soda a great help. Rubbing alcohol is also good, but you must be careful not to spread the alcohol: it may carry some oil particles along with it. An effective old Indian trick is to rub the blisters with scented fern.

You can't get the rash by touching someone else's blisters, except if the outbreak is recent and some oil is still lingering on the skin. For this reason, it's a good idea not to scratch your own rash. You might spread oil to new parts of your body.

Some other don'ts:

Don't bathe. Sitting in the tub may let oil come into the bath water and settle on other parts of your body. A shower, on the other hand, is fine. It washes away the water quickly.

Don't put grease or oil on your rash. It can dissolve and spread the oil.

An old wives' tale says you can develop immunity to poison ivy by eating one of its leaves. But I wouldn't recommend it. One researcher, in the spirit of Dr. Jekyll, tried it to see what would happen. It didn't affect his mouth, but a couple of days later, he got a bad rash at the other end. So much for old wives' tales.

Despite all the problems that poison ivy can cause, I hope you will not try to destroy it wherever it grows. It has a role to play in nature. Many birds and animals eat its berries, leaves and stems. And bees make nonpoisonous honey from its nectar.

Poison ivy also gives us a good reason to keep our eyes open when we're out in the woods. Not really that bad a thing when you think of it.

Originally published in Outdoor Canada *magazine (Toronto).*

Getting rid of poison ivy plants safely

by Jennifer Bennett

Poison ivy (*Rhus radicans*) is a native plant that is "just plain hard to get rid of," according to Susan Cooper, staff ecologist with the National Coalition Against the Misuse of Pesticides (NCAMP) in Washington, D.C. This hardy perennial, with its unique method of self-defence and a tenacious root system, demands determination and respect if it is to be routed out safely.

The old saying "Leaflets three, let it be" warns of a plant that produces urushiol, a resin that causes the production of antibodies in sensitive individuals. The antibodies remain in the bloodstream, so successive incidents cause increasingly severe reactions, ranging from small bumps to large blisters.

Sensitivity to poison ivy is an occupational hazard for Jack Alex, a professor of environmental biology at the University of Guelph. He manages Canada's largest weed garden, an educational project that includes *Rhus radicans*. According to Alex, "All parts of the poison ivy plant at any stage of growth can be poisonous to humans, summer and winter." His first line of defence is simple: "I stay away from it. But if I have to work in poison ivy, I don a complete waterproof cover from legs to neck to tips of sleeves. I have rubber boots and plastic gloves, and I wear a mask."

To get rid of poison ivy, both Cooper and Alex favour digging it up, but the digger must be properly garbed. Thoroughness and persistence are the keys to success. "Be careful to remove all the underground parts," says Alex, "because it can sprout again from what's left in the ground. I would say

probably six to eight inches deep would get rid of most of the reproductive material." The rhizomes can be long: Alex ruefully tells the story of a man who mistakenly thought he had found ginseng. "He dug up a whole tubful of it, and he spoke of the roots running long distances."

Cooper says that according to research by the Bio-Integral Resource Center in Berkeley, California, seedling plants are most easily dug up in early spring after the leaves have unfurled but while the soil is still wet. By fall, the seedlings will have extensive root systems and will be harder to eradicate. Mature plants are easiest to get rid of in late fall after the leaves have fallen and rain has saturated the soil. After the initial digging, check the site monthly, digging up any new growth. Poison ivy that is growing vertically on poles or fences should be snipped close to the base. The vine can be removed immediately or left in place to dry and removed in fall when the leaves have dropped. When new growth springs from the severed base, it must be cut again as often as is necessary.

As soon as the ground is clear of poison ivy, plant a fast-growing ground cover. In most places, a perennial such as periwinkle (*Vinca minor*), English ivy (*Hedera helix*) or Japanese-spurge (*Pachysandra terminalis*) would be suitable and hardy.

Laying down a heavy mulch that is impenetrable to light is another way to eliminate poison ivy. Several layers of newspaper or heavy-gauge black plastic or rubber-backed carpet weighted down at the perimeter will do the job in a year. Lay the mulch in winter or early in spring before the leaves open. To be safe, combine the mulches: a heavy layer of overlapping newspapers covered by large sheets of black plastic, protected from photodegradation by a layer of straw or leaves. Make sure the mulch overlaps the edges of the patch. "If there are healthy plants outside the area you are covering," says Alex,

"they are going to be sending plant foods through the roots to the area under cover."

Goats are sometimes recommended for poison-ivy control, although they will browse above and beyond the patch. Tethering a goat will restrict it to the vegetation within reach, but Alex is skeptical about the plant's attractiveness to other livestock. "In my experience, cattle will browse around poison ivy stands and won't touch it."

Agricultural agents usually recommend herbicides for poison ivy eradication, although chemicals are not the easy answer they might seem to be. The chief problem is their questionable safety: the cure may be worse than the disease. Amitrole, one of the herbicides suggested, is a known carcinogen of laboratory animals and a persistent contaminant of groundwater. Another common suggestion is glyphosate, marketed by Monsanto under the trade names Roundup and Rodeo. Says Cooper, "It has a relatively innocuous reputation. The problem with glyphosate appears to be not the active ingredient but rather the 'inert' trade-secret ingredients, which include something called POEA and a contaminant 1,4 dioxin, which is related to 2,3,7,8 dioxin, with which people are more familiar." A herbicide that has not been proved unsafe is ammonium sulphamate (Ammate or AMS). Painting the herbicide on individual plants is the most selective application method, but several applications are usually required, and it is necessary to wear protective clothing. Also, the dead plants remain toxic and must be removed.

Never burn poison ivy. "Some people have had extremely serious reactions to the ash carried in the smoke by inhaling it, getting it into their breathing passages," says Alex. Instead, pile poison ivy out of the way to compost it, or dump it into garbage bags.

Originally published in Harrowsmith *magazine (Camden East, Ontario).*

Fighting mice is never easy, but persistence can pay off

Doing Battle With a Mouse

by Ronald J. Brooks

Four of every ten mammals in the world are rodents, members of the 1,750 species in the order Rodentia. A modest fraction of this horde comes into conflict with humans, and a select few actually thrive in our company. Like people, rodents seek comfortable surroundings and an ample food supply in order to lead happy lives, and cottages can often provide both.

As they move into such dwellings, rodents modify them to suit their own needs by gnawing holes in walls, pipes, wiring and insulation. They also deposit prodigious quantities of feces — an impressive 18,000 pellets per year per mouse — as well as smaller amounts of very pungent urine, and they consume food we thought was for ourselves or for our pets.

Given these unpleasant habits and the considerable array of diseases rodents carry, it is not surprising that civilization has expended great effort to exterminate the little blighters. The campaign has met with limited success by even the most optimistic assessments; hence, we tend to label all rodents, with the possible exception of the noble beaver, as vermin or pests. This deep-seated aversion to rodents has caused most people to lump rats, mice and field mice into one category. Most indoor problems caused by mice, however, are the work of but one or two species — the others are blameless or should, at least, be blamed only for other problems.

Field mice are not mice at all; rather, they are voles, close relatives of lemmings and muskrats (*Ondatra zibethica*) of our marshes. The common meadow vole (*Microtus pennsylvanicus*), an inhabitant of meadows, marshes, orchards and old fields, weighs one to two ounces and is dark to light brown above, shading to dull grey below. Readily recognized by their short tails (less than two inches), short legs, small, black beady eyes and barely visible external ears, voles are unprepossessing, even comical, in appearance. In fact, homeowners can afford to regard them with detached amusement because voles rarely enter buildings, and if they do blunder inside, they have no interest in climbing, thus eschewing aboveground floors. Though unlikely to damage furniture or other in-house belongings, voles sometimes cause serious damage outside by girdling trees.

There are, however, two kinds of mice that cause damage in both barns and houses. By far the most common and widespread is the house mouse (*Mus musculus*), a relatively recent import from Europe, though the species originated in central Asia. House mice are readily distinguishable from voles because they have long tails (at least four inches) and large external ears. They are extremely mobile and can climb even vertical walls with great speed. A less common and more restricted problem is the attractive-looking deer, or white-footed, mouse, of which there are several quite similar native species under the genus *Peromyscus*. Weighing less than an ounce, they are superficially similar to the house mouse but can be identified by their hairy, bicoloured tails, by the sharp change in colour from brown-grey above to white below and by their larger eyes — remember, though, that all mice have large, bulging eyes when killed in a snap trap. House mice have hairless, dull tails and no clear separation of colour from their back to belly.

With a long history of close association with humans, house mice thrive in a big-city environment, although they are found in the countryside as well. Deer mice usually only invade rural buildings. They are completely nocturnal, and although they accept any food they find in buildings, deer mice probably occupy them primarily for shelter

A deer mouse can be distinguished from the more urban house mouse by its white feet and big eyes.

The field mouse is actually a meadow vole, cousin to the lemming.

and the excellent nest material offered by upholstered furniture, pillows and mattresses. In the course of their activities, they leave a strong and almost ineradicable odour that pervades many cabins, cottages and hunting lodges in the northern forest. Two years ago, a deer mouse moved into the glove compartment of a research vehicle I was driving. When the glove compartment was opened, my companions and I found a neat nest lovingly constructed from the shredded remains of our $60 gas money.

Like most small rodents, mice and voles have short life spans and a marvellous capacity to increase their numbers rapidly. The average house mouse, deer mouse or vole, born in a litter of six to eight only 21 days after conception, is weaned 20 days later and becomes fertile as soon as 10 days after that. Females mate within 24 hours of giving birth, and in the cases of voles and house mice, reproduction can continue throughout the year. Therefore, in a mere 10 generations (five years), assuming each female produces 20 female offspring per generation (well below potential), a single pair of mice or voles could produce more than 10 trillion descendants. Of course, this does not happen: predators, disease, accidents, climate and other factors prevent most females from living long enough to breed at all, let alone long enough to produce 20 successful

daughters. On the other hand, it does not take 10 trillion mice to destroy a cottageful of belongings — a mere dozen can do great damage in a relatively short period of time.

How does one rid one's premises of mice? Humankind has given much thought to this problem; the methods that have been recommended include traps, snares, mouse-proofed walls, flooding, fumigation, ferrets, poison, limes, lures, repellents and viruses, as well as laws at all levels of government. The prevalence of mice and rats today is vivid testimony to the value of a flexible reproductive rate. Trying to control mice by reducing their numbers only works if they are exterminated. Haphazard efforts to reduce other numbers merely fit into their reproductive strategy — a game plan that has been honed to perfection by millions of years of scrimmages with humans and other predators.

Spray repellents may discourage mice, but they are often sticky, toxic or more foul-smelling than the mice. Most often, they simply do not work. Mothballs are often effective in a confined space, but they evaporate and must be replaced regularly; in addition, they are toxic to children. Expensive ultrasonic devices that produce a loud, high-pitched sound have been widely advertised recently. They appeal to our love of technology, but I know of no data that indicate they have any effect on mice, and my own

observations are that mice do not even notice the sound, much less find it repellent. Since these devices produce sound in a range also detected by cats and dogs, they probably irritate pets at least as much as they do mice.

Rodenticides can be used to kill mice, but these substances are toxic to most mammals and must be used with caution. Baits must be replenished regularly, and children and family pets must be prevented from ingesting the poison or the mice it has killed. If checked regularly, traps can be effective, especially against deer mice, who are more easily trapped and less likely to reinvade a building than are house mice. The best method is to bait the traps for a few days before setting those which are being visited. Handle carcasses with gloves or tongs. Exterminating mice or even keeping their numbers at a very low level requires fierce dedication. If one relaxes vigilance even for a short time, the mouse population will burgeon rapidly to problem levels. Usually, a compromise position must be adopted, generally one that favours the rodents.

Cats and other animals kill mice, but they will never exert much control over their numbers. In fact, pet food may provide an excellent food source for the mice. I have watched deer mice empty my dog's bowl of kibble — carrying it off piece by piece as he and I gazed in dumb admiration.

In the end, there is only one solution if you want to store books or padded furniture in a cottage: protect the valuables with a mouse-proofed structure. It must be impervious to gnawing and have no holes greater than ¼ inch in diameter. Metal, metal screen or hard plastic are recommended. Holes may be plugged with steel wool.

Finally, there is no truth yet to the Pied Piper fable. Even if a piper could lure all the rats and mice to a watery grave, mourned by no one, new mice would soon reinvade, or a few tone-deaf individuals would remain behind to replace the fallen.

Originally published in Harrowsmith *magazine (Camden East, Ont.).*

Are those little ants chewing up your cottage?

by Adrian Forsyth

My friend's encounter with carpenter ants began when he joined his children to watch the scurrying insects milling about a pile of firewood stored on his verandah. When he noticed them disappearing under his clapboard, he headed for his bug books.

As it turned out, he had good reason to worry, for he was playing host to a thriving colony of carpenter ants.

Carpenter ants get their name from their nest-building habits, and although some species nest in soil, most excavate a series of cavities, galleries and passageways in wood. Under natural conditions, carpenter ants are found in rotten trees — usually fallen logs or trees that contain dead, rotted wood. Because firm, live wood and sound, dry lumber are too tough for them to dig into, they rarely pose a threat to new buildings, but any older house or structure with rotting and damp wood is a prospect for colonization. Carpenter ants can be found in rural or urban situations wherever there are trees.

A carpenter ant colony gets its start with the flight of a new ant queen from an already established colony. The virgin queen flies into the air and mates with a male, which then leaves the nest and dies. Upon landing, the queen breaks off her wings and begins searching for a suitable nest site, usually under the bark of a dead tree. She then constructs an enclosed cell for herself and begins to lay eggs. Her large flight muscles are self-digested and converted into a nutrient-rich solution, and when the eggs hatch into white, grublike ant larvae, the queen regurgitates the rich fluid for them to eat. This enables her to rear a set of worker ants without ever leaving her cell to search for food.

The first workers are relatively small, but as the colony grows, the worker becomes larger — up to one inch long in some species. The colony may grow until it contains several thousand workers and can last a decade or more. After a couple of years, it will begin producing and releasing new queens and males: over its lifetime, it may produce thousands of them.

Carpenter ants feed on insects and rich sources of sugar. They can often be seen on garden plants and fruit trees, stroking aphids with their antennae, an act of husbandry that causes the aphid to excrete a sugary solution. Each colony jealously guards its aphid herd from other ants, aphid parasites and competing insects such as caterpillars. Sometimes, though, when the ants' need for meat exceeds their sugar requirements, they simply eat some of the aphids. In addition, carpenter ants attack and carry off all sorts of other small insects, but they do not eat wood. Their intricate carpentry is just that — a form of home building.

Like most ants, carpenters have a sophisticated chemical communication system by which they can release scents to alert colony members of an attack by predators or lay down scent trails that guide other workers to rich food sources or new nest sites. It is this ability that makes carpenter ants a threat to homeowners who heat with wood. If firewood that contains carpenter ants is brought into, or stored near, a house, it begins to dry out, and the carpenter ants send out scouts to search for a more suitable nest site. If they happen to find damp wood in the house — around a bathroom, laundry room vent, damp foundation or rotting timber — the scouts lay a chemical trail for the colony to follow.

To get rid of carpenter ants, one needs to do more than simply step on them, for while this may weaken a small colony, a large one can produce new workers almost as fast as the old ones are killed. Chemical fumigation is expensive, hazardous and usually ineffective because the colony and its queen are probably hidden in some inaccessible spot under a damp eave or deep in the foundation. To kill a colony of carpenter ants, the queen must be destroyed, and the easiest way to do this is to let the workers find a sweet poisoned bait. Not only will they lead other workers to the find, but they will carry it home and feed it to the young ants as well as to the queen. The most popular form of this bait is a sugar solution containing boric acid, a relatively mild toxin widely used in making soap and one that poses little threat to humans. Small bottles of this bait are sold in hardware and general stores, and they can be effective, but only if they are set out diligently over a period of weeks, since it may take that long for the colony to die out. There has been some research done using sugary solutions containing hormones that shut down the ant's reproduction, but these products are not yet commercially available.

For those who live in a wooded area, prevention is the best cure. Any house, whether heated with wood or not, is a target for thousands of carpenter ant queens every summer, and they will always be a threat wherever there is damp, soft wood. Prevention means a serious regime of house maintenance that identifies and removes any such wood.

Trying to eliminate carpenter ants from the trees in an area is neither possible nor desirable. They are an important element of any northern forest and a major source of winter food for such birds as the pileated woodpecker. The holes these magnificent birds pound in pursuit of carpenter ants are used by other cavity-nesting birds, such as bluebirds and chickadees.

Originally published in Harrowsmith *magazine (Camden East, Ont.).*

Nature

Treating the orphaned wildfowl that the kids rescue

Caring for a Bird in Hand

by Laura O'Bisco Socha

Most people who find themselves rehabilitating wild birds start off in the same manner — unexpectedly — and your initiation into this phase of ornithology will in all likelihood follow much the same pattern. Rehabilitation is an inevitable side effect of the birding habit. Sometimes it is thrust upon you by a friend or neighbour (or a perfect stranger who heard somewhere of your birding interests), appearing at your door offering a featherless, half-dead baby on an outstretched palm, stammering something about how you know all about birds and will, of course, do something to save this one. Sometimes you initiate it yourself, when you are the one to discover a bird in trouble. Whatever the circumstances, you must make a choice: ignore the situation, or take some type of rehabilitative action.

Most of the literature concerning the rescue and care of wildlife elaborates on the reasons why you should ignore the situation, and in general, these reasons are quite valid.

Caring for distressed birds requires knowledge of diets, medical needs and treatment of injuries, coupled with at least a working knowledge of a bird's natural development, behaviour patterns, proper facilities, an acceptable re-

lease site and a host of other specifics. This is knowledge the average person does not possess, and attempts at rescue, however well intentioned, often end in disaster.

There is also the problem of people wanting to make pets of the wildlife they have successfully raised or nursed back to health. This is not only illegal but immoral as well and can pose a serious threat to the health and welfare of both the animal and its captor.

To discourage the temptation to keep wildlife pets and to discourage rehabilitation attempts by inexperienced persons, federal and, in many cases, state or provincial permits are required of anyone engaged in rehabilitation efforts. In addition, permit holders work in close cooperation with federal and state/provincial fish and wildlife agencies, must maintain accurate records and submit annual reports accounting for the welfare and final disposition of each animal or bird that they have taken under their care.

But however justified the arguments against rehabilitation attempts may be, there are other factors that should be considered. First, with man's increasing encroachment on and destruction of wildlife habitats, contact with displaced and distressed wildlife is inevitable. Pollution, pesticides, oil spills, out-of-control construction, high-tension wires,

windows, cats, dogs, children and automobiles are just a sampling of human-made hazards that have been responsible for bringing avian casualties and would-be rehabilitators together. In recent years, public concern for the conservation of wildlife has increased, and more people are actively expressing that we do have moral obligations in the matter.

A second point to consider is that, regardless of the discouraging statistics and literature concerning rehabilitation attempts, it is certainly not impossible for a person, armed with a little knowledge and a lot of effort, to successfully rehabilitate an injured or orphaned bird. Success may be the exception to the general rule, but it is within reach.

It is difficult, at best, to provide a complete treatise of wild-bird care in the space here. This information is intended to guide you through the basic treatment of the most common casualties and to soften the surge of panic that will accompany the arrival of your first orphan. Most important, realize from the start that the well-being of the bird will be your responsibility and that your goal is to see the bird released back into its natural habitat. And any-

Swamp sparrow nestlings in the wild; humans should duplicate the natural routine as much as possible.

thing less is not successful rehabilitation.

Since baby birds are the most common casualties you will encounter, let's talk about their special requirements first. Before you can hope to successfully raise an orphaned bird, it is important to have at least a basic idea of a bird's natural development under normal circumstances. The following will be very basic in nature, and it is recommended that you take advantage of any publications on the subject for more detailed information.

Newly hatched birds, or "hatchlings," are known as "nestlings" until they are mature enough to leave the nest, at which time they become "fledglings." "Altricial" young are featherless, blind and completely helpless and confined to the nest until they are fully feathered and strong enough to fly, although some species will leave the nest before the skill of flying has been mastered. All passerines are altricial.

"Precocial" young are usually called chicks. These emerge from the egg covered with soft down, leave the nest soon after hatching and are capable of feeding themselves within hours. Precocial chicks depend on the hen for protection and are never far from her side. Ducks and geese are examples of precocial birds.

To confuse matters, there are also semialtricial birds, which are covered with down upon hatching but are completely dependent on the parent birds (hawks and owls are semialtricial), and semiprecocial birds, which are down-covered and able to walk shortly after hatching but remain in the nest and depend on the parent birds for such essentials as food and protection. The chicks of gulls and terns are examples of semiprecocial young.

Because altricial nestlings and fledglings are the birds you will encounter most often, let's look at their development more closely.

An altricial bird hatches from the egg looking as if it should have spent a few more weeks on the inside. It is featherless, except for a few wisps of natal down. Bulging black eyes are tightly closed, the rubbery, swollen beak (usually bright yellow) is too big in propor-

Cedar waxwings deliver chokecherries to their nestlings; altricial young are completely helpless at first but often are ready to leave the nest in 10 days.

tion to the head and seems to have been added as an afterthought. The head itself is somehow supported by a spindly, wrinkled neck that looks as though it will surely break under the strain. The wings are three sizes too small, the belly three sizes too big. The remains of the yolk and bodily functions are visible through transparent skin. Long legs and tangled feet are at the same time too large and too delicate. All in all, the newly hatched bird is not a pretty sight.

Happily, the youngster does not remain in this sorry state for long. A baby bird matures rapidly, and you will see physical improvements every day; in some species, the birds are fully feathered and ready to leave the nest within 10 days of hatching. Timetables vary according to species, but generally, it is safe to say that small-sized species and species that utilize an open nest develop at a much faster rate than larger species or cavity nesters. For example, the young of most wood warblers will fledge in 8 to 12 days of hatching and the young of nuthatches (small cavity

nesters) in 18 to 21 days, while the young of eagles may remain in the nest from 70 to 84 days.

In the wild, the parents will brood the young to keep them warm or shade them from sun or rain by standing over them with wings outstretched. Usually, both parents feed the young, beginning at sunrise and stopping at dusk. This becomes a rotation feeding, with each chick receiving something to eat about every 10 to 15 minutes.

The key to successful rehabilitation is plain old common sense. Familiarize yourself with the type of parental care your orphan would get under normal conditions, and duplicate this care to the best of your ability. Sometimes your duplicated care may be something subtle, like shielding the orphans of cavity-nesting species from bright lights, simulating life in the nest hole. Sometimes it is more direct, such as cutting a mouse into bite-sized pieces for an orphaned owlet.

It is probably safe to say that at least half of the baby birds I have received in the past as orphans were not orphaned or abandoned at all. Most were newly fledged young that had not yet perfected their flying skills and were still, no doubt, under the care of their parents until they were "rescued."

The discovery of a naked nestling is, however, a more serious problem, since it will not live long without food and protection from the elements. But taking the nestling home is not always the only solution.

In either case, returning the misplaced youngster to its nest is the best possible form of rehabilitation. Unfortunately, this is often easier said than done. A naked, helpless nestling discovered on the ground out in the open obviously did not get there of his own accord. If you (and the bird) are lucky, you need only to look above the nestling, into the eaves of the building, the branches of the tree, the bushes or birdhouse to locate the nest the kid has fallen from. If you cannot find the nest, the bird was probably dropped there by a nest-raiding bird or perhaps a child, and in that case, it will need rescuing.

If you can locate the nest, make every effort to put the baby back. The parent birds will not be upset because you have handled their youngster — birds have a poor sense of smell, and they won't even notice. What if the whole nest has been destroyed or is in danger of falling? This often happens to the nests of robins after a rain — the mud used in construction washes away. You can choose a substitute nest, such as a small box, and wire it to the tree as close to the original location as possible. Place the nestlings in it, and go away. Watch from inside the house or at least from a reasonable distance. The parents will not return to care for their young if you are too close.

Fledglings that are discovered on the ground do not always have broken wings. Again, these birds are in a normal, though hazardous, stage of their development. Putting them back in the nest won't really help, because they will only jump out again. You can, however, place them in the branches of a nearby tree or bush, which will afford them some protection against predators and children. If you take the time to

watch from a reasonable distance, you will most likely see the parent birds bringing the food. You need not do anything else.

Always, without exception, you should make every effort to return an uninjured, healthy youngster to its nest or parents. Rescue the bird only after you have determined that the bird will not survive without you, because the chances are very high that it won't survive with you, either.

The first thing most nestling orphans will need in the way of first-aid treatment is warmth. This is especially true if the orphan is newly hatched and still featherless. At this stage, songbirds are essentially cold-blooded, and their bodies adjust to the temperature of the surrounding air. Body-temperature control does not develop until five to six days from hatching in many species. A chilled baby will be listless, will feel cool to the touch and will make little or no effort to beg, or "gape," for food. You can use your own body heat to warm the baby by placing it under your shirt, against your skin, or simply by cupping it gently in your hands. (It is useless to attempt to feed a chilled baby; in fact, you can kill it, so getting the youngster warm should always be your first concern).

Once you have warmed the baby in this manner, you must provide a substitute nest and a more permanent source of heat. Line a small bowl, basket or similar container with 15 or 20 tissues, place the nestling inside, and cover with another tissue to protect it from drafts. Place the "nest" on a towel-wrapped heating pad set on "low," or suspend a 60-watt light bulb about 12 inches above it. Some people use hot-water bottles, but this can result in inconsistent temperatures, as the water cools if not carefully maintained. In any case, keep a thermometer on hand to monitor the temperature. You want to keep the bird warm; you don't want to cook it. For a featherless nestling, it should be around 95 degrees F. A lightly feathered orphan should be kept in an 80-degree environment, and one that is fully feathered will probably need no supplemental heat source unless it is

sick or injured. Soak a sponge in water, and keep this next to the nest to provide some humidity.

Using this method, it will be very easy to keep your youngster clean. Simply remove the soiled tissue on top of the pile and add a few more whenever needed. Avoid the temptation to use a real nest, because these often carry parasites and are much more difficult to keep clean. You are going to be in for a lot of work as is, and you'll find using the paper tissues to be much more convenient.

Now that your orphan is warm and comfortable, you can think about the next priority — food. In the wild, the youngster would be fed a wide variety of high-protein foods: insects, worms, grubs and other similar creatures. Considering the fact that you will be feeding this bird every 10 minutes or so and that you might possibly be raising more than one orphan at the same time, some quick calculations on your part will demonstrate the odds against your being able to collect enough insects to do the job. This will be one area where you will have to alter your duplicated-care techniques for a more convenient system, but the importance of a protein-rich, balanced diet cannot be sacrificed in the process.

There is a convenient alternative. Young songbirds respond well to a diet of soft dog food, supplemented with natural foods as the birds mature. You may use any one of the kibbled varieties, provided you soak it in water until soft, or you may use one of the canned varieties. I find the kibble easier because I can mix a fresh batch when I need it, instead of being faced with a whole can of food that can spoil easily in warm weather. The soaked kibble doesn't fall apart when I'm trying to feed it, as the canned food will do, and the kibbled pieces are "bite-sized" for many birds.

The dog-food diet works well on all songbirds (seed eaters included), woodpeckers, swifts and similar insect-eating species. If fussing makes you feel better, you can also prepare bits of hard-boiled egg yolk, pieces of lean beef, raw beef kidney, insects, mealworms, maggots and earthworms. Don't feed bread soaked in milk, which for some reason seems to be a popular offering among well-meaning rescuers. Remember the common sense mentioned earlier? Where does a wild bird obtain milk to feed her young, and why would she want to, since birds are not mammals? Milk is actually difficult for most birds to digest, and while it may not kill your orphan outright, it can certainly cause it a few digestive problems at a stressful time.

Natural Supplements

As soon as you know what kind of bird you are raising (you may have to wait for some feathers for this) and your orphan is eating well, begin to supplement the dog-food diet, if at all possible, with some of the natural foods the bird would receive in the wild from its parents. You can also offer fruit — blueberries, strawberries, cherries and grapes are always favourites.

If your orphan is warm and comfortable, coaxing it to eat should not be difficult unless the youngster is near death. You may have to force-feed a very weak nestling until it regains its strength. To force-feed, gently press against the side of the beak at the back portion, open the bird's mouth and place the food well down the throat. Be careful not to exert too much pressure on the rubbery beak, since you can easily damage it and cause it to mature deformed. A healthy baby will eagerly open its mouth wide, or gape, as soon as you tap the edge of the "nest." This simulates the parent bird's arrival on the nest. When the nestling's eyes are open and it recognizes you as its food source, you will not be able to come near without setting off a display of wing-fluttering, gaping and repeated "feed me" calls.

If you have ever watched a parent bird feed its young, you probably noticed that the food is unceremoniously stuffed down the nestling's throat. Your method of feeding must closely match the action of the parent. A young bird cannot swallow unless the food is placed well down in the throat, behind the tongue, and this is where many peo-

ple run into trouble. They timidly place a bit of food into the baby's mouth and wonder why it just sits there or continues to gape with a mouth full of food.

Use your fingers, a pair of tweezers or a toothpick, if necessary — if you use anything but your fingers, be gentle — but be firm and get that food down the throat. If you are faced with a very small, weak orphan and are having difficulty opening the beak, you can try the "drop" method. Add water to the food until it is the consistency of thick soup. Dip the end of a toothpick or similar tool into the food, and allow it to collect at the tip. Hold the bird, and let the food "drop" into the crack where the upper and lower mandibles (beak) come together. The bird should make an attempt to swallow the liquid. Continue feeding in this manner until the bird shakes its head, slinging food all over the place and indicating that it has had enough.

A very small nestling may only take one piece of food at a feeding, while larger, older birds may accept upward of 10 pieces at a session. The important thing is to feed the baby as much as it will accept. You cannot overfeed a baby bird that begs for food; it will simply refuse to gape and will go to sleep when it's had enough, but you can easily starve one in a matter of hours with inadequate feedings. Force-feeding is another matter, and you must exercise caution not to overfeed and suffocate the bird.

You should offer food whenever the bird calls for it, or at least every 15 minutes or so at first. As the bird gets older, the time between feedings will lengthen so that you are feeding a fledgling about every 30 to 45 minutes.

Avoid giving the bird water until it fledges and can take the water on its own. It is too easy to accidentally introduce water into the lungs when placing it in a bird's mouth, and the bird will receive enough moisture from the food.

Until the bird fledges, there isn't much more in the way of care that you must provide other than keeping the orphan warm and protected from the family pets and small children.

The day will come when your orphan

will hop on the edge of its nest to have a look around. This is the first step toward fledging, and from this point forward, it is a good idea to put nest and bird inside a spacious cage. The bird may spend a few days just perching on the edge of the nest, but sooner or later, and usually without much warning, it's going to jump. This can be disastrous if the nest is left unattended on a table and the fledgling jumps over the side, since this stage of development often takes place before the bird is capable of flying. It's one thing to leap out of a nest and crash-land on a patch of Mother Earth; but it's quite another to make sudden contact with a hardwood floor.

The cage should provide enough room for the fledgling to move around without injuring itself. Be sure there are one or two sturdy perches within easy reach of the nest. Once the bird fledges, you can remove the nest — it won't return to it anyway. You should now put down a small dish of food and a shallow dish of water, large enough to accommodate a bath. A pie plate works nicely; add a flat stone in the water for added security.

Until now, your orphan has been accustomed to you stuffing the food down its throat at each mealtime, but you should soon notice a change in feeding behaviour. The bird will show more curiosity toward the food you are offering, and it is now time to alter your feeding methods. Instead of automatically stuffing the food, give the fledgling the chance to take it from you. Hold the food in front of its beak within easy reach. The bird will gape and beg as usual but will probably make no attempt to take the food, even though it is right under its nose. After a few seconds, feed the fledgling in the usual manner. Raptors can be stimulated to pick up their own food by touching it to their feet.

The bird will be spending more and more time exploring its surroundings, pecking at perches, the dishes of food and water, the cage bottom and sides and sometimes its own toes. Gradually, this exploratory behaviour will carry over to feeding, and one day, the bird will make a half-hearted stab at the food you are holding before its beak.

When the bird finally does grab the food in its beak all by itself, it most likely will not know what to do with it. This is a new experience for the young bird, and it may stand there holding the food in the tip of its beak, making no attempt to swallow. Be patient; eventually, it will get the hang of it and begin to feed itself.

Since these first feedings tend to be haphazard at best, you should continue feeding the bird in the accustomed fashion until you are absolutely certain the bird is capable of feeding well on its own. Even then, it will continue to gape for food whenever it can. Parent birds continue to feed their young after fledging, ensuring survival while the birds learn to fend for themselves.

The ability to fly is inherited, but coordination and strength require much practice, and your fledgling must be given the opportunity to perfect its flying skills before it can be released. A large indoor or outdoor flight pen is the ideal accommodation, but unless you plan to make rehabilitation a major part of your birding habit, such a pen is probably not practical. An enclosed porch, greenhouse or similar structure will also serve the purpose — or, if all else fails, a room in your home (this could be messy). The major requirement for your flight area is that it be safe from cats and other predators. It should also prevent the fledgling from escaping prematurely. You should also remove anything the bird could accidentally (or purposely) destroy. One northern oriole fledgling I left flying free in my living room spent one afternoon methodically lacerating the leaves on 26 potted African violets. If you must keep the fledgling caged, be sure that it receives a few hours of flying time each day.

If you have raised this bird indoors, begin now to "weather" it by placing the cage outside during the daylight hours and gradually working toward leaving it outdoors overnight. Be sure the cage is out of the reach of cats, raccoons and other dangers and protected from the elements.

Early release is important, but imprinting is not as inevitable as some think.

If at all possible, your fledgling should be banded. The recovery of a banded, hand-raised bird will provide some valuable insight to the success or failure of any rehabilitation project.

Final Rehabilitation Phase

Once your bird is capable of feeding itself (even though it prefers to be fed), is flying well and is reasonably adjusted to the outdoors, it is time to begin the final phase of rehabilitation and the goal of the whole project: release back to the wild. Plan to release the bird when two or three days of fair weather conditions are forecast. Early in the morning, open the cage door. Secure the door in the opened position so that the fledgling can return at will. Provide fresh food and water either inside the cage or nearby it, where the fledgling can locate it easily.

Most likely, the fledgling will not venture too far from "home" in the beginning, but this will vary with species. Cedar waxwings, for example, travel great distances as fledglings and will disappear shortly after their release. Robins will return to you for at least a week, and you will begin to wonder if blue jays

and orioles will ever decide to leave you.

Before you decide that you have a fledgling that is hopelessly "imprinted," be sure that you have allowed ample time under the right conditions for the bird to make the adjustment to living by itself.

Imprinting normally occurs soon after hatching and is the way an infant bird identifies itself as belonging to its parents. When humans are foster parents, a bird can become imprinted on them. The result is a bird that attaches itself to humans. The degree of imprinting varies with species, but in most cases, it can be avoided or outgrown, or the bird can be retrained.

One particular blue jay that comes to mind was nearly retained as an incurably imprinted bird, even though "Blue" had been officially banded and released for several weeks. The bird would disappear for hours at a time but would arrive like clockwork at the back door at mealtime. He showed no fear of anyone, and we never observed him hanging around with other blue jays. We were considering holding him over the winter when, well into the fall migration, he failed to return.

We feared the worst and wondered if he'd made it, and then we received a banding report. It seems our Blue was alive and well, recaptured by a bander in Connecticut. As if to keep in touch with us, Blue managed to get himself caught a few weeks later in South Carolina and again in a third location that escapes me now. There are two points to that story: Get your rehabilitated birds banded if possible, and be sure you have allowed ample time under the right conditions for the bird to make the adjustment. Certainly this is an area for more research.

When you do determine an individual is unfit for release, either by virtue of its being incurably imprinted or through a physical disability, you can usually find a nature centre, wildlife refuge or similar facility where the bird will be welcomed as part of the educational staff. However, if you raise your orphan in the manner I have described, avoid unnecessary handling and allow ample time for adjustment, you should not encounter such a problem often.

It is obvious that not all species can be raised according to the methods discussed thus far. While all species require specific diets and housing, some are decidedly more difficult to care for than others. You would not be able to raise a great blue heron in your living room — nor would you want to. The following species are the most common difficult species you will encounter. Do not attempt to care for these birds unless you can provide the specialized diets, housing and release techniques they demand.

Hawks and Owls

These birds require a balanced diet of fresh meat, with bones, fur, hair and feathers included. In the wild, they obtain this by killing and eating other birds and animals. Hawks usually tear chunks of meat and bone from their prey, while owls tend to swallow their prey whole. In either case, whatever material their bodies do not use (bones, fur, feathers) are regurgitated later in the form of a pellet. The bones, fur and feathers serve as roughage and keep the digestive system functioning properly.

The feeding requirements of raptorial birds are the reason for placing them in this special-care section. While most people have no problem mixing up a batch of dog food for the robin, some do tend to balk when it comes to cutting a mouse into bite-sized pieces. In fact, we sometimes used this technique to persuade would-be "rescuers" to surrender a raptor chick to a rehabilitation centre rather than keeping it at home.

Quite often, we would receive calls from people who had orphaned hawk or owl chicks in their possession and were calling for information on how to care for the birds, which they thought "would be fun to raise." After lengthy conversations about wildlife pets, the law, retraining the birds for life in the wild, along with the other responsibilities associated with caring for such a bird, most people had a better understanding and surrendered the bird to a qualified centre.

There are always a few exceptions, and one particular incident sticks in my mind. The caller was determined to keep the screech owl her son had found in the woods. Dot, a colleague of mine, can be equally determined, especially when the welfare of a bird is at stake. After speaking to the caller on the phone, it was apparent to Dot that this woman did not have the knowledge (or the common sense) necessary to successfully raise the bird. But the woman was persistent. "Just tell me what to feed it, and I'll be all right."

"Do you have a blender?" Dot asked sweetly.

"Yes."

"Fine. What you need to do is catch at least two mice a day. Put them in the blender and chop . . ." The bird was delivered to the rehabilitation centre within half an hour.

Actually, there is truth in the blender technique. Newly hatched raptors respond best to a mouse that's been crushed to a mushy consistency. In an emergency situation, you can feed strips of lean beef, beef heart or chicken parts, but this should be only on a temporary basis until the bird can be brought to a qualified facility. Maintaining a supply of mice can create additional problems,

since a full-grown hawk or owl may consume as many as 10 mice a day. Established raptor-rehabilitation centres sometimes obtain the healthy "control" mice from research laboratories. These are kept frozen, then thawed and warmed as needed. Some also obtain day-old chicks from poultry and game-bird farms to supplement the rodent diet. Fresh road kills also provide a convenient additional food source.

Unlike the passerine birds discussed earlier that learn to feed themselves easily, raptors must practise and master their hunting techniques before they starve to death. The killing instinct is inherited, but the skill required to accomplish it must be learned.

For a bird raised in captivity, this presents still more problems. You must be absolutely certain the bird is capable of feeding itself before it is released, and there is a vast difference between the half-tame, plodding, domesticated mouse you might raise for the purpose and the wild, ever alert lightning-fast mouse the bird will depend on as prey.

Raptor-rehabilitation facilities are equipped with specialized flight cages, allowing the birds room to develop their hunting skills. There are also specially designed holding pens that allow the bird to be raised with minimum human contact, reducing the effects of imprinting. Since raptors mature more slowly, it is sometimes necessary to hold the birds through the first winter to ensure their survival.

With all of the above considerations in mind, there may still be an occasion where you find yourself with a raptorial chick in need of immediate care. Until you can contact a qualified rehabilitation centre, the following guidelines should be followed.

Raptor nestlings should be kept warm and free from drafts. An extra source of heat is usually unnecessary (since the chick is down-covered) unless the chick is debilitated.

Feeding methods are slightly different. Raptor chicks do not gape as vigorously as passerine birds. For the first few times, you may need to force-feed the bird until it realizes you are offering food. To force-feed a raptor, use your fingers, tweezers, chopstick or similar tool. Press the meat gently to the side and back part of the beak. When it opens, gently push the meat to the back of the throat. The bird will swallow and, after a few such feedings, will begin to take the meat. Since raptor chicks do not gape as readily as the passerine nestlings do, it may be necessary to palpate the bird's crop to determine if the feeding is sufficient. The crop should feel "padded" — not stuffed. In any case, stop feeding if the chick begins to regurgitate. Chicks under two weeks of age should be offered food about every hour. Extend feeding intervals to two hours for chicks two to three weeks of age. At four weeks, feeding should be spaced four hours apart and remain so until the bird is fully feathered and fledged. At this point, gradually extend the time between feedings until the bird is receiving one meal a day.

Again, hawks and owls should be referred to a qualified rehabilitation centre as quickly as possible. If you are particularly interested in this area of rehabilitation work, you may want to volunteer some time with an established centre.

Waterfowl and Wading Birds

These species are very difficult to care for properly unless you can offer the water for swimming, wading and feeding that they will require. In an emergency situation, you can use a child's plastic swimming pool or your bathtub.

I once cared for a Peking duck that had been attacked by a dog late in January. As I lacked proper outdoor facilities in the dead of winter, the duck lived in a large box in the bathroom (luckily I had a huge bathroom) while his wounds healed, enjoying daily duck time in the tub. My son called him Donald, and Donald soon became quite possessive of the bathroom, quacking in protest when his "territory" was invaded. It was almost worth having a duck in the bathroom to see the reaction of unsuspecting guests who tried to discreetly use the facilities unnoticed and, instead, had their intentions loudly publicized by a quacking duck. Anyway,

Donald fared quite well under these circumstances and, one morning in March, after much fussing and quacking, presented us with an egg. We had fresh duck eggs for the next few weeks, until the ice broke up on the ponds and "Ms." Donald was released.

Ducks and geese can be fed a mixture of grain, cracked corn, dog food or uncooked oatmeal, but other species are considerably more difficult to house and feed properly. Many fish-eating birds require force-feeding, which can be a two-person job. These birds will also regurgitate their meals if upset, and if you think the fried-fish smell from last night's dinner is causing an odour problem in your kitchen, consider the effects of a regurgitated mackerel across the floor. Herons can be quite dangerous to handle: they will stab at you with their spearlike bills, aiming for your eyes.

If you must care for a heron or similar bird until you can locate a rehabilitation centre, keep the bird in a large, covered cardboard carton (ask your local appliance store for a refrigerator or stove box), place a large basin or bucket of fresh water — weighted with rocks so that it won't tip easily — in a corner of the box, and disturb the bird as little as possible. Remove the water when you are ready to transport the bird to the rehabilitation centre.

If you will be feeding the bird during the time you are holding it, try to obtain some live baitfish from the local sporting-goods store, drop them in the water bucket and leave the bird alone. Few birds will attempt to eat while you are watching. When live fish are unavailable, you can defrost a frozen fish and swirl it around in the water so that it appears to be moving.

I do recommend that you contact a rehabilitation centre or your local fish and wildlife office immediately when dealing with these species.

Precocial Chicks

These birds are probably among the easiest ones to care for, if for no other reason than they will feed themselves. They will require an enclosed area where they are free to roam about yet

are protected from predators. A 25-watt light bulb suspended in the corner of the pen (for very young chicks, a large cardboard box is sufficient) will provide an adequate and low-cost source of heat.

Provide the chicks with commercially sold chicken mash, supplemented with insects, earthworms, mealworms, crickets and similar creatures. Also supply a shallow dish containing grit – commercially sold parakeet grit will serve the purpose. As the chicks mature, the cage should be placed outdoors, but only if the chicks are sheltered and have access to grass and soil.

You may need to teach the chicks to eat. In the wild, the hen teaches her young by "talking" to them, picking up seeds and dropping them in front of the young. By imitating their mother, the chicks soon learn to peck for their own food. If you can "talk" to the chicks in their own language, great, but more than likely, you'll have to teach them by demonstrating the art of pecking. Pick up some food, and drop it in front of the chick to get its attention. With luck, it should respond by pecking at the food you have dropped. Another technique is to tap the floor of the box lightly with your finger or a toothpick in a pecking motion.

If you are certain your charges are not feeding themselves, you may need to use the drop-feeding technique explained earlier.

Pigeons and Doves

These birds do not gape for food, as do the young of altricial birds described earlier. Instead, they are fed by taking a liquid secretion (pigeon milk) from the crop of the parent bird. As a substitute, you can use cooked wheat cereal mixed with an equal amount of water until soupy. Cut the tip off the nipple of a doll's baby bottle, fill it with formula, and offer the cut end to the baby. It will insert its beak into the "soup" and feed. Repeat feedings about every hour.

Reprinted with permission from Birding for the Amateur Naturalist, *by Laura O'Biso Socha,* ©1989, $8.95, The Globe Pequot Press (Chester, CT).

Understanding the haunting cries floating across the lake

The Magic of the Loons' Songs

by Kate Crowley and Mike Link

For as long as people have wandered and lived near northern lakes, they have turned their heads to look for the source of the soprano ululations coming off the waters. These sounds evoke strong feelings of empathy. The Cree heard in them the anguish of a dead warrior denied entry to heaven, and the Ojibwa interpreted the cry as an omen of death.

The loon has a basic collection of four calls that can be given individually or combined to signify the response to conflicting emotions. Very often, the call is given in combination with a physical display — what might appear to be a type of dance. Because we find such emotional and spiritual feelings in the loon's repertoire of calls and displays, it may come as a shock to cottagers to learn that three of the most commonly heard calls are vocalizations of excitation, stress and distress and therefore reflect negative conditions rather than celebration.

In the 1970s, William Barklow undertook a study of the loon's vocal communication. His research resulted in a doctoral thesis and a popular recording, *Voices of the Loon*. Much of what we understand today about the loon's moody music is based on his study.

The four calls are described as wail, yodel, tremolo and hoot. Most people are familiar with the first three calls because they are the most dramatic and easily heard. The hoot is a softer monosyllabic note, with a questioning, tentative sound to it. It is given by an individual bird as it approaches a flock or when surfacing with food for a chick. It appears to be used to locate or keep in contact with nearby birds. On a misty morning, it is a sound one might hear and have trouble identifying, for it has none of the dynamic qualities that we normally associate with the loon. The hoot is the loon call that we hear least frequently.

Most people who have written about the loon, including the earliest naturalists, have described its wild "laughter." While he was on Wrangell Island, John Muir wrote, "A loon flew past as we lingered, screaming and making the solitary place more solitary by his intensely lonely wild laugh." This is the tremolo, a call with the characteristics of a hysterical soprano. Barklow says it can be best described as "a distress call, generally given in situations that are alarming to the bird."

A boat approaching a nest area will almost certainly cause the birds to tremolo, and the pitch and frequency will increase as the perceived danger increases. If a loon on its nest is suddenly disturbed by an approach from land, it will quickly leave the nest and run on the surface of the water, drawing intruders away from the nest, while giving the tremolo call; the tremolo can be heard gradually fading into the distance, but the air continues to vibrate to that staccato syncopation.

A mated pair of loons will perform a tremolo duet if they should be near one another when confronted by a boat or any other threat to their nest or young. When birds duet, it is very difficult to distinguish one bird's call from the other's, for the calls are just marginally spaced apart and very close in pitch — too close for the human ear to distinguish easily. The asynchronous call may add to the intruder's auditory confusion and subsequent distraction.

It is during this type of encounter, when a boat or intruder penetrates a pair's territory and offspring are nearby, that the most dramatic display occurs. Some call it "penguin dancing." In this dance, the loon rushes toward the intruder and rises, with head drawn back and bill almost touching breast, while its feet beat the water and create a spray around its body. The loon then falls forward, raising more water. It may momentarily dive, then rise again and beat the water with its wings, all the while tremoloing loudly.

One or more parents may display in an effort to create a scene of frenzy that

A frantic loon performs its "penguin dance" as human intruders approach; such a display should warn people away rather than attract an audience.

will scare away or distract the threat to their young. To unenlightened human eyes, it is a magnificent demonstration. However, as each year passes, fewer and fewer people who visit northern lakes can claim ignorance of the true meaning of the birds' display. It should be an immediate signal that they have ventured into an area where people are totally unwelcome, and they should quickly withdraw without disturbing the loons further.

When one loon of a mated pair returns to the nest, it may tremolo briefly. In this case, the call may be a means of strengthening the pair bond or

may give reassurance to one another after a disturbance.

Loons in flight, when passing over another loon's territory, generally tremolo, the only call given by a flying loon. It has a distorted quality that contributes to its urgent sound.

The yodel is the most complex of the calls. It is believed to be given only by males, most frequently when establishing or defending territories, and it is considered to be an aggressive call. Anywhere from one to nine repeat phrases may be given — the greater the number, the greater the bird's agitation. It generally lasts four to eight seconds,

similar in length to some of the more complex songs of the warblers but not as cheerful and upbeat. The yodel is the call heard most frequently around dusk, the time of peak flight activity. It appears to be a contagious sound. One loon may begin to yodel after an earlier aggressive interaction, and loons in surrounding lakes will pick up the call until all the woods and the night sky reverberate with echoes of the excited wild sound.

Barklow, through his study and use of sonograms (paper graphs that visually record a bird's call, similar to the machines used to record heartbeats), believed that individual male loons could be identified by their yodel. By recording these calls and playing them back at a slower speed or observing the sonogram, he could distinguish idiosyncrasies in the yodel of different individuals. These appear to remain the same from year to year.

Based on Barklow's research, further study has taken the loon's call into the computer age. Today, another researcher, Ed Miller, at Governor State University, in Illinois, is taking yodel sonograms from loons in the Sylvania Recreational Area of the Upper Peninsula of Michigan and putting them into a computer to more accurately catalogue and identify individual birds. The purpose of this process is to see whether the same loons are returning each year to the same lake. Vocal recording is much easier on people and loons for identification and study purposes than is capture and banding of birds.

A display is associated with the yodel; Lynda Rummel and Charles Goetzinger, who studied loons in Ontario, call it the "crouch-and-yodel" display. The loon hunches low in the water, extends its neck and head so that it rests on the water, tips the bill up slightly and yodels. After vocalizing, the loon returns to the normal alert posture of floating, with head held high. Rummel and Goetzinger observed this behaviour most frequently when there were territorial confrontations between pairs. Loons have also been observed yodelling when floatplanes begin to take off or fly low over a lake.

The last call is the wail, a melancholy, drawn-out sound that is most often compared to a wolf's howl. In 1857, at Walden, Thoreau wrote, "This of the loon — I do not mean its laugh but its looning — is a long-drawn call, as it were, sometimes singularly human to my ear." The wail is structurally like the tremolo but lacks the modulation. It can carry farther on the wind than the other calls. Barklow speculates that the wail may have developed before the tremolo and that over time, as a more specialized communication signal was needed, the tremolo gradually evolved. Loon researcher Judy McIntyre has ob-

served that the first vocalization of a loon chick is the wail.

Unlike the tremolo and yodel, the wail may be given in a variety of situations. In most cases, it is given when interaction is desired but somehow prevented, such as when a bird is searching for a mate or chick or when a parent bird is separated from its chick by a boat. A female will also wail when her mate is having an aggressive encounter with an intruder and while he is giving the yodel.

In early spring and summer, the wail may be the lead-in to a rousing night chorus. The chorus may be initiated by one pair of loons, then taken up by other pairs in nearby territories until sound echoes and fills the night sky. The mixture of yodels and tremolos, varying in intensity and tempo, seems to be tied to the general enthusiasm and excitement of the nesting season. The chorus may fade to a gradual conclusion or stop as abruptly as when a needle is lifted from a record.

Loons are also known to combine calls to cover more complex situations and emotions. It is not understood why, but these combined calls always begin with the tremolo. When it is combined with either the yodel or the wail, there is conflict within the bird — indecision, such as the fight/flight reaction that can be found in many other species. The combined call differs from a chorus in that it is a statement by the bird and not a chorus combining individual calls.

Loons perform one other display, which has the appearance of a stately minuet. It is called the "circle dance," or the "bill-dipping ceremony." It involves two or more loons and is frequently seen in large flocks as a greeting behaviour or an appeasement activity. This ritual also can be seen in early summer as part of the loon courtship. In this dance, the birds swim toward one another, frequently putting their faces in the water in a peering motion. As they draw nearer to one another, they begin quick dives, sometimes together and at other times alternately. They submerge for only a few seconds and then surface very near to one another. They swim slowly in a circular pattern,

occasionally "breast-puffing and bill-tucking," as Rummel and Goetzinger described it. If a bird dives and surfaces too far away, the dance breaks up and the rest of the birds paddle away. For a courting couple, the dance is the lead-in to copulation.

Most of us are familiar with the common loon, but the Pacific and the red-throated loon also engage in their own song and dance. Both have calls that are distinct from the common loon's but difficult to describe. Perhaps the best way to relate to their dances is to let your imagination flow with the descriptive names that researchers have given to the various movements. The Pacific loon displays are called the tuck, threat and upright positions, the splashdive and the threat dance. More inspirationally named are the red-throated loon movements: looking into the water, snake ceremony and plesiosaurus race ceremony.

The loons are showy birds. Their feathers lack flamboyant colours but make up for that with a striking intricate, geometric black-and-white pattern. They dance on the water when consumed with desperation, and they fill the northern regions with echoes of antiquity. They inspire us humans to think deeply about ourselves and this planet. Their song has inspired the Paul Taylor professional dance company to choreograph a dance called "Sunset."

But they are not feathered vaudevillians put here for our entertainment. William Barklow has recorded the wail of the loon as it searches through a thunderstorm for its chick or mate — the sound of rain mixing with that plaintive call. He has recorded coyotes howling near a lake where loons spend the summer and superimposed the howl of the canid with the wail of the water bird. It's powerful enough to send shivers up the spine and tears down the cheeks, a sound we should hear in person, with water lapping at our feet and the pines pressing at our backs. As Bent so aptly said, "And what would the wilderness be without it?"

Excerpted from Love of Loons. *Voyageur Press Inc. (Stillwater, MN).*

Feeding birds over the winter months can be a natural treat

Cold-Weather Dinner Guests

by Clive Dobson

Once when working on the third floor of an urban factory, I watched with macabre fascination as a pigeon slowly slid down the steep, sloping slate roof of an adjacent building, its descent slowed only by the vigorous flapping of its wings. Reaching the gutter, the pigeon appeared to falter and then toppled over the brink — quickly breaking into flight and then circling the building several times before again landing at the peak of the roof. The strange actions became suddenly clear when the bird revealed itself to have but one leg. Once more sliding down the slate surface on its belly, wings beating to maintain balance and speed, the pigeon finally reached the gutter and this time was able to stop, gain a foothold and support itself on its single leg.

Birds often amaze us with their abilities to overcome adversity — not the least of which is the Canadian winter, arriving with the always-surprising first snowfall, which annually causes us to stop and wonder how anything manages to find food in the great white savannah that is this country in winter. Out of a mixed desire to lend a hand to these creatures and, selfishly, to keep their beauty around to brighten the darkest months, growing numbers of

Canadians and residents of the northern United States have established informal feeding stations, providing themselves with untold satisfaction and, in the case of certain species, actually moving the winter range of some birds north into formerly inhospitable zones. Ornithologists report a dramatic increase in the number of birds wintering over in snow-covered areas in recent years.

Bird feeding at its simplest level — scattering stale bread crumbs on the snow — requires little more than a commitment not to build the birds' dependence on you and then cut off their supply in midwinter. Once a casual regimen of bread scraps begins to attract some interesting avian visitors, most bird feeders decide to attempt something more ambitious.

At this stage, one might introduce a bag of commercial feed mix for birds, available in various forms and under different labels at garden centres, hardware stores, pet shops, agricultural feed stores and some supermarkets. These mixes usually contain sunflower seeds, crushed corn, wheat, millet, buckwheat and some lesser grains. Proportions in these mixes differ greatly, but they will give an indication of the types of birds being drawn to your yard and an idea of their eating preferences. If most of the smaller grain is left, you will obviously want to increase the proportions of

crushed corn and sunflower seeds to avoid wastage and satisfy the birds.

Having established a satisfactory menu over the course of a week or so, you will be ready to graduate to bulk purchases of ingredients. Sunflower seeds, whole or crushed corn, peanut hearts, millet, oats, wheat, buckwheat, barley and rapeseed can be bought in economical bulk quantities from feed mills (some items will have to be specially ordered) and better-stocked garden centres.

Midfall is the best time for initiating a bird-feeding program, as it will give the birds time to become acquainted with your location and to include your yard in their feeding territory when severe weather arrives.

While all manner of bird-feeding stations and associated paraphernalia are available, the most direct method of luring birds to a spot near your favourite viewing window is to scatter crumbs, crackers, breakfast cereal, raisins, nuts, seeds, popcorn or a mixture of these in a six-foot-square clearing or packed-down area in the snow.

This done, there is nothing to do but replenish the supplies when necessary. Observe. Be patient. It takes time for wild birds to discover that a new feeding ground is available to them. The endless fascination of an active bird-feeding station, with its own rhythms, rituals and unexpected dramatic arrivals, can quickly provide a new dimension to winter, and most bird feeders rather quickly find themselves creating more sophisticated or at least more permanent facilities for their guests.

Feeders

Each individual bird has its own particular feeding behaviour, and this diversity in eating habits demands a corresponding diversity in feeder design. Cardinals, for example, are more likely to use a feeder that has a perch, juncos prefer ground feeding, and woodpeckers like vertical hanging feeders or something resembling a tree trunk.

If you wish to ground-feed, there are a number of locations appropriate for scattering food. The lower branches of large, thick spruce, fir and hemlock may keep some of the snow from covering your feed. Hollow logs, woodpiles, woodsheds or cleared pathways in the snow can offer some shelter and cover for ground-foraging birds. If feeding near or under evergreens, check to make sure that there is nothing close enough to conceal cats. Cedar hedges may provide good shelter, but they are usually thick enough to hide cats.

There are a number of things to consider before deciding what kind of feeder to buy or build. If you are buying, choose a simple design that is easy to clean and keep stocked up. Better feeders are usually made of rot-resistant redwood or cedar. These woods weather well and turn a silvery-grey colour that blends in well with the landscape. Avoid buying metal feeders, which have sharp edges that can cut and are also subject to rust and to freezing up badly after a slight thaw. The eyes and tongues of birds can freeze to metal surfaces in extremely cold weather if they happen to make contact.

Plastic feeders are available, but generally, I have found them too flimsy and lightweight. They tend to break and blow in the wind, spilling most of the seed on the ground. However, there are some smaller plastic feeders that are quite useful.

All hopper-type feeders (feeders that only allow a certain amount of seed out

at a time) should always be stationary. If they are hung up, they should be secured in some fashion to prevent excessive wind movement, which causes a needless flow of seed to escape. The best solution is to fix them securely on a post, metal pole or directly on the side of a tree (which has the possible disadvantage of providing squirrels with too easy an access).

If you build, don't weatherproof wood with preservatives. Almost all preservatives are toxic. Feeders dry out quickly in the air, and rot should not be much of a problem.

Ground Tables or Platforms

A ground table is extremely simple to make and is effective for feeding ground-foraging and perching birds. It consists of a sheet of plywood or several boards nailed together that make up an area of approximately six square feet (two feet by three feet). Attach the platform to legs to raise it about two feet off the ground (higher in areas of greater snowfall). A wooden lip around the perimeter (a nailed-on slat) will keep the feed from being blown or knocked off. The lip also serves as a grip for perching birds. This type of feeder should be placed in an open but sheltered area of your yard. If the table is placed just slightly off level, it will allow drainage in the event of rain or a quick thaw; make a few holes at the lowest end. Easy access for you should be considered when positioning the table, as you will have to restock this type of feeder daily.

Mixes of smaller seeds (millet, crushed corn, buckwheat, wheat, et cetera) and scratch feed work best with this feeder, as they will appeal more to the birds than the squirrels. If the constant clearing of snow becomes a problem, a shallow pitched roof (shed or double-pitched) can always be added. However, leave the sides open to provide maximum space for entrance and exit routes.

Window-Shelf Feeders

Window shelves are probably the best type of feeders for bird observation. Installation should take place some

time after you have been feeding birds from other feeders built away from your house. Birds that are regulars at your window-shelf feeder will get used to glass surfaces and your movements on the other side more readily than the occasionals. These feeders are merely extensions of exterior windowsills. They should not project out from the wall farther than one foot, as drainage may become a problem. Again, a lip around the outside is a good idea.

Some diagonal bracing may be necessary to provide extra support. If the window does not open, at least be sure you have a door nearby to allow easy access for restocking. This type of feeder may also be adapted to fit the top of an outside deck railing. Larger window-shelf feeders (but not so large they become an obstruction) are useful for apartment dwellers and others who don't have a convenient access to a backyard. If you are building the larger variety, be sure to provide drain holes.

Raised Feeders

Raised feeders have a number of advantages. If they are placed in an open, sheltered area of your yard, they should be about head height (high enough to keep squirrels and cats out). They can be mounted on a wooden post (a fencepost is fine) or a metal pipe. A square or rectangular base can be used, but the surface feeding area should not exceed four square feet (two feet by two feet). Any closed-in side should face the direction of prevailing winds to give additional shelter. A lip is necessary to contain food. This type of feeder is ideal for holding all types of food, including suet cake mixes and suet bags. Provide an eyehook for securing suet bags.

Hopper-Type Feeders

Hopper-type feeders are the most useful feeders for bulk distribution of seed and seed mixes. Depending on how many birds you have attending on a daily basis, it is possible for a large hopper feeder to release its contents slowly and automatically over a period of a week. This feature is most suitable for people who might be absent for a

A large hopper feeder can be filled with seed as seldom as once a week, an ideal solution for cottagers who are away much of the time.

few days at a time. If you plan on winter holidays, a neighbour or friend may only have to refill your feeder once or twice during your absence. It is a good idea to mount the larger types of hopper feeders securely to a rigid post or pole. Avoid gimmicks when buying or constructing this type of feeder. They only cause problems. A good example of this is the popular weather-vane version that has a tendency to seize up. Single-sided hopper types should be mounted directly onto the side of a fencepost or solid tree.

When building these feeders, avoid hinging the roof as a filling device. It weakens the structure, and the joints will inevitably let in water. Instead, drill a hole about one inch in diameter — large enough to insert a funnel for refilling. A slip cap or large cork can be used to close the hole. Use Plexiglas, if possible, instead of glass for the sides to allow visible inspection of the con-

tents. It will make construction easier, stronger and safer. Plexiglas can be drilled and screwed, making it an integral part of the structure. Since these feeders carry more weight in feed than other types, take the time to build them properly. Make sure you leave the right size of gap for feed to escape.

Commercial feeders come in many shapes, sizes, colours and materials. Most of the small hanging types are plastic and only allow room and feeding for one bird at a time. These types are more for fun and amusement than for functional feeding.

Suet Feeders

Suet feeding can be accomplished in a variety of ways. The simplest method is to tie up lumps of suet in small pieces of fishnet or plastic onion bags and lash them to the limb of a tree or fencepost. They may also be tied to an eyehook inside a larger raised platform feeder.

A version of the single-sided hopper can be constructed for suet feeding. Instead of installing glass, you provide some means of lashing in the suet.

Suet Logs

A cedar, fir or hardwood log can make a great suet feeder. The log should be 3 to 4 inches in diameter and 14 to 18 inches long. Holes 1¼ inches to 1½ inches in diameter should be drilled 1½ inches deep. Melted suet and suet-seed mixes can now be packed into the various holes. Hung by a large eyehook at one end, this vertical feeder is a favourite of woodpeckers. If you add some dowels (¼ inch in diameter) for perches below the suet holes, other birds will be able to use it as well.

Rough bark left on the log will also allow birds of various kinds to get a grip while feeding. To avoid injury to birds, make sure that the material you use to hang this feeder is quite visible

— the thick, plastic-covered wire used for household outlets is ideal.

Children and Feeders
Given some guidance, children can enjoy themselves immensely making various kinds of feeders and bird recipes. Revised apple crates or grape crates make good sheltered feeders that can be mounted on trees or fenceposts. Children have fun hanging half-shells of coconuts filled with suet and suet-seed mixes, although this is practical only for smaller birds.

Filling empty grapefruit halves with suet and seeds or pasting up pinecones with peanut butter for hanging outside can occupy kids for hours. How about helping them construct a feeder from an empty milk carton? Children will be quite amazed when they actually see their creations being used by the birds. With a little imagination, very practical feeders can be constructed from the most unlikely materials. Just make sure they are safe for the birds.

Hand Feeding
After you have been feeding the birds in your yard for a period of time, you will find that certain individuals will become accustomed to your presence. When you have established a quiet, consistent rapport with your regulars, offer them your outstretched hand with a few sunflower seeds. Before long, if your patience and calmness last, a few bolder chickadees may find the courage to land. Avoid any abrupt movements while occupying their feeding grounds. Being accepted in this way is quite an honour and accomplishment.

Feed
Corn is eaten by almost all of the winter birds. Use it whole, crushed and milled (cornmeal) for maximum appeal. Corn left standing in your garden through the winter will offer a natural source for some birds skillful enough to penetrate the leafy husks. Stalks of corn done up in sheaf fashion close to tree-lined fields and orchards can offer shelter and food for bobwhites, ruffed grouse and ring-necked pheasants. Some of the corn should, however, be

An ideal device, this weatherproof cylindrical feeder holds several days of food, is made of durable Plexiglas and has perches at the feeding holes.

removed from the stalks and left on the ground underneath. You can count on buying corn, like sunflower seeds, in large quantities. Corn works well in hopper-type feeders, on feeding tables or scattered on the ground. It is also excellent used in scratch feed (discussed later).

Corn is the favourite food of cardinals, cowbirds, crows, doves (rock, mourning, and band-tailed), Canada geese, grackles, red-breasted grosbeaks, slate-coloured juncos, ducks, ruffed grouse, ring-necked pheasants, ravens, sparrows, rufous-sided towhees, hairy woodpeckers, flickers and evening grosbeaks.

Sunflower seed is the best all-purpose seed. It is nutritious (high in protein, fats and carbohydrates), economical and a choice food for almost all winter birds. If you have the garden space and a sunny, protected area, perhaps against a fence or wall, sunflowers are easily cultivated. Grow the commercial variety rather than the ornamental one, as the seeds are larger and more palatable. The whole flower head may be offered once it has been cut off and sun-dried. Keep a large stock of these seeds available in February and March when the greedy flocks of evening grosbeaks strike your feeders. Use in hopper-type feeders, on feeding tables and on window shelves, or scatter these dark seeds on a packed snow surface where they can easily be seen.

You can expect almost all birds to take sunflower seeds at some time, but they are the favourite food of chickadees (boreal, black-capped and chestnut-backed), cardinals, rose-breasted grosbeaks, Steller's jays, slate-coloured juncos, mourning doves, all sparrows, purple finches, pine siskins, grackles, all nuthatches and tufted titmice.

Suet seems to fill the needs of all insect-eating birds. The hard fat that comes from cattle and sheep, suet is a good source of the energy and heat necessary for birds in the winter. Cut off the loose, stringy pieces, and save them for melting down. Take the larger, whole pieces (about the size of a small fist), and wrap them entirely in plastic mesh bags, tied at one end (onion bags are excellent for this). Bags should be securely tied with string or twine to branches or suet feeders.

Melt down the stringy leftovers in a pot, pour into small containers, and leave to set. Plastic or paper cups are more suitable than metal ones, as there is no risk to the birds and they can be discarded after use. Suet served plain in this fashion is fine, or you can add any variety of nuts, seeds, currants, raisins, peanut butter, peanut hearts or corn. It is a great medium for holding together all your birds' favourite recipes. A few words of caution:

☐ Do not use wire mesh, metal screening or wire to secure the suet.

☐ Tie it down securely with twine so that larger birds and squirrels won't disappear with the whole piece.

☐ Remove all old stringy suet from feeders in warm weather to prevent it from turning rancid.

☐ Keep suet out of reach of dogs.

Save the grease and drippings from bacon and oven-cooked meats for use in the same manner as suet. Because the consistency of these fats is generally softer than suet, it is advisable to use them in the suet-recipe mixes mentioned above. Almost all birds will eat suet in one form or another.

Wheat seed, whole or cracked, has a great appeal for a wide variety of birds. If you are fortunate enough to have a pond on your property, you might like to start regular feeding of ducks and geese in the summer months, encouraging them to stay over the winter. Wheat and similar grains are their favourite food. Harvested wheat fields sometimes have patches of knocked-down stalks or small areas the combines have missed. Collect and tie up fistfuls of these stalks. Propped in the snow with the heads exposed, they will provide food for the birds and entertainment for you. At the back of your property, there may be a tree-lined fence where you can tie bunches of wheat together for the pheasants to find.

Wheat seed is the choice food for redwinged blackbirds, snow buntings, cardinals, cowbirds, American crows, mourning doves, pigeons, mallards, black ducks, Canada geese, grackles, rose-breasted grosbeaks, jays (blue, Canada and Steller's), slate-coloured juncos, ring-necked pheasants, most sparrows, rufous-sided towhees and starlings.

Bread is a staple item not only of our diet but of city-dwelling birds too. It is very useful for controlling birds at your feeding station. Start putting out bread at the beginning of winter season, and after the offerings have brought in flocks of starlings and house sparrows, other species are sure to follow. When your bird population starts to get out of hand and overcrowding is becoming a problem, move the bread farther away from feeders and reduce the daily quantities. If the starling and house sparrow population is still too large, try skipping a day or so. The practice of feeding bread to city-dwelling birds is worldwide. Great quantities are fed to pigeons (rock doves), starlings and house sparrows in city parks. Ducks, geese and seagulls are also familiar with the taste of bread and compete with each other for the larger pieces. Scatter the bread widely in an area where there are numerous birds waiting for your charity. Remember that whole-grain bread has more nutritional value for birds.

Crackers, muffins, pastry crust, whole wheat and other breakfast cereals, popcorn, biscuits and hard dog meal may be offered, but you run the risk of attracting dogs, more starlings, crows and squirrels. It may be necessary to scatter such products away from your regular feeding area.

Buckwheat is usually found in prepared wild-bird mixes, but it can also be purchased from feed mills. Having bought a suitable quantity of these small, hard, pyramid-shaped seeds, you will be able to add them to your homemade mixes in a proportion to match the demand.

Buckwheat (the common variety) is a favourite food of cardinals, American crows, ruffed grouse, ring-necked pheasants, mourning doves as well as most sparrows.

Millet comes in several different types, but they all have the same nutritional value and taste appeal. Millet seed, because of its small size, is ideal for including in suet recipes. Scatter millet on the ground or on feeding tables so that it is more accessible to the ground-feeding birds. It is a favourite of cardinals, mourning doves, pigeons (rock doves), purple finches, goldfinches, Canada geese, slate-coloured juncos, mallards, redpolls and most sparrows.

Hemp is also the plant that produces marijuana, so government regulations have made it necessary to blanch and sterilize the seeds before they are put on the market. Although sterilization makes the seeds less desirable for birds, it is still one of the seeds found in wild-bird mixes. This seed should be used in a similar manner as millet. Birds that eat millet will generally take hemp seed as a replacement.

Rice is not as popular as wheat, but it can be used as a substitute. Both cooked and uncooked rice are acceptable to many species of birds. Obviously, brown rice will be more nutritious than the processed adulterated versions. However, the greatest nutritional value of carbohydrates can be derived from all rice types.

Birds that will eat rice include cardinals, red-winged blackbirds, rock doves, most ducks and geese, slate-coloured juncos, most sparrows and mourning doves.

Oats, used in seed form, crushed, rolled or in the form of solidified porridge, will appeal to most blackbirds, cardinals, rufous-sided towhees, most sparrows, ring-necked pheasants, slate-coloured juncos, grackles, grosbeaks and rock doves.

Sorghum seeds are favourite foods of cardinals, mourning doves, grackles, blue jays, slate-coloured juncos and most sparrows.

Rapeseed is a plant belonging to the mustard family and grown extensively in the prairie regions. The seed is a favourite of mourning doves, goldfinches, purple finches, slate-coloured juncos and redpolls.

Scratch feed is generally used commercially for feeding chickens. However, it is a good idea to provide small quantities of it for birds in your garden. The digestive system of birds requires the ingestion of limited amounts of dirt to aid in the digestive process. Fine sand added sparingly to smaller seeds such as millet, sorghum, rapeseed, wheat or crushed corn can provide a good scratch feed. Other essentials for birds, such as salt and calcium (eggshell), may also be added. Offer scratch feed along with other mixes, or scatter it occasionally on the ground.

Nuts are all nutritious, as they contain protein, carbohydrates, fats and vitamins. They are too expensive to offer to birds on a regular bulk basis, but small quantities added periodically may entice some birds that would not otherwise come to your feeders. Collecting indigenous nuts such as acorns, chestnuts, beechnuts and walnuts before the squirrels hide them all will add variety to your feeding program and help keep down costs.

Unshelled peanuts are rather difficult for smaller birds to penetrate. However, you might enjoy the antics of some birds trying to get the nutmeats inside. So that larger birds and squirrels do not walk off with the whole lot, tie several larger peanuts together with thick nylon or linen thread and hang them from your roof eave or the branch of a tree.

One cheap way of purchasing peanuts for feed purposes is in the form of peanut hearts, the small knuckle that falls out when a single nutmeat separates in half. These small pieces are by-products of the peanut industry. Peanut hearts are available at some feed mills. Peanut butter, although costly, can be added in small quantities to suet cakes or spread on the bark of trees or dangling cones for birds to peck at. Making these kinds of treats for the birds is the sort of activity that children especially enjoy. Occasional use of salted peanuts is fine. Salt is one of the items some birds develop a craving for and eat intentionally. Peanuts are a favourite food of most blackbirds, cardinals, catbirds, chickadees, crows, pigeons, purple finches, robins, tufted titmice, wrens, most sparrows, slate-coloured juncos, most nuthatches as well as some woodpeckers.

Fancy nutmeats such as walnuts, pecans, hazelnuts, cashews and almonds should be given only as a special treat; otherwise, you may find that your feeding grounds are overrun with squirrels. Because squirrels covet these nuts so much, it is a good idea to feed them to the squirrels intentionally, unshelled and away from other feeders. They work well as a temporary distraction.

Certain varieties of apples and pears lend themselves better to bird feeding than to human consumption. Wild trees and orchards that have been neglected produce smaller, scabby varieties. It is a good idea to collect baskets of these apples and pears and store them in a cold place for the birds. As long as they keep well, they can be used as feed, cut in half to expose the seeds inside. Crab apples have the same appeal.

Most apples and pears are well received by blue jays, crows, grackles, ruffed grouse, starlings, waxwings, ring-necked pheasants and hairy woodpeckers.

If there are bluebirds in your area, there is a good chance they may be enticed to your feeder by a supply of raisins and currants.

Vegetable seeds, either raw or cooked, usually do not interest most birds. However, save the seeds from your

pumpkins, squashes, cantaloupes and watermelons. Wash them off and dry them. Birds such as cardinals, chickadees, blue jays and nuthatches will eat them.

Feeder Problems

Keeping your feeders from being emptied by greedy squirrels can be most frustrating if you physically have to chase them away every five minutes. An inverted funnel-shaped piece of aluminum or galvanized sheet metal attached to your feeding pole may keep squirrels out of your hopper-type feeders or raised platforms. Small feeders and suet bags should be hung away from branches, rooftops and trees to prevent squirrels from jumping across to them. If they are hung from the middle of a stretched wire (visible and plastic-covered), it will be difficult for squirrels to approach. Slip a five-foot length of hosing over the wire on both sides of the hanging point. This will make the balance even more difficult for squirrels.

Fasten down net-covered suet securely with twine; otherwise, squirrels may run off with the whole sack.

Of all the squirrels, you will find the smaller red squirrels are the most aggressive. Very few defences will foil these squirrels for long. It is fascinating to watch them trying out their latest tactics. As long as your installations inhibit their approach, you will find it unnecessary to chase them away. Don't be too ruthless: squirrels store most of their loot, and their memories are bad, so before long, birds find half of their caches anyway.

Supplying squirrels with a few of their favourite foods (peanuts, suet leftovers) in a special area away from your bird feeders may also distract them long enough to allow the more reserved birds to feed in their absence.

When placing feeders or scattering feed, stay clear of extremely dense foliage and other places where cats can hide. No disciplinary action will ever change the basic nature of a cat. Your own cat should be provided with a bell and a collar (of course, if your cat is decimating the bird population, you shouldn't attempt yard feeding at all).

Collisions with windows are inevitable as bird traffic outside your windows increases. If your feeders are on the brighter side of your house, you may have fewer incidents of birds hitting windows, as the sun should cause some reflection or glare. However, if you are feeding on the shady side of your house, there is the chance that birds will try to fly through a window and out the other side where, perhaps, they can see the landscape. Hanging sheer curtains or drawing curtains on windows where possible can help. A piece of paper 10 inches by 4 inches, fringed at the bottom and taped to the outside of the window, will help prevent birds from flying through.

If a bird strikes your window, it may only be stunned. Carefully pick it up in the palm of your hand. You should feel a fast pulse if the bird is alive. A flapping, spastic bird should be restricted with gentle hand confinement. Place stunned birds in a paper-towel-lined box that allows ventilation. Keep the bird warm, secluded and calm until completely recovered. Restrict the bird's erratic movements, as this will only injure it further. Release the bird in the same location you found it.

If your feeding area has become overcrowded, you might try installing a ground table or another hanging feeder. Expansion may be the answer. However, if most of your guests are house sparrows and starlings, try cutting back on bread and small seeds and temporarily stop ground feeding until their flocks have reduced.

In the early spring, many birds are returning north, but some arrive a little too soon and are caught in a weather pattern of heavy snow or freezing rain. At times like these, scatter a selection of feed far and wide after the storm has subsided. This will offer many more birds food, especially the shy ones or birds unfamiliar with your feeders. West Coast weather can take a sudden turn for the worse anytime during the winter months, dumping a foot of wet snow in a matter of hours. Again, a little extra widespread feeding will help birds until thaw.

Placing feeders in close proximity to trees and bushes will allow birds to survey the safety of a situation before venturing into the open feeding area.

Store feed grains, sunflower seeds, corn, et cetera, in a cool, dry place, preferably in lidded containers such as plastic garbage cans. Some forms of mould in grain and corn are poisonous, so keep feeds dry.

Keep suet refrigerated, and make sure to replace old suet that may have gone rancid. Suet feeders should be in the shade. Remove old or wet feed from feeders. Periodic washing of feeders to rinse off bird waste is a good practice. Avoid feeding birds anything spoiled, mouldy, rancid or tainted, as it could make them sick during a harsh season.

Don't litter your yard with heaps of kitchen scraps. They may rot or might attract some unwanted scavengers.

Beyond this, many people extend their activities well into the spring, planting garden crops, bushes and hedges to attract both song and game birds, in effect turning the winter-feeding activities into a year-round program. Homes with yards and gardens that support a profusion of bird species are special places, and far from being simply a free lunch for the birds, bird feeding is a symbiotic relationship with clear, if intangible, rewards for the human participants.

Excerpted from Feeding Birds in Winter. *Firefly Books (Toronto).*

Are these great swamp singers disappearing or just lying low?

Singing the Bullfrog Blues

by Suzanne Kingsmill

The sun was just dipping behind the trees as the canoe glided quietly into the middle of Nogies Creek, in central Ontario's Kawartha Lakes. For a while, all was idyllic. But as dusk approached, the scene was shattered by the buzzing swarms of mosquitoes that descended on the only two humans unfortunate enough to be there. Joe Cebek and his wife Linda Zernask were trying to catch some bullfrogs for Cebek's master of science thesis on temperature regulation in bullfrogs. "It's really miserable," recalls the tall, lanky biologist and current Ph.D. student, with the relish of one who has suffered and conquered. "No matter how much repellent you use, it doesn't make any difference — you're eating mosquitoes."

But dusk is when male bullfrogs begin to call, serenading females with the deep, booming bass of their love song, which gives away their position not only to their intended but to any eavesdropper as well. The biggest of North American frogs, the bullfrog is a late bloomer, one of the last to fulfill its amorous desires in late May or June. Taking a deep breath, the male clamps its mouth and nostrils shut, forcing the inrushing air to expand its paired vocal sacs. The air is forced over the vocal

chords, and the booming jug-o'-rum call escapes to entice a female to come a-courting.

As the singing began, Joe and Linda moved into action, trying to bag a bullfrog big enough for Cebek's studies. The frogs had to weigh at least 250 grams (half a pound) to be able to carry a 7-to-12-gram radio transmitter, which is implanted under the skin without impairing behaviour. But it was not to be that night.

"There were lots of bullfrogs, literally hundreds that we could see in a night of canoeing," Cebek recalls of his field research five years ago. Yet every one they sneaked up on turned out to be too small. "When you go into the old literature, they talk about bullfrogs of a pound, a pound and a half, even two pounds," says Cebek, spreading his hands wide to indicate the size. "I think the biggest we got up there (at Nogies) was about 150 grams (a third of a pound)."

Although bullfrogs are not rare, biologists and naturalists are becoming increasingly concerned that their numbers are declining. E.J. Crossman, curator of ichthyology at the Royal Ontario Museum (ROM) and one of several researchers who did some tracking of bullfrogs in the Nogies Creek in the late 1970s, says, "Yes, they're declining. I know there are far fewer at Nogies Creek

now. When I was there as a student from 1951 to 1953, you could hardly hear yourself talking during the time when they were breeding, mating and laying eggs, but it became a rather rare occurrence to hear a bullfrog croak in the '70s and early '80s."

In the area around Cebek's home near Little Britain, north of Lake Scugog and 40 miles from Toronto, populations also appear to have declined. "I have gone out every year listening to the chorusing, and in the past couple of years, I haven't heard any," says Cebek. "It's possible I'm just missing them, but whereas before, I could go out on any night in June and listen to a bullfrog, I can't do that anymore."

Bullfrogs are found throughout southern Ontario. Their northern limits are roughly defined by a west-east line from just north of Lake Huron to the Ottawa River. The biggest and best populations live in southeastern Ontario. According to Hans von Rosen, a fish and wildlife management officer in the Ministry of Natural Resources' (MNR) Carleton Place district near Ottawa, various factors have combined to produce ideal habitat for bullfrogs in the southeast. Elsewhere, the pH and depth of the waters, as well as the soil conditions and climate, are not as favourable, and both the number and size of frogs are noticeably smaller.

But the bullfrogs in Carleton Place district are in trouble. In 1977, in response to public concern that populations were declining, district personnel did a census of some 15 areas which bullfrogs were known to inhabit. Says von Rosen: "In 1984 or '85, we repeated the program using the same methods and observed bullfrogs at the same time of year. We found that the populations in these same areas had declined drastically, anywhere from 20 percent to 80 percent per location."

One reason for the decline of bullfrogs is private and commercial hunting — for education and biomedical research, as well as for food. According to John Williamson, regional biologist at MNR's eastern region, the hunting of bullfrogs in Ontario has been regulated for many years. When it was understood that the females laid their eggs much later than was previously supposed and that some populations were declining, the season was shortened to give the females adequate time to spawn. Today, the season runs from late July to mid-October.

All commercial hunting of bullfrogs in Ontario occurs in the southeastern region. It is not a major industry, says Williamson, but is mostly a way to supplement income for people who fish in the spring and trap in the winter. Commercial operators have no bag or size limit in most regions but must report their catch annually and are assigned harvesting areas by MNR. They give the ministry information on the state of the populations in the areas where they harvest. If the harvesters have a bad year and there are few bullfrogs, the ministry will close the relevant areas to harvesting until the bullfrog populations have had a chance to recover. Says Williamson: "Basically it's set up so that the person who had the area this year gets first chance at it next year. So if they're interested in using it from year to year, then the onus is on them not to overharvest." The ministry also monitors the harvest by sending conservation officers into the field, but with a huge territory to patrol and limited staff, monitoring the population is not an easy task.

A well-known, if not romantic, serenader, the bullfrog is facing decimation throughout cottage country as habitat disappears and harvesting increases.

The rules for private citizens are quite different. Individuals must obtain a licence, which is free. They are allowed to catch 10 frogs per day and may have no more than 10 in their possession at any time. However, as von Rosen says, "We have a considerable private harvest, although nobody knows how big it is. People do have to have a licence, and there is a limit, but as long as they eat their catch, then there is no quota, no ceiling." Poaching is also a problem, he says. "The delay of the open season to mid-July applies only to the law-abiding. But those people who were

traditional poachers are going out just the same, because they are drawn by the mating songs, the roaring of the bullfrogs out in the marshes. They sneak out in a canoe at night, and you just don't see them. Conservation officers either find them or they don't. It is a recognized problem, but you can't have an officer behind every tree."

A little farther west, in the Tweed district, north of Belleville, bullfrog populations appear to be holding their own. Over the past three years, numbers harvested have remained fairly steady at 10,000 to 12,000 frogs, says Gary

Brown, a commercial fish and wildlife management officer with MNR in Tweed. "But it's a funny thing," says Brown. "In some instances, you'll talk to people and there are just no frogs anymore, and then the old fella who's been harvesting frogs over the years sends in his return saying, 'It's a very good year, lots of frogs!' It's a hard thing to get a handle on." Crossman concurs. "Declining yes, but in some places, there are still thousands of them. It's very, very odd."

Concern about the impact of hunting on local bullfrog populations is not limited to Ontario. Harvesting of various species of bullfrogs occurs worldwide. Egypt, which exports 35 tonnes to France every month to satisfy the market for frogs' legs, only this year banned the hunting of frogs during breeding season in order to conserve stocks. Most frogs' legs served in Europe, however, come from Asian bullfrogs, which are seriously endangered in Bangladesh and are becoming scarcer in other areas. With a worldwide bullfrog harvest in the mid-1980s of some 200 million annually, it's no wonder that bullfrogs in high-harvest areas are having a hard time maintaining their populations. They're up against extremely tough odds.

It takes a long time to become a mature bullfrog, and the pathway is riddled with pitfalls that make the chances close to 1 in 10,000 that a tadpole will live long enough to reproduce. After choosing the male that suits them, females deposit anywhere from 6,000 to 20,000 eggs, all bound up in one wiggly gelatinous mass. The tadpoles hatch in two to five days, competing with their many brethren for the vegetarian food that makes up their diet. While tadpoles from other species become frogs by summer's end, the large bullfrog tadpoles must overwinter under the ice. By the following summer, if they survive the rigours of winter, some may be big enough (four inches) to begin their metamorphosis. But many others face yet another winter before undergoing the miraculous change that turns them into frogs.

During metamorphosis, the tadpoles outline the history of evolution from fish to the first land vertebrates in just 10 to 12 days. The fishlike tadpole is completely transformed within and without. The water-breathing gills are replaced by lungs, the eyes migrate back and to the sides, hind legs appear, front arms poke out, the tail slowly shortens, the tiny mouth widens into a

---

South of the Canadian Shield, we've already lost 75 to 80 percent of all original wetlands, and it continues to be destroyed . . .

---

typical frog grin as it is structurally rearranged, and the digestive system is transformed to handle the meat diet of adulthood. As froglets, the males will need yet another year before they can breed; the females will need two. As adults, few will live longer than five or six years.

It is, of course, the big bullfrogs that are caught for the dinner table. "Unfortunately, the ones that are most desirable from the consumer's point of view are also the most desirable for maintaining the population," notes Cebek. "When you think about it, there's a direct relationship between egg mass and body size of the female, so it's the big ones that have the greatest reproductive potential. Think of that last breeding season of a five- or six-year-old frog: She's going to be at her maximum size, she's going to deposit more eggs perhaps in that one year than all of the years beforehand, and she's not getting that chance because she's getting nipped."

Many biologists believe that while harvesting may be compounding the problem, it is not the major factor in the decline of bullfrogs. MNR's von Rosen notes that when the Carleton Place office did its bullfrog study, "all the concerns up to that time were directed toward harvest, be it private or commercial. But we found that bullfrogs had also declined in areas where they were never harvested."

Most experts point to habitat loss and degradation as a greater and far more insidious threat. "All the lakeshores and rivershores are being cottaged to smithereens," says von Rosen. "Every time a person builds a cottage, he fills in the near-shore areas and puts up a nice lawn, a cement wall and a beach, if he can get away with it."

Many municipalities are reluctant to pass bylaws that preserve shorelines, leaving the responsibility with property owners. "Everyone is environmentally conscious, except on their own land," notes von Rosen.

"Habitat loss is the killer," agrees Cebek. In the past five years near his home, he has watched bullfrogs vanish from Mariposa Brook, a wide, meandering stream with wetland components. Now local farmers want to dredge the brook to improve the drainage of their land. "If they dredge it out, that will kill it," Cebek warns.

All over Ontario, the draining of wetlands is eliminating the breeding grounds of our native frogs. South of the Canadian Shield, we've already lost 75 to 80 percent of all original wetlands, and it continues to be destroyed at the rate of 1 to 2 percent a year. MNR's Williamson points out that the draining of wetlands was one of the factors influencing the decision to implement a shorter harvesting season on bullfrogs. They are the most aquatic of our frogs and never venture much farther than 6 to 10 feet from water, except during rain. Without suitable habitat, they cannot survive. But their habitat is being systematically destroyed — bulldozed, drained and degraded — in the name of progress.

Flood control may also have a devastating impact on both the tadpoles and the adults. When water levels are controlled through dams, frogs have no way of knowing if the site they have chosen for hibernation will suddenly become a death trap, as levels are lowered in winter and the water above and around them freezes solid.

There are other problems. Highways block migration routes, and various pollutants, including insecticides, find their way into the water where frogs must live.

The impact of pollutants is only just beginning to be understood. Heavy-metal pollution, for example, can decrease reproductive potential and slow reflexes, increasing the odds in an already very risky life. Although the quantities are often not sufficient to be lethal, these substances could adversely affect behaviour. "It seems that for some of these frog larvae," says Cebek, "there's a decrease in activity and response time. When a predator comes along, the larvae may respond in twice the time or not at all, and the predator success rate may skyrocket."

Acid rain poses another problem. Von Rosen says that the study in Carleton Place district confirmed what has been conjectured for some time: "Bullfrogs thrive best where the pH is highest, so they are an animal that is quite sensitive to acidification." The study monitored rainfall in the district and found that the rainwater is highly acidic, with pH ranging from 3.8 to 4.6. Another study on several populations of frogs in central Ontario, including bullfrogs, has showed that there were fewer small bullfrogs in acidic ponds, even though the acidity of the water was not high enough to cause acute harm to eggs or larvae. The study suggests that "chronic sublethal effects in conjunction with the indirect ecological effects of pond acidification may be affecting anuran [frog] populations."

Clearly, the environmental pressures are enormous, and they're not just occurring in Ontario. David B. Wake, a biologist at the University of California, Berkeley, recently chaired a conference addressing the plight of amphibians worldwide. The conference results and Wake's own "Froglog" (a log of information on the world's declining amphibians) indicate there is cause for concern about many of the world's amphibians, including those which have never been hunted by man. In Puerto Rico, three miniature frogs have disappeared since the late 1970s, and one species is now rare; in Norway, declines of the European common toad on islands in Oslo's fjord have been recorded; in Japan, several species are literally losing ground to housing developments and golf courses; in Nova Scotia, a number of species are on the decline, including leopard frogs; the chorus frog of the southeastern United States once thrived along the coast but now either has vanished or is rare; in the western United States, three lowland frogs may already be extinct, and boreal and Yosemite toads, cascade frogs and several species of forest frogs and leaf-breeding frogs are on the decline. The list seems endless.

"The problem is severe enough that some species and many populations have become extinct, including populations that are locked up in presumably secure nature preserves in remote parks," says Wake, who lists parks in the United States, Costa Rica, Australia and Brazil before pausing to catch his breath. A disquieting thought.

"Amphibians are essential components of normal ecosystems," points out Wake. "They're critically important. Their larvae are primary herbivores that consume a tremendous amount of algae and vegetation. As adults, they are the major carnivores in terms of their position in the food chain and form a great deal of biomass." But data on numbers and breeding habits are desperately needed to pinpoint what is happening, where and why.

"Everybody is painfully aware that there is no sustained monitoring effort," says Wake. "We have very little data from the past. Without data, how can you convince people there is a problem, not just locally but globally and not just with bullfrogs but with many species of amphibians?"

People are already collecting data, but it takes time and proper funding to build an extensive data base. R. Bruce Bury and P. Stephen Corn of the U.S. Fish and Wildlife Service in Colorado are publishing "Ribbit," a research letter devoted entirely to the problem of declines in frog, toad and salamander populations in the western United States. They have also started Frog Net, a communications system for the collection of data on declining numbers of amphibians in the west.

Closer to home, the ongoing "Ontario Herpetofaunal Summary" will provide much-needed baseline data that can be used in years to come. Co-editors Wayne Weller and Mike Oldham are collecting and collating vast amounts of data sent in by naturalists and informed members of the public on all of Ontario's herptiles, including bullfrogs. More specifically, MNR staff have recorded their own bullfrog numbers in some areas of Carleton Place district, and according to von Rosen, they hope to follow up on their 1984-85 study sometime in the mid-1990s, provided that funding becomes available.

One of the problems of studying the bullfrog, says von Rosen, is its public profile as a "minor little creature," lacking the glamour of the many bird and mammal species that garner public attention easily. Still, he says, the bullfrog is "something we should not just let slip by."

Von Rosen's comments apply equally well to all amphibians, whose dying populations hold a message for us. Biologists suggest that amphibians, because of their known sensitivity to pollutants and environmental degradation, could warn us of dangers to the environment in much the same way that the canary alerted miners to threats to their health. We need to start listening, because it is not just Ontario's bullfrogs that are speaking through their growing silence. Says Wake, "We have people paying attention to rare and endangered species, we've got people paying attention to pollutants that kill people, but who's taking the temperature of the environment itself?" Unlike the miners, we don't have the option of leaving to avoid the dangers, for, as Wake says, "Where, on Earth, can we go?"

Originally published in Seasons *magazine (Toronto).*

Discovering the beauty of moths after dark

A Flicker of Colour by Night

by Robert Michael Pyle

One late night as I was reading in bed, a great thump at the window drew my attention. There was another thump, then more, as some great batlike object tried to get in. I opened the window, and in it came, eclipsing the light of the lamp and casting huge, improbable shadows as it fluttered about the room. I got to it just before the cat did and picked it up gently so as not to rub off its tawny fur or caramel scales. It was a Polyphemus silkmoth. The big creature struggled — stout furry legs and feathery antennae waving, strong thoracic muscles straining between my thumb and forefinger. Those robust antennae showed it to be male. His wings were the softest tan, rimmed with delicate mauve above, and his big blue eyespots were clear-centred, so I could see through the wing. Below, chestnut bands crossed pink wings flecked with chocolate scales, the eyespots yellow-ringed. I turned out the light and released him, and he sailed out into the night in search of a female calling with her pheromones on the breeze.

In the eastern parts of Canada and the United States, several kinds of giant silkmoths come to porches and windows — Cecropia, Prometheus and Luna, in addition to Polyphemus and others. Any curious, open-minded person would delight in such a night visitor. I know many people, however, who would happily forgo the beauties of these moths and all others: they just don't like moths. A common prejudice. But it means that they miss out on a group of insects similar to butterflies yet much more diverse and extremely interesting in their own right.

How are moths related to butterflies? The question should really be put the other way around. Moths are the most numerous members of the order Lepidoptera, several hundred thousand species in several suborders. Butterflies are but a diurnal, colourful offshoot of one of those suborders, some 15,000 to 20,000 in number worldwide. So moths vastly outnumber butterflies, to whom they have largely surrendered the daylight hours. Since butterflies fly by day, they evolved a great many defences from colour-sighted predators, usually expressed in their colour patterns. Moths, on the whole nocturnal, generally tend to be drabber. Yet there exist moths — such as the Uranias — whose hue and brilliance rival those of any butterfly. Moths tend to have fuller, hairier bodies, but that is not always true. And although most moths hold their wings rooflike while butterflies hold them vertically over their backs, moths of the geometrid family hold them butterfly-like. The one characteristic most useful for distinguishing butterflies from moths is the shape of the antennae. Virtually all butterflies have clubbed antennae (a thickening at the end), while those of nearly all moths, whether ferny, feathery or filamentous, taper to a sharp point. By checking the antennae first, you should always be certain. Soon, with a little practice and watchfulness, you will be able to learn the basic groups of moths by sight: tigers, sphinxes, silkmoths, millers, micros, geometers, and so on.

If moths are so like the universally beloved butterflies, why are they so often looked upon with indifference, antagonism, fear and loathing? As creatures of the night, like bats, moths may seem malicious to some people. There are clothes moths, which are tiny, nondescript members of the microlepidopteran family Tineidae. Most moths' larvae could no more subsist on woollens than you or I could. Of the others, nearly all plant feeders, a number do compete vigorously for resources we value. The gypsy moth, spruce budworm, tussock moths, peach rollers, tent caterpillars and garden cutworms of this world do not endear themselves.

Adult Cecropia moth; a bright porch light beside a white cloth makes observation and collection easy.

Even so, only a small percentage of moth species are considered pests. The rest are benign or beneficial.

Some people dislike the hairiness of moths or worry about getting them in their hair. Like bats, moths have no desire to go there. Others object to their congregating about the porch light. When dense, they can be a nuisance, it's true. I remember a Colorado cabin so full of millers that one had to douse the lights in order to be able to breathe. Nonetheless, moths are mostly misunderstood. They belong to a little-known world of variety, soft beauty and fascination that I would hate to miss. They take butterfly watching on around the clock. Moths, approached without prejudice, offer a great deal of enjoyment.

Diurnal (day-flying) moths may be spotted in much the same ways as butterflies. Some, such as the cinnabar moth, come in bright scarlets and gunbarrel blue — as bright as butterflies, they fly differently. Others, with their whirring grey wings, look instantly mothlike. Many geometers (inchworm family) fly by day, and some of these resemble satyrine butterflies. As a young collector, I often trailed what I thought was a new satyr, only to find it to be a brown striated geometer.

The majority of moths are fly-by-nights, so special techniques are required for locating and observing them. Let's begin at dusk. Go out into the garden. Spy along the rows of four-o'clocks, over the tops of the lilacs, around the edges of the petunia bed. Moths suck nectar like butterflies. The sphinx moths, in particular, have long proboscies and prefer to visit such tubular flowers. What is that, hovering near the four-o'clocks, darting from bell to bell? It looks like a hummingbird as it hangs in midair, a blur; but it is grey and has a long, yellow-spotted body. It is a sphinx moth, so named for the posture assumed by their larvae. Also known as hawk, or hummingbird, moths, sphinxes hover with rapid, invisible wingbeats like those birds, as they probe flowers with their long proboscies, usually three or four inches. One African sphinx, however, visits an orchid with 18-inch nectar spurs — and its tongue is that long!

Moths provide naturalists with a much wider scope for observation than do butterflies; there are over 20 times as many moth species as butterflies.

Rare is the sultry summer dusk that fails to produce a sphinx moth or two hovering over the petunias. One of my early-spring pleasures was watching the immigrant rose-winged white-lined sphinxes coming to glistening lilacs at twilight after a rain.

Sphinxes also come to lights, and light is what you need if you hope to see many moths. Searching flowers with a flashlight may be fairly rewarding — special moths come to evening primrose, which opens just for them — but nothing beats lights for drawing an interesting assemblage of moths where they may easily be seen. In my youth, I used to haunt the local shopping-centre spotlights and go from door to door to glean moths from neighbours' porches. I suppose it was an acceptable activity for a boy, but as I assumed a man's dimensions, I began to draw the attention of patrol cars as I made my rounds.

A safer and more effective technique is to set up your own lights, in the darkest place possible. Mercury and long-wave ultraviolet (black) lights work best. The nearer to a patch of wooded habitat, the better. Hang a white cloth behind the light, or spread it on the ground around the source. If you happen to be merely watching moths, the sheet should be adequate. Collectors employ traps that invite the moths into an orifice but prevent their escape. They can also be used to trap moths throughout the night in advance of leisurely morning examination of the catch. Light traps can be fitted with killing jars, but it is better to fill them with sections of cardboard egg cartons for surface area, footing and hideyholes. The catch can then be looked over and unwanted specimens turned loose. This should be done some distance from the trap, or birds will learn to frequent the spot for easy pickings.

The spectacle of moths gathered around a light in the tropics can be truly astonishing – thousands of winged, scaly fliers of myriad shapes, colours, patterns and sizes. The display at your porch light or black light may not be as spectacular, but the moths of almost any locale will include a rewarding array of interesting species. Most visitors simply take up a perch where the moths may easily be examined. If the moth you wish to look at refuses to settle, catch it in a jar and plunge it into the freezer for a few moments. This will not hurt the moth but will slow it down long enough for a good look. Many moths possess the ability to create body heat by shivering, so they may not remain immobilized long by this treatment.

What is it about lights that attracts moths? The moth to the flame is an age-old image, but only recently have biologists begun to understand the reasons behind it. Moths, like butterflies, have vision sensitive to ultraviolet light. This alone may suggest the attractiveness of UV lights for them. But one theory gaining ground proposes that the light attracts moths less than it dazzles them. In other words, when a moth flies within visible range of the light, its brilliance disrupts the insect's ability to orient using dim natural light. This causes it to begin circling and ultimately to drift in toward the light: the moth to the flame. Far from "liking" lights, then, moths — if capable of so feeling — would be highly frustrated by bright city lights. In fact, it has been suggested that the proliferation of mercury and sodium-vapour street lights has added to the pressure on giant silkmoths and contributed to their decline throughout the urban northeast. Drawn from the country to the bright lights, they spend their nights circling lampposts instead of seeking mates. According to the theory, by thus disrupting their courtships, the powerful lights reduce the big moths' reproductive success. At the same time, moths concentrated around light sources are vulnerable to bats at night and birds in the morning. Whatever the actual relationship between moths and light, the fact that moths come to lights makes it possible for us to observe them closely.

When using lights, one is forced to remain within reach of a power-supply source or else pack heavy batteries around. Moth hunters desiring greater portability often fall back on the other time-honoured attractant: bait. Rotting fruits and other substances may be used to entice butterflies. Moths will come to fruit as well, but they seem to prefer a mixture of sweet-stuffs that practitioners simply call "sugar." At least one recipe exists for each person who makes it. A typical mixture might consist of the following ingredients: a couple of pounds of sugar, a bottle or two of stale beer, mashed overripe bananas, some molasses or syrup, fruit juice and a shot of rum. This unpleasant-sounding brew should be left to ferment in the sun for a few hours, whereupon it becomes even more cloying. I have never been clear as to whether the addition of alcohol enhances the attractiveness of the fluid to moths or merely enhances their watchability or catchability by dulling their reflexes.

The traditional method of sugaring involves painting the sugar on tree trunks, rocks, stumps, fenceposts or any other surfaces in or near a likely-looking moth habitat. Clearings or lanes in deciduous woodland are especially good. The sugar should be applied in the late afternoon and left to "cook" in the last sun of the day but not long enough to evaporate. A sultry, cloudy evening gives the best mothing; clear, cool, breezy and moonlit nights are not as good. When you return to the site as night falls, lantern or flashlight in hand, proceed from sugar station to sugar station, and you should see a succession of moths coming for the bait. If you want to take some back for study or observation, quickly place a jar beneath the drinking moth. Often it will drop right into the jar when disturbed. Otherwise, prod it gently in that direction. Keep the jar in the dark to prevent the moths from battering themselves to bits; or simply enjoy the moths in situ as they probe the cracks in the bark for the dripping liquor, their eyes shining like fiery garnets in the beam of the lantern. Some drinkers become quite besotted and easy to approach, while others sip sparingly and retain their wariness.

Experience will show that some places sugar better than others. One summer, I led sugaring walks for my classes in two disparate localities. In the foothills, we tried a ponderosa pine wood and a quaking aspen grove. Neither yielded many moths. But in a cluster of plains cottonwoods a few nights later, we watched big red underwing moths flicker through the lantern beam, hover by the cottonwood trunks, then settle gingerly and extend their tongues toward the gleaming sugar. Dozens of the beautiful moths came to the bait, giving one the sense that prairie groves are better than mountain forests. Yet on another summer night years earlier, my mother and I enjoyed an excellent night's sugaring among the pines and aspens near a cabin we had taken in a foothills canyon. On that occasion, we added cherry cider to our sugar bait, and it has been one of my central ingredients since then.

Lately, many lepidopterists have become more aware of their impact on the environment. Sugaring the old way can leave unsightly patches on the trees and may attract many other insects that can get stuck or preyed upon. A new way of sugaring that avoids these problems has been gaining acceptance. It involves soaking sponges in the sugar vat and hanging them from limbs of trees, rather than painting the woods. While less pleasing as a moth background, the sponges leave no sticky trace and make collecting much easier. It is best left to your own discretion. But however it is done, I highly recommend sugaring as a uniquely rewarding nature-by-night experience.

Perhaps no author has painted a more evocative scene of a moth outing than W.J. Holland in his essay "Sugaring For Moths," which appeared in his 1904 classic, *The Moth Book*. This casual but suspenseful piece is a classic of period natural-history writing. In it, Holland describes the entire event, from mixing the sugar, daubing the trees and resting for the evening's work through mothing by lantern light, scurrying for the protection of the old verandah as the storm comes and anticipating the morning's labour ahead in setting the catch. He describes the moths themselves and the rising excitement of a pair of lepidopterists (the narrator and his protégé) in terms that inspire the reader's enthusiasm for this naturalist's sport. Here is a sample:

Let us stealthily approach the next tree. It is a beech. What is there? Oho! My beauty! Just above the moistened patch upon the bark is a great Catocala. The grey upper wings are spread, revealing the lower wings gloriously banded with black and crimson. In the yellow light of the lantern, the wings appear even more brilliant than they do in sunlight. How the eyes glow like spots of fire!

When I lead a moth walk, I try to find a quiet and comfortable place where I can read selections of Holland's essay to the group. It adds such flavour that it can make a success of a near-mothless night (it is available in a Dover reprint edition). On one such occasion, I had just come to the part about the thunderstorm when the lightning flashed, thunder crashed and the sky opened so that we, too, ran for shelter. We finished the piece in a rustic lodge, examined our

catch and set them free into the rain-fresh night air. I cannot guarantee that the elements will play true to the script like that, but I can assure you of a worthwhile night out.

Still another method of attracting moths may bring spectacular results. If you can obtain a living female of any of the saturnine (giant silk) moths, such as Cecropia or Luna or Polyphemus, fresh from the cocoon and therefore virginal, you can employ her to attract males. Of course, this works only if these moths live within a certain radius of the female's position. Males have been known

to track calling females from 10 miles away, but 1 or 2 miles is probably much more common. Place the female moth in a room with screened, open windows or, better yet, in a screened cage outdoors. (Specialists construct dainty harnesses of thread with which to tether their moths.) She will release pheromones, which the males pick up with their great feathery antennae. Like Argonauts to a siren, they sail out of the night to surround her. The spectacle of the ardent silkmoths flapping their great wings around the object of their desire is not to be forgotten. Gene Stratton Porter, whose 1912 book *Moths of the Limberlost* captures the charm of moths better than any others for me, described such an experience.

Protecting the night sky

by Terence Dickinson

The most common outdoor light until the 1980s was the familiar pale green glow of mercury vapour. With less than half the efficiency of the more modern sodium lamps, mercury lamps are now seldom chosen for large lighting tasks, but they are still used for smaller parking lots and so-called security lights. Usually, these lights are equipped with a photocell that turns them on at dusk and off at dawn.

Tom Dey, a senior optical-systems engineer at Eastman Kodak in Rochester, New York, says many mercury lamps available for backyard, driveway or farm not only send up to one-third of their light uselessly into the night sky but also have a huge hidden expense. "I got a flyer in with my electric bill at home," he recalls. "It was an ad for a $50 mercury lamp with a $20 discount coupon, a $10 rebate from the manufacturer and another $10 from the electric company. The funny thing was, they forgot to mention that it takes electricity to operate it." Dey calculated that the 175-watt lamp and its 30-watt ballast would consume about

$448.95 worth of electricity over its five-year rated lifetime.

One alternative is to use high-pressure sodium bulbs. These require special fixtures but use only half the electricity to produce the same amount of light as a mercury-vapour bulb. Although most sodium fixtures are equipped with photocells, one bulb can last up to 6½ years. And sodium bulbs give off yellow light, producing far less glare than the green light of mercury vapour. To reduce glare further, select fixtures that are shielded from above to direct the light where you need it rather than have it "leak" into the sky.

A second alternative, if you don't need the light to be on all night, is to install motion-sensitive floodlights in strategic locations, such as the garage, back door, barn or toolshed. When the infrared sensor in the lamp housing detects movement, it switches the light on for a few minutes. "The lights come on when you need them and are off when you don't," Dey says, "so they are on for only a few hours a month." And, Dey asks, "What would deter an intruder more, a bright light on all night or a bright light being turned on?" Lights coming on outside would also alert the homeowner to any activity in the yard.

Originally published in Harrowsmith *magazine (Camden East, Ont.).*

In connection with Cecropia, there came to me the most delightful experience of my life. One perfect night during the middle of May, all the world white with tree bloom, touched to radiance with brilliant moonlight, intoxicating with countless blending perfumes, I placed a female Cecropia on the screen of my sleeping-room door and retired . . . Past midnight, I was awakened by soft touches on the screen, faint pullings at the wire. I went to the door and found the porch, orchard and night sky alive with Cecropias holding high carnival. I had not supposed there were so many in all this world. From every direction, they came floating like birds down the moonbeams. I carefully removed the female from the door to a window close beside me and stepped on the porch. No doubt, I was permeated with the odour of the moth. As I advanced to the top step that lay even with the middle branches of the apple trees, the exquisite big creatures came swarming around me. I could feel them on my hair, my shoulders, and see them settling on my gown and outstretched hands. Far as I could penetrate the night sky, more were coming. They settled on the bloom-laden branches, on the porch pillars, on me, indiscriminately. I stepped inside the door with one on each hand and five clinging to my gown. Then I went back to the verandah and revelled with the moths until dawn drove them to shelter.

Admit one or more of the males to the female's chamber, and she will soon be mated. Eggs will appear, the size of glass pinheads, on curtains or wherever she can crawl. Then you can launch a new generation. The big, beautiful moths have large and striking larvae as well. Cecropias' thick, apple-green caterpillars bear red and yellow and blue tubercles that give them a decorated look. You may be surprised by their appetites. The first batch of Cecropias I acquired as a boy came in the form of a couple of hundred eggs. I began by trying to feed each hatchling individually, but as they outgrew my patience, I tossed them into a washtub with fresh foliage daily. Eventually, I simply slung the lot onto my mother's lilacs, which they nearly defoliated by the time they spun their big-bag cocoons!

Searching for those cocoons in winter makes a fine treasure hunt. Each species has its own distinctive shape. Cecropia makes a drawn-out sack; Promethea's is narrower, wrapped in a leaf. Polyphemus, too, incorporates the leaf, but the cocoon is broad and bulky. The lovely green Luna spins up in a silky ball. When the leaves fall in deciduous woodlands, thickets and hedgerows, these and many moths' smaller cocoons stand out. Since most of the giant silkmoths feed on a variety of broad-leaved trees and shrubs, they occur in many rural and wildland habitats. And according to Gene Stratton Porter, "The Cecropia is a moth whose acquaintance nature-loving city people can cultivate." She noted several bushels of their cocoons in Indianapolis one winter. Well adapted to many ornamental plants, they nonetheless tend to spread out and seldom become pests.

But if Cecropia tolerates cities, an equally beautiful species positively prefers slums. Whereas Cecropia is coloured in shades of russet and robin-red, the Cynthia moth is honey-tan with lilac-pink bands. Imported from Asia as a potential silk source in the 19th century, the moth and its host plant (*Ailanthus*) became naturalized in the east.

The sericulture project faded out, the cocoons being too difficult to unravel, but the adaptable *Ailanthus* continued to spread with its beautiful moth. Known as "the tree that grows in Brooklyn," *Ailanthus* has a penchant for slums, railroad yards, industrial sites, concrete jungles — anywhere it can get a roothold. So these are the kinds of places where the Cynthia lives. The slender cocoons, wrapped in a leaf and lassoed to a twig by a silken tie, may be found in great numbers in these unlikely-seeming locales.

Silk-enclosed cocoons like these should be stored in a cool place and sprinkled lightly with water from time to time. There should be something for the emerging moths to climb on — twigs or rough wood or fabric. If you keep the cocoons in a warmer place indoors, they may hatch early, like forced crocuses. Silkmoths lack mouthparts and live as adults just a few days.

Once you have seen them in their pristine condition, every scale in place, you may prefer to release them. Be sure to do so at dusk, in the proper habitat and well away from strong lights.

I shall never forget the pleasure of keeping Luna moths in my lab at Yale. A friend sent me a batch of cocoons, which I kept over the winter. With spring, they began to eclose: pale green shrouds with moist white mantles crawling out of silken bags sheared open with a tooth concealed in the ermine fur of their thoraxes. As they pumped fluid from their fat bodies into crumpled wings, their long tails unfurled and the green vanes took shape. I was deeply struck by these splendid moths, their sickle-shaped, crescent-tailed wings of the softest jade, rimmed along the leading edge with deep purple. At a frenetic and pressured time in my life, the Lunas brought a very welcome note of tranquillity and beauty, as well as a touch of nature, for which I was grateful. They were the first I had seen alive, and I have still yet to discover the Luna in the wild.

I have been speaking largely of the giant silkmoths of the family Saturniidae, distant relatives of the domestic silkmoth. But there are many other groups of moths worth your attention. Their incredible diversity presents a real challenge in terms of identification. For many years, Holland's *The Moth Book* was the only available reference that named and pictured even a smattering of American moths. Now there are detailed monographs of some families, and selective field guides are beginning to appear. Still, it is no mean feat to identify correctly the moths that you encounter. The family Noctuidae (commonly called millers) alone comprises hundreds of roughly similar species. Our moths as a whole are rather poorly known. Where I live, we haven't the scantiest picture of the moth fauna. Moths will continue to present new frontiers to lepidopterists long after the butterflies have been reasonably well documented. This seems appropriate for these mysterious night fliers. Somehow, with the dark as their curtain, I feel we may never know moths as well as we might like.

I hope you will not let the difficulty of identification discourage you altogether from searching out moths. It is not difficult to get to know the commoner, more conspicuous species and the major families. For those of you who develop a deeper interest, the names will come later as a product of the sort of involuntary research that is the handmaiden to enthusiasm.

Our moths may lack the charming common names with which the English species have been endowed — names like true lover's knot, angleshades, maiden's blush and lesser lutestring. Yet they possess no less charm. If "charm" seems a peculiar word to apply to a moth, I would ask your opinion again after you have seen a few of our elegant underwing moths or followed an eight-spotted forester making its rounds among the phlox. If you admire butterflies, you will be missing out on a great deal if you ignore their closest relatives, the moths — perhaps our most undervalued natural resource.

Excerpted from The Audubon Society Handbook for Butterfly Watchers. *Charles Scribner's Sons (New York).*

Protecting nature's best little insect exterminator

Learning to Love Bats

by Craig Canine

Merlin Tuttle walks through the shadows of a late summer evening, a palm-sized plastic box in his hand. The small device is a "Mini Bat Detector" that picks up vibrations too high-pitched for the human ear and "translates" them into audible sounds — the audio version of an infrared night-vision scope. Like a transistor radio, the bat detector has one dial to adjust volume and another for frequency.

Tuttle has tuned it to 30 kilohertz, the frequency of the Mexican free-tailed bat's sonar blips. (Some bat species "broadcast" at frequencies as high as 150,000 vibrations per second, or 150 kilohertz; the range of human hearing extends to about 20 kilohertz.) As the detector comes alive with static, Tuttle excitedly explains, "There are a lot of bats around. So many that they're jamming the machine."

The detector is chattering madly as we strain to spot bats in the darkness. "There's piles of bats here," he shouts. "People just don't realize that when they go out at night, they're almost always close to a bat. The average batophobe would be totally freaked out if he knew how many bats were around him."

Merlin Tuttle has been around bats for most of his 45 years. He collected and catalogued his first specimens at the age of 9. Since 1982, he has been president of Bat Conservation International (BCI), a nonprofit organization he founded to educate batophobes about the virtues of the order Chiroptera (Latin for hand-wing), the only mammals capable of true flight. He thinks bats are the most misunderstood, needlessly persecuted animals on Earth. Because most bats are nocturnal, their appearance is often startling. "They're so unpopular that few people have studied them," Tuttle says. "We simply don't know much about them. And what we don't know, we fear — and what we fear, we persecute."

Although bats make up a quarter of the world's mammalian population, several species have become extinct, and many others are threatened with extinction, mainly because of human mistreatment. Of nearly 1,000 known bat species, 39 of them are indigenous to parts of the United States and Canada. The most common species in the colder regions of North America are the little brown and big brown bats, the red bat, the silver-haired bat and the hoary bat. Of northern North America's 39 species, 5 are officially endangered, including the eastern big-eared bat and the Indiana bat. Tuttle thinks four or five more of them, such as the western big-eared and Sanborn's long-tongued

bats, should be added to the endangered list. Even species that are still plentiful are vulnerable, he says, simply because they roost in such large colonies. Millions of bats can be, and have been, wiped out with a single human act, such as dynamiting or fumigating an important nursery cave.

Because so little research on bats has been done, the implications of their extinction are largely unknown. One certainty, however, is that bats are by far the most important predators of night-flying insects. A single grey bat (an endangered species native to the southeastern United States) can eat 3,000 or more insects per night. The little brown bat can eat 600 insects in a single hour, making it far more effective at controlling mosquito populations than the purple martin.

"I've got nothing against martins," Tuttle says, "but they go to bed about the time mosquitoes come out. If you really want something that gets rid of mosquitoes, purple martins or bug zappers can't come close to what a colony of bats can do."

While insectivorous bats are vital to worldwide insect control, nectar- and fruit-eating bats play equally important

A big brown bat rests upside down during the day; by night, it will consume thousands of insects.

roles in the pollination and seed-dispersal of economically important plants. Wild bananas, for example, provide genetic material for the development of new banana varieties and depend on bats for their pollination. In the wild, avocados, breadfruit, carob, cashews, dates, figs, mangoes and plantain also rely on bats for survival. By dispersing seeds in deforested tropical regions, small flying foxes — which can eat, digest and excrete a fig in less than 20 minutes — are responsible for 95 percent of all the forest regeneration that occurs in West Africa.

"Bats occupy important niches in ecosystems from the tropics to the sub-arctic," Tuttle says. "In some cases, the disappearance of a single species could trigger a series of linked extinctions of other plants and animals, creating unpredictable shatter effects."

On the island of Guam, for example, the native Chomorros consider fruit bats a delicacy and have harvested them to near-extinction. As a result, fruit that was once eaten by bats now stays on trees until it becomes overripe, providing food for fruit flies and fungi that infest and ruin entire crops. Guam must now import nearly all the fruit in its markets — apparently due to the popularity of bats stewed in coconut milk.

What does the delicacy taste like? "It is reputed to taste like chicken or ham," Tuttle says. "And it is considered horrible etiquette in Guam to leave the fur — they eat everything, bones and all."

In his efforts "to promote bat values," Tuttle's biggest challenge is to clear up the many misconceptions that people have about bats. The following myths, he says, can each be dispelled by some little-known facts:

Bats are flying rodents. Actually, bats are more closely related to humans than to rats and mice. It has recently been discovered that an entire suborder of bats, often called flying foxes because of their reddish brown fur and long, tapering snouts, have the same sophisticated brain pathways that distinguish primates from other mammals. Under a microscope, the brains of flying foxes and lower primates, such as lemurs, are difficult to tell apart. The only way to deny

that flying foxes are primates, according to some scientists, is to claim that primates, by definition, do not fly.

Bats are blind. "There's not a blind species of bat in the world," Tuttle says. Microchiroptera, or microbats (which include all North American species), navigate by echolocation, but they also have good vision and can see at night as well as humans can. Megachiroptera — megabats, or flying foxes — have no echolocation systems. They navigate strictly by using their acute vision.

Bats are often rabid. All mammals, including bats, can and do contract rabies. But fewer humans have contracted rabies from bats than from dogs or cats. In four decades of record keeping in the United States, 10 people died from bat-transmitted rabies, compared with more than 130 human deaths from dog and cat rabies. "We lose far more people every year to honeybee stings than to bat rabies," Tuttle says, "yet we recognize the value of honeybees and tolerate them happily. Bats are just as beneficial, so why do we single them out for persecution?"

Bats are filthy. Like cats, bats spend a great deal of time grooming and preening. They keep themselves immaculate, in part because a speck of dirt on a bat's wing membrane can fatally affect its precise aerodynamic control. Bat guano, which many people believe is a potent medium for disease-causing organisms, is no more pathogenic than bird droppings.

Bats are vicious. "Bats are among the most naturally gentle mammals on Earth," Tuttle says. "If I went out there and caught you a bat, I could hand it to you and it wouldn't bite either of us. In my 25 years as a bat researcher, I've never come across an aggressive bat." Even rabid bats, he says, are not likely to bite unless they are threatened. "Never touch a bat that's lying on the ground," he warns, "because there's a good chance that it's sick. Leave it alone, and it will return the favour."

Bats often get tangled in people's hair. "I've tried to get bats to cling to my hair," Tuttle says, "and they can't get hold of it. They just slide off." Neither is a bat likely to blunder into a person's

hair at night by mistake: bats' echolocation systems enable them to detect and avoid single strands of fine wire. A whole head full of hair is, by comparison, an easily avoided obstacle.

Poisons are an effective means of ridding houses of bats. This one really gets Tuttle going. "By far the worst hazard to public health associated with bats," he says emphatically, "is the misdirected efforts of humans to eradicate them with poisons." The only effective way to rid a house of bats, he points out, is to wait until they leave at dusk and then seal their points of entry.

The two chemicals used most often against bats are methyl bromide and Rozol. Methyl bromide, a chemical that prevents blood from clotting, is, according to Tuttle, "more dangerous to people than cyanide." And Rozol, a "tracking powder" that kills rats and mice after they walk across it, is "83 times more potent than a closely related chemical that is known to cause birth defects," he says.

In one documented case, a pest-control operator blew several pounds of Rozol into the attic of a Minnesota house via an opening in the closet of a young child's bedroom. The child's lung tissue eventually became severely scarred, and his blood-clotting rate resembled that of a haemophiliac. The family moved out of the house but had difficulty selling it because Rozol had sifted into the insulation. "The irony of it all," Tuttle says, "is that Rozol and methyl bromide aren't even effective against bats, because bats roost in high places and the chemicals just accumulate on the floor."

Despite the known dangers of Rozol and methyl bromide, many pest-control companies use them routinely. Tuttle shows me a cost-estimate sheet from a nationally recognized pest-control company, sent to him by a member of Bat Conservation International. The form quotes prices of $75 to plug holes in the BCI member's house and $425 to fumigate the attic with methyl bromide. "The only effective thing on there is the $75 for plugging holes," Tuttle says. "That $425 is pure consumer fraud."

Many bats are aggressive and deadly

vampires. "Vampire bats are not half as gross and dangerous as they're made out to be," Tuttle says. True vampire bats are found only in tropical South America. Their bites pose a threat to cattle, not people, because the small wounds provide egg-laying sites for botflies. Vampires may also carry parasites that spread the blood-borne cattle disease trypanosomiasis.

"Sure, vampires cause substantial economic harm to cattle ranchers in Latin America," Tuttle admits. "But hundreds of thousands of innocent, beneficial bats have been killed in the name of exterminating *vampiros*. Besides, no animal is all bad — or all good. Vampires are known to be among the world's most altruistic mammals when they're among their own kind. They adopt orphans and care for unrelated individuals in need of help. Someday, the vampire may be appreciated for its good qualities."

Rehabilitating the bat's reputation may be a bigger job than one person can accomplish in a lifetime. But Merlin Tuttle is used to defending underdogs. "When I was in grade school," he recalls, "I don't know how many fistfights I got into against big bullies on behalf of friends — me, the class runt. I don't ever remember getting into a fight on my own behalf or with someone my own size." When he wasn't getting into fights, he was slogging around in ponds, creeks and fields collecting animal specimens. Much to his mother's horror, he once brought home a five-foot king snake. He convinced his mother to let him keep his prize until his father could see it. That night, his mother stepped on the snake, which coiled around her leg.

Tuttle's love for animals also caused problems in school. "I essentially flunked out of the fifth grade," he says, "because I spent all my time learning the scientific names of the mammals of California," where he lived during his early childhood. When he was in high school, he began capturing bats, banding them for identification and releasing them. He has since banded more than 40,000 bats. His first four scientific papers, published while he was an undergraduate in college, were based on bat banding he did in high school. He is now the world's foremost authority on the population ecology of the American grey bat, a species put on the endangered list because of his tireless efforts to protect it.

He founded Bat Conservation International because he could not persuade existing wildlife-conservation organizations to take up the cause of endangered bats. "They thought it was too hopeless," he says.

In Tuttle's view, some conservation groups are guided by the "cute-and-cuddly syndrome" rather than by a careful assessment of a species' environmental and economic importance. He points out that 394 species have been declared endangered in the United States — and that half of the money budgeted for wildlife conservation goes to fewer than a dozen of those. Tuttle calls them "glamour species," many of which are so scarce that they became "biologically irrelevant" long ago.

"For a tiny fraction of what has been spent on a few California condors," he says, "BCI has really done something to help bats — a quarter of the world's mammals. I'm all for saving the pandas and the condors and the baby seals. But the fact is that many animals are going to become extinct, and we have to develop priorities."

Originally published in Harrowsmith Country Life *magazine (Charlotte, VT).*

Out of the house and into the yard

Unlike rodents, bats in attics and wall cavities do not chew insulation, wiring or lumber. Their worst offences are noise and piles of guano.

If squeaks and strange smells are keeping you awake at night, you can easily bat-proof your house. The only safe and effective way is to lock the colony out of your house by plugging the bats' point of entry. Watch at dusk to see where bats emerge from the house. Then, over each exit hole, attach one end of a plastic bag that has been opened at both ends. The bags will act as one-way valves, allowing bats to leave the house but preventing their re-entry. After a few nights (not all bats leave the roost every night), seal the holes permanently. The best time to bat-proof is late fall or winter, when most northern bats have migrated from buildings. Do not exclude a bat colony in June or July, when flightless young will be trapped in the house and starve.

To prevent an occasional stray bat from coming indoors, cover chimneys and plumbing vents with screens, repair any loose screens over soffit and ridge vents, install draft guards at the base of doors and seal any possible access holes around windows and plumbing. A bat can squeeze through any hole big enough to admit your thumb.

Bat Conservation International (Box 162603, Austin, Texas 78716-2603), a nonprofit organization devoted to educating the public about bats, offers a ready-made house designed for North American species. The 17-inch-tall house is bottomless, thereby providing easy access for bats but preventing deer mice and squirrels from settling in. Two interior partitions create three crevices of different widths (from about 1⅛ inches to 1⅝ inches), sized in accordance with the latest research on bat preferences. The house is made of ¾-inch western red cedar, a naturally durable wood, rough-sawn and unfinished so bats can cling to it.

Bats are most plentiful near streams, lakes or marshes, though they can be attracted in almost any environment south of the Arctic. You may have to be patient, however: many bat houses remain vacant for as long as a year and a half after they are put up but attract increasing numbers of residents in following years.

Basic map and compass skills made easy

Getting a Sense of Direction

by G.I. Kenney

The first landmark I ever located with the aid of map and compass was the University of Montreal tower, rising from the northwest slopes of Mount Royal, prominent and proudly aloof from the frenetic streets of Jean Drapeau's city far below. The day I "found" the tower still stands out in memory, marking my initiation into the use of the elementary yet fascinating skill of not getting lost in the woods.

My guide for that first expedition was an ordinary city map, with the university tower designated by a tiny red block. My compass was little more than a toy, and imagination played a large part in my achievement: the spire, plainly visible throughout the search, was hidden only in my mind. In my situation, unlike most that call for a map and compass, I was in less danger of losing my way than in being brushed by a low-flying Montreal taxi; emergency sustenance was as close as the nearest *crêperie* or pastrami-on-rye emporium. The challenge was entirely mental as I wound my way through the traffic-ridden streets, across Côte Ste. Catherine and up the hill to the campus.

It was clearly a game of self-imposed illusion, but the satisfaction of arriving at the base of the tower, looking up its imposing 590 feet of brickwork, finding it exactly where my dead-reckoning calculations had said it would be, was very real. Sergeant Preston, tracking his villainous quarry in the dark reaches of the Yukon, ready to pocket his brass compass and utter his classic "I arrest you in the name of the Crown," could have done no better.

Following that first conquest, I have traversed considerably less civilized terrains and found my way to landmarks a bit more obscure and decidedly more attractive than urban towers of brick, steel and concrete. Lakes hold a special fascination for me. To see a body of water marked on a topographical map with no apparent access other than by shank's mare makes that bit of water irresistible — I don't know why. Perhaps it is the vision of the ultimate trout swimming in its cold recesses or the hope of glimpsing a picture of unspoiled, misty wildness nestled in the mountains. I have found many wilderness lakes with a compass, and more than one has yielded its share of speckled trout.

When I first discovered the pleasure of working with map and compass, the word "orienteering" seemed intimidating. It called up images of super-scientific precision, logarithms and cosines and all of the mathematical apparatus of the professional long-distance navi-gator — as well as the dark suspicion that someday soon, we would be told we needed orienteering boots and orienteering pants and an official orienteering T-shirt before we could go out and practise this science.

I prefer the old-fashioned term "bushwhacking," which tends to demystify the whole thing. The first use of the lodestone may be shrouded in antiquity, but it is far from an esoteric art. Basic common sense and a little practice in the field are all it really takes to master the mysteries of the magnetic needle.

The two essential tools of the bushwhacker are the compass and the topographical map — not an ordinary road map (although this might do in an emergency) but a map drawn to a scale of one to 50,000 (in Canada) or one to 24,000 (in the United States) and showing the details of local terrain as well as roads and towns.

The ratios by which such maps are classified mean that one inch on the map corresponds to 50,000 inches or 24,000 inches, respectively, of actual territory in the field. The smaller the ratio, the more detail will be shown on the map. Most of Canada has been mapped on the one-to-50,000 scale, while about 600 individual locations, mainly cities and areas along the heavily populated shores of the St. Lawrence River corridor, have been mapped on a scale of one to 25,000. In the United States, maps of the entire country have been drawn to a one-to-24,000 scale. By contrast, the majority of road maps are drawn to scales of one to 250,000 or one to 500,000.

According to the Canada Map Office, Canadian topographical maps are scaled one to 50,000 to match the measures of the standard military maps used by European NATO countries, on which one centimetre equals one quarter of a kilometre. U.S. maps nonetheless provide an easy-to-multiply round figure on the one-to-24,000 scale: One inch equals approximately 2,000 feet.

Topographical maps are available from the Canada Map Office in Ottawa and from most sporting-goods stores. Maps for U.S. regions can be obtained from the United States Geological Survey offices in Arlington, Virginia, and Denver, Colorado.

Topographical maps differ from standard road maps in other ways besides scale. Road maps are usually white or a light shade of blue, with streets marked in red or black. Only major landmarks are identified, and no attempt is made to indicate surface characteristics. Topographical maps, however, are splashed with colour: green to indicate vegetation, blue for lakes and streams, brown for bogs, white indicating rock or desert, and pink, orange or black used to represent towns and the roads connecting them. Concentric bands, or contour lines, follow the shape of the land, showing where it rises or falls. The closer the bands are together, the steeper the grade.

Topographical maps also carry a declination figure, or diagram, normally printed in the border at the bottom of the map or in the right-hand margin. The declination figure shows the difference in degrees between true north and magnetic north for the part of the continent covered by that map. It comes as a surprise to many beginning bushwhackers, but these two norths are not at all the same.

True north is the direction a traveller would follow from any given point if he were making a beeline for the planet's actual geographical North Pole, the frozen spot in the Arctic Ocean that Robert E. Peary was first to reach in 1909. That spot would correspond to the northern tip of the imaginary north/south axis line running through the centre of the globe. It is also the point through which all longitudinal lines pass.

Magnetic north is the direction a traveller would take to get to the spot where the northern tip of the invisible magnetic field surrounding the planet intersects the Earth's surface. This is the point to which compass needles point in the northern hemisphere. In the southern hemisphere, they point to the south magnetic pole.

Unlike the north and south geographical poles, whose locations are constant, the Earth's magnetic poles are always in motion, shifting at a rate of approximately 1 degree every 10 years. For this reason, maps are updated roughly every 10 years and the declination figure in the margin corrected to account for the magnetic pole's migration over the decade. As of 1980, the magnetic north pole was located approximately 1,300 miles south of the true North Pole, northwest of Hudson Bay.

As for compasses, they come in various sizes and styles and at various prices, ranging from the basic Boy Scout pocket compass to a Plexiglas-mounted, liquid-filled, sight-equipped hiker's model with fluorescent needle and adjustable scales to expensive precision cruiser compasses designed for geologists and other professional explorers. More practical for bushwhacking is the standard "orienteering compass," which is mounted on a square plastic backing and features a liquid-filled housing to prevent the needle from bobbing. A dependable one can be purchased for $10 to $20 in most sporting-goods stores. (If possible, you should buy two just to be safe. It is always a good idea to carry a spare compass in the bush in case one breaks or is lost.)

The standard compass dial is marked off with the 360 degrees of a circle, with the four cardinal directions indicated by the initials N, S, E and W. Decorative models may also include a traditional compass rose, which has 32 points (north-northwest, northwest, west-northwest, and so on) and was used by early mariners. Many marine compasses of today still carry both the 360-degree circle and a compass rose.

Professional cartographers and navigators work in terms of degrees and minutes — the latter represented in writing by a number with an apostrophe — and in precise work, each degree of a circle may be divided into 60 minutes. Such careful measures are unnecessary for hikers, however, and minutes are not marked on field compasses.

Once outfitted with map and compass and a comfortable pair of hiking boots, the apprentice bushwhacker is ready to launch his education in pathfinding. The best way to begin is in fairly familiar territory, with visible landmarks the hiker knows but can pretend not to see. As things become more routine, the apprentice can progress to landmarks shown on the map but invisible from the hike starting point. Today the post office flagpole, tomorrow the world!

Practice is the best teacher. First, find the declination figure for the map being used. Let's assume it is 15 degrees west, namely, that the compass needle will point to a spot 15 degrees west of true north. (If the declination figure includes minutes, simply round it off to the nearest degree.)

Set the compass down on a flat surface away from metal objects, and orient it so that the needle points to 15 degrees west of N on the compass face. The degrees of a compass start at zero at N and proceed clockwise around the circle so that 15 degrees west of north means the needle should be pointing to 345 degrees.

With the compass in this position, N will be facing true north. This is the position in which the compass will always be used while you are working with a map that indicates a declination figure of 15 degrees west plus or minus 30 minutes.

Now, two points must be located on the map — the starting point and the destination. Draw a straight line joining these two points, and extend it three or four inches past the destination. Place the compass on the map so that its cen-

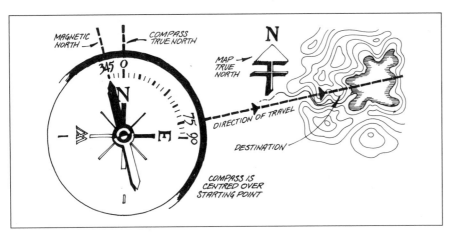

Always take bearings from true north. After finding magnetic north, adjust the compass (according to your map legend) so that true north is at O degrees.

tre is exactly over the starting point, keeping the needle pointing to 345 degrees as before. Next, lift the compass a bit off the map so that it won't move, and orient the map so that its true-north pointer is indicating the same direction as the N on the compass. Take note of the direction of the line just drawn between starting point and destination. This is the direction to follow to reach the destination.

For example, say the destination's heading is 75 degrees, or roughly east-northeast on the old-time compass rose. Sight along that direction in the field, and pick out a landmark — a big tree, a rock or a mountain peak — and start walking toward it. After a few minutes, stop and take out the compass again, orienting it so that the needle again points to 345 degrees (assume, in this case, that the magnetic declination for the area is 15 degrees, as given previously). Take a sighting along 75 degrees, pick out another landmark (or the same one as before if it is still visible), and proceed toward it. Keep doing this every so often during the hike, as a series of directional checks, until you finally reach the destination.

Coming back, the same process is followed, except that it is now reversed. The hiker will be sighting along the heading on the opposite side of the compass dial — 255 degrees — and walking west-southwest.

If detours must be made around obstacles — a lake or a mountain too steep for climbing — several alternatives are possible. The easiest, if the obstacle is a small one, is to pick out a prominent object on the other side of the obstruction that falls in line with the original compass bearing leading to your goal. Walk around the obstacle until the prominent object is reached, then, using the object as a base, make another compass check to get back on the original bearing, and proceed.

If no prominent object presents itself, the triangulation method may be employed. Using the compass dial as a protractor, count off enough degrees to the right or left of the original heading to produce an angle of march (a) that will clear the obstacle. Set the compass so that the direction of travel points to this new bearing and, counting the paces, walk along this line (x) until the obstacle is cleared. Now set the compass back on the original course, drawing an imaginary line (y) parallel to the original line of travel. Count off the same number of degrees used to take the second bearing (a), only this time going in the opposite direction on the compass dial. Using this angle (b), draw a third imaginary line (z) back to your original direction of march, and walk back the same number of paces along this line. You will reach a spot on the far side of the obstacle roughly opposite the point where you were first forced to halt.

Still another method is to use the map, breaking the journey up into intermediate destinations. Pick a landmark to the side of the obstacle, and locate it on the map. Using this new landmark as a second starting point, draw a line from it to your original destination and take a compass bearing on that line. Say the bearing is 350 degrees. After walking from wherever the obstacle first forced you to halt to this second starting point, use the new point as a base and again take out the compass. This time, sight along the new heading of 350 degrees, find another landmark toward which to walk, and proceed once more. You will be moving toward the original destination again.

As the bushwhacker's experience widens, various tricks and shortcuts will suggest themselves to make travelling easier, such as following valleys and streams that lie in the same direction as the hiker's route or noticing the position of the sun after a compass check. By keeping the sun in the same position as he or she walks, a hiker can go much farther between checks without straying off route.

It may also save the hiker considerable time if the topographical map being used has been "struck off" with grid lines showing the direction of magnetic north, as well as the usual grid lines showing true north. Few maps have such magnetic grid marks, however, so the bushwhacker will likely have to put them in by hand. This can be done in a few minutes using a pencil and straightedge. Simply draw lines roughly every inch or two, parallel to the declination figure pointer indicating magnetic north.

Finally, if you ever get lost, or think you are lost, always believe the compass. It may be pointing in the opposite direction from what seems correct, but as long as it isn't sitting on an axe blade or some other piece of metal, it will invariably be right.

The most rudimentary of instruments — a bit of magnetite ore on a floating needle — was sufficient to lead the mariners of yesteryear across trackless oceans to a safe harbour. The modern bushwhacker's compass, too, will guide its owner safely out and home again.

Originally published in Harrowsmith *magazine (Camden East, Ont.).*

Beavers alter the world they live in with dams and teeth

Colonizing the Wilderness

by Adrian Forsyth

The most remarkable adaptations of the beaver are behavioural ones. Beavers build dams, lodges and food caches. When they move into a new area along an unoccupied stream, the first thing they build is a dam. Normally, a dam is placed at a constriction, or narrow place, in the valley. This minimizes the amount of material needed for construction. However, in flat habitats, beaver dams may extend for hundreds of yards. The dam of the beaver is a composite of logs, sticks, rocks and muck that impedes, rather than halts, the flow of water. Most of the outflow percolates through the dam, rather than over the top, so that the current does not continually erode the dam. The dam serves several purposes. It backs up water, giving the beaver easy access to trees and reducing the beaver's need to travel over land, where it is vulnerable to predators. Beavers will also build canals that run for hundreds of feet. They may divert other streams into the canal system and build smaller dams, all to create water access to stands of food. Branches are transported much more easily by towing across water. The dam may be 10 feet high or more, providing adequate water depth to build a secure lodge.

A lodge typically has an underwater entrance close to the pond or stream bottom, making entry difficult for all predators but otters. The interior has a dry raised platform, sometimes created out of the previously emergent stream bank or constructed by layering woody debris and mud to rise above the water level. The roof of the lodge is thickly woven of intermeshed twigs, and before winter, when the lodge is to be occupied, the roof is layered and smeared with muck and mud that freeze into a hard, virtually impenetrable roof. Much of the material used in lodge construction comes from branches that the beavers have already cut and peeled the bark from while eating.

Beavers also build food caches — piles of interwoven branches and sticks placed in the water to which they gain access by swimming under the ice from the lodge. This food caching is an adaptation to the ice cover of northern winters. Southern beaver populations do not cache food.

Beavers will excavate bank burrows for summer use where soil conditions permit. These bank dens may or may not be covered with branches and mud.

Dam construction requires much of the beavers' time and involves continuous maintenance work. The value of the territory created by this work is such that it also requires vigilance against

intrusion of and attempted takeover by other beavers. These two factors have led beavers to develop a territorial and cooperative family unit that maintains its lodges, dams and feeding grounds and excludes nonrelated beavers. All members of the colony scent-mark around the water's edge and along the dam with a musky secretion from the castoreum gland and with urine and possibly oil. Special mounds of vegetation and debris up to a foot high are erected around the colony boundary and marked with these secretions. The castoreum scent gland produces a complex pheromonal mixture of more than 50 different molecules, enough complexity to give every beaver its own unique chemical signature. It is not known how much individual recognition exists in beavers, but it is clear that colony members can smell and distinguish each other's scent from that of outsiders. The dominant male beaver, in particular, becomes highly aggressive if he smells foreign castoreum. The beavers will hiss and slap their tails when they smell the scent and will investigate it. This behaviour is used by trappers, who rub beaver castoreum on beaver traps and never fail to attract the resident beaver. Under normal conditions, a foreign beaver thus detected will be attacked and driven out. Beavers can inflict formidable gouges and bites and have been known to kill intruding beavers in territorial disputes.

The social structure of a beaver colony is based on a monogamous pair of mates. They share a lodge and cooperate in building duties and territorial defence. The female normally selects the home site and generates the social stability of the family unit. If her mate dies, she will remain in the territory and accept a new male. But if the female dies, the territory may be abandoned.

The male and female produce one litter each year and tolerate the presence of previous offspring. How many offspring remain in the colony and for how long apparently varies according to the quality of the habitat. Typically, the male and female pair is accompanied by the immature young of the year and several other juveniles that may be as old as 2½ years. The presence of an extended family of closely related kin explains the use of the tail slap on the water as a warning signal. Even though the slapping draws a predator's attention to the beaver issuing the warning, the beneficiaries of this warning probably will be close relatives.

Most colonies contain five to six individuals, with 12 being a reported maximum. Twelve adult beavers would weigh close to half a ton and would place severe grazing pressure on the surrounding trees. Pressure on the local food resource requires juvenile dispersal, which appears to be instinctive in two-year-old beavers and is not necessarily the result of eviction by the parents. Low-quality habitats have the highest rate of juvenile dispersal. Most beavers move only a few miles during this dispersal phase, but one tagged beaver has been recorded moving 150 miles. It is also possible that one of the juvenile beavers may ultimately inherit the lodge and territory of its parent.

In any case, all juveniles inherit considerable amounts of learning experience from their residency within the parental colony. Young beavers are born in spring in the lodge, usually in a clutch of two to four. They are furred but remain in the lodge and are breastfed for a full month or more before they are weaned. All members of the colony cooperate in bringing food to the young, but the parental male does most of this work, a highly unusual pattern in mammals. The year or more that young beavers spend as members of the parental colony is devoted not just to growth but to learning and polishing the techniques of construction and tree felling. Experience and strength appear to be necessary for a beaver to be successful. Reproduction is usually physiologically impossible until the animal is two years old, an old age as rodents go. Beavers continue to grow for four to five years in the extreme parts of their range and for as long as nine years in more central regions.

Woody Diet

Beavers eat shrubs and weedy vegetation during the summer months, but their tree cutting gives them a unique resource base. Beavers have felled trees close to four feet in diameter. Cutting and harvesting a tree this size requires some special techniques. Beavers are not able to fell trees with any great directional precision, but they may not need to. The direction in which a tree falls depends on its lean, the wind and the presence of obstructions. However, since trees are cut near the pond edge, they will naturally tend to lean toward the open area above the pond or stream surface and usually away from a downhill slope. Thus, on average, most trees fall toward the water. Beavers trim smaller limbs for transport and normally leave the heavy trunk. Although considerable quantities of wood are left behind, most of the nutrients are contained in the young bark and leaves. This felling of large trees allows sun-loving pioneer trees, such as willow and aspen, to sprout. These trees become coppice easily, and many generations of quickly harvested stump sprouts must be taken before the tree dies. Thus the beaver often modifies mature stands of unpalatable hardwoods and conifers to create faster-growing stands of palatable species that are easily harvested.

Few other wild animals, except possibly elephants, modify the landscape as much as beavers do. Prior to the European colonization of North America, an estimated 60 million beavers existed. Colonies require from about ½ to 1½ miles of stream or pond shoreline, so the result must have been many millions of acres of forest and wetland wildlife under the considerable influence of beavers. Although beavers were decimated and entirely trapped out in many regions, they have been restored to most of their former range. However, much of the habitat previously dominated by beavers is now subject to human occupation. At the same time, humans have eliminated many of the large carnivores that once preyed on beavers, and as a result, beavers frequently come into conflict with farmers and other landowners.

Beavers are still heavily trapped in many areas, but in semiurban and farming areas, trapping is often economically as well as aesthetically unattractive, and beavers may become a problem, flooding land, plugging culverts and irrigation canals and cutting valuable trees. Without some form of regulation, populations grow until the beavers deplete their food resources and then become subject to epidemic diseases such as tularemia. But where beaver populations are regulated by natural predation and scientifically based management plans, they provide many benefits.

In addition to their high-quality fur, beavers provide significant ecological benefits. The wetlands they create provide breeding and feeding habitats for waterfowl, frogs, salamanders, fish and mammals such as otter, muskrat and water shrews. Their dams provide erosion control, conserve water and increase the water quality of large rivers by reducing the amount of silt introduced. The open areas that beavers create and then abandon support a distinctive set of plants that depend on disturbance for their continued existence.

The impact of the beaver is so great that many of the ecological dependencies that have developed in concert with the presence of beavers remain to be discovered.

Excerpted from Mammals of the Canadian Wild. *Camden House (Camden East, Ont.).*

Hoarding the forest's harvest for the future

by Adrian Forsyth

Many small rodents cannot hibernate because their metabolism is too high and their body too small to survive a northern winter without feeding. Caching food has been their solution.

The biggest stashes are built by the biggest rodents. Beavers, for example, may cache a mound of tree branches several yards in diameter. The edible part of the cache is bark, which is available all winter long, but by caching it underwater, the beaver minimizes its predation risk. Another winter bark eater — the porcupine — has not evolved caching behaviour, which none of its tropical ancestors needed. Consequently, the porcupine must climb trees to keep feeding all winter and is highly exposed to predators. Fishers can catch large numbers of winter-foraging porcupines, and horned owls will pluck them from the branches. It would seem that porcupines could profit from the use of a cache, even if it were only at the base of a tree with a rock crevice close at hand.

Predator pressure may favour caching in beavers, but most small rodents cache because of energetic necessity. Burrowing root feeders, such as prairie and woodland voles, build large caches of roots and tubers, high-energy foods that store well. One prairie vole cache excavated in Manitoba contained an amazing harvest of 1,176 lily bulbs, 678 onion bulbs, 583 sunflower roots and 417 pasqueflower roots. Such a concentration of resources undoubtedly attracts cache robbers and requires energy in defence. In addition to the depredation by other voles, humans often rob caches. Plains Indians sought

The chipmunk's large cheek pouches make lightning food raids easier.

prairie vole caches, and the Inuit sought those of yellow-cheeked voles. The natives are reported to have trained dogs to sniff out the licorice root stashed by tundra rodents.

The risk of theft strongly influences the hoarding strategies of squirrels. *Sciurus* species, like the grey squirrels, hide each acorn and nut separately and thereby decrease the risk of losing an entire stash. Red squirrels that feed on large piles of conifer seeds, on the other hand, build them into vast central middens containing bushels of cones. Red squirrels can afford to concentrate their food stores because they normally have to defend them only against other red squirrels. Each cone is a small fraction of the total store, and serious losses could not be experienced before being detected by the territorial owner. When their territories overlap those of grey squirrels, the red squirrels must scatter their hoards, for the grey squirrels ignore the red squirrels' threats.

Chipmunks also use scatter hoarding to deal with the problem of theft. The burrow serves as a primary storage site, but nearby chipmunks frequently rob their neighbours' burrows. Large cheek pouches enable a chipmunk thief to run in and quickly carry off prized items such as lily bulbs. Thieving chipmunks

will make repeated trips to a neighbour's burrow as long as they can get away with it. The scatter hoards of the chipmunk are smaller and better hidden than the main burrow hoard. When its burrow is robbed, a chipmunk uses the scatter hoards to replace what it lost from the burrow. These scatter hoards are a kind of theft insurance, and when there is no theft, many scatter hoards are left to rot or sprout if they contain seeds. Chipmunks also place the scatter hoards in spots where they can keep an eye on their burrow while working and rush back if a thief is spotted.

The scatter hoarding of grey squirrels is less easily explained. Flying squirrels in the same forest use piles of nuts in tree holes. The strategy may be related to the fact that flying squirrels are much poorer runners on the ground than grey squirrels, and tree holes for caches are limited and must be filled with several nuts. The flying squirrels trade a risk of theft for greater safety from predators. The day-active and visually acute grey squirrel may suffer less predation and be more concerned about minimizing robbery.

Excerpted from Mammals of the Canadian Wild. *Camden House (Camden East, Ont.).*

Index

acid rain, 45, 201

acidity, 91, 201

Adirondack chairs, 60

Aedes vexans, 163

Aedes vexans canadensis, 163

allergies, 159-161, 166, 167, 169, 172, 113

"alligatoring," 36

angling, 108, 132, 134-136, 138-143, 146, 148, 150, 152

ants, 177

Bacillus thuringiensis, 167

badminton, 76

bait, fish, 136-141, 143, 144, 150, 151

barbecues, 12-16, 17
    gas, 12, 17
    hibachi, 12
    kettle, 12, 17
    vegetarian, 17

bass, 132, 138, 139, 141, 148-150

Bat Conservation International (BCI), 210, 211

bats, 208-211

beavers, 215-217

bee stings, 159-161

bees, 158-161

berries, 85, 89-91, 184

binder resin, 39, 44

biological agents, 103

bird feeders, 97, 191-197

birdhouses, 97, 191-197

birds, 82, 84-88, 91, 100, 180, 182-187, 191-197
    feeding of, 183-187, 191-197
    migration of, 87
    nesting, 84-87, 183
    population of, 87
    rehabilitation of, 180, 182-187, 197
    reproduction of, 84, 87

blackflies, 158, 165-167

blueberries, 18, 19, 89-91, 184

board games, 72, 77, 78

boatbuilding, 121-125

boathouses, 100, 101

boating, 106-110

boats, 121-125, 128

bowriders, 127

brakes, 71, 128, 129

bullfrogs, 198-201
    hunting of, 199, 200
    population of, 199, 200

survival of, 200, 201

butterflies, 202, 205

"candling," 59

casting reels, 144-147

caulking, 36, 40

caustics, 42, 44, 45

chalking, 36

charcoal, 12

chemical fumigation, 177

chicken, 15

children, 23, 78, 117, 118, 121, 125, 146, 164, 168, 169, 194

chipmunks, 217

chromated copper arsenate (CCA), 29-33

citronella, 162, 163

cocoons, 207

compass, 212-214

corn, 15, 194

creosote, 26, 28, 29, 32, 33

crokinole, 72-74

dams, 215

decking, 30, 32

decks, 38

deer ticks, 168, 169

deet, 162-164, 169

desserts, 18, 19

dibasic acid esters (DBE), 45

docks, 100, 101, 141

drainage, 53, 56, 67, 68, 91, 95, 112

earthworms, 85, 152, 153, 183

electric heating cable, 53, 55

endangered species, 82, 201, 208, 211

engines, 106-110, 111, 114, 117, 126
    electric starters, 109, 110, 114, 117
    manual starters, 108, 114

Environment Canada, 109

Environmental Protection Agency (EPA), 52, 162, 164

epoxy glue, 122-124

erosion, 101, 102

feeding birds, 183-187, 191-197

fertilizer, 95, 96, 103

fibreglass, 122, 124, 127, 147

finishes, 37, 38

fish, 100-102, 132-153
    intelligence, 137
    bass, 132, 138, 139, 141, 148-150
    habitat, 140-144, 148, 149
    muskies, 137, 140, 141
    pike, 132, 137, 140, 141
    salmon, 16, 139
    sunfish, 144, 145
    trout, 139
    walleyes, 132, 139, 140, 142, 143

fish senses, 132, 134-137

hearing, 135, 143

lateral line, 134, 135

scent, 136

sight, 132, 134, 143

taste, 136

touch, 137

fishing, 108, 132, 134-136, 138-143, 146, 148, 150, 152
    licence, 151
    rods, 143, 144, 146, 147
    tackle, 146, 147, 150, 151

flotation devices, 120

flowers, 85, 86

forests, 85-87, 90, 168, 172

freezing, 53-57

Friends of the Earth, 109

fruit, 89, 90, 184, 196, 205, 210

games, 76-79

giardia cysts, 48, 50

gross-weight rating (GWR), 70, 71

guarantees, 32, 33, 46

harvesting, 91

hawks, 186, 187

Hedera helix, 173

herbicides, 98, 100, 102, 103, 173

hitches, 70, 71, 128

horseflies, 158

horsepower (hp), 106-110, 117, 126

hull shapes, 125-128

hulls, 117

ice, 53, 57-59
    black, 57-59
    "frazil," 59
    white, 57-59

insect bites, 156, 158-160, 163, 165, 167-169

insect repellents, 162-165, 169

insecticides, 96, 167

insects, 82, 85, 148, 150, 156-161, 165, 183, 208

insulation, 53

jigs, 138-140, 143, 151

kayaks, 118-120

kebabs, 15

ladders, 41

lakes, 57-59, 98, 142, 211

lamb, 15

laneways, 64-69

leaf miner, 97

loons, 188-190

lures, 136-141, 143-145, 150, 151

lye, 44

lyme disease, 168, 169

maps, 212-214

mechanical weed harvesters, 100, 102, 103

melanin, 20, 24, 25
melanoma, 20, 23
mercury, 204-206
methyl bromide, 210
methylene chloride, 42-44
mice, 174-176
Microtus pennsylvanicus, 174
milfoil, 102, 103
Ministry of Natural Resources (MNR), 98, 100-103, 198-201
Ministry of the Environment (MOE), 102, 103
minnows, 136, 141, 143, 150, 151
moisture, 34, 36, 64, 69, 90, 91, 94, 95, 97, 112, 177
Monopoly, 77, 79
mosquitoes, 156, 158, 159, 162-167
moths, 202-207
    attracting, 204-206
motors, 106-110
mulch, 91, 96, 173
Mus musculus, 174
muskies, 137, 140, 141
Mutual Association for the Protection of the Lake Environment (MAPLE), 100
N, N-diethyl-meta-toluamide (deet), 162-164, 169
National Coalition Against the Misuse of Pesticides (NCAMP), 173
National Sanitation Foundation (NSF), 51
nitrates, 51
nitrogen, 91, 96
nurseries, 92, 94, 95, 97
oars, 125
oil injection, 108
Ondatra zibethica, 174
orchards, 97
outboard motors, 106-116, 129
overexposure, 44
owls, 186, 187
Pachysandra terminalis, 173
packaging, 94
paddling, 118, 120
paint, 30, 34-40
    blistering, 36, 38, 42, 43
    latex, 34-40
    oil, 34-40, 44
    scraping, 36, 40, 42, 43
    stripping, 42-45
paintbrushes, 37, 43, 45
painting, 41, 125
parasites, 87
penta, 29, 33
pests, 91, 97, 162-167, 174

pH levels, 91, 201
pigments, 39, 40
pike, 132, 137, 140, 141
pipes, 53-56
plants, 82, 84, 85, 88, 90, 91-98, 170, 173
plants, water, 100, 103
Plexiglas, 193, 213
poison ivy, 170, 172, 173
pollination, 91
pollution, 109, 201
polyethylene vapour barriers, 36
porcupines, 217
potatoes, 15
preserved wood, 26-33, 38
propellers, 106, 107, 110, 112, 114-116, 126
protective clothing, 45, 166, 167, 169, 173
pumps, 55, 56
rash, 44
raspberries, 85
rehabilitation, 180, 182-187, 197
retaining walls, 101
Rhus radicans, 173
rivers, 98
roads, 64-69
rodenticides, 176
roots, 92-95, 98
Rozol, 210
runabouts, 117, 126, 127
salads, 15, 16
salmon, 16, 139
sanctuary, 82, 84-88
sand, 98, 100
scaffolding, 41
Scrabble, 77, 79
seeds, 191, 192, 194, 196
shade, 24, 25, 90
shelterbelts, 88
shorelines, 59, 98-101, 140, 142
snow, 58, 59
soil, 67, 88-92, 95, 96, 98, 152, 177
spareribs, 16
spray guns, 37
squirrels, 217
stains, 30, 37-40
Stizostedion vitreum, 142
storm windows, 36
suet, 193, 195
sulphur, 91
sun protection factor (SPF), 22
sunburn, 20, 25
sunfish, 144, 145
sunglasses, 23, 24
sunscreen, 22-24

suntanning, 20-24
surface preparation, 34, 36, 38, 40, 42, 62, 125
tackle, 146, 147, 150, 151
targets, 77
temperature, 38, 45, 48, 57-59, 183
tongue weight, 129
towing, 70, 71, 128
trailer capacity, 128
trailers, 70, 71, 128, 129
transplanting, 95, 97
tree cavity, 86
trees, 92-97, 100
trout, 139
ultraviolet light, 50, 204, 205
ultraviolet rays, 20, 22, 25, 36
U.V. systems, 50, 51
UVA rays, 22
UVB rays, 22
Vaccinium angustifolium, 90
Vaccinium ashei, 89
Vaccinium australe, 89
Vaccinium corymbosum, 89
vegetables, 16, 17
vehicle towing capacity, 70, 71
Vinca minor, 173
voles, 174, 176, 217
walleyes, 132, 139, 140, 142, 143
water, 46-54, 68, 91, 95, 96, 98, 112, 113, 132, 165-167, 201
    drinking, 52
water filtration, 46-51, 52
    carbon, 48, 49, 51
    distillation, 49-51, 112
    reverse osmosis, 49, 51
water plants, 100, 103
Water Quality Association (WQA), 51
water repellents, 30, 38
water softeners, 48, 49, 51
water, tap, 46
waterfowl, 187
waterfront, 59, 98-101, 140, 142
weeds, 100-103, 140, 141, 143, 148, 173
wells, 49-52, 55
wildlife, 82, 84, 88, 100, 180
windbreaks, 88
winterizing, 53-56
wood, 26, 37, 38, 62, 74, 121-125, 177, 192, 193
wood, preserved, 26-33, 38
wood rot, 26, 39, 86
worms, 85, 138, 147, 150-153, 183

Sources

P.12, Originally published as "Grill Work," *Harrowsmith* magazine, July/August 1988.

P.17, Originally published as "Garden Fresh Grilling," *Organic Gardening* magazine, August 1988.

P.18, Originally published as "Bravo Blueberries," *Organic Gardening* magazine, June 1988.

P.20, Originally published as "Under Cover," *Health* magazine, May 1990.

P.25, Originally published as "Why the Sun Tans Your Skin but Bleaches Your Hair," *Rainbows, Curve Balls and Other Wonders of the Natural World Explained*, Harper Row (New York), 1988.

P.26, Originally published as "Preservative-Treated Wood," *Fine Homebuilding* magazine, October/November 1990.

P.32, Originally published as "New Pressure on Treated Wood," *Harrowsmith* magazine, May/June 1991.

P.34, P.41, Originally published as "In Search of the Perfect Finish," *Harrowsmith Country Life* magazine, July/August 1986.

P.42, Originally published as "Chemical Paint Strippers," *Old House Journal*, January/February 1991.

P.46, P.52, Originally published as "Distilling the Essence," *Harrowsmith Country Life* magazine, September/October 1989.

P.53, Originally published as "Cold Comfort," *Cottage Life* magazine, September/October 1990.

P.57, Originally published as "The Icing on the Lake," *Cottage Life* magazine, November/December 1990.

P.60, Originally published as "Sitting Pretty," *Harrowsmith* magazine, May/June 1989.

P.64, Originally published as "Take Me Home," *Harrowsmith Country Life* magazine, May/June 1987.

P.70, Originally published as "Travelling With Trailers," *Home Mechanix* magazine, July/August 1990.

P.72, Originally published as "They Shoot, They Score," *Harrowsmith* magazine, November/December 1988.

P.75, not previously published.

P.76, Originally published as "Pain in the Name of Fun," *At the Cottage*, McClelland & Stewart (Toronto), 1989.

P.78, Originally published as "Games," *Canadian Consumer* magazine, Issue #11/12, 1990.

P.82, Originally published as "Micro-Sanctuaries," *Harrowsmith Country Life* magazine, May/June 1986. Adapted from *The Audubon Society Guide to Attracting Birds*, Charles Scribner's Sons (New York), 1985.

P.89, Originally published as "Backyard Blues," *Organic Gardening* magazine, June 1988.

P.92, Originally published as "Trees Without Trauma," *Harrowsmith* magazine, March/April 1981.

P.98, Originally published as "Turning the Tide," *Seasons* magazine, Autumn 1990.

P.102, Originally published as "War of the Weeds," *Cottage Life* magazine, May 1990.

P.106, Originally published as "Small Outboard Motors," *Canadian Consumer* magazine, Issue #6, 1989.

P.111, P.114, Originally published as "Care and Feeding of the Savage Outboard," *Cottage Life* magazine, June/July 1988.

P.117, Originally published as "The Aluminum Classic," *Cottage Life* magazine, August/September 1988.

P.118, Originally published as "Paddling Fancy," *Cottage Life* magazine, June 1989.

P.121, Originally published as "A Birthday Boat," *Harrowsmith Country Life* magazine, July/August 1988.

P.126, Originally published as "The Hull Story," *Cottage Life* magazine, March/April 1989.

P.128, Originally published as "Pulling a Fast One," *Cottage Life* magazine, March April, 1990.

P.132, Originally published as "The Senses," *The Art of Angling*, Prentice-Hall (Toronto), 1986.

P.138, Originally published as "Summer Strategies," *Field and Stream* magazine, August 1990.

P.140, Originally published as "Where the Bass Are," *Cottage Life* magazine, August/September 1988.

P.142, Originally published as "A Fish Called Walleye," *Cottage Life* magazine, May 1990.

P.144, Originally published as "A Plug for Sunfish," *Field and Stream* magazine, May 1990.

P.146, Originally published as "Fishing with Small Fry," *Cottage Life* magazine, March/April 1989.

P. 148, Originally published as "Developing an Eye for Big Bass," *Field and Stream* magazine, September 1990.

P.150, Originally published as "Box Steps," *Cottage Life* magazine, June/July 1988.

P.152, Originally published as "Worms," *Fishing: An Encyclopedic Guide to Tackle and Tactics for Fresh and Salt Water*, Outdoor Life/Popular Science Publishing Company (New York), 1975.

P.156, Originally published as "Of Bites and Stings," *Goodbye Bugs*, Grosvenor House (Montreal), 1983.

P.162, Originally published as "Buzz Off!" *Harrowsmith Country Life* magazine, May/June 1990.

P.165, Originally published as "Blackflies," *Goodbye Bugs*, Grosvenor House (Montreal), 1983.

P. 168, Originally published as "Update on Lyme Disease," *Parents Magazine*, July 1990.

P.170, Originally published as "The Big Itch," *Outdoor Canada* magazine, April 1990.

P.173, Originally published as "Touch Me Not," *Harrowsmith* magazine, May/June 1991.

P.174, Originally published as "A Mouse in the House," *Harrowsmith* magazine, May/June 1987.

P.177, Originally published as "Architectural Ants," *Harrowsmith* magazine, January/February 1986.

P.180, Originally published as "Carrying for Injured and Orphaned Birds," *A Bird Watchers Handbook: Field Ornithology for Backyard Naturalists*, Dodd, Mead & Company (New York), 1987.

P.188, Originally published as "Song and Dance," *Love of Loons*, Voyageur Press (Stillwater, MN), 1987.

P.191, Originally published as "Stations of Life," *Harrowsmith* magazine, December/January 1982. Adapted from *Feeding Birds in Winter*, Firefly Books (Toronto), 1982.

P.198, Originally published as "Bullfrog Blues," *Seasons* magazine, Summer 1990.

P. 202, Originally published as "Moths: Learning to Love Them," *The Audubon Society Handbook for Butterfly Watchers*, Charles Scribner's Sons (New York), 1984.

P. 206, Originally published as "Outdoor Lights," *Harrowsmith Country Life* magazine, May/June 1989.

P. 208, Originally published as "Batman," *Harrowsmith Country Life* magazine, January/February 1987.

P.212, Originally published as "Map & Compass Bushwhackery," *Harrowsmith* magazine, December 1980.

P.215, Originally published as "Beaver," *Mammals of the Canadian Wild*, Camden House (Camden East, Ont.), 1985.

P. 217, Originally published as "Caching In," *Mammals of the Canadian Wild*, Camden House (Camden East, Ont.), 1985.

Inside front cover. Adapted from *Exploring the Night Sky*, Camden House (Camden East, Ont.), 1987.

Inside back cover. Adapted from *Exploring the Sky by Day*, Camden House (Camden East, Ont.), 1988.

Publications

Canadian Consumer
Consumer's Association of Canada
Box 9000
Ottawa, Ontario
K1G 3T9

Cottage Life
111 Queen Street East
Suite 408
Toronto, Ontario
M5C 1S2

Field & Stream
Times Mirror Magazines
2 Park Avenue
New York, New York
10016

Fine Homebuilding
Taunton Press
63 South Main Street
Newtown, Connecticut
06470

Harrowsmith
Telemedia Publishing
7 Queen Victoria Road
Camden East, Ontario
K0K 2S0

Harrowsmith Country Life
Telemedia Inc.
Ferry Road
Charlotte, Vermont
05445

Health
Family Media Inc.
3 Park Avenue
New York, New York
10016

Home Mechanix
2 Park Avenue
New York, New York
10016

Organic Gardening
Rodale Press, Inc.
33 East Minor Street
Emmaus, Pennsylvania
18098

Old House Journal
435 Ninth Street
Brooklyn, New York
11215

Outdoor Canada
Canadian National Sportsmen's
Shows Ltd.
801 York Mills Road
Suite 301
Don Mills, Ontario
M3B 1X7

Parents Magazine
Gruner + Jahr Publishing
685 Third Avenue
New York, New York
10017

Seasons
Federation of Ontario Naturalists
355 Lesmill Road
Don Mills, Ontario
M3B 2W8

Credits

Inside front cover John Bianchi
p.3   Ernie Sparks
p.7   Greg Locke/First Light
p.10   John de Visser
p.13   Fred Bird
p.14   Fred Bird
p.18   F.B. Edwards
p.21   Chris Harvey/Focus/Tony Stone
         Worldwide
p.27   Brian Vanden Brink; Margo
         Jones, architect
p.28   Karen Bussolini; Tramontano
         and Rowe, landscape
         architects
p.31   Brian Vanden Brink; John
         Morris, architect
p.35   Barry Dursley/First Light
p.38   Janet Dwyer/First Light
p.41   F.B. Edwards
p.43   Ron Watts/First Light
p.47   Julie Habel/First Light
p.50   Julie Habel/First Light
p.54   Robert Semeniuk/First Light
p.58   J. Evans/Focus/Tony Stone
         Worldwide
p.61   Ron Watts/First Light
p.62   Ian Grainge
p.63   Ian Grainge
p.65   Peter D'Angelo/Focus/ Tony
         Stone Worldwide
p.66   Ray Maher
p.69   Ray Maher
p.80   Linda Burgess/Focus/Tony
         Stone Worldwide
p.83   Robert McCaw
p.84   Robert McCaw
p.87   Robert McCaw
p.90   Robert McCaw
p.93   Derek Trask/The Stock Market
p.96   Ian Grainge
p.99   Tom W. Parkin/Pathfinder
         Productions
p.104   Todd Korol/First Light
p.107   Peter D'Angelo/Focus/ Tony
         Stone Worldwide
p.108   Ron Watts/First Light
p.112   Don George
p.113   Don George
p.115   Don George
p.119   Janet Dwyer/First Light
p.122   Bill Lorenz
p.123   Cathy Bray
p.124   Cathy Bray
p.125   Cathy Bray
p.127   Don George
p.130   Annie Griffiths Belt/First Light
p.133   David Laine
p.134   David Laine
p.139   Todd Korol/First Light
p.143   J. Taposchaner/First Light
p.145   Dwight R. Kuhn
p.147   Steve Smith/First Light
p.149   David Laine
p.151   F.B. Edwards
p.153   Lawrence Manning/First Light
p.154   Dwight R. Kuhn
p.157   Brenda Sun/University of
         Guelph
p.158   Geoff Dore/Focus/Tony
         Stone Worldwide
p.161   P. Morgan/Focus/Tony
         Stone Worldwide
p.163   Dwight R. Kuhn
p.167   Dwight R. Kuhn
p.171   Robert McCaw
p.175   Dwight R. Kuhn
p.176   Dwight R. Kuhn
p.178   Thomas Kitchin/First Light
p.181   Robert McCaw
p.182   Robert McCaw
p.185   Dwight R. Kuhn
p.189   Tom W. Parkin/Pathfinder
         Productions
p.193   Dwight R. Kuhn
p.194   Jessie Parker/First Light
p.197   Robert McCaw
p.199   Dwight R. Kuhn
p.203   Dwight R. Kuhn
p.204   Brian Milne/First Light
p.209   Dwight R. Kuhn
p.214   Ian Grainge
p.217   Dwight R. Kuhn
Inside back cover John Bianchi